Spanish and English of United States Hispanos:
A Critical, Annotated, Linguistic Bibliography

Richard V. Teschner, GENERAL EDITOR
Garland D. Bills and Jerry R. Craddock, ASSOCIATE EDITORS

Center for Applied Linguistics

Z
2695
.D5
S63
1975

467.9
T283

Copyright © 1975
by the Center for Applied Linguistics
1611 North Kent Street, Arlington, Virginia 22209

International Standard Book Number: 87281-042-9
Library of Congress Catalog Card Number: 75-21564

Printed in the United States of America

DEDICATORIA

It is the editors' hope that the present Bibliography contributes to a general dissemination of knowledge about the languages and the linguistic heritage of the United States' ever-increasing Hispanic populations, and that it serves, furthermore, to focus overdue attention on the strengths and the triumphs (as well as the weaknesses) of the considerable body of research already undertaken on the speech and the language behavior of Chicanos, Puerto Ricans and others.

Esta bibliografía la dedicamos, entonces, a toda la comunidad hispana de los Estados Unidos y a los múltiples investigadores de su realidad lingüística.

> Richard V. Teschner (University of Iowa)
> Garland D. Bills (University of New Mexico)
> Jerry R. Craddock (University of California, Berkeley)

TABLE OF CONTENTS

MAJOR CATEGORIES: PAGE

1. United States in general   1
2. Chicanos (Mexican-Americans) in general   20
    3. New Mexico and South-Central Colorado   71
    4. Arizona   116
    5. Texas   134
    6. California   210
    7. Elsewhere (other Colorado, Midwest,
        Northwest)   235
    8. Pachuco/Caló Studies   245

    (Note: 3.-8. are understood to be sub-parts of
    Major Category No. 2, supra.)

9. Puerto Ricans on the United States Mainland   258
10. Cubans   302
11. Isleños (Louisiana Canary Islanders)   315
12. Peninsulares (Spaniards)   318
13. Sephardic Jews (Dzhudezmo, Ladino or Judeo-
    Spanish)   321

    Sub-Categories of All of the Above: (when applicable)

    .1   Bibliography
    .2   Comprehensive/General Studies; Miscellany;
          Anthologies/Festschriften
    .2.1 Sociolinguistics
    .2.2 Textbooks
    .3   Spanish Phonology (includes Orthography)
    .4   Spanish Grammar (Morphology and Syntax)
    .5   Spanish Lexicon (includes Semantics)
    .6   Onomastics (includes Toponymy)
    .7   English Influence on Spanish
    .8   Spanish Influence on English
    .8.1 English of This Particular Hispanic Group
    .9   Spanish Influence on Amerindian Languages
    .10   Code-Switching

TABLE OF CONTENTS (contd.)

LOCATIONS of Categories and Sub-Categories (when applicable)

CATEGORY	PAGE
Dedicatoria	
General Editor's Preface	i
User's Guide	iii
Acknowledgements	iv
INTRODUCTION TO THE BIBLIOGRAPHY: Linguistic Research on U.S. Hispanos--State of the Art	v
General Trends and Emphases	vi
Major Research on Each Variety	x
Chicano Spanish	xi
Puerto Rican Spanish	xvii
Cuban Spanish	xix
Judeo-Spanish (Dzhudezmo)	xx
Louisiana Spanish: isleño	xx
Other Dialects	xx
U.S. Spanish in General	xxi
Concluding Remarks	xxi

CATEGORY	PAGE	CATEGORY	PAGE
1.1	1	3.5	95
1.2	7	3.6	103
1.2.1	14	3.7	106
1.3	16	3.8	110
1.4	17	3.8.1	111
1.5	18	3.9	113
1.7	18		
1.9	19	4.1	116
		4.2	116
2.1	20	4.2.1	119
2.2	26	4.3	122
2.2.1	38	4.4	124
2.2.2	46	4.5	124
2.3	47	4.6	127
2.4	48	4.7	128
2.5	48	4.8	128
2.6	54	4.8.1	128
2.7	54	4.9	131
2.8	55		
2.8.1	65	5.1	134
2.9	68	5.2	134
2.10	70	5.2.1	148
		5.2.2	161
3.1	71	5.3	163
3.2	72	5.4	169
3.2.1	83	5.5	175
3.3	87	5.6	193
3.4	92	5.7	194

TABLE OF CONTENTS (contd.)

CATEGORY	PAGE	CATEGORY	PAGE
5.8	196	9.2.2	288
5.8.1	200	9.3	289
5.10	209	9.4	290
		9.5	291
6.1	210	9.7	292
6.2	210	9.8.1	295
6.2.1	212		
6.3	216	10.1	302
6.4	217	10.2	302
6.5	218	10.2.1	304
6.6	219	10.2.2	304
6.7	221	10.3	305
6.8	223	10.4	309
6.8.1	224	10.5	309
6.9	230	10.6	310
6.10	232	10.7	311
7.2.1	235	11.1	315
7.4	237	11.2	315
7.7	239	11.5	317
7.8.1	242		
7.9	244	12.2	318
		12.2.1	319
8.2	245	12.3	319
8.2.1	246	12.5	319
8.5	247	12.7	319
8.7	256		
8.8	256	13.1	321
8.10	257	13.2	321
		13.3	324
9.1	258	13.4	326
9.2	259	13.5	327
9.2.1	267	13.7	327
Author Index	328		
List of Abbreviations	347		

GENERAL EDITOR'S PREFACE

The present Bibliography hopefully includes all items relating in full or in part to the speech and language behavior of United States residents/citizens of Hispanic background, chiefly Chicanos (Mexican-Americans) and mainland Puerto Ricans but also Cubans, Sephardic Jews, peninsulares (Spaniards) and isleños (Canary Islanders in Louisiana).

In the process of assembling this volume's 675 items (the vast majority annotated in full, many critically and at some length) we have examined material from books, parts of books, doctoral dissertations, masters theses, articles, parts of articles, textbooks, anthologies, Festschriften and monographs, composed by persons from a wide variety of academic disciplines: linguistics in the main but also anthropology, sociology, education, mass communications, onomastics, speech pathology, folklore, literature and psychology. At all times, however, our glance was firmly cast toward the item's relevance to the scientific examination of language. It is logical then that our chief orientation is linguistic and that each of us has approached the material as linguists.

Though it attempts an exhaustive coverage of United States Hispanic language, the Bibliography excludes many items oriented chiefly or exclusively toward language education, especially when these relate to the Mexican-American. But our decision to exclude certain items was a deliberate one and was prompted in part by the welcome news that our fellow bibliographer Prof. Paul Willcott of Pan American University (Edinburg, Texas) had received substantial fiscal support for his forthcoming bibliography of Chicano-oriented applications of linguistics. Since Prof. Willcott's work will not include studies related to non-Chicano Hispanic groups, however, we have been somewhat more liberal in our inclusion of educationally-oriented items pertaining to Puerto Ricans, Cubans and others, provided that these have light to shed on language and language behavior among the target populations. Such studies, though, are always examined from the standpoint of what they have to offer the linguist.

It is well known that the great majority of Spanish-speaking U.S. Hispanos are also bilingual in English (to whatever degree). To exclude from our examination the growing number of items which deal with the English of Chicanos, Puerto Ricans and others would therefore be an artificial exercise. Thus in addition to examining all items that treat the phonology/grammar/lexicon of natively-spoken United States Spanish, we have also endeavored to include all linguistic studies of U.S. Hispano English and all studies of that often typically "bilingual" form of behavior known as code-switching. Our Bibliography also treats the sociolinguistics of U.S. Hispano speech and the influence Spanish has had upon American English and United States Amerindian languages as well as the impact English exerts upon United States Spanish. In addition we have examined all bibliographies (and a few of the more comprehensive "checklists") that deal in full or, as is often the case, to some limited extent with the speech of U.S. Hispanos.

This Bibliography hopes to have continued Prof. Hensley C. Woodbridge's masterful study "Spanish in the American South and Southwest: A Bibliographical Survey for the Years 1940-53" (1954), which in turn is a continuation of the section on U.S. Spanish by Madaline W. Nichols, <u>A Bibliographical Guide to Materials on American</u> [i.e., Western Hemisphere] <u>Spanish</u> (1941). In general terms our own "cut-off date" has been December 1974, though for doctoral dissertations it was somewhat earlier (i.e., the end of <u>DA</u> vol. 34 [June 1974]). It has likewise been our policy to exclude from this work all items which cannot be acquired by the researcher through inter-library loan channels, from commercial distribution agencies, or in a very few cases from the author of the manuscript directly; only in two or three instances do we mention items which have been "lost" or which are otherwise unobtainable.

To the extent that our non-existent materials acquisition budget has allowed, we have examined first-hand the great majority of all items annotated; only if there already existed a readily available, extensive abstract of a given item (typically a doctoral dissertation) did we fail to purchase it; on the other hand, all dissertations directly relevant to U.S. Hispanic language have been purchased and read. While no attempt could possibly have been made to locate all pertinent masters theses (barring receipt of an impressive travel grant, or the resumption by <u>Hispania</u> of its annual listing of masters theses [a practice abandoned in 1950], or an expanded-coverage, retrospective and cumulative separatum to the relatively recent Xerox University Microfilms publication <u>MAAb</u>), several dozen university libraries in Texas, New Mexico, California, Wisconsin, Illinois and Iowa have nonetheless been visited and their public catalogues checked (though only through the summer of 1973 in some cases).

The author of each annotation is identified by his initials, within brackets, following the annotation itself. Each annotator has been solely responsible for the critical content of his particular annotations and has always been free to evaluate each item as he saw fit.

It is inevitable that the present Bibliography will be marked by the lacunae and omissions which always seem to be the fate of works of this type. We stand, therefore, ready to receive amendments and addenda of all sorts and will readily acknowledge our indebtedness, in future, expanded editions, to all who have offered supplemental information.

        Richard V. Teschner, May 1975, Iowa City

USER'S GUIDE

The Table of Contents (supra) will suffice to indicate this Bibliography's organizational format. But a few brief words about the format of the individual item entry will doubtless prove helpful.

Serial publication titles of more than one word are abbreviated in the item entry and a key to their abbreviations (as well as to all others used) is provided at the end of the Bibliography. Following the item citation there appears a bracketed line or two which refers the user to all the item's previous annotations and, occasionally, brief reviews, by the present volume's several precursors, chiefly Nichols 1941, Woodbridge 1954, Serís 1964, Solé 1970 (also 1972 when so marked), Fody 1971, and Craddock 1973; reference is also made there to the existence and location of the item's abstracts (if any) in MLA Abstracts--Linguistics, Language and Language Behavior Abstracts, and occasionally elsewhere; the user is also guided to the location of the abstracts of all dissertations processed by Xerox University Microfilms in the serial DA and to those masters theses Xerox processes and lists in MAAb.

Subsequently cited (also in brackets) are the item's reviews appearing in serial publications. It should be noted that no reviews are listed for items whose relevance to linguistic description is minimal.

Each of this Bibliography's subsections is prefaced by a brief "Reader's Guide" containing two parts: (1) a listing of "Major Items" designed to direct the reader to the material the annotators consider salient, and (2) a cross-referential listing of items annotated in other sections of the Bibliography but which nonetheless pertain in part to the topic of the particular subsection at hand. Abbreviations are used for all items in both (1) and (2); for a key to what the abbreviations represent, as well as an explanation of how they were devised, see the Author Index at the Bibliography's end.

ACKNOWLEDGMENTS

No bibliography of this magnitude can be produced without the assistance of many persons who willingly gave of their time to assist the editors in a myriad of particulars which lie within their various fields of specialization. To the following persons, then, we wish to express our special gratitude for sound advice given, arcane items located, and manuscripts cheerfully lent:

Prof. Anthony F. Beltrano of the Univ. of Montana; Mrs. Bonnie M. Davis of Xerox University Microfilms; Dr. Bruce Gaarder of the U.S. Office of Education; Prof. Roberto Galván of Southwest Texas State University; Prof. Einar Haugen of Harvard University; Prof. George Haley of the University of Chicago; Robert M. Hammond of the Univ. of Florida; Mrs. Maurine Miller of the Library of Baylor University; Prof. Harvey Nadler of New York University; Prof. José R. Reyna of Texas A & I University; Prof. Muriel Saville-Troike of Georgetown University and the Center for Applied Linguistics; Prof. Clarence Senior of the Inter-American University of Puerto Rico; Prof. Frank Joseph Shulman of the University of Michigan, Ann Arbor; and John Terry Webb of the University of California, Berkeley. We are immensely indebted to Dr. Theodore S. Beardsley, Jr., Director of the Hispanic Institute of America, for an early interest in our project and for having supplied us with several dozen references of which we were previously unaware (all items brought to our attention by Dr. Beardsley are marked "[TSBJr.]" at the end of the item's heading).

Special thanks must clearly go to Allene Guss Grognet, Director of Publications, Center for Applied Linguistics, for patient guidance consistently shown throughout the production of this work. The General Editor is also grateful to Dean Charles M. Mason of the Graduate School of the University of Iowa for having funded much of the typing, and wishes to express sincere gratitude to Mrs. Herminia E. de Santizo, Iowa City, for having typed most of the final manuscript with consumate skill.

INTRODUCTION TO THE BIBLIOGRAPHY

<u>Linguistic Research on U.S. Hispanos--State of the Art</u>

The Spanish language is spoken natively in the United States by a large and diversified population. The precise size of this group is difficult to determine, although it is readily conceded to be the largest "alloglottic" minority in the nation. For absolute numbers we can only rely on imperfect census figures. The 1970 Census variously estimates 9.6 million "persons of Spanish language," 9.3 million "of Spanish heritage," or 9.1 million "of Spanish origin." This last estimate, however, was quietly raised to 10.6 million by the Census Bureau in January 1974 as the result of a methodologically distinct recount (as well as some intense political pressure from Hispanic activists). We may guess, then, that there are currently perhaps ten million Hispanos in the U.S.

Although the size of this group makes it extremely important in all facets of American life, it is the diversity within the group that enhances its significance to linguists. Much of this diversity is due to the varied origins of the Hispanic population. Three major subgroups account for two-thirds of the numerical total: the Chicanos, or Mexican-Americans, number roughly five million (4.5 million "of Mexican origin" according to the 1970 Census); the Puerto Ricans total approximately 1.5 million; and the Cubans amount to upwards of 500,000. The last two groups primarily represent relatively recent immigration, with fully 80 per cent of the Cuban population being foreign-born. The Chicanos, however, exhibit much greater heterogeneity, ranging from the estimated 750,000 Mexico-born immigrants to the indeterminable number who trace their ancestral settlement in New Mexico back to as early as Juan de Oñate's colonization party of 1598. In addition to these three major elements, there are also the <u>isleño</u> Spanish speakers of Louisiana, descendants of early colonists from the Canary Islands; the speakers of <u>Dzhudezmo</u> or Judeo-Spanish, who immigrated to the U.S. primarily in this century; and communities of other immigrants from Spain, Central and South America, and even the Philippines. The dialectal diversity resulting from these distinctions of time and place provides a wealth of research opportunities for the linguist.

Beyond such "imported" diversity, the U.S. Spanish situation is also enriched by the sociolinguistic diversity developing out of the distinct sociocultural environments into which these varied Spanish speakers entered. One aspect of this "home-grown" diversity is the evolution of distinctive social varieties of Spanish, including such specialized variants as the notorious Southwest argot known as Pachuco. Another aspect is the exceedingly complex diversity arising from differential language contact and bilingualism. Everywhere the clash of Spanish and English has produced varied interlingual influences and intriguing sociolinguistic phenomena. Contact with Native American languages in the Southwest, with French in

Louisiana, and with other languages of less prominence--as well as the contact of different dialects of U.S. Spanish--have further contributed to linguistic heterogeneity. The topics of interest and significance in the areas of bilingualism and bi- or multi-dialectalism are virtually unlimited.

The diversity of U.S. Spanish, then, has long presented exciting opportunities--indeed challenges--for linguistic research. How have language scholars responded? The answer to this question yields good news and bad. The quality and quantity of reported research is as mixed and uneven as the target itself. For some varieties of U.S. Spanish there has been a long history of attention from linguists; for others an equally long history of neglect. Within each variety, some topics have been extensively explored while others are hardly noted. In order to assay the "state of the art" of language research on U.S. Hispanos we shall briefly examine its prominent characteristics and then survey the major research contributions for each variety.

General Trends and Emphases

Although studies of U.S. Spanish have been quite diverse, most work fits under one or more of three dominant characteristics or "trends": (1) a peculiarly Hispanic orientation to the study of language, (2) a concern for the education of the Spanish speaker, and (3) an interest in the sociological aspects of bilingualism.

The most striking characteristic of the gamut of U.S. Spanish research is the first trend: the dominance of what we will call the "Hispanic tradition" of language study and the relative lack of influence of contemporary scholarship in American and European linguistics. Typical traits of this Hispanic tradition are: (1) interest in the accumulation of speech fragments with little concern for linguistic or sociological context; (2) almost exclusive interest in deviations from standard Spanish; (3) historical explanation of deviations in philological-comparative terms; and (4) a lack of interest in theoretical issues regarding the analysis of language data or the implications of these data for the understanding of language as a human phenomenon.

The Hispanic tradition is superbly exemplified by the work of Aurelio M. Espinosa, Sr., the most prolific of U.S. Spanish language scholars. Although a founding member of the Linguistic Society of America and a contributor to the first volume of its journal Language, Espinosa remained aloof from the trends of American linguistics and himself made no impact on those trends (indeed, his death was not even noted with an obituary in Language). His tripartite masterwork, Studies in New Mexican Spanish (1909-1915, with the Spanish translations in 1930 and 1946) is hailed throughout the Hispanic world as one of the major contributions to the linguistic description of Spanish, but significantly only the first part was ever published in the United States (1909aa). The work of Espinosa was, it appears, nourishment intended largely for pan-Hispanic consumption.

Though few U.S. Spanish researchers have come close to matching the standards set by Espinosa, up to the present time the Hispanic tradition has been the dominant approach. This approach has had both positive and negative results. The emphasis on simple observation of bits of language without regard for analysis of the whole has resulted in numerous works on morphology (primarily lexical) and phonetics, but virtually nothing on syntax or semantics. Such interest in "oddities" has produced abundant descriptions of <u>nonstandard</u> forms but little on the standard aspect, i.e., the bulk of the language. The concern for diachronic rather than synchronic analysis has resulted in much erudition but scant creative thinking, and has reinforced the emphasis on phonological and lexical study and the neglect of syntax and semantics. Finally, the atheoretical, amethodological bent of this tradition has contributed to works filled with data and relatively free of polemics and terminological obfuscation, but too frequently abounding in linguistic naïveté.

The impact of the Hispanic tradition is most prominently noticed in studies of those varieties of Spanish with the longest history of language description: Southwest Chicano Spanish, <u>isleño</u>, Judeo-Spanish and to some extent Cuban Spanish. Since the majority of the descriptions of these varieties are immersed in this tradition, they deal in consequence with phonology and vocabulary and thereby emphasize archaisms, English influence, and other evolutionary departures from standard Spanish.

The Hispanic tradition's dominance is so great that it is simpler to illustrate with exceptions than to attempt enumeration by citing major works. Most exceptions are those works that either fit solely under one of the other two trends (to be discussed below) or those that are strongly influenced by American structural linguistics. Major taxonomic (structuralist) linguistic research did not occur until this "neo-Bloomfieldian" approach was already reeling in its confrontation with syntactic problems. J. Donald Bowen was the first to embrace, daringly and most apologetically, this "new" taxonomic approach in his severely analytical dissertation on "The Spanish of San Antonito, New Mexico " (1952). But followers were few; most simply grafted chance taxonomic insights onto hoary Hispanic traditions. After Bowen's work, all important taxonomically oriented contributions appeared in the period when the taxonomic approach was no longer the central focus of American linguistics, e.g., M. Kindig's thesis on Hawaiian Puerto Rican English phonology (1960), R. Phillips' dissertation on Los Angeles Spanish (1967), and V. Poulter's dissertation on Texas Spanish phonology (1973). Only now, more than fifteen years after its ascendancy to the throne of American structural linguistics, is the transformational-generative approach finally being pursued in the study of U.S. Spanish. In phonology this is examplified by J. Harris' limited forays into New Mexican Spanish and by J. Guitart's dissertaion on his own idiolect of Cuban Spanish. Transformational treatment of syntax remains unexplored except for S. Said's pro forma thesis (1970) and F. Hensey's very general essay (1973). The major study of U.S. Spanish syntax still remains Robert Phillips' "Los Angeles Spanish: A Descriptive Analysis," which in 1967 was still a loose blend of neo-Bloomfieldian and Hispanic traditions. These few studies stand in marked contrast with the host of major works, strictly within the Hispanic tradition, that continue to demonstrate the salience of this trend.

The other two trends are characterized by orientations primarily educational or sociological, and resemble each other in several important ways. Both have shown major concern for the functional levels of bilinguals' language capabilities. Both have developed slowly out of nonlinguistic disciplines over many years. And both have become very prominent since the middle of the 1960's.

The educational current has contributed substantively to the description of the Spanish as well as the English of the Spanish-heritage population. These descriptions are often simply "traditional" in linguistic orientation, though are sometimes freely blended with the Hispanic tradition or with American structuralism (either taxonomic or generative). Typically, the chief topic examined is the language of the child.

Education-oriented descriptions of Spanish have been limited almost solely to Chicano Spanish. The interest in teaching Spanish to the Spanish-speaking, for example, has resulted in a number of pedagogical theses (e.g., F. Roots 1936, J. Mellenbruch 1954) and textbooks (e.g., P. Baker 1953, M. Barker 1970) that necessarily but indirectly give some information on Chicano Spanish. More specifically descriptive of the Spanish of the (Chicano) child are a few laudable vocabulary compilations and studies (e.g., L. Baugh 1933, L. Tireman 1948a, R. Cornejo 1969, E. Carrow 1971) and a smaller number of significant phonological-grammatical descriptions (Gustavo González 1968 and 1969, Matluck and Mace 1973). In recent years, several excellent studies have appeared in the form of dissertations discussing the acquisition of the morphology and syntax of Chicano Spanish: M. Brisk 1972, Gustavo González 1970, J. Martínez-Bernal 1972, and A. Toronto 1972.

Although the teaching of English to the Spanish-speaking child has been a topic of concern for many years, the description of the child's English was generally ignored until the 1970's. K. Lynn's early (1940) study of Chicano English phonology in Arizona has gone conspicuously unheralded; this otherwise unimportant dissertation remains the only work of its kind to date, and stands alone as a crumbling, primitive monument to the disinterest of U.S. linguists toward this little-known variety of English. Today, however, interest in the topic is growing rapidly (see for example N. Broussard 1972, C. Willard 1971, C. Benítez 1970, Ricardo García 1973, P. Van Metre 1972, and B. Hoffer 1974). Hopefully these works merely mark the forefront of linguistic research on vernacular Chicano English.

Like the educational current, the sociological trend was largely dormant until the 1970's. While many early sociological reports on the acculturation of Hispanic groups (especially Puerto Ricans and Chicanos) do not fail to mention language usage and attitudes, no major work of linguistic-language substance appeared until after World War II, when George C. Barker (1947) and his disciple C. Barber (1952) authored unique and penetrating examinations of the "social functions" of different language codes as used in Tucson, Arizona. These, however, were maverick inquiries whose seminal nature went unappreciated for two decades. Barker's complete dissertation and the essence of Barber's thesis were finally published in 1972 and 1973, respectively, at last receiving the attention they deserve as pioneers of the sociological trend.

The mid-1960's sociocultural essays on language function in the Southwest by Christian/Christian, Voegelin/Voegelin/Schutz and others gave some advance warning of the rising tide of enthusiasm for the sociology of language. Again, attention was directed primarily toward Chicano Spanish, but the surge of interest was due in no small measure to the influence of the gargantuan project directed by Joshua Fishman (1967/71) which set as its goal the full examination of Puerto Rican bilingualism in Jersey City, New Jersey. The ready accessibility of the project's reports appears to have made the multidisciplinary Fishmanesque "sociology of language" approach (as generally distinct from the type of sociolinguistics principally fostered by William Labov) the leading model for other such broad-gauge research efforts.

"Sociology of language" studies have concentrated on determining, in specific areas, the domains of usage of Spanish and English and the factors associated with Spanish language loyalty and maintenance. Thus A. Buitrago Hermenet 1971 and V. Patella 1971 examine the relationship between ethnic identification and language use and preference among (respectively) Puerto Ricans and Texas Chicanos; R. Thompson provides a masterful study of Spanish usage and generational maintenance in Austin, Texas; A. Brekke studies Anglo and Chicano reactions to Anglo and Chicano English varieties; and N. García explores the attitudes of subjects, co-workers, and employers toward Texas Chicano English. These are dissertations for the most part, and are typical of the sociology of language trend, emphasizing as they do the correlation of sociological variables with language choice and attitudes.

Unfortunately, however, the correlation of specific linguistic elements with sociological variables (i.e., Labovian sociolinguistics as opposed to the Fishman variety, language sociology) has hardly been explored. New York-area Puerto Rican English is sociolinguistically probed in several recent works (e.g., Wolfram 1972 and 1973, Shiels 1972, and Silverman 1972; all zero in on Puerto Rican adoptions of vernacular Black English phonology), but the English of other Spanish speaking groups remains untapped by sociolinguists, while sociolinguistic treatments of U.S. Spanish are marginally represented at best (next to nothing except for Ma and Herasimchuk 1971), though Phillips incorporates several crude social distinctions into his description of Los Angeles Spanish (1967), G. Keller (1974) correlates social and situational variables with the use of tú and usted by young New Yorkers, and an intriguing sociolinguistic study of attitudes toward slang and standard Spanish in El Paso is presented by K. Ramírez (1973). But until such time as sophisticated sociolinguistic research is undertaken on a broader scale, our knowledge of the social dialects employed by U.S. Spanish speakers will remain as it is today: minimal and fragmentary.

The total picture is further complicated by the general observation, tentative but nonetheless necessary, that in the past few years the two otherwise placid currents of "educational" and "sociological" linguistic emphasis have discovered each other and have merged into streams that casual observers readily perceive as raging floods, spewing debris (largely in the form of unpublished theses and dissertations) here and there over the academic landscape. This hybrid trend often focuses on assessment of the bilingual's control of his two languages. Studies in this area mainly deal with Chicano Spanish and are largely oriented toward bilingual education. They are invariably in the language sociology mold, treating such topics as language preference, dominance, attitudes, and proficiency. Several of the better examples of these recent dissertations will suffice to illustrate the direction of this research: A. Cohen's evaluation (1973) of a bilingual education program's effectiveness in promoting Spanish and English usage and proficiency; G. Mallory's attempt to ascertain participant influence on the child's choice of language (1971); L. Gutiérrez's survey (1972) of parents' Spanish usage and attitudes toward bilingual education; and Rodolfo García's examination of the standard English proficiency of migrant children (1973).

In sum, then, these three major "trends"--Hispanic, educational, and sociological--accommodate virtually all significant language research on the U.S. Spanish-speaking population. There are, to be sure, occasional intractable studies that defy such characterization; some salient examples have been noted above. It is also possible to discern two secondary trends, reflected in research on Spanish influence on (1) Native American languages and (2) American English. The first shows an anthropological orientation with strong sophistication in American structural linguistics and will be considered separately in the discussion of Chicano Spanish below. The second is characterized largely by the sort of popularistic "Anglic tradition" illustrated on the pages of the journal American Speech and exhibits little linguistic sophistication except in the realm of traditional dialect geography (e.g., J. Sawyer 1957, E.B. Atwood 1962, E. Bright 1967). But these exceptions merely serve to heighten awareness of the distinctiveness and limitations of U.S. Spanish research: its independence, for the most part, from the currents of American and international structuralism in linguistics and its concern, in the main, for the societal problems of bilingualism.

Major Research on Each Variety

The study of the several varieties of U.S. Spanish is as distinctive and limited as the trends themselves. But there is also great disparity between the varieties with regard to trends emphasized and amount and quality of research produced. A cursory examination of the major works on each variety (in order of the quantity of research available) will clearly add considerable perspective to an understanding of the "state of the art."

Chicano Spanish. Chicanos form the largest group of U.S. Spanish speakers. Though the present Chicano population derives predominantly from the immigration of Mexican nationals in the 125 years or so that the Southwest has been a part of the U.S., it is important to emphasize that the ancestors of an important number of this group had settled in the Southwest long before it became United States territory and, indeed, long before there existed a U.S. or a Mexico. Because of this 400 year history of fluctuating but continous immigration, the group is highly heterogeneous. Sociologically it may still defy unitary classification, but linguistically (at least for present purposes) we must treat it as a unit nevertheless.

At this point it is essential that some justification be offered for our choice of the potentially offensive label "Chicano" to refer to the group and the language variety alike. Various terms--Mexican, Chicano, Latin American, Latin, Mexican American, Spanish American, Spanish, Hispano, Spanish-surnamed, and others-- are used for non-pejorative ethnic identification by different segments of the group and by outsiders as well. However, a term acceptable to some is offensive to others. Ignoring such sensitivities, "Mexican," the label selected by Cárdenas (1970), could be justified on the groups that the group is characterized by ancestral residence within Mexico's borders (either present or else pre-1848). The label "Mexican Spanish" is not, however, nearly precise enough to distinguish it from the Spanish of Mexico (even though it may well be a subdialect of the latter). Consequently, the term "Mexican-American" is often employed (e.g., by J. Craddock 1973), but it is rejected here because of increasing negative in-group reaction to such hyphenated terms. "Chicano," on the other hand, carries the general sense of "Mexican" (the two forms apparently derive from the same source) while also referring to the distinctively "American" variant thereof. Although objectionable to some because of militancy and/or criminality, the term "Chicano" now seems appropriate not only because of its increasing acceptance by diverse members of the group (well documented for a strongly anti-"Mexican" sentiment by J. Metzgar, "The Ethnic Sensitivity of Spanish New Mexicans," NMHR 49.49-73 [1974]) but also because it is associated with the sociological solidarity of the linguistically unified group that we wish to label.

Chicano Spanish is readily the best described of U.S. Spanish varieties. This is due no doubt to the size of the group, its heterogeneity, and the depth of its roots in the region. But the length of the roots can often be seen to correlate to a large degree with the volume of research. For this reason it will be useful to survey the situation according to somewhat arbitrary geographical boundaries: New Mexico and southern Colorado, Arizona, Texas, California, and "elsewhere" (includes northern Colorado, the Midwest, the Northwest, etc.). Pachuco Spanish, and Spanish influence on Native American languages (two topics having an indubitable non-geographical unity) will be treated separately.

The Spanish dialect of northern New Mexico and southern Colorado, traditionally called New Mexican Spanish, holds the distinction of being the most extensively researched of all Chicano Spanish variants and is, indeed, perhaps the most exhaustively investigated of any Spanish dialect anywhere. It is also the subject of the earliest substantive linguistic descriptions. The first to appear was the thrice-published 1906 dissertation on phonetics and morphology by E.C. Hills. But it was Hills' mentor, Espinosa, who launched in 1909 the half-century of publications that are largely responsible for making New Mexican Spanish the meticulously described dialect that it is. And his renowned three-part Studies on phonology, morphology, and English influence was highly influential in establishing the dominance of the Hispanic tradition in New Mexican (and Southwestern) Spanish descriptive linguistic research right up to the present day. The only significant departure from this tradition up until the recent spate of sociological-educational research is another classic in its own right, Donald Bowen's comprehensive structuralist description of the phonology, morphology, and lexicon of "The Spanish of San Antonito, New Mexico." This 1952 work remains one of the two finest post-Espinosa linguistic studies of U.S. Spanish; the other is Phillips 1967.

The host of other important works on New Mexican Spanish are primarily of a phonological or lexicographical nature. Prominent studies of the phonological stripe include: Espinosa's precise description of "Syllabic Consonants in New Mexican Spanish" (1925); J. Rael's "A Study of the Phonology and Morphology of New Mexican Spanish Based on . . . 410 Folk-tales" (1937), an Espinosa-directed dissertation that is admittedly as sweeping but not nearly as exacting as the master's work; the detailed historical treatment of [š] by R. Duncan (1956); and J. Harris' recent papers (1974a, 1974b) on several morphophonemic peculiarities viewed from the generative phonology perspective. The major lexicographical contributions are: Espinosa's learnèd discussion of several distinctive forms (1930); the jointly-bound vocabularies by F. Kercheville (1934) and G. McSpadden (1934); the listing by S. Gross of lexical items from the published works of Espinosa; the Espinosa-directed thesis by Trinidad García on Anglicisms in southwestern New Mexico, especially noteworthy as the only major study for the southern half of the state; L. Tireman's dictionary of the Spanish of four preschool children (1948a); L. Trujillo's vocabulary, based chiefly on Rael's folktale collection; L. Kiddle's excellent article on "'Turkey' in New Mexican Spanish" (1951-52), the only dialect geography research yet performed on U.S. Spanish; the peculiar but valuable vocabulary study submitted jointly as a thesis by Shoban and Singer; and R. Murphy's sociolinguistic investigation into the "Integration of English Lexicon in Albuquerque Spanish" (1972). Syntactic studies are practically non-existent; M. Brisk's valiant attempt to describe the syntax of the preschool child is the only major contribution.

The Spanish of Arizona has been scantily researched at best. All major works are at least twenty years old and deal almost solely with the Tucson area; only three significant descriptions of the Spanish language can be cited. The sole description of phonology and grammar is the dated work of Anita C. Post, whose MA thesis on phonology and morphology (1917) and dissertation on phonology (1932) poorly imitate the work of Espinosa, who directed the 1932 work. The only lexical contribution of note is A. Trejo's thesis listing Tucson nonstandard forms. Arizona Spanish has simply not been studied outside the confines of the Hispanic tradition.

But distinctive early work in two other areas--language sociology and vernacular Chicano English--provide Arizona with a certain measure of importance in the study of the speech of U.S. Hispanos. K. Lynn's quite ordinary 1940 dissertaion, "A Phonetic Analysis of the English Spoken by Mexican Children in the Elementary Schools of Arizona," provides more information than is yet available elsewhere on the phonology of an English dialect spoken by many Chicanos. In similar fashion the previously-mentioned works of G. Barker and C. Barber constitute pace-setting studies of the social functions of language in bilingual and trilingual areas of Tucson. The works of Barker and Barber and the comprehensive survey of the multilingual situation in Arizona by Voegelin/Voegelin/Schutz (1967) give Arizona Spanish a language-sociology descriptive basis that is unsurpassed elsewhere. It is rather surprising, then, that the current surge of interest in language sociology has so far failed to have much impact in Arizona.

The Spanish of Texas is second only to that of New Mexico in total amount of major research. The chief difference is that linguistic studies of Texas Spanish are largely of more recent vintage (the past thirty years) and consequently are often more sophisticated. But in Texas too the Hispanic tradition has been dominant. Predictably, then, much of the research has been on vocabulary; leading the pack is the valuable though mechanistic Vocabulario español de Texas (Cerda/Cabaza/Farias 1953) on the Spanish of South Texas; it is doubtless the most comprehensive lexicographical work so far published on any single variety of U.S. Spanish. Of major importance too are the equally comprehensive though sadly unpublished studies of San Antonio Spanish lexicon by R. Galván (a thesis in 1949 and a dissertation in 1955) and the various theses on Texas Spanish lexicon by students of Galván's at Southwest Texas State University (see Frausto 1969 et al.). Similarly meriting mention are M. Fody's glossary of nonstandard forms (1969) and two studies of the Spanish vocabulary of preschool children: the early thesis by L. Baugh (1933) and the more comprehensive dissertation by R. Cornejo (1969).

One is surprised to find that good detailed phonological descriptions of Texas Spanish are nonexistent. We can mention only: V. Poulter's dissertation on Fort Worth-Dallas Spanish (1973), a work with ample data but serious methodological and analytical flaws; the same author's nicely executed comparison of English and Spanish voiceless stops as produced by bilinguals (1970); and Gustavo González's too short report on the phonology of Corpus Christi children (1969).

There have also been few comprehensive studies of the structure of Texas Spanish. Although M. Patterson's 1946 study of San Antonio

Spanish and M. Marrocco's lengthy attempt (1972) to describe Corpus Christi Spanish must be noted, the most sophisticated overview is Rosaura Sánchez's perceptive and wide-ranging article on the Spanish of Chicano college students (1972). But in the area of morphosyntax the description of Texas Spanish is sparse. In addition to the preceding general descriptions, especially the lucid morphosyntactic observations of Sánchez, F. Hensey's article on El Paso grammatical variables (1973) and S. Said's Austin-based thesis (1970) provide unique though limited transformational examinations of syntax. The salient contributions, however, have been the work of Gustavo González, including his thesis sketch of the morphology and syntax of the Corpus Christi first-grader and his subsequent meticulous explorations of children's acquisition of Spanish grammar.

The influence of Spanish on English has a longer a more fertile history of description in Texas than anywhere else. The study of Spanish borrowings in Texas English begins with H. Tallichet's early lists (1896) and culminates with E. Bagby Atwood's *The Regional Vocabulary of Texas* (1962), a truly signal contribution to American English dialect geography. The study of vernacular Chicano English has also been admirably pursued in recent years--a follow-up, so to speak, of Janet Sawyer's pace-setting 1957 dissertation, "A Dialect Study of San Antonio, Texas," which has long been kept in the public eye by a well-orchestrated series of spin-off articles. Noteworthy among more recent work is B. Heiler's careful thesis on stress placement, C. Benítez's commendable thesis on phonological and grammatical deviations, and B. Hoffer's probing article on developmental stages in the acquisition of English syntax.

In Texas Spanish as elsewhere, research on language sociology and bilingualism has been seriously pursued in recent years. D. Lance's *A Brief Study of Spanish/English Bilingualism* (1969 and ff.), documenting multiple aspects of language usage, has become the standard reference work, especially with regard to code-switching. Also important for our understanding of the sociological functions of Spanish vis-à-vis English are the numerous studies emanating from Texas A & M University, e.g., R. Skrabanek (1967 and ff.) and the several excellent works of Kuvlesky and Kuvlesky/Patella. But the single outstanding language sociology contribution is Roger Thompson's "Language Loyalty in Austin, Texas: A Study of a Bilingual Neighborhood" (1971), a dissertation that carefully and comprehensively surveys language usage in Austin's Chicano community and draws penetrating conclusions on local trends in the maintenance of Spanish. Other studies cover a wide range of language sociology topics, for example: E. Carrow's analysis of Spanish-English comprehension by preschoolers (1971), N. García's examination of language attitudes and employment, R. Jordán de Caro's essay interrelating loyalty to Spanish language and folklore (1973), and J. Reyna's sociolinguistically-oriented collection of jokes and anecdotes.

As concerns California it is most unpleasant to report that
the state with the largest absolute number of Spanish-speaking
inhabitants--almost 2.4 million "persons of Spanish origin" (an
astounding one quarter of the national total)--exhibits a veritable poverty of research on Chicano language. But while there
is only one significant descriptive study of California Spanish,
that one work is fortunately the most all-inclusive <u>grammatical</u>
description yet written on any brand of U.S. Spanish: R. Phillips'
1967 dissertation on the phonology, morphology and lexicon (but
especially the syntax) of the Spanish spoken in East Los Angeles.

All other important California works have appeared since
Phillips' and, with the exception of A. Blanco's encyclopedic
socio-historical account of <u>La lengua española en la historia de
California</u>, all are products of the recent sociological/educational
concern for Spanish-English bilingualism. Especially notable for
descriptive linguistic value is A. Beltramo's 1972 dissertation,
a skillful study of English lexical influence and related aspects
of phonology and morphology. Gumperz and Hernández-Chávez (1972)
present a probing pragmatic examination of code-switching. Educational in its orientation is the most thorough evaluation yet made
of bilingual schooling for Spanish speakers, A. Cohen's recent
Stanford University dissertation; other recent works that deserve
mention are Allan Metcalf's "Mexican-American English in Southern
California" (1972), A. Brekke's dissertation (1973), and two MA
theses: N. Broussard's graphemic-phonemic study of Chicano highschoolers' English spelling errors, and C. Willard's study of the
grammar of English compositions of Chicano junior college students.

Very little research has been performed on Chicano Spanish
outside the Southwest. Except for N. Humphrey's notable early
assessment of language loyalty and attitudes in Detroit (1943-44),
major research contributions have been quite recent. Four doctoral
dissertations and one MA thesis stand out. The influence of
English is explored in two dissertations cast largely in the Hispanic tradition but blended with American structuralism: S. Tsuzaki's study of the phonology and morphology of Detroit Spanish
(1973 [published in 1971]) and R. Teschner's lexical study of
Anglicisms in Chicago Spanish (1972). The other works have all
been cast in the educational-sociological molds. A. Toronto 1972
examines the development of morphosyntactic structures in the
Spanish of Chicago preschoolers, while Rodolfo García (1973) reports on the oral English proficiency of Mexican American migrants
in Michigan. The remarkable thesis by B. Mace (1972) provides a
huge language usage and English proficiency survey of Seattle's
preschool population, which includes a sizeable number of Spanish
speakers.

"Pachuco," the Southwest Spanish argot that gained national
notoriety in association with gangs of Chicano delinquents during
the 1940's, is referred to by several other names (<u>caló</u>, <u>tirilí</u>,
etc.) but the well-established term will be used here. Like all
argots, Pachuco deviates from general Chicano Spanish primarily
as regards its lexicon, which derives from a number of sources.

Studies of Pachuco, therefore, have naturally been devoted for the most part (and in the finest Hispanic tradition) to the collection of nonstandard vocabulary items and to their etymological exegesis. Though preceded by several collections of lexical oddities, the first major report is G. Barker's separate publication on Tucson Pachuco (1950), notable as much for its discussion of usage and attitudes as for its vocabulary list. The long-ignored M.L. Wagner (1953-54), however, is the first scholarly piece to examine significantly the varied Romance and other historical origins of Pachuco lexicon. A more thorough documentation of the links between Pachuco and other contemporary Hispanic argots is provided by A. Trejo's excellent compilation of Latin American argot forms (1968). The most extensive vocabulary of Pachuco is also one of the best lexicographical efforts on U.S. Spanish: Lurline Coltharp's 1965 dictionary of El Paso Pachuco, a work that also contains minor comments on phonology. In addition to these major works, two recent MA theses are oriented primarily toward establishing the currency in other areas of the forms cited by Coltharp: W. January's 1970 study of North Texas Pachuco lexicon is also distinctinve in providing data on usage by different age groups, while L. Katz (1974) is a more naive treatment of Pachuco forms in Los Angeles. An exceptional piece of research is K. Ramírez's restricted examination of the usage of and attitudes toward Spanish and Pachuco forms in the El Paso area (1971, 1973), a pace-setting work that signals the fruitful potential of exploring the social aspects of U.S. Spanish dialect variation.

The study of the influence of Chicano Spanish on Native American languages is both unique and generally atypical of the trends in U.S. Spanish research as a whole. This particular field has been largely the province of anthropological linguists, often prominent names in mainstream American linguistics, whose central concern in Amerindian culture contact and acculturation. The outstanding acculturation study is E. Dozier's contrastive examination of the distinctive patterns of Spanish cultural contact with (and resultant linguistic influence on) Yaqui and Tewa. Most work of this type has dealt with phonological, lexical, and semantic aspects of borrowing. Salient studies emphasizing phonology are those of W. Miller (1960) on Acoma and G. Trager (1944) on Taos. The outstanding lexical study is W. Bright's examination of loanwords for domestic animals in the Native American languages of California (1960). Although morpho-syntactic influences have hardly been considered. the pioneering studies by J. Johnson 1943 and J. Lindenfeld 1971 deserve acknowledgement. Scholars of the Hispanic tradition have occasionally ventured into this field, but with a distinct orientation; notable are the sojourns of the indefatigable A.M. Espinosa, typified by his study of the loanword "Castilla" in several Pueblo languages for the purpose of drawing implications about the colonial pronunciation of ll in Spanish (1932). Also noteworthy is the historically-oriented article by L. Kiddle (1964) that ended a long polemic about the source of the word for "cat" in many Southwest Indian languages.

The greatest flaw in research on Chicano Spanish influence on

Amerindian languages is that the researcher typically has a command of the language and linguistic literature of only one of the two groups in contact. A meeting of the minds of American anthropological and traditional Hispanic linguistics (not only in the U.S. but elsewhere in the New World as well) is clearly needed to produce any substantive research in this area.

To conclude this section, a brief comment on the more general aspects of research on Chicano Spanish is now in order. It is clear that there have been few "pan-Chicano Spanish" studies made. Most such attempts are simple surveys of a few aspects of the language situation with an emphasis on the sociocultural and educational aspects of bilingualism, as in the ground-breaking essay by Christian and Christian (1966) and the recent articles by J. Ornstein (especially 1970 and 1972). Other more sociologically-oriented works, such as Grebler/Moore/Guzmán 1970 and W. Kuvlesky 1973, present insightful information on language usage and loyalty but can hardly be considered pan-Chicano since they are based on research in just two areas (Texas and California and Texas and Colorado, respectively).

With regard to descriptive linguistics, no noteworthy work has dared to attempt a description of the parameters of Chicano Spanish as a single phenomenon (ignoring D. Cárdenas' cursory outline [1970] of the major varieties of U.S. Spanish). There have been, however, innumerable--usually insignificant--publications that discuss particular aspects of Chicano Spanish or some unidentified variant thereof. Notable are the discussion by Gustavo González of E. García's 1971 analysis of several linguistic markers and the treatment by Matluck and Mace of diverse Chicano Spanish phenomena, especially English influence.

Thus while works of analysis are abundant for local variants of Chicano Spanish, works of synthesis are notably lacking. This is as true in lexicography as in phonology and grammar. The influence of Chicano Spanish on the vocabulary of English is well documented in such works of synthesis as the American English dictionaries of Craigie and Hulbert (1938-44) and Mathews (1951). A dictionary of Chicano Spanish, however, has yet to be produced. This lack can be said to stem from a variety of reasons both linguistic and sociological; some of the linguistic problems are trenchantly discussed and illustrated in R. Teschner (1974a).

Puerto Rican Spanish. Puerto Ricans on the U.S. mainland are a relatively recent phenomenon. While a certain number of Puerto Ricans moved to New York before World War II, the great majority of the present population is a product of post-World War II entry, the heaviest migration coming in the late 1940's and throughout the 1950's. According to the 1970 Census, over 95 per cent of the mainland Puerto Rican population report the island as their own birthplace or as the birthplace of a parent. New York City is the present home of most mainland Puerto Ricans--perhaps as many as two-thirds of the total. The nature of this sudden influx is critical in explaining the fact that the study of Puerto Ricans has been

directed almost exclusively toward sociological and educational
concerns, often of an immediately pressing sort. Language considerations figure primarily within these contexts.

Although sociological studies in the 1930's and 1940's--e.g.,
L. Chenault 1938, P. Gosnell 1945--loosely refer to language factors, works more specifically concerned with Puerto Rican language
have appeared only in the past twenty-five years. Few have dealt
with the description of Puerto Rican Spanish. The few significant
works that have reported on Puerto Rican Spanish usually deal with
phonology or the lexical nature of English influence, typically show
a great concern for the bilingual's usage of his two languages, and
generally avoid any discussion of the Puerto Rican Spanish of New
York City! The only major phonological descriptions are two MA
theses that examine small communities nowhere near New York City:
B. Decker 1952 (Lorain, Ohio) and M. Kindig 1960 (Hawaii). Noteworthy studies examining the lexical influence of English are (most
prominently) Charles Kreidler's careful dissertation (1957) and the
MA theses of Ana Porges and C. Craig; Carlos Varo's popularizing and
angry treatment of New York Puerto Rican "Spanglish" (1971) may also
be cited as representative of a special class of works. While most
of these items fit the Hispanic tradition, some show considerable
taxonomic influence as well (especially the Kreidler dissertation).

Coincident with but usually overshadowing these scattered descriptions of Puerto Rican Spanish are the relatively numerous "educational" items, produced especially in New York and addressed invariably to such topics as language dominance and preference, acculturation, attitudes, English and Spanish proficiency, and so
forth, with the incorporation of little specific language description. Noteworthy examples of such works are Anastasi and de Jesús
(1953) on Spanish communicative proficiency, F. Mayans (1953) on
environmental influences in the learning of English, A. Buitrago
Hermenet (1971) on ethnic identity and language usage, and K. Kendler
(1972) on language usage in schools and at home. In the early 1970's
the linguistic description of Puerto Rican English was seriously
and substantively pursued along the lines of Labovian sociolinguistics--S. Silverman (1971), W. Wolfram (1972, 1973), and M. Shiels
(1972) all focusing primarily on phonology and the occasional Black
English influences on the English of some Puerto Ricans. Also important for the description of Puerto Rican English is George Williams' generative-transformational study of phonology and grammar
in spontaneous speech (1972).

Capping off all work on the language and language behavior of
the mainland Puerto Rican is, of course, the ambitious and comprehensive survey by Joshua Fishman and his associates, a project that
lead eventually to the influential volume of reports and workpapers
entitled <u>Bilingualism in the Barrio</u> (1971). This massive study of
the language situation in a bilingual neighborhood in Jersey City
explores a wide range of sociological and psychological aspects of
language sociology--usage and domains, attitudes, dominance, and so
forth--and even attempts a sociolinguistic treatment of selected
phonological variables in Puerto Rican Spanish and English. Multi-

faceted and multidisciplinary, the study aims to set high standards for the investigation of language in bilingual settings. It is not likely that other research on U.S. Spanish in the immediate future will begin to attempt the catholicity of the Fishman project.

<u>Cuban Spanish</u>. There have been enclaves of Cubans in the U.S. for over a hundred years, but the bulk of Cuban immigration has been very recent, arriving in the main since the 1959 Castro revolution. The 1970 Census indicates that approximately 80 per cent of the Cuban population in the U.S. was born in Cuba. One would therefore not expect a great amount of research so far. That is indeed the case. Only a few scattered studies over the years have dealt with the language of the earlier immigrants; the modest amount of work of the past ten years is largely devoted to the speech of the post-1959 group. Most of this and previous research has been performed on Cuban Spanish in Florida, the principal locus of Cubans in the U.S.

The Hispanic tradition has dominated the study of Cuban Spanish, but the influence of American structuralism, both taxonomic and transformational, has also been felt in recent years. Phonology and lexicon are once again the central areas of research. Studies of English influence (mostly lexical) have been particularly manifest; a few of the major works are: C. Ortiz's early MA thesis on Tampa Spanish (1947); a Washington D.C.-based thesis by M. Castellanos (1967); an article on Anglicisms in the speech of the early Cuban settles of Key West by T. Beardsley (1972-73); B. Varela de Cuéllar's consideration of "La influencia del inglés en los cubanos de Miami y Nueva Orleans" (1974); and R. Fernández's 1973 study of written and spoken Anglicisms in Miami. Two other works deal with Cuban Spanish slang and proverbs: a thesis by C. Navarro (1963) and a 1966 booklet by A. Cherry.

Occasional items give noteworthy descriptions of U.S. Cuban Spanish phonology. The early article by D. Canfield (1951) considers a couple of phonetic aspects of Tampa Spanish, but little more has been done for Florida, though Profs. Melvyn Resnick, Bohdan Saciuk and other Florida-based scholars are now directing several theses and dissertations on Florida Cuban phonology; one of these that has recently come to our attention is R. Hammond's impressive-sounding MA study of the systemic consequences of /s/ → [∅] among Miami's Cubans. A. Lamb (1968) gives an excellent linguistic (and partly sociolinguistic) description of the Spanish phonology of Cubans in Chicago, and a careful generative analysis of one idiolect is presented by J. Guitart (1973). No significant work has been done on Cuban Spanish grammar or (as yet) on the Spanish-influenced English of Cubans. Surprisingly enough we have yet to find any major examples of "educational" or "sociological" currents, even though much of the important work on bilingual education and curriculum development has been produced for speakers of Cuban Spanish. We can note just two works that approach the sociolinguistic: the above-mentioned study by Lamb (1968) and B. Vallejo's 1970 dissertation, a sociolinguistic and dialect-geography examination of selected phonological variables in the speech of exiles recently arrived from Havana and elsewhere in Cuba.

Judeo-Spanish (Dzhudezmo). The Sephardic Jews, most of whom arrived in the U.S. in the twentieth century, are dispersed throughout the country though the heaviest concentration is in New York. It is impossible to ascertain either the total number of U.S. Sephardic Jews or the number of those who still speak Judeo-Spanish (variously though not definitively termed "Ladino" or "Dzhudezmo" as well). In the mid-sixties R. Renard estimated that U.S. Ladino speakers numbered 15,000, and it is generally conceded that use of the language is rapidly declining here. Unfortunately, this variety of U.S. Spanish is disappearing with too few--and too limited--linguistic descriptions accomplished.

Perhaps because of the many implications of Judeo-Spanish for the study of the history of the Spanish language, research on U.S. Dzhudezmo has been entirely in the Hispanic tradition, with the emphasis on peculiar forms in phonology and vocabulary. Studies of New York Judeo-Spanish are most prominent, ranging from M. Luria's pioneering article on "Judeo-Spanish Dialects in New York City" (1930) to F. Agard's cursory overview of phonology, morphology, and lexicon (1950, with corrections by H. Besso 1951) and the two wide-ranging linguistic descriptions by R. Hirsch (1951) and D. Levy (1952), both doctoral dissertations. Outside of New York, we may only note the early comments on archaisms in Seattle Judeo-Spanish by Umphrey and Adatto (1936) and the recent etymological study by I. Bar-Lewaw (1968) of Ladino vocabulary used in two southern cities.

Louisiana Spanish: isleño. The speech of the isleños, early Canary Island colonists who settled in what is now Louisiana, is in an even sadder state of documentation. This dialect of Spanish is known solely through the work of R. MacCurdy in the late 1940's, as reported in his dissertation (1948) and the publications derived therefrom. Subsequent fieldwork resulted in a brief article on lexicon (1959) with cursory comments on French-Spanish-English trilingualism in the area. MacCurdy's work is heavily and quite narrowly within the Hispanic tradition and woefully lacking in an awareness of scientific linguistics. Nonetheless, and in the absence of more linguistically sophisticated research, the studies by MacCurdy represent an invaluable contribution on a unique variety of U.S. Spanish. Any future research can ill afford delay; the estimated 5,000 isleño Spanish speakers at the time of MacCurdy's research has declined to perhaps half that number today.

Other Dialects. The few additional remaining varieties of U.S. Spanish have been scarcely documented by linguists. The only major language study of immigrants from Spain is the dissertation by M. Gutiérrez (1971) which loosely examines Spanish-English bilingualism among Gallegos in New York City. The previously cited Florida-based studies by Ortiz, Canfield and Cherry comment on Asturian as well as Cuban Spanish. A few other works marginally comment on other varieties of Spanish, e.g., Mace's study of non-English speaking preschoolers in Seattle (1972) and G. Keller's report (1974) on the use of tú and usted by a variety of New York immigrants, some from Central and South America.

U.S. Spanish in General. Given the tremendous diversity within U.S. Spanish, it is quite understandable that little attention has been given to the treatment of the topic as a whole. Quite naturally, bibliographical works are most prominent. Although the present Bibliography is the only attempt to annotate all linguistic studies of all varieties of the speech of U.S. Hispanos, the valuable article-length bibliography by H. Woodbridge (1954) and the supplement by M. Fody (1971) are important contributions for the Spanish of the South and Southwest regions. Only one survey of research is noted: J. Craddock's superb critique (1973) of major contributions to the field between the years 1953-1970. The single work that has attempted to assay the many facets of the Spanish presence in the U.S. is the imposing volume by C. Fernández-Shaw (1972), though as regards language its presentation is necessarily superficial. Of the many generalist statements of an educational or sociological nature, none is sufficiently comprehensive to merit mention as studies of U.S. Spanish as a whole.

It is even more to be expected that little has been done in the realm of descriptive linguistics. Indeed, only one work can be cited: the summary treatment by Daniel N. Cárdenas of the "Dominant Spanish Dialects Spoken in the United States" (1970), a sometimes quixotic contrastive description of selected linguistic features of four varieties (Chicano, Puerto Rican, Cuban and Peninsular). Other researchers have coincidentally included speakers from two or more Spanish speaking groups in their samples, but have failed to explore the issues of heterogeneity or homogeneity of language. Clearly, then, works of synthesis are sorely lacking. But perhaps of more value to our understanding of the science of language is the work that could be done on the linguistic contact between speakers of different dialects of U.S. Spanish--Puerto Ricans with others in the New York area, Chicanos and Puerto Ricans in urban areas of the Midwest (see for example our annotation of Toronto 1972), Cubans with others in cities throughout the country, Chicanos with Central Americans in San Francisco, and so forth. Such topics (and many others of a more general sort) have yet to be considered, much less dealt with.

Concluding Remarks. We now return to our central question: how have language scholars responded to the research opportunities in U.S. Spanish? If nothing else, this present brief survey of past research should provide both an awareness of the difficulty of answering this question with any precision and, at the same time, a general idea of the positive and negative aspects of any response. Let us simply highlight here the central points.

The good news is that a fair amount of research has indeed been performed on U.S. Spanish. This research has largely been in the form of phonological and lexical observations on the Spanish of isolated communities, especially on Southwest Chicano Spanish but also on all other varieties. In recent years some stimulating research has been undertaken on the multitude of factors involved in assessing the role of Spanish in the numerous bilingual areas of the U.S. The works in these and other areas have therefore built a solid foundation of knowledge about U.S. Spanish.

The bad news is that the work on U.S. Spanish has been much less than one would expect for such a numerically significant language. By way of contrast, the largest of the U.S. Native American languages, Navajo, shows a bibliography with almost three-fourths as many entries as the present work (see James Kari, "Navajo Language Bibliography: Preliminary Edition," Albuquerque: Univ. of New Mexico, 1973), though the Navajo population amounts to less than two per cent of the Spanish-surnamed population.

The worst of the bad news is that much U.S. Spanish research is of poor quality, resulting both from the often inadequate training of researchers and the frequent disinterest in this language on the part of those in the mainstream of American linguistics. Most of the remainder of the bad news (lack of research on syntax, semantics, sociolinguistics, theoretical issues, and so forth) can be said to derive from these lacunae.

Finally, then, it is both fortunate and unfortunate that past research has left so much for the future researcher. And this is the "news" that will most concern the users of the present Bibliography. There is hardly an endeavor--analytic or synthetic, documentational or theoretical, pure or applied--that does not go begging for additional study. Basic descriptive linguistic research is needed everywhere, though perhaps most urgently on isleño Spanish and Judeo-Spanish, given their imminent prospects for extinction. There are also total voids in knowledge based on past research, such as the isolation and description of social and geographical dialect variations, especially with regard to Chicano Spanish (and English). In more general terms, the tremendous complexities of assessing the linguistic, sociological and psychological aspects of bilingualism vis-à-vis Spanish speakers provide topics sure to keep fieldworkers and theoreticians fruitfully occupied for many years to come.

In these and other future efforts, then, we hope this Bibliography will serve as a useful guide, linking past to porvenir, in the unending drive to understand the multiple manifestations and ramifications of United States Spanish language and Spanish-English bilingualism.

Garland D. Bills, May 1975, Albuquerque, New Mexico

SECTION 1 (UNITED STATES IN GENERAL)

1.1 BIBLIOGRAPHY

Major Items: Haug-1973; Nich-1941; Wood-1954.

See also these items elsewhere (consult Author Index for location):
(none)

BRENNI, Vito J. American English: A Bibliography. Philadelphia:
   Univ. of Pennsylvania Press, 1964. 221 pp. [Rev. JEGP
   64.574-578 (1965) (R. McDavid); MLR 61.657-658 (1966) (H.
   Hargrave); AS 43.69-71 (1968) (S. Baum).]

   Just five entries pertaining to "Spanish Language: loan words
from" are found through a consultation of this work's author/
subject index; only one (Bentley 1932) is annotated briefly.
Readers alert to other categories that bear on English Hispanisms
will also check "The Language of the Cowboy" (p. 155, a subsection of sec. 6, "Slang") and the entries under "Dictionaries of
Americanisms" (most of these are annotated, at times copiously).
   In general, reviewers have not thought highly of this bibliography; see especially McDavid 1965. [RT]

HAUGEN, Einar. "Bilingualism in the Americas: A Bibliography and
   Research Guide." PADS 26.entire issue (159 pp.) (Nov. 1956).
   (Rept. 1964.) [Rev. Hispania 40.502-503 (1957) (J. Palermo);
   BSL 53:2.41-42 (1957-58) (E. Benveniste); Language 34.91-93
   (1958) (H. Hoijer); Anglia 76.427-429 (1958) (W. Leopold);
   JCLA 4.94-98 (1958) (W. Mackey); MLR 53.458 (1958) (S. Potter);
   Monatshefte 50.93 (1958) (C. Reed); SL 13.81-82 (1958) (G.
   Trager); PJ (1959).357-363 (1959) (W. Cienkowski); RR 50.156-
   158 (1959) (L. Pap); RPh 13.84-86 (1959-60) (W. Shipley).]

   Haugen's superlative "bibliography and research guide" in
reality is much more than that, and effectively constitutes the
single best available discussion of the many diverse aspects of
Western Hemisphere native and immigrant bilingualism, linguistic
interference, attitudes toward multilingualism, political and
educational policies toward speakers of non-official languages,
etc., etc. But inevitably, and given the vast territory the author
was obliged to cover in a limited amount of space, the relatively
narrow topic of United States Spanish could not (at that moment
in time) receive more than peripheral attention; it is for this
reason alone that we do not assign the status of major contribution to Haugen's work. Passing mention of U.S. Spanish and especially of Espinosa Sr.'s earlier writings occurs on pp. 29 and
53-59; Espinosa's work is reviewed in detail in sec. 3.4.3 (51-52).
Other authors Haugen discusses or mentions are Agard 1950, Anas-
tasi/Jesús 1953, Barber 1952, Barker 1947, 1950, 1951, Bentley 1932,
Besso 1951, Canfield 1951, Casagrande 1954-55, Cerda et al. 1953,
Dockstader 1955, Dozier 1956, Espinosa 1909 and v.d., Fitz-
Gerald 1921, Friedman 1950, Gamio 1930, Gray 1912, Griffith 1947a,

Hayes 1941, Heflin 1941, Hills 1906, Hirsch [Weinstein] 1951,
Kercheville 1934, Kiddle 1952, Lynn 1945, Lynn 1949, MacCurdy
1950a, 1950b, McSpadden 1934, Nichols 1941, Ornstein 1951, Ortiz
1941, Porges 1949, Post 1933, 1934, Sorvig 1952, 1953, Tallichet
1896, Tireman 1948, 1951, Titiev 1946, Trager 1939, 1944, Trager/
Valdez 1937, Tuck 1946. [RT]

HAUGEN, Einar. "Bilingualism, Language Contact and Immigrant
Languages in the United States: A Research Report 1956-1970."
CTL 10.505-591 (1973).

Apparently in order to avoid duplicating the work assigned
elsewhere in CTL 10 to Craddock (1973), Haugen pays relatively
little attention to U.S. Spanish in what is in all respects another superb example of the fine work that one has come to expect
from the dean of American bilingualists. The report is nevertheless of interest to students of North American Spanish for its
good discussions of Joshua Fishman's major writings, especially
the "Bilingualism in the Barrio" project (1968/71) in sec. 5.2
and Fishman 1966 (Language Loyalty . . .), treated at some
length in sec. 5.3. In 3.2 Haugen pays more than passing attention to Lance 1969 as concerns the phenomenon of code-switching;
others not escaping notice are Tsuzaki 1963 (3.4), Lozano 1961
(2.1) and Grinevald-Craig 1968-69 (2.2). The last-named section
is entitled "Non-English Languages and Dialects" and discusses
"only those studies . . . that aimed at a deeper understanding of
the contact situation and were not just an analysis of isolated
phenomena;" in its short sub-section on Spanish Haugen comments
briefly on two authors he deals with elsewhere: Lance 1969 and
Fishman 1968/71. [RT]

KENISTON, Hayward. "Notes on Research in the Spanish Spoken in
the United States." BACLS 34.64-67 (1942).

A well-written description of who has done what, with emphasis
on the publication history of the works reviewed. With the
exception of the massive efforts of the senior Espinosa, which are
chronicled in sufficient detail, the general paucity of publications explains the brevity of Keniston's contribution, although
one notes with surprise the absence of any reference to Juan B.
Rael, who had already done considerable work on New Mexican
Spanish by the end of the 1930's. [RT]

KIDDLE, Lawrence B. [1943a]. "A propósito de A Bibliographical
Guide to Materials on American Spanish, de Madaline W. Nichols."
RevIb 7.213-220 (1943). (Cf. Kiddle 1943b and Nichols 1941.)

This article defends Madaline Nichols' 1941 bibliography
against an unfavorable review by Amado Alonso. In his entry no.
14873, Serís makes the mistake of assigning the title of Kiddle's
"Bibliografía adicional para la obra de la señorita Nichols" to
the pages covered by Kiddle's "A propósito . . . " The two are
actually separate articles although they have a common reference.
[RT]

KIDDLE, Lawrence B. [1943b]. "Bibliografía adicional para la obra de la Srta. Nichols." RevIb 7.221-240 (1943).

Here Kiddle provides a checklist containing 141 items which Nichols did not include (cf. Kiddle 1943a). Of the 141, 8 relate to United States Spanish, the majority of them in re "Fauna and Flora." [RT]

NICHOLS, Madaline W. A Bibliographical Guide to Materials on American Spanish. Cambridge, Mass.: Harvard Univ. Press, 1941. 114 pp. [Rev. RFE 25.432-433 (1941) ("M.C."[?]); RFH 4.85-86 (1942) (A. Alonso); HR 10.352-355 (1942) (J. Gillet); HAHR 22.183-185 (1942) (L. Wright); RR 34.285-287 (1943) (S. Rosenbaum); ZRPh 63.220 (1943) ("W."[?]). See also the review article by L.B. Kiddle 1943 and the same author's extensive addenda to Nichols' work.]

For years this work remained the standard reference guide to all aspects of Western Hemisphere Spanish; in recent times it has served as the point of departure for several excellent annotated bibliographies on the Spanish of the various Republics.[1]

The Guide's contents are succinctly described by a note on its cover: it "lists the outstanding studies on the Spanish language in the several Spanish American countries. It includes a brief historical account of the growth of an American Spanish; a special section on the work of the American language academies and philological institutes; and approximately twelve hundred annotated entries, covering general studies of the language of each country, dictionaries and vocabularies of local terms, words borrowed from other languages, geographical nomenclature, and flora and fauna."

United States Spanish is covered in a brief section (pp. 98-100) containing 17 separate entries; while some of these are annotated at length, especially those of Espinosa 1930 and Rael 1939, the majority are described laconically. Nichols' subcategories for U.S. Spanish are "General," "[Dictionaries and] Vocabularies," and "Influence of Other Languages." Nearly all the

---

[1]These are: Hensley C. Woodbridge, "Spanish in the American South and Southwest: A Bibliographical Survey for 1940-53," Orbis 3.236-244 (1954); Woodbridge, "An Annotated Bibliography of Mexican Spanish for 1940-1953," KFLQ 1.80-89 (1954); Woodbridge, "An Annotated Bibliography of Publications Concerning the Spanish of Bolivia, Cuba, Ecuador, Paraguay and Peru for the Years 1940-1957," KFLQ 7.37-54 (1960); and Jack Emory Davis, "The Spanish of Argentina and Uruguay: An Annotated Bibliography for 1940-1965," [I:] Orbis 15:1.160-189 (1966), [II:] 15:2.442-488 (1966), [III:] 17:1.232-277 (1968), [IV:] 17:2.538-573 (1968), [V:] 19:1.205-232 (1970), [VI:] 20:1.236-269 (1971); and Davis, "The Spanish of Mexico: An Annotated Bibliography for 1940-69," Hispania 54.624-656 (1971).

reviews describe Nichols' coverage as generally exhaustive, and while substantial additions are put forth by Gillet, Wright, Rosenbaum and especially Kiddle 1943 few of these pertain to U.S. Spanish although for that section Kiddle suggests eight additional titles, the majority in "Fauna and Flora" or "Toponimia."

The Nichols bibliography gave rise to the famous polemical review by Amado Alonso 1942, who took the work to task for not serving adequately as a "guide to materials," as its title promised it would; Alonso's point was that bibliographer Nichols' lack of preparation in linguistics precluded the judicious culling out, sorely needed by students, of the many amateurish materials that crowded the field. In response to this, Lawrence Kiddle pointed out that since Alonso served as one of the project's advisory editors (along with Hayward Keniston and Tomás Navarro Tomás), he should have provided the guidance himself. [RT]

SERÍS, Homero. Bibliografía de la lingüística española. Publicaciones del Instituto Caro y Cuervo, No. 19 (Bogotá: Instituto Caro y Cuervo, 1964). lviii, 981 pp. [Annot. Solé no. 17. Rev. RJB 16.363-366 (1965) (K. Körner); RPh 20.107-112 (1966-67) (H. Woodbridge); PhP 10.125 (1967) (S. Hamplová); GRM 17:48.442-444 (1967) (H. Schneider); RRLing 13.165-170 ("Una bibliografía de lingüística española"-- review essay) (1968) (T. Şandru).]

This indispensable Magnum Opus has been reviewed from all angles by Woodbridge, Schneider, Şandru and the others and will only be discussed here in re United States Spanish. The pertinent section (pp. 752-758) includes 60 entries, unannotated in the main; in some instances the decision as to what to annotate was impeccable (e.g., the judicious citations from reviews of Espinosa 1930/1946), in others eccentric (thus nearly all of p. 754 is given over to a series of quotations on resistance to English which come from four disparate sources and appear to be motivated by entry no. 15517, cited [with the occasional lapses and the archaic format that typify Serís] as "Salado Álvarez, V., Nuevo Méjico todavía no es [norte] americano, RevIbBA, 1930."). While Serís takes great pains to point out errors in and omissions from the work of Nichols 1941, he himself has sometimes made the errors typical of any list which amasses items without checking them; thus Wagner 1953-54 is misleadingly annotated as discussing "El 'pachuco' o jerga de Arizona, Los Ángeles y California del Sur, de influencia mexicana," and Galván 1954 is wrongly cited as "Arispe Galván, Robert;" D. Lincoln Canfield's brief "Diphthongization in the Spanish of the Anglo-North-American" does not belong in a list that deals with natively spoken Spanish; and "15525. Chrétien, D., The dialect of the Sierra de Mariveles Negritos, Berkeley, 1951. (Univ. of California.)" does not belong in a list that deals with Spanish at all,

since in fact the monograph (UCPL 4:2.61-109 [1951]) has solely
to do with problems of classifying an Oceanic dialect spoken by
the cited group on the Philippine island of Luzon. [RT]

SOLÉ, Carlos A. Bibliografía sobre el español en América 1920-
    1967. Washington D.C.: Georgetown Univ. Press, 1970. 175
    pp. [Rev. HLAS 34 (1972) no. 3056 (Canfield); AdL 8.258-261
    (1971) (Moreno de Alba)]

   "Excellent bibliography and review of works on the Spanish
of America. Arranged first of all by general categories such as
bibliographies; general studies on pronunciation, morphology,
syntax; and vocabulary . . . Important aspect is that author has
written critical comments on many of works listed and has included review in résumé of many books and articles on Latin
American Spanish." (Canfield) Solé's section on "Estados Unidos
de Norteamérica" runs from pp. 106-111 (items 944-1007.A). Of
these 65 items, 15 are not found in Serís including 7 issued before 1960; but while Solé has deleted close to 10 of Serís's 60
entries he has not corrected several of the latter's errors such
as the inclusion of Chrétien 1951, the title of Donald Bowen's
PhD dissertation, et al. Solé's brief annotations of 12 of the
more important items are succinct and generally spotless. [RT]

SOLÉ, Carlos A. "Bibliografía sobre el español en América:
    1967-1971." AdL 10.253-288 (1972).

   This is a continuation of Solé 1970. The majority of the 327
items are not annotated. Of the 9 which pertain to United States
Spanish, 2 items are repeated from Solé 1970: Phillips 1967 (in
the present listing Solé locates the dissertation's Abstract in
the DA) and Cerda et al. "1971." (Solé does not indicate that
this latter item is an unrevised reprinting of the 1953 edition,
reference to which is also found in Solé 1970.) [RT]

[ANON.] The Spanish-Speaking People in the United States: A
    Guide to Materials. Washington D.C.: The Cabinet Committee
    on Opportunities for the Spanish-Speaking People/GPO, 1971.
    187 pp.

   This checklist is arranged strictly according to the nature
of the items' issuance, whether as "books and monographs" (pp.
5-58), "articles, reports, speeches" (59-80), "dissertations and
other unpublished materials" (81-104), "government publications:
state and federal" (105-114), etc. A check through pertinent keywords in the subject index (169-187) turns up little of interest
to linguists; most of the items under "Spanish" or "language,"
etc., have solely to do with bilingual education and similar
pedagogical concerns. This work's chief value to students of U.S.
Spanish will lie in its "Listing of Spanish Language Radio & TV

Stations and Programs (State-by-State)" (145-164) and to a lesser extent in its "Listing of Currently Published Serials (State-by-State)" (137-144). [RT]

STECK, Francis Borgia. A Tentative Guide to Historical Materials on the Spanish Borderlands. Philadelphia: The Catholic Historical Society of Philadelphia, 1943. 106 pp.

This is a catalogue (for the most part unannotated) of books, articles and documents which deal with the Hispanic phases of the history of Florida (1561-1819), Louisiana (1763-1803), Texas (1689-1836), New Mexico and Arizona (1581-1846), and the period of "discovery and exploration, 1513-1561." A list of "general and comprehensive materials" is also given. Steck is an historian writing for historians, and thus at first glance there is little here that will interest linguists. But many of the items included are documents originally written in Spanish (some appearing, alas, in English translations only); these might prove valuable to philologists eager for testimonies as to the sort of language the literate class "took along" on its colonizing missions. [RT]

TESCHNER, Richard V., comp. [1974c]. Spanish-Surnamed Populations of the United States: A Catalog of Dissertations. Ann Arbor, Michigan: Xerox University Microfilms, 1974. vii, 43 pp.

Lists but does not annotate nearly 1200 doctoral dissertations pertaining to the various Hispanic groups of the United States, most notably Chicanos, Puerto Ricans (island as well as mainland) and Cubans. Dissertations encompass all the several disciplines of the Social Sciences, the Humanities and Education as well as those realms of Science which bear directly upon human concerns. The subsection "Language" lists 59 items (pp. 32-33); scattered additional works of some interest to linguists are also found throughout the bulky Education sections (15-31). An Author Index appears on pp. 39-43. This catalogue has attempted to be all-inclusive through volume 34 (June 1974) of the Dissertation Abstracts listings. [RT]

WOODBRIDGE, Hensley C. "Spanish in the American South and Southwest: A Bibliographical Survey for 1940-1953." Orbis 3.236-244 (1954). [Annot. Serís no. 15507; Solé no. 959.]

A lucid, concise and valuable descriptive survey by the dean of American Spanish bibliographers of two dozen books, articles, doctoral dissertations and occasional masters' theses on Mexican-American, Cuban and isleño Spanish (Louisiana) was represented solely by the work of Porges 1949 and was thus not included as a separate category. With this bibliography and several others (see fn. to our annotation of Nichols 1941) treating Mexico, Central and South America Woodbridge continued and up-dated the

work of Nichols 1941, although his entries are usually more
thorough and more accurate than those of his predecessor, who
lacked Woodbridge's background in philology. A typical Woodbridge annotation quotes resumatory lines from the work itself,
at times extensively (see the good summations of Ortiz 1947,
MacCurdy v.d., Sorvig 1952, Bowen 1952, Barker v.d., and Hustvedt
1948). The survey concludes with recommendations for future research, which Woodbridge feels should direct more attention to
U.S. Spanish syntax and slang which "except for Pachuco . . .
has been but little studied." (243) The passage of time has not
diminished the value of this work, which continues to serve as a
model bibliographical study. [RT]

1.2 COMPREHENSIVE/GENERAL STUDIES; MISCELLANY; ANTHOLOGIES/
    FESTSCHRIFTEN

Major Items: CARD-1970; CRAD-1973

See also these items elsewhere (consult Author Index for location):
TESC-1972.

AARONS, Alfred C., Barbara Y. Gordon and William A. Stewart, eds.
    "Linguistic-Cultural Differences and American Education."
    FFLR 7.(entire issue) (Spring 1969).

    Contains the reprint of Troike 1968, reviewed elsewhere in
this Bibliography. [RT]

CANFIELD, D. Lincoln. East Meets West, South of the Border.
    Carbondale: Southern Illinois Univ. Press, 1968, xiii, 137 pp.

    Very brief overview (pp. 72-73) of New Mexican Spanish phono-
logy and, to a lesser extent, the phonological oddities of "the
Spanish of the border, except New Mexico," and of Florida (Tampa).
Prof. Canfield's lifelong interest in dialect patterns as manifestations of immigration periods is reflected in his judgment
that "Arizona, California, and Texas, if they resemble any other
settlement, are reflections of an earlier type of Andalusian
Spanish imported bodily from Mexico in more recent times. In a
sense they are Spanish of 1850-1950 from Mexico, while New Mexico
represents 1600-50 from Spain." (72) [RT]

CANNON, Garland. "Bilingual Problems and Developments in the
    United States." PMLA 86.452-458 (1971). [Abs. LLBA 6.7200881;
    HLAS 34 (1972) no. 3077 (Canfield).]

    A good, comprehensive survey of bilingualism and bilingual
education in the United States as of the year 1970. While the
article offers no information on language per se, it will still
be of interest to persons seeking insights into the various

sociolinguistic ramifications of Mexican/American and Puerto Rican bilingualism, especially as these compare with bilingual situations elsewhere. [RT]

CÁRDENAS, Daniel N. "Dominant Spanish Dialects Spoken in the United States." Washington, D.C.: Center for Applied Linguistics, 1970. iii, 46 pp. [Available ERIC: ED 042 137; abs. RIE 6.16 (Jan. 1971).]

A very general attempt to highlight the differences between the "four major Spanish dialects in the United States: Mexican Spanish, Puerto Rican Spanish, Cuban Spanish, and Peninsular Spanish." (p. 1) Following an overview of the distribution of these groups, he provides a summary description, mostly phonological, of standard Spanish and points out a very few examples of how the four U.S. varieties and sub-varieties diverge from this standard in phonology and morphology. The survey ends with a five-page, grossly simplistic and speculative commentary on intonation and a brief discussion of vocabulary variations that gives too few examples. [GB]

CÁRDENAS, Juan Francisco de. Hispanic Culture and Language in the United States. New York: Instituto de las Españas en los Estados Unidos [Casa de las Españas, Columbia Univ.], 1933. 40 pp. [TSBJr.]

An address delivered by Spain's ambassador to the U.S. upon being made Doctor honoris causa at the University of Missouri. The original English appears on pp. 1-23; a Spanish translation follows. Neither offers much of interest since Cárdenas mostly speaks in ringing generalities; as a possible stimulus to Anglo learning of Spanish, all manner of 16th century explorers from Ponce de León to Juan de Oñate are cited briefly. [RT]

CRADDOCK, Jerry R. "Spanish in North America." In CTL 10.305-339 (1973).

In his exemplary and extensive review of linguistic research (1953-1970) on United States Spanish (Mexican-American, Puerto Rican, Cuban, Louisiana isleño and Sephardic Jewish, together with brief descriptions of studies of Spanish influence on American English and U.S. AmerIindian languages), Prof. Craddock takes pains to present not only the details but also the general thrust of "current trends," wherever discernible. The chief of these springs from "the rapidly developing field of bilingualism, thanks mainly to the efforts of men best described in this context as 'sociolinguists,'" (306) among whom he cites William Labov, Joshua Fishman, Jacob Ornstein and John Gumperz, researchers whose efforts are directed toward "redressing the long-standing imbalance between pure descriptivism excessively given over to abstract

models of linguistic structure and the social realities governing
the use of language." (ibid.) Prior to what he terms the
"sociolinguistic revolution" of the middle 1960's, work on U.S.
Spanish "had lapsed into a state of relative decline and stagna-
tion" and consisted largely of "a discouraging sequel to the
flourishing of U.S. Spanish studies brought about by Aurelio M.
Espinosa, a movement that began in the first decade of the
twentieth century, and lasted well into the 1950's." (ibid.)
Craddock notes that the socio-linguistic revolution paralleled
(or was stimulated by) the sociopolitical turmoil within American
minority groups, including Mexican/Americans and Puerto Ricans.

Craddock's review is especially useful for the full-length
discussions it gives of the works he considers important or those
he feels are in need of critical commentary; thus Craddock is
indispensable for analyses of Fishman 1968/71, MacCurdy v.d.,
Sawyer v.d. Lozano 1961, Gumperz and Hernández-Chávez 1969
and v.d., Coltharp v.d. Sharp 1970, and especially Phillips 1967.
[RT]

FERNÁNDEZ FLÓREZ, Darío. The Spanish Heritage in the United
    States. "Claves de España" Series No. 3 (Madrid: Publica-
    ciones Españolas, 1965). 362 pp.

Perhaps a "precursor" of Carlos Fernández-Shaw 1972, although
worth consulting in its own right (and especially for the more
concise form in which it presents some of the same information),
Fernández Flórez's work deals with "The History of Spain in
North America" in part one and "The Spanish Heritage in the
United States" in part two (subdivided into "Spain's Legacy to
American Literature" and "Spanish Influence on Art in the United
States"). Three short sections treat U.S. Spanish language and
folklore. The first, pp. 253-259 ("The Development of Instruc-
tion in Spanish in the States") is basically a summary of Manuel
Jato Macías 1961, as the author himself admits. Pp. 263-264
("Hispanisms in American English") make passing reference to
Harold Bentley 1932 but incorporate little of his information;
two paragraphs (p. 263) allude to Aurelio Espinosa's work on New
Mexican Spanish and cite the dialect's more outstanding archaisms.
A more complete résumé of the salient literature is given in
"Spanish Folklore in the United States," pp. 291-294. Most of
p. 293 concerns the Hispanic heritage of Florida, with specific
reference to the St. Augustine Minorcan colony, regarding which
the following (probably ill-informed) statement is made: "The
language, soft-toned Mahonese, the songs and the customs of the
beautiful Balearic island are still zealously guarded in Florida
by the descendants of those original immigrants;" cf. the comments
of other observers of the Florida scene (sec. 10, passim). [RT]

FERNÁNDEZ-SHAW, CARLOS M. Presencia española en los Estados Unidos. Madrid: Ediciones Cultura Hispánica, 1972. 932 pp., supl. (maps). [TSBJr.] [Rev. Hispania 57.186 (1974) (M. Nason); REH 8.147-148 (1974) (E. Florit); RIB 23.451-452 (1973) (J. Itelguera).]

This gargantuan book, the incredible product of investigations that can only be described as encyclopedic into fields as diverse as history, economics, language, agriculture, folklore and statistics (Fernández makes use of nearly 500 secondary sources; these are listed in the bibliography, pp. 817-834) was written chiefly to document the degree that Spain (and, to a lesser extent, the Hispanic world in general) has participated and continues to participate in los asuntos EE UU. F first provides background material in the form of chapters treating Spanish contributions as a whole; he then goes on to discuss Hispanic heritage and contemporary presence in each of the fifty states (at times this becomes a bit forced, as with various parts of New England and the Middle West, when F necessarily turns to a mere recitation of touristic commonplaces). Invariably the most pages are devoted to the "Spanish borderland" regions.

Linguistic and sociolinguistic concerns appear throughout the work and are discussed superficially in some cases, in depth and with sophistication in others. F summarizes natively-spoken U.S. Spanish on pp. 74-75 and gives a good résumé on pp. 75-76); reference is made to recent legislation which permits Spanish-speakers to "vote" in Spanish in the state of New York; reference (possibly ironic) is also made to the Treaty of Guadalupe Hidalgo (1848) "que convirtió, en verdad, a los Estados Unidos en una nación bilingüe." (76) The former Spanish-speaking settlement at Florida's St. Augustine is dealt with on pp. 214-215; considerable space is given over to contemporary Hispanic colonies in Miami (p. 219) and Tampa-Ybor City (231-232; here F waxes lyrical, perhaps because many of the colonia's residents are immigrants from Spain itself; he even asserts that Ybor City's "numerosos italianos allí residentes hablan perfectamente el castellano sin apenas acento," [231] and carefully catalogues the area's clubs, restaurants, businesses, periodicals and radio stations). Fernández's information on the two Spanish-speaking corners of Louisiana is taken from the publications of Raymond MacCurdy (v.d.). Allusion is made throughout sections on Nevada, Idaho and Wyoming to immigrant Basque sheep-herders and the language they retain (see esp. pp. 497-498). Of the fifty chapters on the individual states the New Mexican one is clearly the most comprehensive (413-447); "el idioma castellano" is discussed at length but rather superficially on pp. 419-420, and the state's various Hispanic tradiciones are chronicled subsequently. Surprisingly, language is not alluded to in the chapters on California and Texas and is given short shrift in the Colorado and Arizona sections.

As part of Appendix "D" (pp. 761-777) F provides a fairly thorough list of U.S. radio stations that transmit in Spanish. The same appendix also lists a variety of U.S. periodicals published partly or entirely in Spanish. (This list is nowhere as complete as it might be.) [RT]

FISHMAN, Joshua A., ed. <u>Language Loyalty in the United States: The Maintenance and Perpetuation of Non-English Mother Tongues by American Ethnic and Religious Groups</u>. The Hague: Mouton, 1966. 478 pp. [Rev. JAUMLA 27.145-147 (1967) (M.G. Clyne); <u>Orbis</u> 16.572-577 (1967) (G.G. Gilbert); <u>MLJ</u> 52.166-118 (1968) (P. Wexler); <u>Language</u> 44.198-201 (1968) (J.B. Rudnyckyj); <u>Lingua</u> 22.261-266 (1969) (N. Hasselmo); <u>Anglia</u> 87.441-444 (1969) (K. Lubbers).]

The variegated essays included in this volume by Fishman, Vladimir Nahirny, John Hofman, Robert Hayden, Heinz Kloss and others focus on the themes alluded to in the work's subtitle. Discussed, in short, is the entire background of U.S. linguistic assimilation (or lack of it); as Einar Haugen notes in his brief Introduction (pp. 9-11), the authors "have shown how the immigrant responded to the threatening loss of ethnic identity from the moment of immigration to the last of his ethnically conscious descendants.... They have given us overall statistics on language maintenance, where these exist. They have scrutinized in detail certain large linguistic groups and have set up cross-group hypotheses of great interest." (10) For these and many other reasons, <u>Language Loyalty</u> will long remain a sine qua non for all students of ethnicity in American life.

Of the work's fifteen chapters, only four discuss the "maintenance" efforts of specific ethnic groups, in this case Germans, French Canadians, Ukrainians, and Mexican Americans. The chapter dealing with the latter (Christian and Christian, 1966, "Spanish Language and Culture in the Southwest") is analyzed separately in the present Bibliography. But passing reference to Hispanos is found elsewhere throughout the work as well, especially in Ch. 4 (Mary Warshauer, "Foreign Language Broadcasting"), where much attention is paid to Spanish radio for the valid reason that it constitutes about 2/3 of all U.S. non-English programming. (Warshauer's statistics were based on data collected in 1960; for a somewhat more up-to-date review of Spanish broadcasting see Teschner 1973.) A certain attention to U.S. Hispanos is also paid in Chs. 1 (Fishman, "The Historical and Social Contexts of an Inquiry into Language Maintenance Efforts") and 15 (Fishman, "Language Maintenance in a Supra-ethnic Age: Summary and Conclusions"); see also the various Tables of Ch. 2 (Fishman and Hofman, "Mother Tongue and Nativity in the American Population"). A frequent conclusion about U.S. Hispanos is that they alone have truly "maintained" their native tongue and that for a variety of reasons there is strong likelihood they will continue to do so. [RT]

GILBERT, Glenn G. "The Linguistic Geography of Non-official Languages in the United States." ACIL 10:2.203-208 (1967/1970).

Summary reference is given Spanish in this theoretically-oriented discourse; Gilbert includes it among the "few non-English languages in the United States [which] have survived well enough into the present to merit making a linguistic atlas of them." [RT]

HELM, June, ed. Spanish-speaking People in the United States. (Proceedings of the 1968 Annual Spring Meeting of the American Ethnological Society, Detroit.) Seattle: Univ. of Washington Press, 1968. (Contents pertinent to language or sociolinguistics [Paredes 1968; Smith 1968] are reviewed separately in the present Bibliography.)

JOHNSTON, Marjorie C. "Spanish-Language Newspapers and Periodicals Published in the United States." Hispania 34.85-87 (1951). [TSBJr.]

Gives titles, addresses, names of publishers, subscription rates and frequency of issue for more than 100 Spanish-language publications (or publications mostly in English but with regularly-appearing sections in Spanish). Some are Spanish translations of English-issued originals (e.g., Ingeniería sanitaria, El automóvil americano) designed for export abroad; others are religious publications (La Esperanza et al.), while still others (perhaps a fourth of the total) are authoctonous publications apparently written by Hispanos for Hispanos (e.g., La Opinión of Los Angeles, La Voz de México of Chicago). [RT]

LOPE BLANCH, Juan M. El español de América. Madrid: Ediciones Alcalá, 1968. 150 pp. (Trans. into English as "Hispanic Dialectology," CTL 4.106-157 [1968].) [Annot. Solé 1970 no. 36a. Rev. ZRPh 85.647 (1969) (K. Baldinger); Hispania 53.343-344 (1970) (D. Cárdenas); RevIb 38:78.161-164 (1972) (S. Hess; general review of CTL 4, with discussion of Lope Blanch's contribution on p. 163).]

This compact, comprehensive, and stylistically obtuse bibliographical survey of works on American Spanish dialectology since World War II devotes less than four pages (85-89; 140-142 in the English translation) to U.S. Spanish, mostly of the Southwest. Pachuco merits one paragraph (119) in the chapter on "Argot" (a chapter not included in the English translation). Only a few of the major publications are mentioned. [GB]

MALKIEL, Yakov. "Hispanic Philology." In CTL 4.158-228 (1968).
[Rev. RevIb 38:78.161-164 (1972) (S. Hess; for Malkiel, see
p. 163).] An expansion and up-dating of "Hispanic Philology"
appeared as Linguistics and Philology in Spanish America:
A Survey (1925-1970), The Hague: Mouton, 1972. 179 pp. [Rev.
Hispania 57.1022-1023 (1974) (D. L. Canfield).]

This erudite survey of philological research in Latin
America contains only a few references to U.S. Spanish, primarily
with regard to Spanish influence on American Indian languages
(pp. 194-195). [GB]

SAVILLE-TROIKE, Muriel R. "Spanish." Part (pp. 125-127) of the
author's "Language and the Disadvantaged," in Reading for the
Disadvantaged: Problems of Linguistically Different Learners,
edited by Thomas D. Horn. New York et alibi: Harcourt,
Brace & World, Inc., 1970. Pp. 115-134 (Ch. 6 of Horn).

A brief but succinct discussion of some of the various structural differences between English and Spanish and how these create
problems for youngsters just becoming familiar with written and
spoken English in the classroom. Saville-Troike's contrastive
comments deal equally with phonology and grammar. Passing note is
taken of the great diversity of U.S. Spanish: the language problem seems very complex "when one considers that there are social
dialects within the regional ones." [RT]

TESCHNER, Richard V. "The Feasibility of Using U.S. 'Ethnic'
Radio in the Foreign Language Classroom." LBRIGN 1:4.4-5
(May 1973).

Oriented towards pedagogical concerns, this report nonetheless
presents useful statistics on Chicago Spanish-language radio and
television: which stations offer how many hours of programming,
what general "types" of programs are transmitted, etc. Teschner
criticizes much ethnic programming for "its tendency to run the
same advertisements over and over again, day after day, week
after week," but admits that this otherwise numbing feature is a
boon for the neophyte language student who can always count on a
"repeat" of an ad not initially understood. [RT]

1.2.1 SOCIOLINGUISTICS

Major Items: GAAR-1971

See also these items elsewhere (consult Author Index for location):
KELL-1974

GAARDER, A. Bruce. "Language Maintenance or Language Shift: The
  Prospect for Spanish in the United States." Paper presented
  at the Conference on Child Language, Chicago, November 1971
  though not included among the collection of Conference papers
  distributed in October 1971 (Preprints: Conference on Child
  Language, Montreal: Centre International de Recherche sur le
  Bilinguisme [Laval Univ.], 1971). (The present item was ac-
  quired privately.) To appear in Theodore Andersson and W. F.
  Mackey, eds., Bilingualism in Early Childhood, Rowley, Mass.:
  Newbury (in press).

  Gaarder seeks to answer the question, "Will Spanish survive
as a language of United States Hispanos, or will [these] go the
way of all previous non-English-speaking groups and become English-
monolinguals?" He discusses at length the linguistic and sociocultural factors which favor the shift and also some which
guarantee resistance to it. Among the former are struggles for
social justice (housing integration, par-level employment, etc.),
the "bridge-to-English" orientation of most current bilingual
education programs, the extent to which both languages are employed in similar domains and with other Hispanos, etc. Factors
encouraging Spanish maintenance will largely involve a conscious
opting for the converse of the above, i.e., resistance to integration, along with a maintenance of the sentiment that Hispanos
must strive to view themselves as culturally distinct (hence linguistically separate) in order to survive what appear to be Anglo
attempts to achieve government-ordered racial balance by mixing
blacks with browns (who are conveniently defined as whites for
the purposes of the moment!). Gaarder notes that U.S. Hispanos,
unlike previous groups, could well employ "renewal from the
hinterlands" as one device to effectively forestall the shift to
English, but appear loath to do so because of what they see as
academic and trans-Rio Grandian contempt for the inevitable language "mixing" and "decay" that is said to typify U.S. Spanish; in
this sense Gaarder notes that many Chicano Studies Programs
actively denigrate "world standard Spanish" and insist that for
their purposes the only languages needed are English and "Barrio
Spanish." [RT]

[ANON.] U.S. Bureau of the Census, Current Population Reports,
  P-20, No. 250, "Persons of Spanish Origin in the United
  States: March 1972 and 1971." Washington D.C.: U.S. GPO,
  1973. iii, 34 pp.

According to this report, "the majority of Spanish origin [i.e., all Spanish-surnamed] persons live in households where Spanish is the current language, as 6.0 million of the 9.2 million persons of Spanish origin, or 65 percent, reported Spanish as the language currently spoken in their home. . . . There was some evidence that the proportion. . . was even higher for persons of Puerto Rican origin, as 73 percent of these persons were in Spanish language homes," (p. 2) as opposed to 65.2 per cent of Mexican-Americans. However a careful look reveals that the question asked of all persons who "reported any one of the Spanish origin categories" applied to the <u>entire household</u> as a unit; (p. 8) "therefore, not all persons reported in such households necessarily now speak or ever spoke Spanish themselves. Nevertheless, this item provides some information on the number of persons for whom the Spanish language has a relatively strong influence or who are exposed to Spanish language usage in the home." (ibid.) Seven of the document's 48 tables contain specific statistics on this "language usage," chiefly as it pertains to a wide variety of variables; some titles: "4. Persons of Spanish origin reporting Spanish currently spoken in home by age and type of Spanish origin, for the United States: March 1972;" "10. Years of school completed by persons of Spanish origin 14 years old and over by age, sex, type of Spanish origin, and Spanish language usage . . ." [RT]

WARD, James H. "Spanish Teachers and Spanish Speaking Minorities." <u>Hispania</u> 55.893-895 (1972).

For the most part Ward is busy chiding Spanish teachers for doing things wrong or not at all, but bits and pieces of sociolinguistic information are here for the finding, e.g., "A student who comes from a Spanish-speaking minority often associates Spanish with 'old fashioned ways' and perhaps even with poverty and discrimination. There is a resentment against being asked to learn any Spanish other than what he has picked up at home and in the street." (p. 894) "The cultural isolation of the Spanish-speaker may be intentional at times, stemming from a perverse or confused pride in ethnocentricity. Some radical students want to speak only Caló." (ibid.) [RT]

1.3 SPANISH PHONOLOGY (includes ORTHOGRAPHY)

Major Items: RESN-1968

See also these items elsewhere (consult Author Index for location):

CANF-1968

CANFIELD, D. Lincoln. La pronunciación del español en América: ensayo histórico-descriptivo. Publicaciones del Instituto Caro y Cuervo, No. 17 (Bogotá: Instituto Caro y Cuervo, 1962). 107 pp., 8 maps.

This short general survey of selected phonetic aspects of New World Spanish (just 40 pages beyond prologue, preface, and bibliography) contains only occasional references to U.S. Spanish, based primarily on personal observations in Arizona, Florida, and New Mexico and such works as Espinosa 1930a, Hills 1938, MacCurdy 1950, and Post 1934. [GB]

CÁRDENAS, Daniel N. "The Geographic Distribution of the Assibilated R RR in Spanish America." Orbis 7.407-414 (1958).

A general essay on New World Spanish; for U. S. Spanish the author cites from Bowen 1952, Espinosa 1930a, MacCurdy 1948 diss., and Post 1934. [GB]

RESNICK, Melvyn C. "The Coordination and Tabulation of Phonological Data in American Spanish Dialectology." PhD Diss., Univ. of Rochester [New York], 1968. ix, 400 pp. [DA 29 (1968) 1887-A.]

This sweeping analysis of existing phonological studies of New World Spanish concentrates especially on eight major phonological variables for the purpose of establishing a precise data base for Latin American dialectology. Data on U.S. Spanish are taken from Alonso 1951, Alonso and Lida 1945, Bowen 1952, Canfield 1962, Cárdenas 1958, MacCurdy 1950, and Post 1933, inter alia. A computer print-out index to documentation of the variables, with brief notes on frequency and types of speakers, is found for U.S. Spanish on pp. 329-333. Despite the reliance on minor and secondary sources, this study is useful for its relating of U.S. Spanish to the broader Latin American phonological scene and for its lengthy bibliography in this respect. [GB]

1.4 SPANISH GRAMMAR (MORPHOLOGY AND SYNTAX)

Major Items: KELL-1974

See also these items elsewhere (consult Author Index for location):
(none)

KELLER, Gary D. "La norma de solidaridad y la de poder en los pronombres de tratamiento: un bosquejo diacrónico y una investigación del español de Nueva York." BilR 1.42-58 (1974).

A meticulously executed contribution to our knowledge of Spanish second-person pronominal usage in general and hypothetical English influence on U.S. Spanish in particular (none is adduced). Following a very thorough discussion (pp. 42-53) of "la evolución diacrónica, es decir, histórica, de estos pronombres [tú and Ud.] dentro del medio-ambiente sociolingüístico de las lenguas romances, particularmente el español" which is complemented by a digest of psycholinguistic theory concerning human relationships typified by power norms vs. norms of solidarity, Keller presents the results of a recent investigation carried out among 100 self-defined lower-class "alumnos hispanohablantes procedentes de los siguientes países: Puerto Rico, República Dominicana, el Ecuador, Colombia, El Salvador, Cuba y algunos nacidos en los Estados Unidos aunque de ascendencia hispana" (p. 54) whose average age was 14; all were bilingual "o al menos conocían bien el inglés." (ibid.) K's self-administered questionnaire recorded data on tú or Ud. used in addressing and being addressed by: informant's mother, father, older brother/sister, younger brother/sister, grandfather/-mother, teacher, friend, uncle/aunt, priest/minister, store clerk, and unknown person encountered in public. Numerical totals and percentages are presented on pp. 55-56; answers are tabulated according to respondent's sex. Some specific findings: "En relación con la madre, solamente 51 % de los adolescentes emplearon tú, mientras que 87 % de las madres lo emplearon con sus hijos. Obviamente la norma asimétrica todavía conserva algún vigor dentro de la familia." (57) K had informants check one of five possible answers ranging from "tú (definitivamente)" through "posiblemente tú, posiblemente Usted (definitivamente)," though the intermediate classification was disallowed statistically. No allowance was made for situational variations from "definitivamente" norms, nor were informants asked to quality "probablemente" usage, e.g., mother addressed as Ud. outside the home but as tú within it, etc.

In general K found Ud. usage to be high, and though it was logical to suppose that overall English-ambient pressures towards the deterioration of the mother tongue and specific influences of the "omnibus," socially-nondistinctive English pronoun you would bring about a greater use of tú, this was not found to be the case among K's informants, whose average length of residence in the U.S. was three years and four months. [RT]

1.5 SPANISH LEXICON (includes SEMANTICS)

Major Items: (None)

See also these items elsewhere (consult Author Index for location):
(none)

KANY, Charles E. American-Spanish Semantics. Berkeley: Univ. of
   California Press, 1960. 352 pp. (Spanish trans. by Luis
   Escobar Bareño, Semántica hispanoamericana, Madrid: Aguilar,
   1962. xvi, 298 pp.) [Annot. HLAS 24 (1962) no. 4740 (D.
   Wogan); Serís no. 15058a; Solé 1970 no. 177. Rev. Hispania
   44.191-192 (1961) (D.L. Canfield); HAHR 41.457-458 (1961)
   (D.L. Canfield); BHS 38.313-314 (1961) (R. Gebbett); MPh 60.75-
   76 (1962) (D. Cárdenas); ASNS 199.133-134 (1962) (García);
   HR 30.351-353 (1962) (J. Lope Blanch); SL 17.54-59 (1962) (B.
   Malmberg). BHi 64.342-343 (1962) (M. Molho); BFUCh 14.235-242
   (1962) (R. Oroz); Language 39.125-128 (1963) (R. Diebold); RPh
   17.179-184 (1963-64) (S.L. Robe).]

   This general reference work on lexico-semantic variation in
the popular Spanish speech of the New World occasionally documents
forms from Louisiana, Texas, and New Mexico drawn from Cerda et
al. 1953, Gaarder 1944, Kercheville 1934, Kiddle 1951-52, 1952,
MacCurdy 1950, and Wagner 1953-54. [GB]

1.7 ENGLISH INFLUENCE ON SPANISH

Major Items: (none)

See also these items elsewhere (consult Author Index for location):

   TESC-1972

MCHALE, Carlos F. Spanish Don'ts: A Reference Book on Correct
   and Defective Spanish. New York: J.J. Little and Ives, 1939.
   xii, 98 pp. [Annot. Serís no. 13299. Rev. Hispania 22.339
   (1939) (A. Coester).]

   This delightfully arrogant and puristic listing of somewhat
over 400 Anglicisms used by U.S. Spanish speakers, learners of
Spanish, and Latin Americans is a convenient guide to prominent
lexical errors produced under the influence of English, but unfortunately the regional identity of the villain in particular
cases is rarely specified. One sample entry: "MARQUETA, A most
execrable anglicism for mercado, frequent in Northern Mexico,
Texas, etc. It is the English word market that has been given
Spanish form." [GB]

1.9 SPANISH INFLUENCE ON AMERINDIAN LANGUAGES

Major Items: (none)

See also these items elsewhere (consult Author Index for location):
(none)

TAYLOR, Allan R. "Spanish manteca in Alaskan Eskimo." RPh 16.30-32 (1962).

    A speculative postscript to Shipley 1962 suggesting that Eskimo mantikaq was borrowed from Spanish via Tagalog-speaking Filipino canning laborers. [GB]

SECTION 2 [CHICANOS (MEXICAN-AMERICANS) IN GENERAL]

2.1 BIBLIOGRAPHY

Major Items: CLAR-1970; FODY-1971

See also these items elsewhere (consult Author Index for location): (none)

BARRIOS, Ernie, ed. Bibliografía de Aztlán: An Annotated Chicano Bibliography. San Diego [State Univ.]: Centro de Estudios Chicanos Publications, 1971. xix, 157 pp.

Studies on Chicano language are not included here although in the section "Educational Materials" (pp. 9-35) the reader will find a partial selection of works dealing with bilingual education which mention language peripherally. Militant in tone, and seeking to provide an index of material which will be acceptable for Chicano Studies courses, this bibliography has naturally concentrated on socio-cultural writings and especially on works pertaining to Chicano politics and history. [RT]

CLARK Y MORENO, Joseph A. "A Bibliography of Bibliographies Relating to Mexican-American Studies." El Grito 3:4.25-31 (Summer 1970).

_____. "A Bibliography of Bibliographies Relating to Studies of Mexican Americans." El Grito 5:2.47-79 (Winter 1972). (Cf. Ray Padilla 1971-72.)

When placed alongside the supplementary material appearing at the end of Padilla 1972, Clark's very exhaustive checklist of 475 items will surely remain the most complete catalogue of the apparently boundless plethora of Chicano bibliographies, checklists, materials guides (selective and otherwise), inventories of collections, holdings lists and so forth for at least several years to come. Of Clark's two publications only the second (1972) need be consulted as it contains all the items listed initially in the first (1970). Clark arranges his list author-alphabetically; each item is numbered and none is annotated. Pagination is given for items appearing in serial publications but not for others. Occasional items first found in the 1970 list are reprinted in revised fashion in the 1972 list. Nearly all entires have bearing on Chicano concerns, although from time to time Clark includes items which do not (e.g., no. 455, Hensley Woodbridge, "An Annotated Bibliography of Mexican Spanish for 1940-1953," KFLQ 1.80-89 [1954]; surprisingly the same author's 1954 "Spanish in the American South and Southwest . . . " is not included). Many of Clark's entries appear to deal with pedagogical matters; others cover a wide range of concerns from history through folklore, the fine arts, guidance counseling, militancy, economics and literature. A few items give the impression of being quick "highlights" compilations of longer works and could probably be disregarded by even the most thorough of researchers. Other items (especially those "topical holdings lists" so often mimeographed by miscellaneous municipal libraries) might prove very hard to obtain; it is clearly to Clark's credit that he has located so many of them. [RT]

FODY III, Michael. "The Spanish of the American Southwest and Louisiana: A Bibliographical Survey for 1954-1969." Orbis 20:2.529-540 (1971).

In format a compromise between the bibliographical essay and the straight item-list bibliography. Fody's work summarizes "publications and dissertations produced between 1954 and 1969" which deal with the Southwest (none were found for Louisiana), and it is therefore a supplement to Woodbridge 1954. Fody's material is listed alphabetically by author within the following categories: "General (including articles in part dealing with Colorado and Utah, as well as those dealing with this entire region), California, Arizona, New Mexico, Texas and Louisiana." (529) Within these categories Fody includes studies of toponymy and folklore along with items more specifically germane to linguistics itself. Reviews of major works are cited occasionally, and critical commentary accompanies items that Fody finds of more than passing interest. Despite the desired omniinclusivity there are the usual lacunae and "omissions," especially in the areas of folklore, onomastics, and California Spanish; but for the most part Fody has proceeded with diligence, and his section on Texas Spanish is especially complete through 1967.

My only criticism is that Fody devotes more space than necessary to material at best ancillary to linguistics; thus two paragraphs are spent on a brief piece appearing in an anthology entitled The Disadvantaged Learner: Knowing, Understanding, Educating, whose thrust seems to be that a lack of English is a psychological handicap. [RT]

JABLONSKY, Adelaide. Mexican Americans: An Annotated Bibliography of Doctoral Dissertations. ERIC/IRCD [Information Retrieval Center on the Disadvantaged] Doctoral Research Series No. 1 (New York: Columbia Univ. Teachers College and Washington D.C.: ERIC, 1973). vi, 83 pp. [Available ERIC: ED 076 714. Annot. RIE (Sept. 1973) 136.]

A total of sixty-two items are annotated in this descriptive bibliography of all dissertations processed through DA/Xerox University Microfilms from 1965 through June of 1972 which "clearly related to educational programs for the disadvantaged." (p. v, "Preface") The bibliography therefore focusses on items whose central concerns are bilingual education, reading and mathematics achievement, self-concept, classroom behavior, relationships

between selected socioeconomic factors and school achievement,
etc., although six of the items Jablonsky annotates (all included
in the present Bibliography) also bear on language and linguistics
(see especially Jameson 1967 and Peña 1967). In some instances
Jablonsky's annotations appear to supplement the information contained in the DA abstract itself. [RT]

JORDAN, Lois B. Mexican Americans: Resources to Build Cultural
 Understanding. Littleton, Colo.: Libraries Unlimited, Inc.,
 1973. 265 pp.

This "selective bibliography of materials suitable for young
adults" cites, with usually one-sentence annotations, 1,028 "books,
16 mm films, 35 mm filmstrips, 8 mm film loops, recordings, slides,
transparencies, and other audiovisual media which provide information on the historical backgrounds, cultural heritage and contemporary social, economic and political problems of Mexican
Americans" (p. 3). The emphasis is on books; a section on Mexican
Americans in the U.S. contains 195 entries and a section on
Folklore and Mythology contains 37 entries, but virtually no
language works are included. Appendix C includes a list of
"Periodicals and Newspapers of Interest to the Mexican American"
(international and local), and Appendix D provides a list of
bibliographical works. [GB]

MICKEY, Barbara H. "A Bibliography of Studies Concerning the
 Spanish-speaking Population of the American Southwest."
 Colorado Series, No. 4 (Greeley: Colorado State College,
 1969). 42 pp. [Available ERIC: ED 042 548.]

Aimed at the anthropologist and sociologist, this simple
alphabetical listing of 544 works from the period 1888-1968 is
interspersed with only a few entries relating to linguistics,
language, and language-related educational problems. An example
of the poor language coverage is the fact that the only Espinosa
work cited is Espinosa 1909aa. [GB]

NOGALES, Luis, ed. The Mexican-American: A Selected and Annotated Bibliography. 2nd ed. (1969; Stanford, Calif.: Stanford
 Univ., Center for Latin American Studies, 1971.) xii, 162 pp.

This is a competently-executed bibliography, easily the best
yet written on a wide variety of Mexican-American-related materials, whose sole defect is its near total ignorance of the substantial body of studies on Chicano language and especially Chicano
Spanish. Of the ten contributors to both editions the majority
are social scientists and the remainder are graduate students
in communications, education, history and Latin American studies.
Given the disciplinary bias, it was inevitable that the editorial
policy should be informed by mendacious statements such as the

following: "Most entries appear because of their scholarly merit, some because they are the best sources in the areas they cover. The social sciences are far better represented than the humanities not because we would necessarily have it that way but because of the nature of the materials currently available." (p. v)

As a consequence the Stanford bibliography includes perhaps ten entries which bear peripherally on language per se. Proportionately greater attention is paid to topics of immediate interest to educators, such as bilingual education (perhaps a dozen worthwhile entries) and "bilingualism," a catch-all category used for everything from casual mentions of the fact that many Chicanos speak two languages, to more germane studies on the emotional consequences of being a Spanish-speaker or on the ever-touchy topic of English-language intelligence tests and the role played in performances on these by Spanish-dominant bilingualism.

The bibliography contains 444 entries arranged author-alphabetically, a subject index, and then a somewhat redundant "field index" which reproduces the subject index'es entries in twelve sub-categories the largest of which are anthropology, education, history and sociology. The field index is followed by a partial guide to Chicano periodicals (pp. 156-162). [RT]

OSBORNE, Zelda L. et al., comps. Mexican-Americans: A Selected Bibliography. Houston: Univ. of Houston Libraries, Office of the Assistant Director for Collection Development, 1972. 73 pp. (plus supl.) [TSBJr.]

Items in this unannotated checklist are arranged according to the following divisions: Historical and Cultural Background, Social/Anthropological/Economic Development, Education, Literature, Journal Articles, and Bibliographies. Journals and Newspapers containing material on Mexican-Americans are listed separately. There is little here that pertains specifically to linguistics, but the compilers have assembled an impressive number of items from the "popular" press culled from the Reader's Guide to Periodical Literature, the Public Affairs Information Service, the Education Index, and elsewhere, and passing references to Chicano language will surely be found in some of the many short articles on Chicanos to appear since 1965 in such publications as Time Magazine, Business Week, Newsweek, School and Society, Saturday Review, Ramparts, the Nation, National Elementary Principal, Texas Outlook, Christian Century et al. [RT]

PADILLA, Ray. "Apuntes para la documentación de la cultura chicana." El Grito 5:2.3-46 (Winter 1971-72).

This critical and frequently combative bibliographic essay discusses nearly a hundred bibliographies and checklists, always from the standpoint of each item's relevance to the Chicano movement. Thus Padilla takes great pains to establish the "audience" for whom each compiler wrote, and which Ethnic Universe has in-

formed the spirit of the bibliography. Bibliographic production
is divided into three periods: 1848-1919, 1920-1959, and 1960-
[1971]. Linguists will glean much from Padilla's analyses of
other language-pertinent bibliographies reviewed on these pages,
esp. R.C. Jones 1942, MacCurdy 1951, Sánchez and Putnam 1959; also
Nichols 1941 (pp. 18-19), of whom Padilla says: "the material . . .
even includes a very small section on the U.S. Although depart-
ments of Spanish in the U.S. have traditionally ignored and even
looked down on Chicano Spanish, the topic is extremely vital to
the survival and development of Chicano culture. For Chicanos,
this work may at least be suggestive of what can and needs to be
done in the uncharted area of Chicano Spanish." For the most
part, though, linguistics takes a back seat to history, sociology,
anthropology, ethnography, etc.; in this sense one notes absence
of reference to Henríquez Ureña 1938, Keniston 1942, Woodbridge
1954, and Serís 1964. Of concern to researchers in early New
Mexican written Spanish is Padilla's discussion of R.E. Twitchell's
The Spanish Archives of New Mexico (1914); Padilla says that since
"many of these documents were misplaced, lost, or destroyed by
Gabachos ["Anglo-Americans" (pej.)] who had them under their
custody, [and since] forgeries were not uncommon. . . perhaps
México City, Guadalajara or Sevilla would be better hunting
grounds for locating duplicates of misplaced or stolen New Mexican
land grant documents." (8-9)

Padilla's views on the recent state of the bibliographic art
are also worth quoting: "a rash of 'Chicano bibliographies' appeared during 1969 and 1970 which purport to demonstrate the cultural
contributions of the Chicano . . . Many of them are mere listings of titles in the form of mimeographed handouts. Others are
voluminous compilations of highly specialized materials, often
espousing the Gabacho viewpoint. Certain bibliographies are
simple adaptations or extractions from other bibliographies. . . .
Fortunately [however,] the Chicano asserted himself and toward
the end of the decade said basta! Chicanos now claim the right
to compile Chicano bibliographies." (27-28) [RT]

RÍOS, Herminio and Lupe Castillo. "Toward a True Chicano Bibliography: Mexican-American Newspapers: 1848-1942." El Grito
3:4.17-24 (Summer 1970). [Cf. Romano-V./Ríos 1972.]

This is a list of nearly 200 daily, weekly and semi-monthly
newspapers published in Spanish in Arizona, California, Colorado,
New Mexico and Texas from the first year of United States
sovereignty through the somewhat arbitrarily-chosen date 1942.
The authors note that the copious number of publications constitutes "a damning blow to those myopic historians who have led some
to believe that the Mexican-American had no history, or to believe what history he has had was not recorded by Mexican-Americans
themselves." (p. 17) While a fair number of the newspapers did
not enjoy more than a decade of publication, an important quantity

have been rather longeved, inter alia Tucson's El Fronterizo, Los Angeles' La Opinión, San Francisco's Las Américas, Albuquerque's El Independiente, Santa Fe's El Nuevo Mexicano (founded in 1862), Laredo's El Demócrata Fronterizo and others. Ríos and Castillo's manner of listing years of publication is not fully satisfactory in all details (although in this instance any drive for full accuracy would surely be hindered by the antiquity of some publications and the limited circulation of others): while "a question mark indicates that the termination date of publication is unknown" (18) as in the case of El Progreso del Valle of Phoenix ("1887-?"), many entries bear both date of termination and question mark (thus Las Vegas [New Mexico]'s El Sol de Mayo "1882-1892-?") while others (such as San Antonio [Texas]'s La Prensa) carry the following type of notation: "1913-1942-continuing," which may indicate a hiatus at some point after 1942 or may indicate that the paper has been in continuous publication since 1913. [RT]

ROMANO-V., Octavio Ignacio and Herminio Ríos C. "Toward a True Chicano Bibliography: Part II." El Grito 5:4.38-47 (Summer 1972).

This is a continuation of the list of Mexican-American newspapers begun by El Grito in 1970 (see Ríos/Castillo 1970). The compilers here add 185 titles to the list, bringing the total to 380 and thus showing that "it is patently evident by now that the stereotype of the non-literate and non-literary Mexican-American has been an academic absurdity promulgated by sociologists, historians, and would-be 'experts' on Chicano literature. In fact, many of the titles of the newspapers themselves offer striking and revealing evidence that also destroys the stereotype of the 'passive' and 'fatalistic' Mexican-American." (p. 39) Among the new titles: Regeneración of Los Angeles (published 'weekly, weekly with interruptions' from 1905-1918) and El Malcriado and Revolución of that same city, El Paladín and La Trompeta of Corpus Christi, Texas, San Antonio's Amigo del Pueblo and El Vacilón, and others. This new list adds publications which appear in both English and Spanish such as the Zapata County News or which seem to have merged with English-language locals (such as El Hispano-Americano of New Mexico, "published as section of Belén News" from 1925-?). In contradistinction to Part I's practice, titles now run through the 1950's in some cases. [RT]

SÁNCHEZ, George I. and Howard Putnam. Materials Relating to the Education of Spanish-Speaking People in the United States: An Annotated Bibliography. Austin: Univ. of Texas Press, 1959. v, 76 pp.

We have not classified this otherwise seminal volume as a major item because of the relatively scant attention it pays to language/linguistics (but then its title would not encourage us to expect major emphasis in that area). Of the 29 items listed under

"Spanish" in the Index (pp. 75-76), only ten actually report on
language usage. In all the bibliography includes some twenty
entries pertaining to language (half of these are not listed sub
"Spanish," e.g., nos. 481 and 716). The title's reference to
"Spanish-Speaking People" is misleading, as Sánchez admits in
the Foreword [iii], since little attempt was made to include
materials on non-Chicano groups.

The work lists 882 items, the great majority cogently but
briefly annotated, in most cases by just a sentence or two.
Items are listed author-alphabetically according to the following
natura formae editionis classification: books, articles, "Bulle-
tins, Monographs, and Pamphlets," bibliographies, "Courses of
Study" (typically Curriculum Guides issued by local school boards
or state agencies; the authors are to be commended for unearthing
these as well as many other arcane items), and MA Theses/PhD Dissertations. Most of the classroom-related material is found
under the last two categories; a healthy share of the "books,
articles" etc. have to do with sociology, race relations, current
events, migrant worker exploitation and the like. Not all annotations were Sánchez's or Putnam's own; as Sánchez admits in his
"Foreword," some were written by the unnamed dozens of graduate
students who collaborated on this project. [RT]

2.2   COMPREHENSIVE/GENERAL STUDIES; MISCELLANY; ANTHOLOGIES/
      FESTSCHRIFTEN

Major Items: GONZ-Gu-1973a; HERN/etal-1975; MATL/MACE-1973;
     TURN-1973

See also these items elsewhere (consult Author Index for location):
     BARK-M-1973; LANC-1972; STEI-1969; TROI-1968

BILLS, Garland D., ed. [1947a] Southwest Areal Linguistics. San
    Diego: Institute for Cultural Pluralism, San Diego State
    Univ., 1974. 315 pp.

The proceedings of the April, 1973, Workshop on Research Problems in Southwest Areal Linguistics II in Albuquerque, New
Mexico. Included are papers by Bowen, Brisk, Gingràs, González,
Hensey, Merz, Metcalf, Murphy, Ornstein, Ramírez, Teschner,
Thompson, Webb, and Willcott; each of these is annotated separately on these pages. The volume also includes several other papers
not directly concerned with Spanish in the Southwest. [GB]

BLACKMAR, Frank W. [1891b]. Spanish Institutions of the Southwest. Johns Hopkins Univ. Series in Historical and Political Science, Vol. 10 (Baltimore: The Johns Hopkins Press, 1891). xxv, 353 pp. [TSBJr.]

It was never Blackmar's intent to discuss language use in the Southwest, and indeed he would have done well to avoid the topic altogether, for the brief section he devotes to SW Spanish (pp. 271-273) can only be considered a remarkable reflection of an egregious series of prejudices. According to Blackmar the Southwest contains "two dialects of the Spanish language." (271) The first of these is "the old Castilian language, still used by the few remaining aristocratic families of pure blood;" (ibid.) this dialect "differs but little from modern continental Spanish, for the Spanish language, as compared with other modern languages, changes but little from century to century." (271-272) The "second dialect" is termed "Mexican;" it is "quite extensively used in New Mexico and California by the great majority of the people of Spanish blood and their native converts to Christianity," (272) and is a source of great worry to Blackmar, for "it is through the language of the common people, through the Spanish language clipped and degraded by the commingling of unlettered Spaniards with an inferior race, that words find their way into English." (ibid.) Blackmar sternly objects to Hispanic lexical inroads ("There are many short phrases in [Southwestern] common speech which are temporary in use, such as mucho frio, mucho caliente, poco tiempo, muchas gracias, si Señor, etc. Their chief influence is exercised in detracting from the use of good English" [277]); fortunately this stance does not prevent him from specifying (pp. 273-277) a few Spanish words which "seem to admit of universal use, and appear indispensable to an intelligent expression of thought" such as adobe, cañón, tule, rodeo, loco, burro, etc. [RT]

CÁRDENAS, Daniel N. "Compound and Coordinate Bilingualism/Biculturalism in the Southwest." In Ewton and Ornstein 1972, pp. 165-180.

This essay on the linguistic and cultural problems of Mexican Americans in the process of assimilation into American society will provide provocative reading for the language engineer, but provides little descriptive information on the Spanish language. Cárdenas cursorily mentions (pp. 175-176) several aspects of English-Spanish interference: his own youthful tendency to overstress the subject pronoun I in English, the assimilation of push and watch into Southwest Spanish, and intrasentential code-switching. [GB]

CHRISTIAN, Chester C., Jr. "Criteria for Cultural-Linguistic Subdivision in the Southwest." In Turner 1973, pp. 39-49.

The meaning, use, and history of such classificatory terms as pachuco and chicano are marginally discussed on pp. 41-43. [GB]

DOBIE, J. Frank, ed. Puro Mexicano. Publications of the Texas Folk-Lore Society, No. 12 (Austin: Texas Folk-Lore Society, 1935). x, 261 pp.

This collection of 20 articles on Mexican and Mexican-American (primarily Texan) folklore is devoted largely to English translations of folktales, although there are some proverbs, songs, and stories in Spanish. The only article from this volume that has been annotated here is Crook 1935. [GB]

EYRING, Edward. "Spanish for the Spanish-Speaking Student in the United States." MLF 22:138-145 (1937).

Of little interest to the linguist except for Eyring's subjective and unillustrated evaluation of Southwest (chiefly New Mexican) Spanish ("A cursory survey of the dialect of the Southwest does not reveal its greatest defect: its limited vocabulary. In their isolation these people have preserved that portion of the Spanish used here a hundred years ago which has to do with the routine of their daily activities, but they have never enriched it [except] through the adoption of Anglicisms" -- p. 138), this lengthy editorial bluntly espouses an effective bilingual society, strongly criticizes United States policy towards Spanish-dominants and monolinguals, and in general advocates plans which only began to be actualized thirty years later. Eyring was way ahead of the times. [RT]

FITZ-GERALD, John D. "The Bilingual-Biracial Problem of Our Border States." Hispania. 4.174-186 (1921).

While Fitz-Gerald recognizes that since Hispanic settlement antedates Anglo-American settlement in the Southwest, New Mexico's Hispanos have a right to retain their native language, he nevertheless advocates that every attempt be made to replace Spanish with English, at least in schools and other public spheres. His reasoning is that History has proven repeatedly the tendency of linguistic minorities to betray the fatherland; Fitz-Gerald cites several World War I-era incidences of this, e.g., Quebec resistance to Empire conscription, growing demands among Catalans for separation, the enthusiasm of Irish nationalists for the restoration of Gaelic, etc. He therefore recommends that the United States follow "the French practice," i.e., that teachers use the national language exclusively, with the exception of the times they must make "supplementary remarks" in the children's home language so that the child knows what the teacher is saying! New Mexico's Hispanos, says Fitz-Gerald, have long been "eager to master English;" it is only the general lackadaisicality of the state's educational system that prevents them from doing so. This is not the case, however, with other American linguistic minorities, such as Scandinavians, Jews, and especially Germans, who have "stubbornly resisted" all efforts to make them "absorb American ideals and identify themselves with our hopes and plans." (176) [RT]

GARCÍA, Ernest. "Chicano Spanish Dialects and Education." Aztlán 2:1.67-77 (Spring 1971). (Cf. González 1973a.) (Rpt. in HERN/et al-1975, pp. 70-76.

Very generalistic discussion of language variation and educational approaches to nonstandard dialects with a focus on Southwest Spanish. Cites only a few phonological/morphological examples (pp. 71-72) taken from Bowen 1972, along with several English loanwords (73). [GB]

GONZÁLEZ, Gustavo. [1973a]. "The Analysis of Chicano Spanish and the 'Problem' of Usage: A Critique of 'Chicano Spanish Dialects and Education.'" Aztlán 3.223-231 (1973). (Cf. Ernest García 1971.)

This is a highly competent, well-written and sometimes trenchant critique of the methods and conclusions of García 1971, whom González takes to task for stating that such forms as hablates, comites and vivites result from the transfer of internal -s- from penultimate syllable-final to word-final position. G argues (convincingly) that since in addition to these forms Chicano Spanish also employs other variants that retain s in penultimate syllable-final position (hablastes etc.), any analysis must allow for the subjection of the 2.p.sing. preterit to two possibilities: "(1) regularization, in which the final -s- is added in conformity with all other 2nd person singular forms; and (2) deletion of the internal -s-." (224) Thus for hablastes only the first rule applies; for hablates both apply. In any event, "the above analyses are not really new at all [since] Ramón Menéndez Pidal . . . cites evidence of existence of such forms in the early eighteenth century [and] proposed the same rules posited above." (ibid.) González also discusses García's treatment of such deviations as verbal first-person plural marker -mos > -nos when the stress is placed on the antepenultimate syllable, the rearrangement of the infinitive of certain "radical-changing" verbs to conform to the changed root, the probable "causes" of pader 'pared' (not dissimilation to avoid homonymity with [paré] but simple metathesis, for whatever reasons), the "reduction" of el and la to l before any word beginning with a vowel, etc.

Various intelligent comments on the issue of accepting Chicano Spanish dialects in the schools follow the strictly linguistic discussions. The author advocates correcting such "baby talk" overgeneralizations as sabo, ero and pongaba on the grounds that "our guide should be the language spoken by the adult Chicano community;" (228) for that reason, then, pidí and siguí are classroom-acceptable, which is not to say, though, that their "standard" alternates pedí and seguí should be banned, since "failure to learn (at least passively) other forms of Spanish will limit the Chicano in his exchange of ideas with other people--especially the writings of our ancestors. Or should we wait for the English translation?" (227) González also speaks against the acceptance of code-switching in the classroom on the grounds that its greatest danger "would be the tendency for the pupils to revert to the stronger of their two languages instead of attempting new things in the language being learned." (229) [RT]

HENRÍQUEZ UREÑA, Pedro, ed. El español en Méjico, los Estados Unidos y la América Central. BDH, No. 4 (Buenos Aires: Univ. de Buenos Aires, 1938). lxi, 526 pp. [Annot. Nichols no. 89; Serís no. 15617; Solé 1970 no. 44. Rev. MLR 34.282-283 (1939) (W. Entwistle); RF 53.123-124 (1939) (A. Zauner); BHi 42.59-62 (1940) (J. Bourciez); Language 16.60-61 (1940) (U. Holmes).] (Rpt. of Henríquez' Introduction in RCu 11.147-160 [1938].)

The only specifically U.S. Spanish study in this volume is the excellent translation and revision of Hills 1906.
Henríquez' "Introduction" (pp. ix-xxii) provides a few brief remarks, based on the studies of Espinosa Sr. and Hills, on Spanish in the Southwest, primarily indigenismos. He also sketches the sociocultural situation of Southwest Spanish. The Bibliography (pp. xxvii-lxi) includes a section on the "Sudoeste Hispánico de los Estados Unidos" (with additions on pp. 383-384) which contains many linguistic and folklore works of the late 19th and early 20th century, occasionally with a note on content.
Elsewhere in the volume scattered references to New Mexican and Arizona Spanish (primarily as documented by Espinosa, Hills, and Post) occur in notes to other articles and in two of the articles by Henríquez: "Datos sobre el habla popular de Méjico" (pp. 277-324) and "Mutaciones articulatorias en el habla popular" (pp. 329-379). The detailed indexes to persons and places (pp. 397-415) is helpful in tracking down these references. The exhaustive index of words (pp. 415-519) may also be useful. [GB]

HENSEY, Fritz G. [1974a]. "The Development of Research Instruments for Mexican American Spanish." In Bills 1974, pp. 85-95.

This plain and unremarkable survey of methods for the collection of sociolinguistic data discusses the techniques of simple observation, informant self-report, and response to specific stimuli, but provides no primary language data. [GB]

HERNÁNDEZ-CHÁVEZ, Eduardo, Andrew D. Cohen and Anthony Fred Beltramo. El lenguaje de los Chicanos: Regional and Social Characteristics of Language Used by Mexican-Americans. Arlington, Va.: Center for Applied Linguistics, 1975. 265 pp. [Rev. Bills 1974b.]

This important anthology includes the following items (all reviewed on these pages): Barker 1947, Bowen 1952 (in part), Ernest García 1971, Gumperz/Hernández v.d., Lance 1969, Ornstein 1951, Peñalosa 1972, Post 1933, Rael 1939b and Sawyer 1969. Appearing for the first time in print are several other items not available for review at the time this Bibliography was compiled. [GB]

HYMES, Dell H. (ed.). Language in Culture and Society: A Reader in Linguistics and Anthropology. New York: Harper and Row, 1964. xxxv, 764 pp.

Contains articles by Hoijer 1948, Trager 1939, and Dozier 1956, each annotated separately on these pages. [GB]

HYMES, Dell H. and William E. Bittle. Studies in Southwestern Ethnolinguistics: Meaning and History in the Languages of the American Southwest. The Hague: Mouton, 1967. ix, 464 pp. 2 maps.

An anthropologically-oriented collection of papers dealing almost exclusively with American Indian languages. The contributions by Dozier 1967 and Voegelin et al. 1967 give some consideration to Spanish. [GB]

JATO MACÍAS, Manuel. La enseñanza del español en los EE. UU. de América. Madrid: Ediciones Cultura Hispánica, 1961. 80 pp. [TSBJr.]

This book attempts to sum up the various ways in which schools throughout the United States teach Spanish. Given the vastness of the topic and the slimness of the volume, a certain superficiality of treatment is unavoidable. For students of U.S. Spanish the following short chapters (which all discuss, anecdotally, the Spanish-as-a-Second-Language programs that schools have set up in hopes of thereby ameliorating conflicts between local Anglos and Chicanos) are of passing interest: 5 ("Enseñanza del español en las escuelas del Sudoeste"), 6 (Texas), and 7 (California.) In the first of these Jato zeros in on the town of Deming, New Mexico, "[que] se divide entre anglo-americanos y méjico-americanos. Antes de iniciar la enseñanza del español había fricciones

entre los niños de ambos grupos, que degeneraban en peleas. La
solución de este problema la encontró la ciudad de Deming intro-
duciendo la enseñanza del español en los ocho grados de las escuelas elementales. Treinta minutos diarios se dedican al español . . . Los alumnos llegan a ser bilingües antes de gra-
duarse . . . Por los informes obtenidos se sabe que los viejos
antagonismos han desaparecido . . . " (pp. 36-37) [RT]

MATLUCK, Joseph H. and Betty J. Mace. "Language Characteristics
of Mexican-American Children: Implications for Assessment."
JSPsych 11.365-386 (1973).

Good reviews and occasional critiques of the literature
dealing with the two pertinent sections "Characteristics of
Spanish Spoken" (pp. 366-371) and "Characteristics of English
Spoken" (371-379). (The third part discusses classroom testing
and will not concern us here.) Much of the material on Spanish
was taken from Cornejo 1969, Lance 1969, Blanco 1971 and Gustavo
González v.d. Following a synopsis of "developmental" errors
(i.e., baby-talk), the authors catalogue lexical, morphological
and syntactical influence from English; of interest is their
vigorous assertion (368) that "to affirm, as do the studies of
Cárdenas [1970], Lance, González, Cornejo, Blanco and others . . .
that the Mexican-American's Spanish syntax is 'almost unaffected
by English' is to do a grave injustice to the facts;" several
dozen syntactical Anglicisms are cited. Matluck and Mace then
get very involved in what appears to be a heated debate concerning
the status of [v] as a "variant of" /b/ in Chicano Spanish; (369)
their point is that [v] is "not a regular, systematic, predictable allophone" of /b/ since "one has only to look at the diffi-
culties--sometimes almost insurmountable--that most Hispanic
speakers, from this or any other area, have in producing" the
/b/:/v/ contrast in English. A competent synopsis of code-switching studies follows (chiefly Lance, Cornejo, and Gumperz/Hernández
1969). The main point of the well-written "English" section is
that linguists and educators have overlooked the young Chicano's
English perception problems while overconcentrating, perhaps, on
problems of production; pp. 375-378 nicely contrast Spanish and
English sounds so as to acquaint teachers with these matters.
Fn. 10 (372-373) sums up studies on language dominance (it seems
that only rural youngsters are truly Spanish-dominant); an encapsulation of material ("unmistakable grammatical influence from
Spanish") from González 1973b appears on p. 374. [RT]

ORNSTEIN, Jacob. [1971a] "Language Varieties Along the U.S.-
Mexican Border." In Perren and Trim 1971, pp. 349-362. [Also
available though EDRS: ED 032 520.]

This general survey of the Southwest linguistic situation is
oriented largely toward Spanish. Sociocultural milieu, bilingual-

ism, sociolinguistics, dialect geography, calós and pidgins, and educational linguistics are briefly discussed. Included is a short conversation in "Southwest Spanish street argot" (Pachuco) with an accompanying glossary. [GB]

ORTEGO, Phillip D. "Perspectives in Language, Culture and Behavior." ILR 15:52.9-16 (Spring 1969). [Abs. LLBA V-836.]

Towards the end of the article the author refers to the Southwest and its Mexican-Americans, to the fact that they speak a variety of Spanish dialects and that Educators are generally intolerant of brands of English which reveal signs of Spanish influence. He takes "linguists and anthropologists" to task on several counts: "[Their studies] have concentrated on the quaint, the curious, and the queer, specifically the language of the Curanderos, the Pachucos, and the Tirilongos, three hardly representative groups. But the various dialects of the four-and-a-half million Mexican Americans of the Southwest have been ignored for the most part." (p. 15) [RT]

ORTEGO, Philip D. "Some Cultural Implications of a Mexican American Border Dialect of American English." SL 21.77-84 (1969-70).

A perceptive but diffuse sociologically-oriented survey of the educational problems of Southwest Chicanos and a plea for needed research on language as an aid to educators. Although there are some loose, off-hand comments on a Chicano "dialect" of English heavily influenced by Spanish, no language phenomena are cited. [GB]

PERREN, G. E. and J.L.M. Trim, eds. Applications of Linguistics: Selected Papers of the Second International Congress of Applied Linguistics, Cambridge 1969. Cambridge: University Press, 1971. xviii, 498 pp.

Contains the herein-annotated Ayer 1971 and Ornstein 1971a. [GB]

RAMÍREZ, Karen G. "Socio-cultural Aspects of the Chicano Dialect." In Bills 1974, pp. 79-82.

This emotional non-linguistic note linking pride in the use of Southwest Spanish with cultural identification offers only vague generalities on the languages of the Chicano. [GB]

RODRÍGUEZ DEL PINO, Salvador. "El idioma de Aztlán: una lengua que surge." Univ. de Méx. 27:6.16-19 (feb. 1973).

Included in a popularizing issue devoted solely to "Chicanos/ Braceros," this piece gives several insights into what its author terms "bioconceptualismo" (see his discussion [p. 19] of "algunas palabras [que] al ser traducidas, cambiaban de concepto de acuerdo con el contexto cultural" such as Christmas/Navidad), but is badly marred by an embarrassing number of fictitious generalizations such as: "Algunas lenguas se prestan más que otras para asimilar en su estructura a palabras de origen extranjero. El español chicano tiene varias maneras de asimilación [léxica] sin caer en reglas formales;" and "El español chicano no se escribe con acentos ni se tilda la ñ [two accents nonetheless make their way into the sample of Pachuco jargon with which the author begins the article]. La b y v son intercambiables así como la J y la g." (19) Rodríguez characterizes as peculiarly Chicano a number of features typical of rural Spanish throughout Mexico and elsewhere: "la supresión de la y o ll como en caie, gaina [gaína?]; la inclusión de la Y como en: me cayi aier; la e final se convierte en i: huarache-warachi," and attributes "el cambio de dos vocales fuertes a fuerte y débil: real - rial" to "influencia inglesa [porque] en inglés no existe la pronunciación de dos vocales fuertes." (ibid.) That the five-item Bibliography lists only two works which deal (peripherally) with Chicano Spanish is a probable reflection of the author's know-nothing claim that the dialect "no ha sido objeto de estudios amplios por parte de lingüistas o estudiosos de la lengua española . . . . Esto se debe al concepto social que se tiene sobre las lenguas 'bastardas' o mezcladas . . ." (16) [RT]

SAMORA, Julian, ed. La Raza: Forgotten Americans. Notre Dame, Ind.: Univ. of Notre Dame Press, 1966. xvii, 218 pp.

This collection of eight papers plus an introduction by Samora "attempts an assessment of the status of a minority population in the Southwestern United States." (xi) Only the contribution by George Sánchez 1966 has anything to do with language. [GB]

SÁNCHEZ, George I. "History, Culture, and Education." In Samora 1966, pp. 1-26.

This general discussion of bilingualism and the retention of Spanish in the Southwest and historical antecedents provides no specific consideration of language. [GB]

SPOLSKY, Bernard, ed. The Language Education of Minority Children: Selected Readings. Rowley, Mass.: Newbury House, 1972. 200 pp.

Contains a reprint of Lance 1970, pp. 25-36. [GB]

SPOLSKY, Bernard and Garland D. Bills, eds. "The American Southwest." <u>IJSL</u> 2.(entire issue) (116 pp.) (1974). <u>IJSL</u> 2 is identical to <u>Linguistics</u> 128 [1974].)

This collection of linguistic papers includes the herein-annotated Southwest Spanish articles by Brisk 1974b, Metcalf 1974b, Murphy 1974b, Teschner 1974b, and Thompson 1974b, as well as a review article by Bills on recent publications in Southwest sociolinguistics. [GB]

STEINER, Stan. La Raza: <u>The Mexican Americans</u>. New York: Harper & Row, 1969. 418 pp.

A journalistic account of the life and times of Chicanos published at the very moment their protests were first capturing national attention, this work includes one short section on "The Language of La Raza" (pp. 216-224). After dealing with Aztec culture, Spanish conquistadors, student strikes in Los Angeles, and bilingual education, Steiner gets around to making a series of sweeping, imaginative, lyrical and truly misinformed statements about language. "The language of La Raza is more than 'hybrid language' that unites English and Spanish. [It is] a new language . . . with a distinctive vocabulary, its own borrowed and re-created grammar, and a unique usage, which combines the Castilian Spanish of the conquistadors and the frontier Americanisms of English with the ancient and modern languages of the Indians . . . " (222-223) One aspect of "this language" is Pachuco, "neither Spanish nor English [but instead] the creation of the barrios. 'Placa' for 'police' cannot be traced to the popular Mexican 'placa' that means 'baggage check,' or the old Spanish 'placa' that means 'star, or insignia of knights,' nor any English equivalent." (223) Not so. Placa, according to the Santamaría <u>Diccionario de mejicanismos</u> (1959), does not mean 'baggage check' in Mexico but rather (inter alia) 'lámina pequeña con rótulo o inscripción . . . para vehículos, con número de registro o de orden, etc.' From this to 'the plate, the badge' as a designation for motorized, badge-wearing police officials is just a matter of synecdoche, a well-known semantic device. But there is more to come: "Even the proper Spanish spoken in the barrios is not truly Spanish. It never was. The ordinary, everyday words, such as <u>tortilla</u> and <u>chili</u>, are of course not Spanish at all, but are from the languages of the Mexican Indians . . . " (ibid.) Sic! With ennui one turns to Corominas' <u>Diccionario crítico etimológico</u> (1954) in re <u>tortilla</u>, the diminutive form of <u>torta</u> 'bread' ("TORTA, palabra común a todos los romances, y ya documentada en el latín tardío"); <u>chile</u> and not <u>chili</u> is the universal pan-Hispanic form, its Nahuatl etymon čilli notwithstanding.

Steiner acerbly takes the National Education Association to task for "misspelling" the Spanish in the title of its 1966 "impassioned appeal for bilingual education, . . . The Invisble Minority--Per [sic] No Vencibles," (224) and then goes on to refer to "the first anthology of modern Chicano writing, El Espeso (The Mirror) . . . " (ibid.) Sic!

It is very, very disturbing to discover that even though they are now "telling the Chicano story like it is," today's Relevant writers continue to propagate the exact same falsehoods and fairy tales about language that their less-than-liberal forerunners had long held as fact. [RT]

TOVAR, Inés. "The Changing Attitude of La Raza Towards the Chicano Idiom." In Hoffer and Ornstein 1974, pp. 63-74.

Citing examples of what she terms her people's formerly subservient attitude towards language and consequent denigration of everything that constituted folk speech, the author then presents multiple quotations from recent Chicano literature which show just how much the worm has turned. Tovar defines the Chicano idiom broadly as a "spectrum of speech" that includes all forms of verbal expression, and asserts that an individual Chicano often "has command of neither language and so improvises and creates a new code from what he knows of both languages." (66) The speech spectrum then becomes a rallying point: "As the Mexican-Americans fight for the survival of their people and their people's culture, they fight also for the Chicano idiom, because Chicanismo and the Chicano idiom exist simultaneously and inseparably." (72) [RT]

TROIKE, Rudolph C. "Social Dialects and Language Learning: Implications for TESOL." TESOLQ 2.176-180 (Sept. 1968). [Abs. LLBA III-545.] (Rpt. in Aarons, Gordon and Stewart [1969], pp. 98-99, 165.) (All references here are to the reprint.)

The author devotes several paragraphs to Chicano Spanish on p. 99, mentioning that there is considerable variation in the Spanish spoken throughout the Southwest and that "there are in fact several native dialects of Spanish spoken in Texas alone-- even in a single city such as San Antonio or El Paso--and most of these are simply local varieties of the much larger regional dialect of North Mexican Spanish." But these varieties have implications for the classroom; for example /č/ is rendered variously as [š] or [ĉ] (sometimes one variant exclusively, at other times both variants in complimentary distribution), and so "if [š] is the norm of pronunciation, it is [ĉ] which must be introduced and contrasted." Troike also mentions the absence of the inflected future (e.g., cantaré) in some dialects, which use the periphrastic voy a cantar exclusively. [RT]

TURNER, Paul R., ed. Bilingualism in the Southwest. Tucson: Univ. of Arizona Press, 1973. xv, 352 pp.

This anthology of writings contains the following selections wholly or partly pertinent to Mexican-American language (all are annotated here separately): Christian 1973, Olstad 1973, Cornejo 1973, Young 1973, Coltharp 1973, Carroll Barber 1973 and Ornstein 1973. The anthology also contains various selections of concern to educators and sociologists. Turner's brief "Preface" (pp. xiii-xv) presents valuable information on the connotations of two key words ("The choice of the term 'multilingualism' also might be preferred since 'bilingualism' has been used in the Southwest in a pejorative way to refer to someone who is linguistically and socially disadvantaged") alongside an embarrassing goof ("Los Angeles [is] reported to have the third largest concentration of Spanish speakers in the New World only exceeded by Mexico City and Guadalajara"). [RT]

VALDÉS-FALLIS, Guadalupe. "[Letter to the Editor:] Spanish as a Native Language." Hispania 56.1041-1043 (1973).

Though mostly pedagogical in orientation, the "letter" does note that "caló or 'dialect'" is often used in class "especially when the student gets excited and argues a point." (p. 1042) Valdés argues cogently that while typical Chicano students are often lacking in Spanish lexicon of the more advanced sort, they "eagerly absorb patterns and constructions in imitation of the teacher conducting the discussion" (ibid.) and even come around to requesting "rules" for grammar and composition. [RT]

*WHITE, Opal Thurow. "The Mexican American Subculture: A Study in Teaching Contrastive Sounds in English and Spanish." PhD Diss., Univ. of Oklahoma, 1972. 185 pp. [DA 33 (1973) 5874-A.]

The Abstract of this anastomotically entitled dissertation informs the reader that Chicanos have yet to become assimilated "into the main stream of American life. In large part, this lack of assimilation is due to the persistence of the use of Spanish." The tail having wagged the dog, the study goes on to analyze why Spanish has persisted, "and the resulting educational problems in Texas." Subsequently discussed are various Texas "special education" programs, theories of language acquisition, ESL methodology; the work appears to conclude with a bit of popularized contrastive analysis or as the author puts it, "a simplified version of English phonetics and contrastive points in Spanish phonetics that could be used in a course for Speech for the Classroom Teacher for prospective teachers who have no Spanish language background and a limited knowledge of English phonetics." [RT]

2.2.1 SOCIOLINGUISTICS

Major Items: CHRI/CHRI-1966; GREB/etal-1970; HOFF/ORNS-1974;
    KUVL-1973; ORNS-1970; ORNS-1972b

See also these items elsewhere (consult Author Index for location):
    MCWI-1949; PEON-1966; RUBE-1968; SKRA-1967-70

*AJUBITA, María Luisa. "Language in Social Relations With Special Reference to the Mexican-American Problem." MA Thesis, Tulane Univ., 1943. ? pp.

   From the Tulane library we learn that the sole copy of this thesis has been lost. [RT]

AYER, George W. "Language and Attitudes of the Spanish-speaking Youth of the Southwestern United States." In Perren and Trim 1971, pp. 115-120.

   Brief impressionistic remarks on the renascence of Spanish among Chicanos, along with an overview of the various types of Spanish characteristic of high school students. These general comments on phonology, morphology, syntax, and lexicon are oriented largely toward the influence of English. [GB]

BILLS, Garland D. [1974b]. "Review Article." In Spolsky and Bills 1974, pp. 101-111.

   Review of Ewton and Ornstein 1972, Turner 1973, Barker 1972, Gilbert 1970, and a preview of the anthology by HERN/etal-1975. [GB]

BROOKS, Bonnie S., Gary D. Brooks, Paul W. Goodman, and Jacob Ornstein. "Sociolinguistic Background Questionnaire: A Measurement Instrument for the Study of Bilingualism." 2nd ed. (1970; El Paso: Cross-Cultural Southwest Ethnic Studies Center, Univ. of Texas, El Paso, 1972). 40 pp.

   Several recent papers by Ornstein (esp. 1972b) discuss and describe the purpose of this 103-item questionnaire, one of the first fruits and the basis for many continuing efforts of the SSSB project at the Univ. of Texas at El Paso. The first 44 questions request personal information on the individual and his family, including whether the individual speaks Spanish and how often. Questions 45-69 require an estimate of Spanish and English usage in varied domains and roles and with varied persons (e.g., "45. At home speaking to your parents," "51. When you write letters to your friends," "60. When you attend church"). Questions 70-89 attempt to gather information on the subject's attitudes toward the two languages (e.g., "71. Which language is most beautiful?",

"75. With which language is it easier to get a job?"). Questions 90-99 inquire into the respondent's ability in the two languages, including notions of stylistic variation and correctness. The last four questions are sociological/attitudinal. [GB]

CHRISTIAN, Jane MacNab and Chester C. Christian, Jr. "Spanish Language and Culture in the Southwest." In Fishman 1966, pp. 280-317.

An excellent sociocultural assessment and overview of Southwest Spanish, but with no primary linguistic data other than several examples from Espinosa 1909aa. The authors survey the history and present status of Spanish speakers and the Spanish language, examine multiple factors involved in the contact of Spanish and Anglo culture and society, and close with speculations on the future. Although this is a superb language sociology survey, it is (perhaps inevitably) heavily laced with linguistic, sociological, and cultural clichés and overgeneralizations, e.g., "New Mexican Spanish . . . remained much as Cervantes and Coronado had used it in the 16th century." (p. 280) [GB]

GREBLER, Leo, Joan W. Moore and Ralph C. Guzmán. The Mexican-American People: The Nation's Second Largest Minority. New York: The Free Press-Macmillan Company, 1970. xviii, 777 pp.

Since this work's orientation is chiefly socio-economic and historical, one finds only sporadic allusion to language throughout this definitive study, the outgrowth of the various "Advance Reports" published by the University of California-Los Angeles as the initial offshoots of its "Mexican-American Study Project," undertaken between 1963 and 1968. Nevertheless it is impossible to underestimate the importance of the brief sections which do discuss language ("The Persistence of Spanish," pp. 423-428, and "Reasons for the Persistence of Spanish," 428-432; these form part of Ch. 18, "The Tenacity of Ethnic Culture"), since the sociolinguistic material they present is based largely on extensive door-to-door surveys of households in San Antonio and Los Angeles and also on a thorough survey of "media preferences" in Chicano neighborhoods. Many of the conclusions offer fresh points of view on this ever-controversial topic of language loyalty and are bound to stimulate further discussion. The reported situation is complex and does not admit generalizations, but "in general" monolingual Spanish speakers were most predominant in the poorer barrios, and loyalty to Spanish declined, at least in metropolitan areas, in direct proportion to generation of residence in the United States and to degree of upward socio-economic movement. [RT]

HELLER, Celia S. *Mexican American Youth: Forgotten Youth at the Crossroads.* New York: Random House, 1967. 113 pp.

Sociologist Heller devotes two short sections to the language of Chicanos in a work which is chiefly concerned with providing explanations as to "why they are the way they are." In her quick glance at pachuco (pp. 59-60) she relies heavily on George Barker (v.d.). The sociolinguistic information on pp. 29-32 is largely taken from the writings of other sociologists; what will interest the reader most are Heller's own observations that "frequently Mexican American youths are deficient in informal English . . . Still, they do not . . . seem to encourage the rare efforts of Anglo Americans to speak Spanish to them, but tend to respond in English." (30) [RT]

HOFFER, Bates and Jacob Ornstein. *Sociolinguistics in the Southwest.* San Antonio, Texas: Dept. of English/Trinity Univ., 1974. 131 pp. (mimeographed).

This excellent little volume contains five items pertaining to this Bibliography's areas of concern; all five (Hensey 1974b, Hoffer 1974, Ortego 1974, Ornstein 1972b and Tovar 1974) are annotated separately on these pages. [RT]

KUVLESKY, William P. "Use of Spanish and Aspirations for Social Mobility Among Chicanos: A Synthesis and Evaluation of Texas and Colorado Findings." Paper Presented at the Rocky Mountain Social Science Association Meeting, Sociology Section, Laramie, Wyoming, April 1973. 18 pp. + 10 pp. appendices, mimeographed. (Copies of this paper, which forms part of the Texas Agricultural Experiment Station research project H-2811 and USDA-CSRS Regional Project, S-81, "Development of Human Resource Potentials of Rural Youth in the South and Their Patterns of Mobility," are available upon request from the author, Texas A & M Univ., College Station.) (See also Patella and Kuvlesky 1973.)

Gathered in a 1967 study of Spanish-language usage among 600 Mexican-American teenagers in four rural counties near Laredo, Texas, Kuvlesky's cogent data convincingly demonstrate that Spanish is the language spoken in most of the "variety of life situations [they] were likely to experience." (p. 3) But while almost all those surveyed spoke Spanish exclusively with parents, "the frequency [declined] as the contextual situation moved from the home, to the neighborhood, and finally to use outside of class in school." (8) While about three-fourths listened to Spanish language radio programs to some extent, only about one per cent admitted to frequent reading in Spanish. When Kuvlesky compared his findings with those of an as-yet unpublished study of El Paso Chicano highschoolers undertaken in 1973 by Moisés Venegas of New Mexico State University, he found striking similarities in language preferences: thus "it would seem that these patterns can be generalized across the entire border area of Texas and it can be inferred that [they] are not changing quickly, if at all." (10) Rather different results, however, were obtained from yet a third study of Mexican-American adolescents in the mountains of southern Colorado, where it was found that only one-fourth prefer Spanish over English. (11) Relative isolation of the region, and the fact that it receives little or no immigration from Mexico may well account for this.

Kuvlesky's findings on the use of Spanish and the level of individual aspiration seem to show that "Spanish is too commonly known and used among most Mexican American populations" (17) to serve as a yardstick in measuring desire to change class and improve income. [RT]

LEVINE, Harry. "Bilingualism: Its Effect on Emotional and Social Development." JSE 44.69-73 (1969).

This is putatively a review of the literature on the relationship between bilingualism and social/emotional adjustment, a topic which the author claims has not been researched sufficiently. Passing mention is made of the Mexican-American bilingual, whose "case" differs from that of other U.S. immigrants; proximity of the Southwest to Mexico and a continued influx of fellow Spanish-speakers constitute the difference. [RT]

*LÓPEZ, Melitón. "Bilingual-Bicultural Education and the Self-Concept of Mexican-American Children." PhD Diss., Wayne State Univ., Detroit, 1972. 158 pp. [DA 33 (1973) 6019-6020-A.]

From the abstract it appears that López concerns himself exclusively with "self-concept" and its resultant pedagogical implications, but it is nonetheless revealing to learn (among other things) that both Mexican-American _and_ Anglo children participating in bilingual programs "reported a more enhanced self-concept than their counterparts in regular educational programs." [RT]

MANUEL, Herschel T. Spanish-speaking Children of the Southwest: Their Education and the Public Welfare. Austin: Univ. of Texas Press, 1965. xii, 222 pp.

This excellent examination of the social, cultural, and economic background of the Mexican American and related educational problems and opportunities is replete with references to language, primarily of a casual language-sociology nature. Chap. 11 (110-129) is devoted to "The Problem of Language" in education; although thoughtful and sympathetic, it is not very sophisticated linguistically. This work contains no primary language data beyond the inclusion of letters by parents, teachers, and high school students addressing the educational problems. [GB]

NALL, Frank C. II. "Role Expectations: A Cross-cultural Study."
    RS 27.28-41 (1962).

Nall is largely interested in quantifying various theories of sociologist Talcott Parsons which do not concern us here. Language usage, however, is one of Nall's "variables," and thus the article has bearing on the sociology of bilingualism. Within a given population of Mexican-Americans (locale not specified) three subgroups were examined: those who spoke Spanish to peers, those who spoke English, and those who spoke both. "It was concluded that the data . . . are congruent with the hypothesis that speaking Spanish to peers implies integration or identification with the traditional ethnic complex of social relations and that speaking English to peers implies integration or identification with the dominant Anglo-American patterns of social relations." (pp. 38-39) The bilingual group, however, was far less easy to pigeon-hole; Nall's data did not allow him to infer clearly whether it is in the "process of transition or whether this represents integration or identification with an emergent pattern of social relations," (39) i.e., a "distinct pattern of role orientations within the context of the ethnically subdivided community." (38) [RT]

ORNSTEIN, Jacob. "Sociolinguistics and New Perspectives in the
    Study of Southwest Spanish." In Ewton and Orstein 1970,
    pp. 127-184. [Rev. GLing 11.175-178 (1971) (D. Lance);
    Craddock 1973 p. 315.]

The first of a series of articles by Ornstein attempting to delineate the problems and needs in sociolinguistic research on Southwest languages, especially Spanish. The initial section of the paper reviews the broad scope of the field of sociolinguistics with only occasional reference to the Southwest. The second part is concerned almost solely with the Southwest, surveying some of the body of existing linguistic, educational, and sociological data on Southwest Spanish (especially of the El Paso area, and hence particularly relevant to Pachuco) and suggesting the needs in further study. Ornstein also describes the goals of a sociolinguistic questionnaire (see Brooks et al., 1972) under preparation by the long-range SSSB project at the Univ. of Texas, El Paso. An idealized diagram of the "Language Situation in the United States Southwest" is given (p. 167), and a very few examples of Southwest Spanish are noted (151, 165). [GB]

ORNSTEIN, Jacob. [1971b]. "Sociolinguistic Research on Language
    Diversity in the American Southwest and Its Educational
    Implications." MLJ 55.223-229 (1971). [Abs. LLBA V-1536.]

This disjointed article briefly surveys the Southwest sociolinguistic situation with special regard for Spanish. The principal topics discussed are bilingualism and language variation

and the speech of young schoolchildren. Ornstein includes a
working list of nine Spanish and ten English linguistic variables
(almost all phonological) which he feels "may be of particular
significance" in the study of linguistic variation in Spanish-
English bilingual areas. The article closes with a list of seven
applied sociolinguistic topics that need greater exploration.
[GB]

ORNSTEIN, Jacob. [1972a]. "Mexican-American Sociolinguistics:
A Well-Kept Scholarly and Public Secret." Paper presented
at the 4th Triennial Conference of Symbolic Processes,
Washington, D.C., April, 1972. [Author informs that the
paper will be published in the proceedings of this conference.] Also published, revised, in Hoffer and Ornstein
1974, pp. 91-111, together with "Brief Bibliography [Check-
list] of Mexican-American Sociolinguistics and Related
Topics," (112-118) two appendices (119-121), and a "discussion incorporating remarks made at The Sociolinguistics
Panel, Annual Meeting of the Linguistic Association of the
Southwest (LASSO), Tulsa, Okla., Oct. 1972 (122-131).

This very generalistic paper, "intended primarily to help
force a better and more realistic realization of the significance
of sociolinguistic work on Mexican-Americans," (p. 1) reports on
the accomplishments and aspirations of the SSSB project. The
tentative list of linguistic variables given in Ornstein 1971b
is repeated here with the addition of one Spanish variable (9).
[GB]

ORNSTEIN, Jacob. [1972b]. "Toward a Classification of Southwest
Spanish Nonstandard Variants." Linguistics 93.70-87 (1972).

The variety of problems and needs in Southwest Spanish
sociolinguistic research are further considered here. Ornstein
is specifically concerned with what he labels "General Southwest
Spanish," which excludes the northern New Mexico-southern Colorado
variety, is highly homogeneous, and is "for the most part a subdialect of, or better, an extension of the northern dialect of
Mexican Spanish" (p. 71). The bulk of the article discusses and
illustrates (but poorly explains) a tentative taxonomic framework for the classification of nonstandard linguistic variables.
Four binary criteria are used in this classification: open or
closed class phenomenon, internal change or interference, occurrence in monolingual communities, and occurrence in bilingual
communities. Ornstein provides incompletely specified examples
for six of the supposedly eight possible types of nonstandard
items (in fact, the four criteria permit 16 possible types).
Three of the examples, all taken from the speech of students at
the Univ. of Texas, El Paso, are cited in sentence context.

A discussion of Pachuco in the article introduces a sample utterance (18 words in length) for which the gloss and origin of each nonstandard lexical item are briefly noted. [GB]

ORNSTEIN, Jacob. "Toward an Inventory of Interdisciplinary Tasks in Research on U.S. Southwest Bilingualism/Biculturalism." In Turner 1973, pp. 321-339.

A cursory review of needs in the study of southwestern languages, especially Spanish, culminating in a list of sixty major tasks, largely sociolinguistic in orientation. This contains no specific linguistic information, but does have an ample bibliography. [GB]

ORNSTEIN, Jacob. "The Sociolinguistic Studies on Southwest Bilingualism: A Status Report." In Bills 1974, pp. 11-34.

A history of the author's activities with the SSSB project. Included is the list of Spanish-English linguistic variables from Ornstein (forthcoming), an interesting discussion of socioeconomic-linguistic correlations, subjects' oral and written performances in both Spanish and English, and attitudes toward Spanish and English varieties in the Southwest. The paper concludes with an explanation of the six series of corpora gathered in the SSSB activities. [GB]

ORTEGO, Phillip D. "Sociolinguistics and Language Attitudinal Change." In Hoffer and Ornstein 1974, pp. 75-80.

Extemporaneous remarks on code-switching, the ways in which the structure of a language encourages "linguistic chauvinism," and the need for linguists to commit themselves and their professional organizations to the achievement of social democracy. For Ortego "it does not do any good to discover that a Chicano does a lot of code switching and to make some determinations that he does so because of this and because of that. The question is, how is he further disadvantaged, and how is he further debilitated because he happens to speak that way." (75-76) [RT]

PEÑALOSA, Fernando. "Chicano Multilingualism and Multiglossia." Aztlán 3.215-222 (1972). (Rpt. in HERN/et al-1975, pp. 164-169.)

A tentative theoretical investigation of the cited phenomena, using as points of departure the insights of Ervin-Tripp, Ferguson, Fishman, Gumperz, Hymes, Kloss and Lambert. Peñalosa rejects "bilingualism" as a descriptor of Chicano realities and suggests instead the term "complex diglossia" to describe "those societies such as the Chicano, which are characterized by both in-diglossia and out-diglossia;" (p. 217) the latter coinages are Kloss's and refer respectively to "a relationship between closely related languages" and one between "languages not closely related." (216)

P agrees with Barker (1947 and v.d.) that the barrio is home to three types of Spanish (standard Mexican, rural-lower-class uneducated Mexican, and Pachuco argot) but argues for the recognition of a fourth code, infelicitously baptized "Pochismos," that refers to the manner of speech characterized by widespread code-switching. P questions previous explanations of code-switching (notably Chacón 1969) and asks: "Is 'pochismos' Spanish with English interference, English with Spanish interference, simple code switching, all of these, or a separate code that can properly be said to act as 'mother tongue'?" (219) [RT]

SCHEFF, Thomas J. "Changes in Public and Private Language Among Spanish-Spanish Migrants in an Industrial City [Racine, Wisconsin]." IntMig 3.78-85 (1965).

Other researchers' findings about immigrant language shift suggest that acculturation occurs more slowly in the "internal system" (especially the home) than in the "external system," and that "change in the internal system is related to age, education, length of residence, and income of the migrants." (p. 84) Scheff's data support this proposition. Among Racine Mexican-Americans (mostly recent Texas migrants), "change appeared to be occurring in the language of the children and associates of the migrants, but was virtually nil in the language spoken in the home." (ibid.) Scheff found a one per cent net change toward English as home language between 1959 and 1960; in 30 years, at this rate, "the majority [of the adult generation] still will not speak English in the home." (82) For the group as a whole he noted a "tendency to use Spanish in private settings and English in public settings." (ibid.) Somewhat to his surprise Scheff found that "a substantial proportion of respondents showed a move toward Spanish over the year period: 17 per cent for home language, 18 per cent for children's language, and 27 per cent for friends' language." (81) While this may be due in part to "changes in the family circumstances" such as "Spanish-speaking parents and relatives moving into the house" or a sudden influx of Spanish-dominants into the immediate neighborhood, Scheff hazards that "most of these responses are probably due to the unreliability of the response categories" (ibid.) which indeed were rather broad-gauged. Or possibly the findings were jeopardized by the fact that responses were simply respondents' self-estimates or by the degree to which the "carefully trained, bilingual interviewers" (79) were Spanish- or English-dominant themselves. [RT]

TUCK, Ruth D. Not With the Fist: Mexican-Americans in a Southwest City. New York: Harcourt, Brace & Co., 1946. xx, 234 pp.

Language and language usage are only discussed on three separate occasions in this classic, pull-no-punches essay on the lives and circumstances of the Chicano colony in the medium-sized city of "Descanso," though Tuck is careful to employ Spanish words for Chicano-culture referents whenerver possible. <u>Colonia</u> attitudes toward the local Spanish-language magazine are detailed on pp. 165-166; Spanish-language retention as an adjunct of "culture survival" is given brief mention on p. 118. Most valuable for the sociolinguist, though, is the discussion of usage attitudes on pp. 97-98: "The use of Spanish in public ranked foremost, far above all other reasons given by Anglo-Americans as a cause of friction and ill-feeling between the two populations . . . 'Most of our playground fights,' said a junior high school principal, 'between the two groups start because Mexican boys were speaking Spanish in a mixed group. The others, because they don't understand, are sure they're being insulted.'" (97) Even the liberal Ms. Tuck has sided with Anglo opinion in this instance with her recommendation (ibid.) that "many Mexican-Americans could exercise greater tact and courtesy regarding the use of Spanish in situations where Anglo-Americans might feel excluded from side-eddies of conversation." An interesting note is that certain young local <u>malcriados</u> consistently avoid even mild swearing in English though <u>chingar</u> is a verb of high frequency whenever they speak Spanish in school. [RT]

2.2.2 TEXTBOOKS

<u>Major Items</u>: BAKE-1953/66

<u>See also these items elsewhere</u> (consult Author Index for location): (none)

BAKER, Paulline. <u>Español para los hispanos</u>. 2nd ed. (1953; Skokie, Illinois: National Textbook Co., 1966.) 116 pp.

Although Baker necessarily presents her material in the form of "lessons," her textbook will interest students of Chicano Spanish in the same way that the <u>Appendix Probi</u> interests Romance philologists, especially the lengthy Ch. 3, "Barbarismos," (19-54) which gives copious examples of "arcaísmos," "anglicismos," "palabras confundidas" (e.g., <u>chanza</u> 'oportunidad'), "letras omitidas" (<u>cencia</u> 'ciencia'), "letras añadidas [e] intercambiadas," "errores con <u>f</u>, <u>h</u>, y <u>j</u>," and "pachuquismos;" in the latter section one finds close to 100 entries, many of which are also used in a brief "conversation" (50-51). Morphological deviations from the standard are presented and corrected in Ch. 4 ("Faltas gramaticales"); the textbook's other chapters deal with such topics as orthography, punctuation, the composition of business letters, "organización de un club," etc. Baker's largely error-free work confesses to be a "texto auxiliar cuyo fin preciso es ayudar a los alumnos hispanos a corregir sus errores comunes al hablar y escribir," and while some critics will disagree with the author's

philosophy ("estamos presenciando una decadencia lamentable del
español de los Estados Unidos . . . cada día se hace sentir más
la necesidad de corregir los errores del mal español que se deben
evitar"--"Prefacio," n.p.), none will doubt the text's utility
as a reflection of regional Spanish. [RT]

BARKER, Marie Esman. Español para el bilingüe. Skokie, Illinois:
National Textbook Co., 1970. 340 pp.

In the work's dedication Barker indicates that she collaborated on its initial stages with Paulline Baker (q.v. 1953/66);
thus it is no surprise to find that Barker is to a great extent
an expanded version of Baker's text and that the central purpose,
linguistic correction, has remained unaltered. But where Baker's
was largely a texto auxiliar, Barker has aimed to provide a full
textbook, complete with protracted supplementary readings and
lengthy pattern drill exercises. While these aspects of the work
are alien to the purposes of the present examination, future reviewers of Barker qua textbook will not be able to avoid commenting upon the unfortunate amount of pedagogical misinformation it
contains (one example: "los grados de comparación" are explained
solely as "positivo: califica nada más," "comparativo: compara,"
and "superlativo: cuando se exagera una cualidad" [68]). Where
Baker's correcciones de lenguaje are largely concentrated in discrete sections, Barker's presentation of the same material is
spread throughout the book: thus nearly all 21 chapters include
scattered information on phonological and morphological aberrancies under the section-heading "Pronunciación." The most concentrated list of lexical variants is given on pp. 46-47 ("Barbarismos"), but this reproduces Baker's Anglicism list almost in toto,
with the addition of saxofón and various omissions: Crismas,
lonchar, lonche, mapa 'mop,' piquenique, tíquete, troca, etc.
Instead of Baker's charife and mistir Barker gives the more commonly used cherife and mistiar. [RT]

2.3 SPANISH PHONOLOGY (includes ORTHOGRAPHY)

Major Items: (none)

See also these items elsewhere (consult Author Index for location):
    (none)

ALONSO, Amado. "La ll y sus alteraciones en España, y América."
    In Estudios dedicados a Menéndez Pidal, II (Madrid: CSIC,
    1951), pp. 41-89. Incorporated in Amado Alonso, Estudios
    lingüísticos: Temas hispanoamericanos [Madrid: Editorial
    Gredos, 1967], pp. 159-212.

This detailed study includes consideration of phonetic data
on Arizona and New Mexico Spanish from Espinosa 1930a, Hills 1938,
and Post 1934.

2.4 SPANISH GRAMMAR (MORPHOLOGY AND SYNTAX)

Major Items: (none)

See also these items elsewhere (consult Author Index for location):

GONZ-Gu-1973a

LOZANO, Anthony Girard. "Grammatical Notes on Chicano Spanish." BilR 1.147-151 (1974).

Following a summary of the author's thoughts on the dialectal divisions of Southwestern Spanish, random notes appear which discuss and exemplify some of the features which Chicano Spanish (excluding or perhaps including the "subdialect" of New Mexican/Southern Coloradan Spanish?) does not share with "Standard Mexico City Spanish." These include analogical assignment of gender to learnèd lexical items, choice of prepositions after verbs with direct objects (e.g., soñar de, of probable English inspiration), redundant marking of possession in such sentences as Ponte tu abrigo, Se me quebraron mis anteojos (at this point the author comments on what he terms exclusive Chicano Spanish use of quebrar for 'to break;' romper is 'to tear'), and the deletion (through English influence perhaps, or else because failure to insert does not always create ambiguity) of the preposition a as a marker of animate direct objects. Various English calques are then cited: Me fui pa' atrás a San Antonio, Hice mi mente pa' arriba 'Llegué a una decisión,' and the like. Lozano notes that while personal investigations into Colorado Spanish reveal conformity to standard subjunctive usage following optative verbals, "Southwestern Spanish" shows a "complete lack of subjunctive verb forms after an environment with feature [+] dubitative in the main clause," (p. 148) e.g., No creo que todavía lo sabe, Ignoro que lo hizo, Su padre negó que era asaltante, etc. (151) [RT]

2.5 SPANISH LEXICON (includes SEMANTICS)

Major Items: GALV-1973; STRO-1958

See also these items elsewhere (consult Author Index for location):
(none)

*BARKER, Marie Esman. "The Purdue Perceptual Motor Survey: The Spanish Edition, Development and Standardization." EdD Diss., New Mexico State Univ., Las Cruces, 1973. 126 pp. [DA 34 (1974) 5614-5615-A.]

Barker produced and then administered a Purdue test version capable of being given in the varieties of Spanish familiar to Chicanos. The varieties were patterned after those common to El

Paso, Texas. "With respect to language, the [overall results of test administration] demonstrated that this Spanish edition . . . is equivalent to the English in eliciting desired performances." (Abstract) So as to allow for local variation Barker presents alternate words and constructions alongside standard ones when necessary. She further adds that since the specific purpose of the test is to determine perceptual characteristics, mixtilingüe and code-switching should not be eschewed if the child's language background has conditioned him to expect code-switched speech as standard: " . . . commonly accepted hispanizing or anglicizing patterns of speech generally employed by Spanish-speaking Mexican Americans of the Southwest [should] be used to provide alternate forms for maximum efficiency in assessing perceptual-motor development [and] to convey the full meaning of any task where performance hinges on knowledge of Spanish vocabulary." Thus linguists will find this dissertation valuable for the "glosses" it provides. [RT]

COBOS, Rubén, ed. Southwestern Spanish Proverbs: Refranes españoles del sudoeste. Cerrillos, New Mexico: San Marcos Press, 1973. 144 pp.

A delightful, but linguistically meager, alphabetical listing of 1697 dichos with loose English glosses and an occasional equivalent English proverb or comment on intent. The entries were collected from throughout the Southwest, but the geographical distribution of particular entries are not provided. An attempt was apparently made to italicize regional lexical items (e.g., ajuma, destornuda, asegún, servites, though not guajolote, truje, pa, etc.). [GB]

ESPINOSA, Aurelio Macedonio. "[Review of Rodolfo Lenz,] Los elementos indios del Castellano de Chile. Estudio lingüístico y etnolójico. Diccionario etimilójico de las voces chilenas derivadas de las lenguas indíjenas americanas, Primera parte. Santiago de Chile: Imprenta Cervantes, 1904-1910)." RDR 2.420-424 (1910).

The substance of this "review" is a commentary on a number of words cited by Lenz that also are used in the Southwest, primarily in New Mexico and Colorado. He mentions 13 such words: atrincar, cacha/cachero, camote, caracho, coribe, chambón, chango, chara, chicote, chiripa, chueco, machi, and sorochi. An example of his comments: "camote: significa en Méjico y en Nuevo Méjico 'patata dulce,' pero en Colorado y Alta California significa 'betavel silvestre.' En Nuevo Méjico también se usa esta palabra con el significado de 'travieso' ó 'querido'" (p. 422). [GB]

ESPINOSA, Aurelio Macedonio, Jr. "Problemas lexicográficos del español del sudoeste." Hispania 40.139-143 (1957). [Annot. HLAS 21 (1959) no. 3638 (D. Wogan); Fody p. 530.]

Lamenting the lack of a comprehensive study of Southwest Spanish lexicon, Espinosa Jr. discusses the problem in most general terms under three headings of historical origin: Spanish forms (divided into archaisms and derivatives from regions of Spain, semantic changes, and new coinages), American Indian influence, and "extranjerismos." Numerous lexical examples are given, especially in the first and last groups, but rarely with specific regional identification and often with inadequate glosses. A few derivational affixes are mentioned and exemplified. [GB]

FRIAR, John G. and George W. Kelly. A Practical Spanish Grammar for Border Patrol Officers. 2nd ed. (1949: Washington, D.C.: U.S. Dept. of Justice, Immigration and Naturalization Service, U.S. GPO, 1969). vi, 225 pp. (All page references are to the first edition.)

The first 110 pages represent a traditional Spanish grammar textbook, but subsequent pages contain some Southwest Spanish lexical items of interest. In the Vocabulary pp. 168-194), for example, entries considered "colloquialisms used on the Mexican Border" (primarily Anglicisms) are cited in italics in the English-Spanish section. The "Practice Material" section (114-138) contains interview transcriptions and autobiographical statements that are laced with lexical forms typical of Mexico and the Southwest.
The 1969 edition is considerably revised in form but not in substance. [GB]

GALARZA, Ernesto. Barrio Boy. Notre Dame: Univ. of Notre Dame Press, 1971. 274 pp. (Glossary pp. 267-275.) [Rev. RIR 3.220-222 (1973) (C. Senior).]

The glossary of this well-written autobiography of childhood and early adolescence in Mexico and central California defines ca. 175 words which appear in Spanish in the English-language text and whose meaning might not be familiar to the reader with only an "academic" knowledge of Spanish. Most of the words are common Mexicanisms but a few of these appear used in a manner not necessarily familiar, e.g., arrimados 'poor relatives or friends who stayed with a family temporarily when they had no place of their own,' bola 'any group of persons who got together to overthrow the establishment or to inflict upon it anguish or alarm.' Galarza's definitions are often amusing (comadre 'a lady's relationship to parents whose baby she has presented for baptism . . . comadres frequently became intimate to the point of not being on speaking terms') and occasionally biting (enganchador 'an agent who went about the country recruiting workers for railway construction with promises of high wages, comfortable quarters, and steady promotion; the process being known as the <u>enganche</u> or hooking, which produced the <u>enganchado</u> or hooked one'). Only a few definitions are dubious, such as the overly narrow <u>barrio</u> 'a neighborhood within a city containing an underground society of young males who regarded the area as their exclusive territory.' [RT]

GALVÁN, Roberto A. "Chicano, vocablo controvertido." <u>Thesaurus</u> 28.<u>111-117</u> (1973).

A cogent, copiously documented and at times uproarious discussion of some possible explanations as to why the word <u>chicano</u> has given rise to controversy among "United States citizens of Mexican ancestry." Militants prefer the word because of all the referents it is the only one unsullied by Anglos, but Galván notes that "[si] el angloamericano no lo ha mancillado todavía . . . el mexicano-americano mismo viene usándolo humorística- o despectivamente desde hace tiempo;" (p. 2) there follows a long recital of <u>chicano</u> used <u>in situ</u> (2-4). According to Galván, a major reason the word is held in low esteem by some is the resemblance that its three syllables show, separately or in a variety of combinations, to lexemes of distinctly scatological reference: "<u>chi</u> 'orina' + <u>ca</u> < 'cagar' + <u>ano</u> (la <u>a</u> se usa dos veces) 'orificio por el cual se expele el excremento.'" (5) Galván also suggests certain formal resemblances between <u>chicano</u> and the word <u>mecachis</u> (cited by Kany, <u>American-Spanish Euphemisms</u>, 1960, p. 151): "Advierta el lector, además, que el <u>mecachis</u> . . . lleva los dos primeros componentes de <u>chicano</u> en forma invertida: <u>mecachis</u> = <u>me</u> <u>ca</u>(go) (y) (hago) <u>chis</u> // <u>chicano</u> = (hago) <u>chi</u> y (luego me) <u>cago</u> (por el <u>ano</u>)." (6) [RT]

GAMIO, Manuel. <u>Mexican Immigration to the United States.</u> Chicago: Univ. of Chicago Press, 1930. 262 pp. (Rpt. New York: Arno, 1969.)

Only one section of this well-written and authoritative volume will be of direct interest to the linguist and that is Appendix VI, "The Linguistic Contact," pp. 230-234. Here Gamio exemplifies various <u>pochismos</u> such as <u>guachar</u>, <u>chansa</u>, <u>troca</u> and <u>marqueta</u> and provides instances of "a great many Spanish words incorrectly used" by Mexicans who have lived in the United States; these include many words which other authors would merely term "Mexicanisms" or else "northernisms," and although most are fairly common coin, some (such as <u>changuira</u> and <u>carranclan</u>) are rare items, unlisted by Santamaría and others, and bear further investigation. [RT]

KEEVER, Mary, Alfredo Vásquez and Anna Padilla. <u>Glossary of Words and Expressions, Irregular in Form or Meaning, Encountered in the Examination of Spanish Mail on the Mexican Border</u>. El Paso, Texas: El Paso Office of the United States Office of Censorship, 1945. vii, 46 pp. (mimeographed). (Loc. Library of Congress PC 4832 .U5.)

    This unusual Spanish-English glossary grew out of the U.S. government's efforts to censor foreign mail during the Second World War in order to catch spies and prevent security leaks. It "represents the examination of tens of thousands of letters [by the El Paso Office]" (p. i) which passed across the border from December, 1941 through November, 1945; since censorship "revealed almost from the outset that many letters contained words which either in form or usage were to be found in no dictionary," (ibid.) the compilation of an ad hoc glossary was a prime desideratum. The glossary gives no bibliography of works consulted; apparently, then, the translation equivalentes were all elicited from local Spanish-speakers.

    Following a brief general sketch of common orthographic errors and semantic deviations designed to aid "the reader of poorly written Spanish" (iii-vii), the work glosses close to 700 words and expressions; some of these have subsequently been included in other publications on Chicano lexicon or Pachuco slang, e.g., <u>agüitado</u>, <u>al alba</u>, <u>alivianarse</u>, <u>apucha</u>, <u>arranar</u>, etc., while others fall into such categories as "typical Mexicanisms," common metatheses, additions or deletions of sounds, "vulgarisms," Anglicisms, or simple spelling errors. There are surprisingly few of the latter, which may show that "border" Spanish is not as poorly written as was thought.

    Although now partly superceded by recent works, the Censorship list continues to be an important guide to some of the less well-known aspects of Spanish lexicon as well as a possible source of "first appearances" for the items it lists. [RT]

PEÓN, Máximo [pseud.?]. <u>Cómo viven los mexicanos en los Estados Unidos</u>. México: Costa-Amic, 1966. 249 pp.

    Various autobiographical or second-hand anecdotes constitute the majority of the various short <u>cuentos</u> which go to make up this readable little volume. "Peón" has travelled the length and breadth of the western two-thirds of the United States, chiefly with braceros but also with Mexican criminals and other down-and-outs. Language-related material is almost non-existent but the following encapsulation of what the author assures us is a letter to a bracero from his wife in Mexico will be of interest to etymologists and lexicographers: "Fíjese usted, don Máximo . . . Apenas acababa yo de enviarles <u>dos milagros</u> o sean cuatrocientos dólares, mi <u>garfila</u> tuvo dificultades con dos <u>piusas</u> que <u>la traían con ella</u> . . . Un día, en que <u>se pusieron al brinco</u> más de lo

debido, mi vieja sacó su alfiler y les dio varios piquetitos . . .
El caso es que vino la chota y se las llevó al bote, donde mi
changa tuvo que azotar con los milagros . . . Y yo que me quería
comprar un tacuche, unos buenos cascorros y dos limas. Pero ya
no se va a poder . . . " (pp. 183-184) "Peón" has an explanation
for this "lenguaje que usaban muchos braceros y que usa la mayoría
de los pochos. Esto se debe a que desde tiempo inmemorial se han
internado a los Estados Unidos, huyendo de la justicia mexicana,
muchos criminales y rateros. Posteriormente, se coló entre los
braceros esta calaña, que propaló sus modismos y su caló entre los
trabajadores honrados." (184) [RT]

SANTAMARÍA, Francisco J. *Diccionario de mejicanismos.* México,
D.F.: Porrúa, 1959. xxiv, 1197 pp.

Though this thick tome is hardly classifiable as a major
source for strictly Mexican-American lexical references, diligent
researchers will want to consult it with care, since from time to
time one indeed runs across a north-of-the-border reference,
chiefly to Anglicisms such as cranque ("Pochismo norteamericano,
que ha invadido el país en su frontera setentrional, por cigüeñal,
particularmente de automóvil"), troca and the like, but also to
words not of English origin such as chutama ("Vocablo usado como
vulgar de una planta burserácea, de la cual hay varias especias,
en el noroeste del país y suroeste de Estados Unidos. . . . ").
At times Santamaría's etymologies are not all that they might be,
e.g., curia "Vulgarismo apochado californiano, por curiosidad.
(Seguramente tomado del inglés curious.)" In all probability
curia is a spelling pronunciation of Eng. curio 'article valued
as a curiosity,' with the feminine gender a probable result of
analogy with curiosidad. [RT]

STROUT, Clevy Lloyd. "A Linguistic Study of the Journals of the
Coronado Expedition." PhD. Diss., Univ. of Colorado, 1958.
viii, xv, 950 pp. [*DA* 19 (1959) 2608-2609-A.]

This noteworthy philological lexicographic effort documenting
the first use of Spanish in the Southwest is a detailed examination of six of the chronicles of Coronado's 1540-1542 expedition
through the Southwest. The bulk of the work is the first chapter,
"A Coronado Lexicon" (pp. 1-782), which contains all lexical items
encountered. For each of the 2,900 entries every distinct meaning
and spelling is recorded and up to ten sentential examples are
cited. This is followed by a 25-page chapter discussing the breakdown of the vocabulary into special groups: military-organization,
geography, flora and fauna, Indian borrowings (only 33, mostly
Nahuatl), and so forth. A 35-page conclusion focuses on the (practically nonexistent) impact of the new environment on the language
of the chronicles. [GB]

2.6 ONOMASTICS (includes TOPONYMY)

Major Items: (none)

See also these items elsewhere (consult Author Index for location):
   AUST-1933

PEARCE, Thomas Matthews. "Spanish Place-name Patterns in the
   Southwest." Names 3.201-209 (19-5). [Annot. Fody p. 531.]

   A very general and disjointed consideration of "categories"
of naming (terms of description, possession, commemoration,
incident, etc.) illustrated with numerous examples from throughout the Southwest. [GB]

2.7 ENGLISH INFLUENCE ON SPANISH

Major Items: (none)

See also these items elsewhere (consult Author Index for location):
   AYER-1971; MENC-1919/36

ADKINS, Patricia G. "Reverse Borrowings of English Corruptions of
   Spanish." SpT 17.331-333 (1968).

   The author mentions various Hispanisms in English and then
goes on to comment, briefly and at times confusingly, upon Spanish
words corrupted by native English speakers and then presumably
reborrowed in corrupted fashion by Spanish speakers. One learns
for example that "Spanish speakers . . . freely use hoosegow to
mean jail, although the Spanish word for jail [is] cárcel;" (332)
from this it is not clear which form is actually used in Spanish-
hoosegow (English pronunciation) or the original juzgado. Other
borrowings and reborrowings are also treated in this fashion:
lariat, ten gallon (hat), ranch(o), cake, etc. [RT]

ALATORRE, Antonio. "El idioma de los mexicanos." Univ. de Méx.
   10.1-2, 11-15 (1955).

   The article bears largely on the language of Mexico itself but
brief sections (notably pp. 13-14) deal with Chicano Spanish as
well. Alatorre astutely compares Chicanos to the mozárabes of
medieval Spain and intimates that the former, like the latter,
have served to introduce many foreignisms into Spanish. Thus
Mexico has witnessed the indubitable spread of certain terms from
what he considers the Anglicism-saturated speech of the "pocho,"
defined as "el mexicano que se deja seducir por la American way
of life y para [quien] las cosas mexicanas son siempre despreciables
y las norteamericanas siempre inigualables." (p. 14) Like many
Hispanic commentators Alatorre is quite critical of any Spanish

that smacks of English; thus he refers disparagingly to "ciertos
grupos fronterizos que han creado una especie de dialecto o
lengua criolla en que se funden elementos del inglés y del español;
(ibid.) as an admittedly extreme and perhaps apocryphal example
of this "dialect or creole" he presents the following: "¿Juasu
mara con la doga anoche? Run pallá run pacá pa nasin. Sámbari
vino y se llevó la leña del boiler." (ibid.) Alatorre observes
that in the 1940's and early 1950's many English elements from
"pocho" and pachuco speech were popularized in Mexico by the
comedian Tin Tan, who used them for humorous effect. [RT]

BLACKMAR, Frank W. [1891a]. "Spanish American Words." MLN 6.91-
97 (1891).

A brief list of Hispanisms in Southwest English notable more
for its relatively early date than for its content. All the
forms discussed, with the exception of tules (pl.) 'large bul-
rushes of the genus Scirpus' (col. 93) and vacquero [sic] (col.
94), continue to be part of every-day western English (adobe,
cañon [sic], corral, etc.). The "short phrases in common speech"
mentioned in col. 96 (including the ungrammatical mucho caliente
and poco tiempo) do not, on the other hand, seem to be generally
current nowadays. [JC]

2.8 SPANISH INFLUENCE ON ENGLISH

Major Items: BENT-1932; CRAI/HULB-1938/44; MATH-1951; MENC-
1919/36; SALA-1924; SORV-1952; SORV-1953

See also these items elsewhere (consult Author Index for location):
ADK1-1968; BLAC-1891b; WOOD-1950

ADAMS, Ramon F. Cowboy Lingo. Boston: Houghton Mifflin, 1936.
x, 257 pp.

Entertaining and useful anticipation of his major work on the
language of the cowhand (Adams 1944). As expected, the number of
Spanish loanwords is high. An index (pp. 241-257) facilitates
locating them. As an example of the author's philological prowess,
I quote his diachronic analysis of caballado (sic) 'set of horses
used by a cowboy in a day's work'--"from the Spanish which Mexicans
degraded into 'cavayer' or 'cav-a-yah', and the American cowboy
pushed farther into 'cavvieyah,' 'cavvy,' or 'cavvoy'" (p. 80).
The word in question is caballada, pronounced [kabayá:] in colloquial Mexican Spanish. I would guess that the cowboys Adams
heard were saying something like [káevijà(d)], often spelled
cavvyard. [JC]

ADAMS, Ramon F. Western Words: A Dictionary of the Range, Cow, Camp and Trail. Norman, Okla.: Univ. of Oklahoma Press, 1944. 182 pp. (2nd ed. rev. with new subtitle: A Dictionary of the American West. 1968. 355 pp.)

This alphabetical wordlist, expanded in the second edition to include terms relating to mining, logging, trapping and other typical western occupations, contains many Hispanisms. Each item is carefully defined with occasional references to secondary literature. Since the author relied on live informants (at least for the first edition) his glossary has no strictly historical dimension (compare Bentley 1932). In 1944, with impressive defiance of common sense, the Castilian pronunciation of Spanish loanwords was indicated in parentheses: ación 'stirrup leather' (ah-the-on'), p. 3, zorrillas 'cattle of the early longhorn breed' (thor-reel-'lyahs), p. 182, rather than the way cowhands say them. Rare exceptions included coyote (co-yo'tay) "pronounced by the Westerner ki 'yote" (p. 44; in my experience [Kájòt] is standard alongside the more rustic [kàyóti]), and mesquite (meth-kee'tay or ma-skeet') (p. 99; of course only the latter [miskít] will ever be heard on the range). In the second edition these pointless transcriptions were wisely deleted but no hint as to Southwest pronunciation has taken their place.
When Adams ambles onto philological ground, he often gets his spurs tangled up. He offers as plain fact Barker's humorous reconstruction of hackamore's phonological history (p. 71 [2nd ed. p. 173; in both places the Portuguese form is given as laco]). Some blunders were corrected in the second edition (compare the entries hoosgow [p.79/153], quirt [p. 122/242] and honda [p. 78/ 151]) but the atrocious solecism muy gracias continues to mar the introduction (p. xvii in the 2nd ed.). These minor points notwithstanding, the work remains a valuable repository of Southwest Hispanisms. [JC]

AUSTIN, Mary H. "Geographical Terms from the Southwest." AS 7.7-10 (Oct. 1933).

A popular, naive prose explanation of perhaps 50 Spanish words, concluding with a simple glossary list of 30 additional terms. Most of the forms are geographically descriptive and drawn from toponyms; Austin presumptuously states that "practically all. . . [are] anglicized for general use in the Southwest." (p. 9) [GB]

BARKER, S. Omar. "Sagebrush Spanish." New Mexico 20.18-19, 32-33 (1942).

Extremely entertaining account of Spanish loanwords in cowhand parlance. Many of the forms mentioned are familiar enough (buckeroo [sic], hackamore, etc.) but this brief essay documents a trend worthy of further study: the conversion of the Spanish words into similar-sounding proper names. For instance, Theodore

'supplementary looped cord . . . run from the bosal (nose stall)
of a hackamore up over the horse's head between his ears for
added security' < fiador 'that which secures, guarantor,'
McCarty < mecate 'thong of rawhide, length of braided horse-hair
for hogtying calves or steers,' and, most curious, Dolly Welter
'the taking of a hitch or hitches around the saddle horn' < dale
vuelta (2nd p. sg. imperative) 'give it a turn, turn it around.'
The spellings suggest an original southern U.S. English suppression of implosive r; if McCarty and Welter represent the pronunciations [mɨkáti] and [wélte], the phonological relationships
between source and loanword seem somewhat more straightforward.
[JC]

BENTLEY, Harold W. A Dictionary of Spanish Terms in English with
Special Reference to the American Southwest. Columbia University Studies in English and Comparative Literature (New
York: Columbia Univ. Press, 1932). 243 pp. [Rev. Hispania
16.234 (1933) (C. Coester).]

The dictionary of some 400 entries follows a long introduction (pp. 1-81) that discusses the basic types of loanwords absorbed into English from Spanish, the historical background of
English/Spanish contacts from the time of the Catholic Kings to
the present (i.e., 1932), and the literary monuments most likely
to contain Hispanisms. For each vocable surveyed the author
supplies both the Spanish and English pronunciations, detailed
definitions with occasional etymological information, and a chronological list of textual citations, if available. The appendices
(pp. 221-240) offer lists of words of Amerindian origin, Spanish
place names in the U.S., bullfight terms, and a group of letters
written by bilinguals. A remarkably inadequate bibliography concludes the work.
  Bentley was no phonetician; indeed, the claim (p. 139) that
the American English pronunciation of gente de razón 'responsible
and reliable people' is identical to the Spanish seems wildly
absurd (he alleges many such supposedly equivalent pronunciations).
Transcriptions like [le: fú: ga:] for Sp. ley fuga 'the right to
kill a prisoner attempting to escape' (p. 156) show how little
the author was versed in the elements of Spanish phonology. The
glosses are in general accurate, but it is difficult to imagine
how a person born and raised in northern Mexico could have made
the following remark: "cabron is, in the mind of the Mexican, as
strong as English 'fool' or even 'damn fool.'" (p. 110)
  Such details aside, Bentley's glossary remains one of the most
useful in the field, particularly since he sought to limit his purview to those forms that could be considered naturalized loanwords
rather than include any and all occurrences of Spanish lexical material in southwestern writings without regard to their currency
in the Anglo vernacular. [JC]

BRÜCH, Josef. "Ein spanisches Wort im amerikanischen Englisch: 'bronco.'" *Wiener Beiträge zur englischen Philologie*, 62 (*Anglo-Americana: Leo Hibler Lebmannsport zum siebzigsten Geburtstag*, edited by K. Brunner), pp. 5-26 (1955).

With excessive confidence in the OED's attestations, Brüch uncautiously assumes that the noun bronco 'untamed horse' was abbreviated in the years 1883-1884 from the phrase a wild bronco. Had he consulted Bentley 1932 or Mathews 1951 he would have discovered that the unmodified noun is on record as early as 1850. It seems that the nominalization occurred already in the Spanish of the Southwest (thus Corominas 1954-57:1.526a26). As for the origin of Sp. bronco (adj.) 'rough, coarse, hoarse,' Brüch accepts the generally recognized starting point Lat. bro(n)cus/ brocc(h)us (adj.) 'buck-toothed (animal)', but proposes a blend with Gk. rhynchos (noun) 'snout, muzzle' in place of the traditional assumption that the interfering lexeme was Lat. truncus 'stump' (Meyer-Lübke 1935, §1337). Corominas rejects Brüch's notion out of hand (1954-57:4.948). [JC]

CARLISLE, Rose Jeanne. "A Southwestern Dictionary." MA Thesis, Univ. of New Mexico, 1939. v, 398 pp.

A list of perhaps 2,500 forms fills the 398 pages of this labored, perfunctory thesis that is "intended as a key to the usages of typical Southwestern words in their literary settings." (p. i) Each entry contains a part of speech designation, a general classification (slang, Spanish, Indian, etc.), a brief definition, and an example sentence from the earliest work in which the form was encountered. Unfortunately, no mention is made of the number or kind of works examined and indeed, no bibliography is provided. Each word of Spanish origin is given an uncareful phonetic spelling (supposedly reflecting Southwest Spanish pronunciation) that is of no value whatsoever. [GB]

CRAIGIE, Sir William Alexander and James R. Hulbert, joint eds. *A Dictionary of American English on Historical Principles*. Chicago: Univ. of Chicago Press, 1938-44. 4 vols. xii/ix/ ix/xi, 2552 pp. [Rev. *BSL* 127.86-87 (1946) (Mossé); *English Studies* 27.186-190 (1946) (Zandvoort).]

The "Prefatory Notes" to each of the four volumes of this lexicographical classic contain partial though often healthy extractions of a wide variety of entry types; thus readers desirous of learning which Hispanisms the work includes can locate most by simply consulting the Prefaces. In all Craigie and Hulbert appear to list close to 130 Hispanisms. [RT]

DILLARD, J. L. "Language Contact in the American West." RIR 2.68-71 (1972).

The gist of Dillard's communication is that everyone on the American frontier was forced to use Pidgin English to some degree. Thus Pidgin, however defined, appears to have "mediated between Spanish and English on the frontier," (p. 69) or at least this is the conclusion Dillard draws from one example in the California-based Overland Monthly, 1893 (no further citation), which "qotes [sic] a Digger Indian who has been offered shoes: /La misma oso. Me no quiero zapato. / which makes no sense in Spanish unless it is considered as a literal translation from Pidgin English / Allee samee bear. Me no want shoe. /" (69-70) How literal a translation this is must remain moot, as must the meaning of the first part of the pidgin model itself, to one not initiate in these matters. Elsewhere (70-71) Dillard makes mention of various well-known Hispanisms in English (wrangler, hoosegow, hackamore, corral, etc.). [RT]

DILLARD, J.L. "The Lingua Franca in the American Southwest." RIR 3.278-289 (1973).

Intriguing examples of words used occasionally (according to the testimony of various early and mid-nineteenth century travellers) by Indians throughout the West lead Dillard to conclude, initially, that some sort of lingua franca-like "contact variety of Spanish" (p. 285) was used by whites and redskins alike during the initial years of Anglo domination. One shortly learns, though, that not a Spanish-based but actually a more general Mediterranean (or probably Portuguese-based) lingua franca, the very same lingua franca that is traceable back to the medieval Crusaders, was the immediate source for most of what Dillard controversially assures us are the "so-called" Hispanisms of southwestern American English. (Cf. Dillard 1972.) His argument is that English could not possibly have interpreted as [û^w] the unstressed Spanish [o] of vamos to 'vamoose,' lazo to 'lassoo,' and the like. Dillard thus presumes their etyma to be Portuguese, or Lingua Franca, but does not consider an equally valid explanation, namely, that o > u^w came about through (1) assignment to [o] of primary stress to counteract schwah, and then (2) raising of the tense vowel by one degree in both stressed syllables. Instead, Dillard insists that since for such words "the accepted Spanish etymologies simply will not work," (289) it is logical to conclude that the first Anglo settlers of Texas (inter alia) "may very well have learned at least some of what may have been at the time a French-based Creole--or, on the other hand, it may have been an international Romance Lingua Franca [which] would have served some of their purposes in contact with Spanish speakers, and it would have helped them along with the Frenchmen and the Indians," (288) who, Dillard suggests elsewhere (287) had learned their lingua franca from runaway black slaves. In short, an intriguing, speculative,

ultra-Creolist hypothesis. Hispanists, though, will chide
Dillard for several errors and misinterpretations within their
own province alone; for example Dillard's rejected Spanish etymon
for wrangler is given as "caballarengero [sic, 'caballerango'];"
for dally he posits dar vuelta ("phonetically rather unlike the
Spanish source" [28]--so why not darle [vuelta]?). He also refers wrongly to "Jesse [sic, 'Janet B.'] Sawyer" and speaks of
"el chalke, el trucke" as being "said" by San Antonio Chicanos.
[RT]

DON ? . "Vaquero Lingo." The Western Horseman 2:5.11
(Sept.-Oct. 1937).

The author, whose full name I was unable to discover, attempts
to inculcate the proper meaning of three terms: remuda 'drove
of saddle horses kept up handy, so a change of mounts can be made'
(the same as cavvyard?), manada 'herd of brood mares,' and
caponera 'herd of geldings.' [JC]

JENKINS, Thelma Adams. "A Study of Cowboy Diction with a Glossary
of Terms." MA Thesis, Univ. of New Mexico, 1931. ii, 127 pp.

The bulk of this uninspiring work is a vocabulary list of over
750 "cowboy" words extracted from 15 popular books "written by
men who spent the early part of their lives in the saddle." (p. 2)
This unadorned list provides a part of speech designation, the
source-work and a sample sentence from it, and a classification
of the form as cowboy "dialect" or "slang" or as being of English,
Spanish, or Indian origin (but with no broader etymological attempt). A large number of the words are from Spanish. Preceding
the glossary, Jenkins offers a trite description of the cowboy and
some crude comments on his language "style," "bad grammar," and
propensity to use borrowings and metaphor. [GB]

MATHEWS, Mitford M., ed. A Dictionary of Americanisms on Historical Principles. Chicago: Univ. of Chicago Press, 1951. xvi,
1946 pp. [Rev. MLR 47.565-567 (1952) (N. Eliason); SNPh 25.53-
54 (1952-53) (S. Liljergren); RES 4.197-201 (1953) (B. White);
Philologica 8.42-44 (1956) (J. Peprník).]

This monument to the science of lexicography appears to contain nearly all the Hispanisms which found their way into written
American English (the author limits his compilation to items
documentable in printed sources). For Mathews an Americanism is
"a word or expression that originated in the United States. The
term includes: outright coinages, as appendicitis, hydrant,
tularemia; such words as adobe, campus, gorilla, which first became English in the United States; and terms such as faculty,
fraternity, refrigerator, when used in senses first given them in
American usage." (p. v [Preface]) Of interest to the Hispanist
will be Mathews' discussion of alcalde on p. vii. The author's

method of listing is to present the form, assign it one or more
figured pronunciations (using for the most part the symbols of
the International Phonetic Alphabet), specify (at times) the
part of the United States in which it enjoys currency, provide an
etymology (or several) and then a definition, and lastly to give
multiple in situ quotations from sourceworks (often travel lore,
fiction, poetry, songs, journals, periodicals and the like).
The bibliography (pp. 1913-1946) is a "partial" listing designed
to "facilitate identification of such sources as may be obscure
in the forms cited." (1913) [RT]

MCWILLIAMS, Carey. North From Mexico: The Spanish-Speaking
    People of the United States. Philadelphia: Lippincott, 1949.
    (Rpr. with new Introduction by the author, New York: Green-
    wood Press, 1968.) 324 pp.

   In what remains no doubt the most readable introduction to the
whole subject of the Hispanic presence in the Southwest,
McWilliams takes up linguistic matters in two sections of Chap. 16,
"By Any Other Name" and "Words That Fit" (pp. 290-296). The
former stresses the impact of English on Southwest Spanish and the
"pachuco patois," while the latter discusses the numerous Hispanisms that have penetrated the English of the same region. The
material is all second-hand and rather carelessly presented, but,
in the main, accurate. Other linguistic obiter dicta include
discussions of loanwords in the terminology of mining (pp. 137-
138), cattle raising (pp. 153-155) and mule driving (p. 166). [JC]

MENCKEN, H.L. The American Language. New York: Knopf, 1919.
    4th ed. 1936. xxix, 769 pp. Supplement One: New York: Knopf,
    1945. xxxv, 739 pp. Supplement Two: New York: Knopf, 1948.
    xliii, 890 pp. (All three volumes were revised and abridged
    into one by Raven I. McDavid, New York: Knopf, 1963. 777 pp.)
    [Supplement Two annot. Woodbridge p. 236.]

   Mencken discusses Hispanisms as a group in each of the three
chronological divisions he established for the history of English
in the United States: pp. 111-112 in Chap. 3, "The Beginnings of
American," pp. 151-152 in Chap. 4, "The Period of Growth," and
pp. 220-221, in Chap. 5, "The Language Today." The Supplements
follow the same outline, so that further comments appear in
Supplement One, pp. 197-199, 312-313, and 436. However, individual
loanwords crop up here and there in all three volumes; they can
be traced by means of the excellent indices provided, both for individual words and for subjects, e.g., "loanwords from Spanish,"
and the like. In this connection, one should also note the jargon
of cattlemen presented on pp. 741-742 of Supplement Two.
   U.S. Spanish receives brief treatment on pp. 647-651 of the
main work; the author was mainly interested in the impact of
English on Spanish in the Southwest, but there are also allusions

to the Puerto-Rican Spanish of New York City.

Most of what Mencken had to say has stood the test of time remarkably well. Among many details worthy of note, I will mention only the etymology of (to) mosey (along) < vamoose 'beat it!'< Sp. vamos 'let's go!,' a derivation supported by the earliest attestations in Mathews 1951 which suggest swift movement, especially that involved in beating a hasty retreat. The progeny spawned by the allegedly Cuban Spanish cafeteria is truly astonishing (The American Language, pp. 176-177). By way of criticism, I should point out that phonological adjustments consisting of prosthetic and epithetic vowels (S.-W. Sp. lonche < lunch, estequi < steak) do not qualify as "suffixes" or "prefixes" (The American Language, p. 649). Am.-Eng. frijole (Supplement One, pp. 312-313) resembles neither the singular nor the plural of the Spanish form (frijol/frijoles) but something in between, perhaps extracted from the plural by false analogy (note also tamale < Sp. tamal/tamales). [JC]

NORTHROP, Stuart A. "Terms from the Spanish." AS 12.79-81 (1937).

Brief notes on two topographic Hispanisms common to the English of the U.S. Southwest: mesa and arroyo. Northrop is chiefly interested in achieving as precise a description as possible for each term. For mesa, two long paragraphs from a U.S. geological survey report are cited and for arroyo the author relates the nature of the fluvonym and concludes that "there exists considerable vagueness in the meaning and connotation of arroyo." (p. 81) [RT]

PEARCE, Thomas Matthews. "The English Language in the Southwest." NMHR 7.210-232 (1932).

An enthusiastic and literate treatise on English lexical innovations in the Southwest due to the new environment and borrowings from Spanish and American Indian languages. It is a philological work drawing solely on written records and is intended primarily to show shortcomings of American English descriptions regarding Southwest words. His presentation is flowing and florid and not always objective, e.g.: "acequia, analogous to English 'irrigation ditch,' but infinitely to be preferred from the standpoint of succinctness, beauty, and appropriateness." (p. 216) Many Southwest Spanish words are cited with explanations of their meanings. [GB]

PEARCE, Thomas Matthews. "Trader Terms in Southwestern English." AS 16.179-186 (1941).

A simple listing of selected vocabulary items drawn from nine mid-19th century popular books and manuscripts. Approximately 120 terms, over one-third marked as Spanish or of Spanish origin, are presented in four groups: On the Trail, In the Market Place, On

Pleasure Bent, and Descriptive Metaphors and Slang. The entries
specify the source language or other historical aspect, a minimum
gloss, and occasionally an example sentence from the source document. [GB]

PEARCE, Thomas Matthews. [1958b]. "Three Rocky Mountain Terms:
Park, Sugan, and Plaza." AS 33.99-107 (1958).

This discussion of the diffusion of these American English
dialect words in the Rocky Mountain area includes a brief and
nonspecific commentary on plaza (pp. 105-106), the only Spanish
term of the three. The article concludes with a mention of other
terms of possible English dialect geography distinctiveness in
the Southwest, including such Spanish terms as bosque, acequia,
ciénaga, terrones, and vigas. [GB]

PEÑUELAS, Marcelino C. Lo español en el suroeste de los Estados
Unidos. Madrid: Ediciones Cultura Hispánica, 1964. 295 pp.

This is a popularizing though genuinely informative synthesis
of the various facets of the Southwest's Hispanic heritage.
"Lenguaje" is treated in a separate chapter (pp. 173-192) and
"Folklore del Suroeste" subsequently (q. v. for good samples of
New Mexican Spanish arcaisms contained in various romances and
cuentos populares). Peñuelas' quick overview of New Mexican
Spanish and its Anglicisms is largely an encapsulation of material
from Aurelio M. Espinosa, Sr. (v.d.); the chapter on language is
of primary interest for its survey of "Influencias del español en
el inglés" (178-186). The author notes that many Hispanisms first
entered English through the newspaper reports of Mexican-American
War correspondents (1846-1848); in this as in other realms Peñuelas notes his debt to Bentley (1932), whose extensive citations
from cowboy literature are freely repated here. At times the
"dated" nature of this second-hand information is only too apparent;
for example: "Everyone [in cattle country] says 'agua' when meaning 'water.'" (185) [RT]

SALADO ÁLVAREZ, Victoriano. "Mexicanismos supervivientes en el
inglés de Norte América." AnMN 19.111-179 (1924). Published
as a separate vol. with new title [Méjico peregrino], México:
Museo Nacional de Arqueología, Historia y Etnografía, 1924.
173 pp.) [Annot. Nichols no. 974.]

Since, as far as I know, so few Mexican scholars have concerned themselves with the topic discussed in this book (originally an
inaugural lecture to the Mexican Academy), it seems particularly
unfortunate that it remained unkown to authorities like Mencken
and Mathews or the bibliographers like Brenni 1964. Like Mencken,
Salado surveys Hispanisms in English from the time of the earliest
contacts up to the moment he was writing. While most of his
material is drawn from well-known sources, his own readings have

occasionally supplied curious data; for instance note his remarks concerning the vocabulary of mule driving (p. 36) where he draws on a source (H.W. Daly) lacking in both Mencken and Mathews (cf. McWilliams 1949, p. 166). When it appeared, I believe this was the only monographic treatment of the subject in any language; though much of the etymological information must be disregarded, the observations concerning meaning and usage in Mexico retain their value.

A group of apendices present a discussion of the name of California, (99-111), a letter concerning the reconstruction of the railroads in northern Mexico, (112-114) a study (115-118) of the word barbacoa > barbecue (also on 29-32), a note (119-134) attributing Gypsy origin to the word chingar 'to fuck,' brief glossaries of Hispanisms current in Texas and California, (135-148) drawn in the main from Tallichet 1890 and H.H. Bancroft, California Pastoral (San Francisco: 1888), and several observations on the influence of Spanish on Nahuatl. [JC]

SORVIG, Ralph W. "A Topical Analysis of Spanish Loanwords in Written American English of the American Southwest." PhD Diss., Univ. of Denver, 1952. 295 pp. [Annot. Woodbridge p. 239.]

Easily the finest lexical work in the field of Hispanisms in U.S. English, far superior in plan and execution to Bentley 1932, yet unaccountably unpublished, Sorvig's dissertation concentrates exclusively on written sources traceable to the core of the Southwest, the states of New Mexico and Arizona together with southern Colorado. The Introduction, pp. 5-40, after stating the purpose of the work, reviews previous studies (omitting, as usual, Salado Alvarez 1924), lays out the theoretical foundations underlying the notion of lexical borrowing and prepares the reader for the style and format of the lexicon.

The lexicon is organized along very broad sense groups ("Topography," "Flora and Fauna," etc.) with the second just mentioned constituting the most substantial part of the whole (see Sorvig 1953). An abundant list of sources (256-271) and a word index (273-293) facilitate comparative study and permit the identification of original citations.

My criticisms are relatively trivial and few in number. Mary Austin should not have been used as a source for Spanish words without independent verification of every form she made use of. The comments on mining terminology (p. 24) would have benefitted from McWilliams 1949, pp. 137-138 while I find the terms "corruption" and "confusion" utterly inappropriate to describe loanwords like calaboose (p. 26). It is unfortunate the quotations could not be included, but at least the contexts can be retrieved by means of the source list. [JC]

SORVIG, Ralph W. "Southwestern Plant Names from Spanish." <u>AS</u>
   28.97-105 (1953). [Annot. Woodbridge p. 239.]

   The author presents here a selection of the plant names
analyzed in his dissertation (Sorvig 1952, pp. 56-113), i.e.,
those that are either wanting in Mathews 1951 or those for which
Sorvig was able to supply more adequate information than the <u>Dictionary of Americanisms</u>. The method followed is the same as in
the larger work; the author makes a good case for including rare
and nonce forms on the ground that they too provide information
concerning "the nature of the cultural relationship between two
or more language groups." I agree wholeheartedly; far better that
the lexicographer err on the side of overinclusiveness, since in
any case the linguistic specialist would have to use independent
data to establish currency, phonological variants, etc. [JC]

2.8.1 ENGLISH OF THIS PARTICULAR HISPANIC GROUP

<u>Major Items</u>: GARC-Ro-1973

<u>See also these items elsewhere</u> (consult Author Index for location):
   MATL/MACE-1973; ORTE-1969-70

*CARROW, Sister Mary Arthur [Elizabeth]. "A Comparative Study of
   the Linguistic Function of Bilingual Spanish-American Children
   and Monolingual Anglo-American Children at the Third Grade
   Level." Ph.D. Diss., Northwestern Univ., 1955. 222 pp. [<u>DA</u>
   16 (1956) 400-A.]

   Carrow examines language and language-related abilities of a
group of third-grade Chicano children who "had been exposed to the
Spanish and English languages in the home from infancy, could communicate in both languages by the age of three, and preferred the
English language at the time of testing," (abs.) compares their
text scores with those of a group of English-monolingual children
of shared age, socio-economic background, and intelligence, and
concludes that the bilinguals are at a relative disadvantage, especially as regards English phonology. Monolinguals were, for example, "significantly superior to the bilingual group in oral
reading accuracy and comprehension, hearing vocabulary, arithmetic
reasoning, mechanics of English, and the extent of speaking vocabulary, arithmetic reasoning, mechanics in English, and the extent
of speaking vocabulary as measured by the number of different
words used. . . . Fifty-two per cent of the bilingual children
had articulation defects; whereas the percentage of the monolingual
children with such problems was 14." (ibid.) "The bilingual
children made 80 per cent more grammatical errors than the monolingual children," especially in verbal conjugation, prepositional
usage and the appropriateness of lexical choice. There was, however, no significant difference between the two groups in "silent

reading vocabulary and comprehension, spelling, oral reading rate, number of words spoken per three minute period of time [as extracted from a 'three-minute sample of oral language'], clause length, degree of subordination, and complexity of sentence structure." Carrow suggests that the bilinguals' deficiencies "were related to a paucity of linguistic and experiential stimuli to vocabulary development and [to] the presence of confused and incorrect languge and speech patterns in the home." While these conclusions seem to fly in the face of more recent findings by Wallace Lambert regarding the relatively advantaged position of the young bilingual, one notes that Carrow's subjects acquired their "second" language (here, English) in a far less systematic manner than did Lambert's (see Wallace G. Lambert and G. Richard Tucker, Bilingual Education of Children, Rowley, Mass.: Newbury, 1972); thus not bilingualism per se but the circumstances of acquisition may well be held accountable for the striking differences between the two sets of findings. [RT]

GARCIA, Rodolfo. "Language Interference and Socioeconomic Status as Factors in the Acquisition of Standard Oral English of Mexican-American and Anglo Migrant Children." PhD Diss., Ohio State Univ., 1973. ix, 1972 pp. [DA 34 (1973) 2162-A.]

This well-executed pioneering study sought to determine whether the English of Chicano and white Anglo migrant children differed significantly. Given the fact that both groups shared the same (very low) socioeconomic background, it was hypothesized that any greater approximation of the Anglo group's speech to Standard English (as measured comparatively through a second control group, the children of relatively affluent professionals in the suburbs of East Lansing, Michigan) would be proof that bilingualism and/or Spanish interference was responsible for the difference. The sample involved 228 six, seven, eight- and nine-year-old children from summer migrant schools in various parts of Michigan and from two elementary schools in suburban East Lansing. Roughly one-third of the 228 belonged to each of the three groups. Oral proficiency was measured through the MOLPT (Michigan Oral Language Productive Test [in somewhat revised form]).

García found that Chicano migrant children (largely from Texas) are less proficient than their Anglo migrant counterparts, and that "the large number of '0' responses . . . indicates that many children did not comprehend the questions or were not proficient enough in English to respond." (p. 126) Socioeconomic status was also a speech determinant: Anglo non-migrants were indeed more proficient than their migrant opposites (but since the latter were all from southern or south Midland dialect zones, regional as well as class differences may have accounted for lack of approximation to a Standard). The conclusion therefore is that "language interference is a greater factor in the oral Standard English proficiency of Mexican American migrant children than is socioeconomic status." (128)

With regard to the migrant groups' speech styles themselves
(these are examined, as selected MOLPT-elicited variant forms)
in largely statistical terms in Ch. 4, pp. 69-122), García concludes that Chicanos do not learn English from their migrant schoolmates, given the marked distance between the two styles. This is
not surprising, though, since "Appalachians" constituted a distinct
minority within the Michigan migrant stream (perhaps 10 per cent)
while Mexican-Americans comprised more than 85 per cent; the remaining few are blacks. Then too, migrants travel in largely
self-contained "family units" and the average child seldom spends
more than two weeks in one single school, so the opportunity for
more than transitory contact between the two groups may well be
limited. [RT]

WAKEFIELD, Mary W. and N.J. Silvaroli. "A Study of Oral Language
Patterns of Low Socioeconomic Groups." ReadT 22.622-624, 663
(1969).

"Natural speech" was elicited from a random sampling of twenty
lower-class first-graders (Anglos, blacks, and Chicanos, the
latter from schools in Phoenix, Arizona) by having them describe
or talk about five stimulus pictures. The authors sought to
corroborate Basil Bernstein's deficit theories which relate "deficient speech" to low socioeconomic status ("The study attempted
to gain insight into whether a difference . . . is influenced
more by ethnic or economic backgrounds of the children in these
subgroups" [p. 622]). Transcripts were analyzed for kinds and
frequencies of basic sentence patterns and also for mazes
(hesitations, false starts, meaningless repetitions). Variance
analysis revealed that "mean scores for the three ethnic groups . . .
were not significantly different" except that Chicanos used the
request/command pattern more frequently than did Anglos and
blacks. The findings thus indicate similarity among the groups,
but since the researchers included no control group(s) of middle
class children, it does not follow from their data that "the
economically disadvantaged child comes to school and is over-
whelmed with the overall language system; consequently, there is
little language production." (663) [RT]

2.9 SPANISH INFLUENCE ON AMERINDIAN LANGUAGES

Major Items: KIDD-1964

See also these items elsewhere (consult Author Index for location):
DILL-1973; DOZI-1956

BRIGHT, William. [1960b]. "A Note on the Southwestern Words for Cat." IJAL 26.167-168 (1960).

 A paragraph-length response to Landar 1959 suggesting Spanish moza 'cat' as "the most likely explanation for Hopi mó·sa and its congeners." [GB]

CROWLEY, Cornelius J. "Some Remarks on the Etymology of the Southwestern Words for Cat." IJAL 28.149-151 (1962). [Annot. Fody p. 530.]

 A brief follow-up on Landar 1961 simply raising problems of etymological derivations from Vulgar Latin. [GB]

DOZIER, Edward P. "Linguistic Acculturation Studies in the Southwest." In Hymes and Bittle 1967, pp. 389-402.

 Although this short paper presents no language data, it is a good critical review of recent studies of southwestern interlanguage influences (mostly Spanish influence on Native American languages) and a probing examination of the purposes of such research. [GB]

HALL, Robert A., Jr. "A Note on Taos k'owena horse." IJAL 13.117-118 (1947).

 This brief response to Trager 1944 suggests that this form does indeed derive from Spanish caballo and cites similar reflexes in 15 other U.S. Indian languages (some quite distant from areas of Spanish domination) to bolster the argument. [GB]

KIDDLE, Lawrence B. "Spanish Loan Words in American Indian Languages." Hispania 35.179-184 (1952).

 A general illustration of the study of loanwords as an aid in cultural and linguistic research. Limited examples of Spanish loans in the domains of religion, material culture, domestic animals, and money are taken from Chiricahua Apache, Hopi, Keresan, Navajo, and Yaqui as well as other Indian languages of Central and South America. [GB]

KIDDLE, Lawrence B. "American Indian Reflexes of Two Spanish Words for Cat." IJAL 30.299-305 (1964).

This short but scholarly article (over 100 references!) documents the Romance and Spanish history of the two Spanish words miz and mozo and lists the reflexes of the two forms in numerous New World languages, including Navajo, Hopi, Zuni, Jemez, Cochití, Acoma, Santa Ana, San Felipe, Santo Domingo, Taos, Tewa, Obispeño Chumash, and others. [GB]

KIDDLE, Lawrence B. "Hispanismos en las lenguas indígenas de América." In ACILFR-11 4.2069-2083 (1968).

This very general discussion of Spanish loanwords in Native American languages from southern Chile to northern California considers in cursory fashion various aspects of cultural diffusion and borrowing. Exemplification is provided by citing the reflexes in a multitude of languages of just eleven Spanish words in four semantic categories. Southwest language examples are given for Keres, Chiricahua, Tewa, Coahuilteco, Yaqui, Wappo, Miwok, Nisenan, Yuma, Patwin, Navajo, Maidu, Zuñi, Chico, Comecrudo, and Cotoname. [GB]

LANDAR, Herbert J. "The Diffusion of Some Southwestern Words for Cat." IJAL 25.273-274 (1959).

Perfunctory and unenlightening but fecund remarks (spawning Bright 1960, Landar 1961, Crowley 1962, and Kiddle 1964) on the Spanish-derived, or perhaps English-through-Spanish-derived, mosi-type words for 'cat' in Navajo, Hopi, Zuni, Keresan, Tewa, and Taos. Landar's intent is to show that "facile statements concerning the diffusion of Spanish and English words for cat in the Southwest are risky if not rash." (p. 274) [GB]

LANDAR, Herbert J. "The Southwestern Words for Cat." IJAL 27.370-371 (1961).

Brief note accepting the suggestion of Bright 1960 and also suggesting that Native American words with u as the first vowel may derive from forms of the Late Latin musio 'cat.' [GB]

SPICER, Edward H. "Spanish-Indian Acculturation in the Southwest." AmA 56.663-684 (1954).

Although devoid of any primary language data, this article (with following comments by Florence Ellis and Edward Dozier) provides an excellent general overview of cultural contact in three major patterns as exemplified by the Pueblo, Apache-Navajo, and Yaqui-Mayo groups. For each group Spicer discusses the contact situation and the resultant cultural and orientation changes. [GB]

2.10 CODE-SWITCHING

Major Items: (none)

See also these items elsewhere (consult Author Index for location):

CARD-1972; MATL/MACE-1973; PEÑA-F-1972

3. [CHICANOS:] NEW MEXICO AND SOUTH-CENTRAL COLORADO

3.1 BIBLIOGRAPHY

Major Items: (none)

See also these items elsewhere (consult Author Index for location): (none)

CHÁVEZ, Fray Angélico. "Some Original New Mexico Documents in California Libraries." NMHR 25.244-253 (1950).

A brief listing of original Spanish language manuscripts of the Spanish and Mexican periods contained in the Ritch Collection of the Huntington Library in San Marino and the Bancroft Collection at the Univ. of California, Berkeley. [GB]

CÓRDOVA, Gilbert Benito. "Bibliography of Unpublished Materials Pertaining to Hispanic Culture in the New Mexico WPA Writers' Files." Santa Fe: New Mexico State Department of Education, 1972. 44 pp.

Minimally annotated list of 581 manuscripts located in the State Record Center and Archives and the History Library of the Museum of New Mexico in Santa Fe. A large portion of the entries deal with folklore, but almost none with linguistic description. There are author and subject indices. [GB]

POTTER, Helen Rose Lavignino. Social and Economic Dimensions of Health and Illness Behavior in New Mexico: An Annotated Bibliography. Albuquerque: Univ. of New Mexico Press, 1969. ix, 220 pp.

Although oriented toward medical studies and containing few entries dealing solely with language, this bibliography of 825 items is laced with numerous demographic and sociological works useful as secondary references for students of New Mexican Spanish. The annotations are brief (usually one or two sentences) and oriented to health. The index for "Spanish American" cites four works on general demography, 26 on population statistics, 36 on folk medicine, and 115 on socio-cultural setting. [GB]

SHELTON, Wilma Loy, comp. "A Check List of New Mexico Newspapers." UNMBSS 2:2 (entire issue) (31 pp.) (Dec. 1935).

This list of 575 newspapers, arranged by towns and with the dates of publication and the place where files were known to exist, includes 115 published in Spanish. The earliest New Mexican newspaper is stated to be the Santa Fe New Mexican Review, established in 1848 (but see Wagner 1937). [GB]

WAGNER, Henry R. "New Mexico Spanish Press." NMHR 12.1-40
(1937). (Also published as separatum by the Historical
Society of New Mexico, 1937.)

A survey of some very early publications from the earliest in 1834 to 1845, with explanations and notes on the locations of extant copies. [GB]

3.2 COMPREHENSIVE/GENERAL STUDIES; MISCELLANY; ANTHOLOGIES/
    FESTSCHRIFTEN

Major Items: BOWE-1952; HILL-1906aa; HILL-1929; HILL-1938;
    MCSP-1934a; MCSP-1934b; RAEL-1937

See also these items elsewhere (consult Author Index for location):
    FITZ-1921; JOHN-L-1938; PEÑU-1964

BOWEN, J. Donald. "The Spanish of San Antonito, New Mexico."
PhD Diss., Univ. of New Mexico, 1952. xiii, 373 pp. [Annot. Woodbridge p. 240.] (Abridgement of sec. on "Adaptation of English Borrowing" rpt. in HERN/etal-1975, pp. 115-121.

This is readily the finest descriptive study ever done of the overall structure of the Spanish of a single rural Southwest community. It is a rigorously taxonomic linguistic analysis based on tape-recorded fieldwork performed in a small town just east of Albuquerque.
The work contains essentially four chapters: "Introduction," (pp. 1-19) "Phonology," (20-75) "Morphology," (76-125) and "Vocabulary." (126-322) The lack of a chapter on syntax is noteworthy and indicative of the linguistic approach at that time. Also included are a meticulously prepared sample of phonetically and phonemically transcribed texts (323-369) and a short bibliography (370-373).
The first seven pages of the Introduction are an apologia to the philologist for such a blatantly structuralist approach to the description of Spanish (this Spanish Department dissertation was directed by the eminent structural linguist Stanley Newman of the Anthropology Department). The rest of this chapter provides a description of the methodology used and of the town and its inhabitants. Included is a careful list of the 21 informants with name, age, birthplace, other residences, knowledge of English, occupation, and schooling. There is also a useful, but generally nonlinguistic, overview of the Spanish of San Antonito: the influence of English, the roles of the two languages, and social variation (including the use of Pachuco).
The phonological description in Chap. 2 is detailed and extremely careful. Presented in order are: the phonemes and their allophones; a description of accent and pitch that is priceless because of its rarity; phoneme distribution and frequency count;

a discussion of English borrowings that delves into morphology, syntax, and semantics as well as phonology; and a section on morphophonology. The beginning of this last section is a boring attempt to smooth out wrinkles resulting from the approach (though he also tackles wrinkles that would now intrigue the generative phonologist), but most of the section is a lucid treatment of phonemic changes in three conversational styles.

Chap. 3 provides a description of the morphological "system" that is the most precise, comprehensive, and well-organized available. Dealt with in order are (a) nouns and adjectives--number, gender, gender classes, and derivational affixation and compounding; (b) pronouns--personal, demonstrative, interrogative, relative, and indefinite; (c) verbs--inflection (an elegantly complex treatment), derivational affixation, enclisis (clitic pronouns), and compounding; (d) adverbs, conjunctions, and prepositions; and (e) exclamations. This chapter concludes with a brief but invaluable statement on intonation patterns in three speech styles.

The Vocabulary contains over 4,000 words and phrases, "all words contacted in the course of the study." (126) This is a major contribution for the lexicographer, though the rigor of the analysis makes it a reference for the dedicated professional, not the amateur. For one thing, the citation of entries only in phonemic form can be frustrating (e.g. iwál 'igual,' yúbya 'lluvia,' xwír 'huir,' wéa 'huella,' uyár 'aullar'). Nouns are provided with an indication of gender, and verbs are cited with full cross-references to details of conjugation, though in a most laconic form that presumably can be tracked down in the verb section of Chap. 3. Occasional notes on social usage are included. [GB]

BOWEN, J. Donald. "Local Standards and Spanish in the Southwest." In Ewton and Ornstein 1972, pp. 153-164.

This article is a plea for the acceptance of Southwest Spanish as a valid speech form and a condemnation of the educational disparagement of the language exemplified by the Baker text (1953/66). A few selected aspects of the morphology and phonology of New Mexican Spanish are included (pp. 158-159), primarily to illustrate that the regularity of this nonstandard speech provides an efficient simplification that could be useful in teaching. A "leave your language alone" discussion of loanwords permits the mention (by listing only) of 26 English borrowings in New Mexican Spanish (160). [GB]

COSTALES, Dionisio. "Spanish Games in New Mexico." MA Thesis, Univ. of New Mexico, 1937. 113 pp.

An unpolished and amateurish discussion, with ample exemplification, of various traditional games: nursery rhymes, children's outdoor games, games of skill and competition, and parlor games. The games were apparently gathered from all over the state; no explanation is given of means of collection other than that the materials were "obtained through personal research and investigation and received mostly by word of mouth." (p. 3) The descriptions of the games and associated rhymes and jingles are given in Spanish in standard orthography; there are only minimal comments on language per se. [GB]

EDMONSON, Munro S. "Los Manitos: Patterns of Humor in Relation to Cultural Values." PhD Diss., Harvard Univ., 1952. 289 pp.

Published without substantive changes in language/linguistic content as Edmonson 1957. [GB]

EDMONSON, Munro S. "Los Manitos: A Study of Institutional Values." MARI 25.1-72 (1957). [Reprinted 1968.]

This revised version of the author's dissertation (1952) is an excellent anthropological study of Hispanic culture and values in New Mexico (the dissertation's focus on humor is de-emphasized here). The work contains a slight amount of linguistic information, almost solely lexical: group identification terms (pp. 14-15), Catholic exclamations (18), kinship terms (27-33), religious terms (33-43). A laconic Glossary (69) lists some 160 entries. Edmonson distinguishes and discusses in a linguistically unsophisticated fashion four major dialects of Southwest Spanish--Mexican, Border, New Mexican, and Pachuco. There is also a brief note on "cifra," the New Mexican Spanish Pig Latin (17). [GB]

ESPINOSA, Aurelio Macedonio. The Spanish Language in New Mexico, and Southern Colorado. Historical Society of New Mexico, Publications, No. 16 (Santa Fe: Historical Society of New Mexico, 1911). 37 pp. [Annot. Nichols no. 1134; Serís no. 15514.]

This simple and readable little monograph is a popular presentation of Espinosa's vast store of knowledge. Although it is inteded for the nonspecialist, it contains much useful linguistic information.

The work is divided into a Preface and six parts. The Preface attempts to erase some popular misconceptions about the local Spanish and contains a plea for more teaching of Spanish in the schools. The first part very briefly comments on the historical origins of New Mexican Spanish. The second section discusses the distinguishing characteristics of the dialect, commenting on only the most prominent phonological and morphological features. The next part is a short consideration of "The Nahuatl and Other Indigenous Elements," while the fourth part deals with "The English Influence." Both of these sections contain lists of vocabulary items. Some 70 words are also listed in the following section on "The Influence of Spanish on the English Language."

The last section discusses the need for the study of New Mexican Spanish folklore and includes a number of short samples from his collection. [GB]

FICKINGER, Paul Lawrence. "A Study of Certain Phases of the Language Problem of Spanish-American Children." MA Thesis, Univ. of New Mexico, 1930. ii, 42 pp.

A simple experiment with Tularosa children to determine if the use of Spanish in giving instructions would produce better results on nonverbal IQ tests. The author concludes that there is no significance attached to the language of giving instructions except in the case of a few who had only a minimal grasp of English. The transcript of the Spanish instructions (8-14) provides some interesting examples of orthography, e.g., <u>handan</u> for <u>andan</u>, <u>voltellen</u> for <u>volteen</u>, <u>haber</u> for <u>a ver</u>, <u>cosas que pertenesen juntas</u> to render English 'things that belong together.' [GB]

GONZÁLEZ, George Adelberto. "The Development and Preliminary Testing of a Theoretical Spanish Language Instructional Model for Bilingual Education." Ph.D. Diss., Univ. of New Mexico, 1973. xiii, 149 pp. [<u>DA</u> 34 (1974) 6516-A.]

A deceptively titled report on the testing in northern New Mexico of an instrument to evaluate the teacher's competence in Spanish at five different speech "levels": local dialect, classroom expressions, terminology in traditional subjects, professional jargon, and knowledge of writing and "grammar." A terribly amateurish discussion (pp. 44-48) deals with aspects of the local dialect (anglicisms, archaisms, "letter" changes, etc.) with minimal exemplification; 150 of the 1,000-plus dialect items are listed (108); and the 30-item multiple choice test items concerning the local dialect are cited (117-121). [GB]

GONZÁLEZ, Nancie L. <u>The Spanish-Americans of New Mexico: A Heritage of Pride</u>. 2nd ed. (1967; Albuquerque: Univ. of New Mexico Press, 1969). xv, 246 pp.

Intended to provide "an up-to-date synthetic account of the sociocultural system," (p. xiv) this good background reference is of little direct value to the linguist. Chap. 2, "Language, Race, and Culture," (15-32) gives only a general sociological-demographic overview of the language situation. Aside from occasional citation of terms in the text, a list of 30 Spanish and English words and phrases of gang jargon appears on p. 177. [GB]

GRAY, Edward Dundas McQueen. "The Spanish Language in New Mexico: A National Resource." UNMBSS 1:2.entire issue (pp. 37-52) (1912). (Reprinted Las Vegas, New Mexico: La Galería de los Artesanos, 1972. 7 pp.)

This thoughtful and compassionate but often naive essay by the president of the University of New Mexico expounds on the need to give greater impetus to the role of Spanish in the state. No language data are provided. [GB]

HILLS, Elijah Clarence. [1906a]. "New Mexican Spanish." Ph.D. Diss., Univ. of Colorado, 1906.

Published as Hills 1906aa, the original manuscript is missing from the Univ. of Colorado Library. [GB]

HILLS, Elijah Clarence. [1906aa]. "New Mexican Spanish." PMLA 21.706-753 (1906).

This first of three printings (see also Hills 1929 and 1938) of Hills' dissertation (1906a) is primarily of historical importance as the earliest fully linguistic study published on Southwest Spanish. As Hills acknowledges, this work is an "incomplete and fragmentary" contribution on the Spanish of New Mexico and Southern Colorado. The study is based on notes on rural speech (the speech of Albuquerque and Santa Fe was not considered) recorded during six months in New Mexico and three and a half years in Colorado. He considers the speech of the region to be highly homogeneous: "the differences in vocabulary and pronunciation seem to be in the individual or in the family, rather than in the locality." (pp. 706-707) He reports virtually no English influence, but "a strong Indian influence."

The study is divided into four parts: Phonology (710-725), Morphology (725-738), "Expressions" (i.e., Syntax; 738-739), and Vocabulary (739-753). In the first two parts Hills' approach is to provide a short descriptive statement of the particular phenomenon and cite several examples. His few attempts at explanation are often based on gross assumptions, e.g.: "There are many Italians in this region, and the final e [after r, l, n] may be due to their influence." (724)

The section on phonology is nicely detailed in phonetics, though the inconsistent transcription and lack of sophistication in sound/letter distinction is bothersome at times. Hills discusses the phonetic realization of each vowel and consonant in varied environments. The section closes with a mercifully brief note on writing with examples of spelling areas common in the region.

The morphology part devotes just four pages to the non-verb parts of speech, and this consists mostly of phonological phenomena. The remainder of the section deals with the verb and amounts primarily to a long list of conjugation paradigms and notes for regular and irregular verbs. The syntax section gives simply a dozen or so examples of "a few common expressions" of a non-standard nature.

The vocabulary section begins with a comment on how the contact with English has caused adaptations in New Mexican Spanish; a few examples of loan translations and meaning extensions are cited. The vocabulary list itself contains some 350-400 commonly used words that differ from standard Spanish in meaning or form, "not including those that differ in form according to regular phonetic laws." The entries are brief, listing only the standard form (or other origin) and a new meaning where necessary. Occasionally a contrastive comment on usage is provided, e.g.: "zoquete, m., mud (lodo rare)." (753)

Hills' little study set the tone for the study of New Mexican Spanish for the next forty years, both in organization and in content; Hills surveyed the subject and later scholars tried to fill in the details. [GB]

HILLS, Elijah Clarence. "New Mexican Spanish." In Hispanic Studies by E.C. Hills (Stanford, Calif.: AATSP, 1929), pp. 1-46.

Hills 1906b is reprinted without revision in this collection of the author's works. [GB]

HILLS, Elijah Clarence. "El español de Nuevo Méjico." In Henríquez Ureña 1938, pp. 1-73. [Annot. Nichols no. 1137; Serís no. 15511; Solé 1970 no. 983.]

This translation and revision of Hills 1906b by Henríquez Ureña is a considerable improvement over the original work. The translation is generally quite faithful; the major improvement rests in the refinement of the phonetic transcription (including the establishment of a distinction between sounds and letters) and the correction of typographical and other errors. Revisions are minor, for example, some organizational shuffling in the treatment of consonants. Most significant are Henríquez' additions in the form of footnotes, an occasional note in the body of the text, and further notes and corrections on pp. 384-387 of the volume. These notes provide cross-references within the paper, supplementary comments drawn mostly from Espinosa 1930a, and extensive philological-linguistic comparative documentation and references to works on other varieties of Spanish. [GB]

JIMÉNEZ, NÚÑEZ, Alfredo. "Panorama etnológico de la presencia española en el suroeste." In Homenaje a D. Ciriaco Pérez Bustamante. Vol. 1 (Introd. by Carlos Seco Serrano.) Madrid: CSIC/Instituto Gonzalo Fernández de Oviedo, 1969. Pp. 279-302. [TSBJr.]

A general discussion of the culture, the history and the geography of northern New Mexico, where the author, a Spaniard, resided

for six months in 1964-65. Language is mentioned in passing
(pp. 284-285); reference is made to the declining use of Spanish
across the years because "el español de [los hispanos] no resulta
en muchas situaciones un instrumento efectivo de comunicación
debido a lo reducido de su vocabulario técnico y a que los anglos
no lo conocen y son el grupo dominante." (285) Jiménez devotes
the greater part of the article to folklore and religious customs;
the hermanos penitentes are also spoken of at length. Jiménez
concludes by commenting editorially upon the Hispanos as a viable
and culturally distinctive group: "Su seguridad sería mayor y la
conservación de su propia cultura podría aparecer ante [ellos]
como un objetivo possible y deseable si la dejaran de considerar
ellos mismos como la cultura de una minoría étnica equiparada por
la sociedad americana a las demás minorías de color . . . para
considerarla parte de la gran tradición cultural hispánica de
alcance universal." (301) [RT]

KANY, Charles E. American-Spanish Syntax. 2nd ed. (1945; Chicago:
Univ. of Chicago Press, 1951.) xiii, 467 pp. [Annot. HLAS 11
(1945) no. 2893 (C. Kany); Serís no. 15033; Solé 1970 no. 119.
Rev. of 1st ed.: MLR 41.336-337 (1946) (W.J. Entwistle);
Thesaurus 2.372-385 (1946) (L. Flórez); HR 14.360 (1946) (J.
Rael); BSS 23.83 (1946) (N. Young); Hispania 30.140-142 (1947)
(F. Alegría); HR 16.182-183 (1948) (Y. Malkiel); AIL 4.301-314
(1950) (F. Krüger); NRFH 4.57-67 (1950) (A. Rosenblat). Rev.
of 2nd. ed.: Thesaurus 8.215-217 (1952) (L. Flórez); BFUCh
7.391-410 (1952-53) (L. Cifuentes); RPh 7.366-372 (1953-54)
(L. Kiddle).]

This general reference work on morphological, syntactic, and
often lexical variation in the popular Spanish of the New World
occasionally cites New Mexican Spanish forms drawn from Espinosa
(1911a, 1912a, 1913a, 1930a, 1930b, and 1946), Kercheville 1934,
McSpadden 1934, and Rael 1940. [GB]

LÓPEZ, Thomas R., Jr. "Prospects for the Spanish American Culture
of New Mexico: An Educational View." Ph.D. Diss., Univ. of
New Mexico, 1972. ix, 335 pp. [DA 33 (1972) 2745-A.]

A nice, strictly library-researched historical analysis of the
Spanish Americans of northern New Mexico and a speculative essay
on their future as a distinct cultural entity. Passing references
are made in quite diffuse, naive fashion to language and language
problems, but there are no specific language data beyond occasional lexical forms in the body of the text. [GB]

MCSPADDEN, George E. [1934a]. "Some Semantic and Philological
Facts of the Spanish Spoken in Chililí, New Mexico." MA Thesis,
Univ. of New Mexico, 1934. 62 pp.

Published without significant revision as McSpadden 1934b. [GB]

MCSPADDEN, George E. [1934b]. "Some Semantic and Philological Facts of the Spanish Spoken in Chilili [sic], New Mexico." UNMBLS 5:3.71-102 (1934). [Annot. Nichols no. 1138. Rev. Hispania 18.230 (1935) (J. Rael).]

This short but excellent monograph (bound in one volume with Kercheville 1934) is a humble attempt to "illustrate a practical method of assembling material for a dictionary" of "Spanish forms and usages which differ from the Castilian standard." (p. 73) The study begins with a note on the "Location and History" (77-79) of Chililí, a small, isolated, and insulated town some 40 miles southeast of Albuquerque. The second part, "Semantics," (81-94) is the important part of this work. It contains some 80 words, each listed with grammatical classification and notes; differences from Castilian in form or meaning, with occasional explanatory comments; usually an example or two of sentences taken directly from conversations; and identification of the form as being general in New Mexico, general in the Albuquerque region, or confined to Chililí. The final section is a jumbled collection of "Miscellaneous Notes on Phonology and Morphology." (95-100). With regard to verb forms McSpadden simply notes that the important paradigms that he collected agree with those of Hills and Espinosa. A nice discussion of the "Postfixing of e" (95-97) humbly and with laudable documentation suggests that this frequently occurring New Mexican Spanish phenomenon, downplayed by Espinosa and poorly explained by Hills, must be an archaism. Included in this section is a list of 39 words of Spanish origin derived largely by affixation, five archaisms, ten Anglicisms, and 15 "Words of Uncertain Origin"--including espauda 'baking powder' (once better known as 'yeastpowder') and the interjection pucha! [GB]

ORNSTEIN, Jacob. "The Archaic and the Modern in the Spanish of New Mexico." Hispania 34.137-142 (1951). [Annot. HLAS 17 (1951) no. 2252 (C. Kany).] (Rpt. in HERN/etal-1975, pp. 6-12.

A generalist discussion of the Spanish of New Mexico with an emphasis on lexicon. Three major points are considered: speech differences between the northern and southern parts of the state, Pachuco, and English influence. Ornstein briefly notes several grammatical forms of the Las Cruces region (p. 137) and provides several lexical items contrasting northern-southern speech (137-138). He also lists some 75 general Spanish words and phrases (138) and about 85 Pachuco forms (139-140) that he found used in the Las Cruces area. A discussion of English influence is illustrated primarily with examples taken from the Santa Fe newspaper El Nuevo Mejicano.

A short discussion by Daniel Wogan (141-142) predictably criticizes Ornstein's use of the term "New Mexicanisms" and applauds his remarks on Pachuco. [GB]

RAEL, Juan B. "A Study of the Phonology and Morphology of New
    Mexican Spanish Based on a Collection of 410 Folk-Tales." PhD
    Diss., Stanford Univ., 1937. 7 vols. 2235 pp. total. (Vol.
    1: 241 pp.)

   Rael's purpose as stated in the first volume is "to supplement
the work of Dr. [Aurelio M.] Espinosa [Sr., his dissertation ad-
visor] by furnishing documentary evidence in corrobation of the
phonetic tendencies which he points out . . . ." (p. 19) The
study is based on the over 2,000 pages (vols. 2-7) of folktales
that he collected in the central area of northern New Mexico and
southern Colorado in 1930. No information is given on the informants other than that they were "elderly persons and persons
living in small towns, farms, or mountain ranches." (23) Virtually all of the tales were taken down "directly from the lips of
the narrator" in a sort of regional orthographic form. Although
he states that the collection "represents the speech of the average person of normal intelligence and contains few of the extreme
phonetic changes recorded by Dr. Espinosa," (26) he apparently
paid no attention whatsoever to phonetic detail in the transcription. His few comments on phonetics seem to derive solely from
his intuitions about the dialect.
   This is essentially a study of vocabulary, with some description of affixation and brief remarks on phonology. It is a careful examination of all the forms in the tales that differ from
the standard in taxonomic phonemic (or perhaps, very broad
phonetic) shape (and most forms do have standard equivalents; he
found for example only 41 Anglicisms in the entire collection).
The topical arrangement is patterned after Espinosa's <u>Studies</u>.
Each phenomenon is documented with usually abundant examples and
references to the number and page of the folktale in which it is
found. All examples are taken from the tales, although he occasionally footnotes additional interesting forms that he knows to
exist. The examples are entered with the standard form first followed by the New Mexican form in orthography and (for what it is
worth) phonetic transcription. It is much to Rael's credit that
he distinguishes whether the deviant New Mexican form is simply
derived from the standard or alternates with it. It is unfortunate however that the lexical items are rarely glossed. For each
phenomenon he usually attempts an explanation (most commonly
analogy or influence of the phonological environment) and provides
considerable comparison with other dialects, historical Spanish
and other Romance, and Espinosa's <u>Studies</u>. The work is much more
philological than linguistic.
   In addition to the Introduction (18-28) and Bibliography (236-
241), the study has two central parts, Phonology (29-165) and
Morphology (166-235). The first part considers phonological deviations from the standard under various topics: accentuation,
simple vowels, vowel clusters, consonants, addition and deletion
of sounds, metathesis, interference through analogy and blending,
archaisms, Anglicisms, and doublets. The lexical contribution
here is great, but one wishes that the phonetic statements could

be trusted. He notes for example that [v] does not occur (77), that [s̨] occurs only in English loans and new formations (78), and that the epithetic e/i is rare, being prominent only "among the ignorant." (126) Illustrative of his lack of concern for phonetics is the fact that y/ll receives no discussion beyond the statement that it is "more open, weak and relaxed, often disappearing in intervocalic position." (79)

The part on morphology is largely a re-ordering by form classes of much of the discussion of the first part. He deals in order with articles, nouns, adjectives, pronouns, particles (adverbs, conjunctions, prepositions, and interjections), and verbs. He discusses deviations in form in the more closed classes and deviations in gender and affixation for nouns and adjectives. The bulk of this part is devoted to the verb, with considered explanation of generalized changes in the verb system, especially nonstandard affixation, and an apparently exhaustive treatment of all nonstandard stem forms encountered in the folktales. [GB]

RANSOM, Helen. "'Manitos' and Their Language." Hispania 36.310-313 (1953). [Annot. HLAS 19 (1957) no. 4540 (D. Wogan).]

A shallow, rambling and cute discussion of the peculiarities of New Mexican Spanish, illustrated mostly with lexical items. [GB]

RICHARDSON, Rupert N. and Carl C. Rister. The Greater Southwest: The Economic, Social and Cultural Development of Kansas, Oklahoma, Texas, Utah, Colorado, Nevada, New Mexico, Arizona, and California from the Spanish Conquest to the Twentieth Century. Glendale, Calif.: The Arthur H. Clark Company, 1934. 506 pp. [TSBJr.]

Anecdotal and "boosterish" for the most part, and in any event largely concerned with history and economics, this large book nonetheless contains items of interest to the linguist, such as the description of New Mexican sheep-ranching customs and their attendant vocabulary (pp. 364-365), and the quick overview of language relations in New Mexico in 1905 ("A journalist . . . stated that interpreters were required in the courts to interpret Mexican testimony to the American half of the jury, and American testimony to the Mexican half. He stated that he was astonished to find an interpreter thus fulfilling his duties in such a way as to mimic the lawyer presenting the case; his jestures and tone of voice were as much like those of the attorney as he could make them." [p. 480]). [RT]

WALTER, Paul Alfred Francis, Jr. "A Study of Isolation and Social Change in Three Spanish Speaking Villages of New Mexico." PhD Diss., Stanford Univ., 1938. x, 343 pp.

This historical-sociological examination of three small villages just north of Albuquerque contains passing comments on the (declining) role of Spanish and scattered vocabulary and phrases of a sociological nature, but spellings such as <u>major domo</u>, <u>machina</u>, and <u>barracho</u> and naive statements such as "In language the people speak an idiom more archaic than the Spanish found elsewhere in the world" should serve to indicate the absence of linguistic value in this work. [GB]

YOUNG, Rodney W. "Semantics as a Determiner of Linguistic Comprehension Across Language and Cultural Boundaries." PhD Diss., Univ. of New Mexico, 1971. xvi, 174 pp. [<u>DA</u> 32 (1972) 5216-A.]

This excellent piece of basic research on Spanish-English and Navajo-English bilingualism is an incisive experimental examination of the relative difficulty of various comparative constructions in the two languages of some northern New Mexico children and provides a stimulating discussion of the causes of differential performance on a strictly linguistic basis. The work contains no Spanish language data beyond the test sentences in the instrument (106-107). [GB]

YOUNG, Rodney W. "The Development of Semantic Categories in Spanish-English and Navajo-English Bilingual Children." In Turner 1973, pp. 95-105. (Also a preprint of <u>Conference on Child Language</u>, Chicago, November 1971, edited by Theodore Andersson. Québec: Les Presses de l'Université Laval, 1971. Pp. 193-208.)

A summary of the basic procedures and significant findings of Young 1971. [GB]

ZUNSER, Helen. "A New Mexican Village." <u>JAF</u> 48.125-178 (1935).

This rambling, personal anthropological description of the inhabitants of the town of Hot Springs in northeastern New Mexico contains intermittent and very minor notes on language and bits of songs in Spanish. The final 20 pages are a selection of folktales in broken English (apparently as recorded from the lips of the informants). [GB]

3.2.1 SOCIOLINGUISTICS

Major Items: HOLL-1973

See also these items elsewhere (consult Author Index for location):
SERI-1964

*CARRILLO, Rafael Abeyta. "An In-depth Survey of Attitudes and Desires of Parents in a School Community to Determine the Nature of a Bilingual-Bicultural Program." PhD Diss., Univ. of New Mexico, 1973. 121 pp. [DA 34 (1973) 3013-A.]

   The abstract informs us that among other things the study proposed "to ascertain by interview the language currently spoken in home and community of a given public school [in the "Old Town" neighborhood of central Albuquerque], and to determine the extent of use of both Spanish and English." Information regarding parental attitudes towards existing and future school programs was also sought. Carrillo first mailed a questionnaire containing 19 statements (which apparently dealt with pedagogical concerns) to a random sampling of 112 Spanish-surnamed and 45 Anglo families; "these . . . were picked up by paid bilingual women, who with this visit, collected selected demographic data and data regarding language used with [?] the child in the domains of home, neighborhood, and church. In addition, an opportunity was given the respondent to tell why he marked selected questions the way he did." Among the non-pedagogical conclusions: "That English was used equally in the home [of bilingual families] with an increase in the use of English as the children moved into the community." [RT]

DONOFRIO, Rosalie S. Maggio. "Situations and Language: A Sociolinguistic Investigation." Ph.D. Diss., Univ. of New Mexico, 1972. x, 92 pp. [DA 33 (1973) 5614-5615-A.]

   This language sociology study contains no primary language data. It reports on a not well controlled experiment on the English communicative performance of 40 Chicano children (half lower-class, half middle-class) subjected to different interviewers (Chicano male, Anglo female) and distinct types of questions (standard language on a middle-class topic, nonstandard on a Chicano topic). The subjects' responses were analysed on the basis of simple counts of sentences, words per sentence, running words, and interviewer cues. The results show rather hazily a better performance by the middle-class children in all situations; the poorer Chicanos performed best in response to the Chicano male asking nonstandard English questions on Chicano topics. [GB]

GONZALES, James Lee. "The Effects of Maternal Stimulation on
   Early Language Development of Mexican American Children."
   PhD Diss., Univ. of New Mexico, 1972. xi, 169 pp. [DA 33
   (1973) 3436-A.]

   A nicely conceived but very limited study of the communicative
competence of six two-year-olds in three groups: lower-class,
lower-class with special training of parents, and middle-class.
The analysis considers such things as words per utterance and developmental sentence types, and the results are very hazy. Language data in this work are limited to sample parent-child protocols
(pp. 107-116), examples of developmental sentence types (150-155),
and a brief vocabulary list of words used by four children at one
session (158-162); most of the language samples are English with
some Spanish. [GB]

GUTIÉRREZ, Lorraine Padilla. "Attitudes Toward Bilingual Educ-
   ation: A Study of Parents with Children in Selected Bilingual
   Programs." Ph.D. Diss., Univ. of New Mexico, 1972. x, 170 pp.
   [DA 33 (1972) 2692-A.]

   This work contains no primary language data, but does present
interesting statistics on the use of Spanish by 220 Albuquerque
parents and their attitudes toward bilingual education, the use of
Spanish in the classroom, and biculturalism. [GB]

*HOLLOMON, John Wesley. "Problems of Assessing Bilingualism in
   Children Entering School." PhD Diss., Univ. of New Mexico,
   1973. 387 pp. [DA 34 (1973) 3026-3027-A.]

   From the abstract of this impressive-looking work we learn
that Hollomon sought to assess both domain assignment and proficiency of usage of a bilingual Spanish-surnamed population in an
Albuquerque _barrio_ and also attempted to assess proficiency of
usage within domains (school, community and work as well as home,
church and entertainment). Both parents and children were tested
for domain assignment; children but not parents were tested for
proficiency within domains. The tests used (word-naming, verb-
production, sentence imitation-repetition, and also "unstructured"
or natural speech) aimed "not to determine how much of each language the subjects knew, but to determine their abilities to operate
in specified sociolinguistic situations with specified ease or
effect." Also tested were sociolinguistic attitudes and self-
concept.
   Hollomon found that "the older the generation the greater the
relative amount of Spanish usage; . . . that Spanish is presently
used more in the homes than English, but less than that used five
years ago; that parents used more Spanish than English in the domains of the church and the movies. The parents' attitudes were
more favorable toward Spanish and the Spanish-surnamed Americans

than toward English and Anglo-Americans." The children themselves "used more Spanish than English with the older generations (and older siblings) in the domain of the home, followed by the domain of the church." But degree of usage does not always correlate with proficiency: while children used "mostly English with peers in the domains of the neighborhood and school," they were found (surprisingly) to be most proficient in Spanish in the domains of school (as well as home) but least so in the domain of neighborhood. With this information in mind one is initially confused by the statement that the children were also "more proficient in English in the domains of the home" followed by the neighborhood (and then the school); a possible explanation is that their general proficiency of production in whichever language was directly related to the degree to which the domain was viewed as not "threatening;" for English to be the language whose proficiency suffers most in the domain of "least familiarity" is a possible indication that even the younger members of this particular population are still Spanish-dominant, despite the fact that "the mean scores of bilingual ratings ranged from one English monolingual to one Spanish dominant." But then Hollomon used only six youngsters as informants and so it is really not possible to generalize. [RT]

MALLORY, Gloria Griffin. "Sociolinguistic Considerations for Bilingual Education in an Albuquerque Community Undergoing Language Shift." Ph.D. Diss., Univ. of New Mexico, 1971. xii, 103 pp. [DA 32 (1972) 6008-6009-A.]

The thrust of this work is clearly stated by the author: "This study is concerned with whom a child will speak to in Spanish, not with how a child will speak Spanish." (p. 5) After a general discussion of bilingual education, diglossia, and methodological procedures, Mallory reports on her original research into the sociolinguistic behavior of children in a bilingual program in contrast with the behavior of their older siblings and parents. The data were collected from role-simulation activities, responses to talking pictures depicting persons of different socioeconomic and ethnic characteristics, and attitudinal measurements. The study concludes with a consideration of the implications of these interesting language shift facts for the structure of bilingual education programs. [GB]

OLIVER, Joseph D. "Diatype Identification in a Bilingual Community." AL 14.361-367 (1972). [Abs. LLBA 7.7302472]

This obscure article identifies six language "diatypes" (formal, informal, and casual Spanish and English) used in the village of Los Ojos in northern New Mexico. The identifications are based on interpersonal relations, attitudes, delivery speed, and such, but explicitness of explanation is glaringly absent. Oliver provides no language data whatsoever. [GB]

*SALADO ÁLVAREZ, Victoriano. "Nuevo Méjico todavía no es (norte) americano." <u>RevIbBA</u> (1930). [Sic]. [Annot. Serís no. 15517.]

 The editors of this Bibliography have been totally unable to identify a journal by the name of <u>Revista Iberoamericana</u> published in Buenos Aires during the year indicated. Serís, apparently quoting from an offprint, provided no further data than those listed above; the few sentences his annotation cites are similar, but not identical, to material found in Salado Álvarez 1924 (q.v.) p. 89, there attributed to "un autor que en estas páginas llevo citado largamente." From the Serís annotation one gathers that Salado successfully demonstrated the loyalty to Spanish of New Mexico's Hispano population, as of the year of composition. [JC]

TIMMINS, Kathleen M. "An Investigation of the Relative Bilingualism of Spanish Surnamed Children in an Elementary School in Albuquerque." PhD Diss., Univ. of New Mexico, 1971. xi, 91 pp. [<u>DA</u> 32 (1972) 3680-3681-A.]

 Remarkably, this work presents no language data whatsoever. It is a report of research on language proficiency in relation to domains and number of years in school, as measured by a language usage and domain interview instrument and word-naming and picture-response tasks. [GB]

TIREMAN, Loyd Spencer. [1948b]. <u>Teaching Spanish-speaking Children</u>. Albuquerque: Univ. of New Mexico Press, 1948. x, 218 pp.

 This textbook for schoolteachers discusses bilingualism as a general phenomenon (Chap. 1) and its educational implications (Chap. 2), the situation in New Mexico (Chap. 3), the teaching of English in kindergarten (Chap. 4), primary school (Chap. 5), and secondary school (Chap. 6), the teaching of Spanish (Chap. 7; exceedingly general), and Tireman's favorite topic, the community school concept (Chap. 8). Scattered throughout the text are minuscule comments on potential problems faced by the Spanish-speaker in learning English (e.g., pp. 77, 81-82, 116-117, 147-148). [GB]

3.3 SPANISH PHONOLOGY (includes ORTHOGRAPHY)

Major Items: DUNC-1956; ESPI-1909a; ESPI-1909aa; ESPI-1909aaa; ESPI-1925; ESPI-1930a; HARR-1974a; HARR-1974b

See also these items elsewhere (consult Author Index for location): ESPI-1911-12-13; ESPI-1946; GARC-T-1939; MILL-1959-60

ALONSO, Amado. "Problemas de dialectología hispanoamericana." BDH 1.315-469 (1930).

See Espinosa 1930a.

ALONSO, Amado and Raimundo Lida. "Geografía fonética: -l y -r implosivas en español." RFH 7.313-345 (1945). (Incorporated as "-r y -l en España y América" in Amado Alonso, Estudios lingüísticos: Temas hispanoamericanos [Madrid: Editorial Gredos, 1967], pp. 213-261.)

A comprehensive survey of syllable-final liquids in Peninsular and American Spanish, including New Mexican Spanish as reported by Espinosa 1930a and Hills 1938. [GB]

DUNCAN, Robert M. "Algunas observaciones sobre la fonología de la s palatal en el español de Nuevo Méjico." ActSal 2.223-228 (1956). [Annot. Solé 1970 no. 991. Rev. HLAS 24 (1962) no. 4724 (D. Wogan); Craddock 1973 p. 318.]

This is a rambling discussion of the many historical aspects of [š] in New Mexican Spanish. Duncan lists a number of words cited by Hills 1938 and Espinosa 1930 that contain this sound, and he adds four additional Nahuatl-derived words. He divides these into six groups on the basis of historical origin and comments on the variation between [š], [č], and [x] in certain Nahuatl-derived words in various parts of New Mexico and southern Colorado. He cites eleven other words from Nahuatl that he finds pronounced with [x] consistently. In discussing [š] as an allophone of /č/ in words of Spanish origin, he notes that such a pronunciation is most common along the Rio Grande valley south of Albuquerque; he correctly identifies this [š] as a natural tendency in Spanish and not simply the result of contact with English. [GB]

ESPINOSA, Aurelio Macedonio. [1909a.] "Studies in New Mexican Spanish. Part I: Phonology." PhD Diss., Univ. of Chicago, 1909. 115 pp.

Published as Espinosa 1909aa and 1909aaa.

ESPINOSA, Aurelio Macedonio. [1909aa]. "Studies in New Mexican
    Spanish. Part I: Phonology." UNMBLS 1,2.47-162 (1909).
    (cf. Espinosa 1909a, 1909aaa.)

Like the other two parts of Espinosa's Studies, the scope of this magnificent and oft-published part (see Espinosa 1909b, 1930a) is the Spanish of "all of New Mexico north of Socorro, with Santa Fé as a center, and the San Luis Valley in Southern Colorado," a region then containing about 150,000 Spanish speakers. The comprehensiveness of the task and the precision of the descriptive-historical analysis make this study the most scholarly and most valuable phonological contribution ever for the Spanish of the United States.

In addition to six central chapters on phonology, this work contains a Preface (p. 47), a Bibliography (48-52), a map of "The New Mexican Spanish Territory" (52), an Introduction (53-56), and a Word Index of three parts listing words cited of Spanish, English, and Nahuatl origin (156-161). The Introduction provides a brief description of the Spanish settlement of New Mexico and a cursory explanation of the peninsular sources of New Mexican Spanish (primarily the Castilian, Andalusian, Northern Spanish, Galician, and Western Spanish-Portuguese dialects of the 16th and 17th centuries). Very brief mention is also made of the influence of Nahuatl and English on New Mexican Spanish.

The six chapters of the body of the study are a masterpiece of organization and presentation. Espinosa notes in the Preface that his "method throughout will be comparative, and the subject is studied in the light of historical Spanish Grammar." (47) He fails to point out explicitly, however, that his work is above all else descriptive. His phonetic description is minutely detailed and carefully explicit (e.g., six allophones of /o/ are cited). Although the description is based on the letters of the alphabet, the organization and treatment are in terms of articulatory phonetics. This description is then compared with "standard modern Castilian" and deviations from this standard are discussed and amply supplemented with historical documentation and dialectal comparisons.

Chap. 1 is a short consideration of "Accent," (57-59) dealing exclusively with the nonstandard placement of primary stress. The second chapter, "Vowels," (59-96) begins with a careful description of the vocalic system, including a lengthy discussion of nasalized vowels. Differences from standard Spanish are then discussed for simple vowels and vowel clusters in stressed and unstressed positions and in varied environments. A final section on "Juxtaposition" provides additional consideration of the phonetic realization of adjacent vowels.

Chap. 3 treats "Consonants" (97-134) in an equally admirable fashion. A phonetic description of each consonant is followed by an explanation of deviations from the standard in initial, medial, and final positions in the word. Following sections provide further details on the aspirated s, the ll, the y/i semivowel, Nahuatl-derived consonants, and syllabic consonants. A final section deals with the vocalization and deletion of consonants.

Chap. 4 considers "Various phonetic changes," (134-141) primarily the addition and deletion of vowels, consonants, and syllables in various positions. Metathesis is also briefly treated. Chap. 5, "Phonetic changes in words of English origin," (141-150) is a short, lucid description of adaptations in stress, vowels, and consonants.

Chap. 6 contains a few verse and prose "Texts in phonetic transcription." (151-156) More importantly, however, the first page of this chapter acknowledges three major dialect areas for the region (Santa Fe, Albuquerque/Rio Grande Valley, and San Luis Valley) and summarizes the most distinctive characteristics of each. Two four-line verses are cited in three phonetic transcriptions to illustrate the three dialects. [GB]

ESPINOSA, Aurelio Macedonio. [1909aaa]. "Studies in New Mexican Spanish. Part I: Phonology." RDR 1.157-239, 269-300 (1909).

This work is an exact duplicate of Espinosa 1909aa.

ESPINOSA, Aurelio Macedonio. "Cuentitos populares nuevomejicanos y su transcripción fonética." BDR 4.97-105 (1912). (Incorporated in Espinosa 1930a, pp. 286-313.)

Fourteen stories in dialectal orthography and narrow phonetic transcription: El padre chiquito, San Sebastián, La paloma y sus pichones, Los viejitos y su güertesita, El predicador y el borracho, El viajeru hambriento, Los tres hermanos, El Jones, El viajero y l' ov' e menudo, Los nuevomejicanos y las semitas, Los güevos blanditos, El duende, Los dos compadres, and five Maño Fašico stories. A brief introduction comments primarily on vowel phonology. [GB]

ESPINOSA, Aurelio Macedonio. "Nombres de bautismo nuevomejicanos: algunas observaciones sobre su desarrollo fonético." RDR 5. 356-373 (1913). (Incorporated in Spanish trans. in Espinosa 1930a, pp. 260-280.)

This study examines the phonetics of Spanish and English first names used in New Mexican Spanish. The article is divided into nine parts. The first seven parts describe the realization of, respectively, stressed vowels, vowel clusters, unstressed vowels simple consonants, consonant clusters, "adición y supresión de sonidos," and stress changes. The basis for comparison is the standard written form. The description is phonetically careful, but the occasional attempts at explanation are too often speculative and indeed many of the examples represent rare or infrequent rather than generalized pronunciations. The eighth section briefly notes the confusion existing in the use of the Spanish diminutive suffix with given names. The final part is an alphabetical word index to the names cited. [GB]

ESPINOSA, Aurelio Macedonio. "Syllabic Consonants in New Mexican Spanish." Language 1.109-118 (1925). (Incorporated in Spanish trans. in Espinosa 1930a, pp. 208-219.)

In a typically Espinosian plunge into phonetic minutiae, this article describes in precise articulatory detail the syllabic m, n, l, and r heard in such forms as the possessive mi, the articles un, una, uno, in the second syllable of camita, palito, perrito, etc. His discussion of the origin and development of these consonants is laced with extensive comparative Romance notes. [GB]

ESPINOSA, Aurelio Macedonio. [1930a]. Estudios sobre el español de Nuevo Méjico. Parte I: Fonética. Trans. and revised by Amado Alonso and Angel Rosenblat. BDH, No. 1 (Buenos Aires: Univ. de Buenos Aires, 1930). 472 pp. [Annot. Nichols no. 1133; Serís no. 15513; Solé 1970 no. 976. Rev. RLR 66.172-175 (1930) (C. Pitollet); AORL 5.313-318 (1932) (R. Aramon i Serra); Language 8.315-323 (1932) (H. Richardson); BHi 35.178-181 (1933) (J. Bouzet).]

Pp. 19-313 of this volume are devoted to the work of Espinosa, almost exclusively the translation of his 1909 monograph, but with the incorporation of: 1912b (pp. 286-313) as a supplement to Chap. 6 of the original; 1913b (260-280) replacing the original Chap. 5 on English elements, which is incorporated into Parte II (1946); and 1925a (208-219) expanding on the original treatment of syllabic consonants. Other differences from the original are very minor, usually of a historical-comparative cross-reference nature and mostly added by Alonso, though occasionally by Espinosa. The descriptive information is virtually unchanged.

Pp. 315-469 of this publication contain nine appendixes by Alonso on "Problemas de Dialectología Hispanoamericana." These consist largely of data cited from throughout the Spanish speaking world that bear on specific topics raised by Espinosa: stress changes, nasals, assimilation and dissimilation, consonantalization of u, the cirgüela form, así forms, señor/señora forms, syllabic consonants, and consonantal replacements. [GB]

ESPINOSA, Aurelio Macedonio. "El desarrollo fonético de las dos palabras todo y en la frase con todo y + substantivo en el nuevo-mejicano." InvLing 2.195-199 (1934). (Condensed and incorporated in Spanish trans. in Espinosa 1946 [pp. 35-38] and fn. 88.) [Annot. Nichols no. 1132.]

A detailed "explanation" of the three dominant free variants [tói], [twí], and [tí] as "leyes fonéticas generales y españolas en particular." [GB]

HARDMAN, Martha James. "The Phonology of the Spanish of El Prado, New Mexico." MA Thesis, Univ. of New Mexico, 1956. 59 pp.

This is a very modest contribution, both in scholarship and in length. It is a taxonomic phonemic analysis of tape-recorded informal conversations and formal narrations gathered from seven principal informants from a rural area just north of Taos. Background information on age, birthplace, other residences, occupation, schooling, and knowledge of English is provided for each informant (pp. 5-6). The brief phonological analysis (9-25) provides a description of the allophones of each phoneme, a calculation of phoneme frequencies, phoneme distributions in the syllable, word linkage, accent, and English influence. The presentation is detailed in many ways, especially phonetically, but lacks adequate explanations. The reader may note, for example, the lack of /r̄/ in the phoneme list, but he can only ascertain inferentially that Hardman feels this phoneme is absent in this dialect (an observation that throws suspicion upon the rest of the study). The major portion of this thesis is devoted to textual samples of the author's phonetic and phonemic transcriptions (26-54), followed by a glossary of just 17 possibly unfamiliar words found in these samples. (57-58). [GB]

HARRIS, James W. [1974a]. "Morphologization of Phonological Rules: An Example from Chicano Spanish." In <u>Linguistic Studies in Romance Languages: Proceedings of the Third Linguistic Symposium on Romance Languages</u>, edited by R. Joe Campbell, Mark G. Goldin, and Mary Clayton Wang (Washington, D.C.: Georgetown Univ. Press, 1974), pp. 8-27.

A rare substantive treatment of Southwest Spanish from the point of view of generative grammar, this article examines the diphthongization of e and o (> ye and we) in verb forms used by a New Mexican informant (Rogelio Reyes, a Harvard graduate student). The purposes of the paper are "(1) to call attention to Chicano Spanish . . . , (2) to add one example to the tiny sample of cases of rule morphologization discussed in detail in generative studies, and (3) to make a small contribution to the nascent but long overdue study of morphology in generative grammar." (p. 9)
Following a detailed examination of diphthongization in standard Mexican Spanish (10-17), a section on "Diphthongization in Chicano" (17-20) points out that "if ANY form of ANY a-theme... verb has the diphthong [we], then ALL forms do, regardless of the position of stress," (18) but all other verbs have the standard vowel/diphthong alternation. Consideration of a number of forms and exceptions leads to the formulation of a rule with both phonological and morphological restrictions. Harris notes that Espinosa 1946 found such extended diphthongization rare and characteristic only of child language, leading Harris to conclude that "we have caught Chicano Spanish in the act" of an apparently ongoing linguistic change. [GB]

HARRIS, James W. [1974b]. "Two Morphophonemic Innovations in Chicano Spanish." [Unpublished paper distributed by:] Bloomington: Indiana Univ. Linguistics Club, 1974. 12 pp.

    A skillful generative-transformational treatment of the interrelated -nos for -mos and antepenultimate stress on first person plural verb forms in New Mexican Spanish. A firm explanation is not attempted for the first-topic and a minor rule simplification is stated to explain the second topic. Both phenomena are used as arguments for the importance of morphology as well as phonology in language change. [GB]

3.4 SPANISH GRAMMAR (MORPHOLOGY AND SYNTAX)

<u>Major Items</u>: BRIS-1972; ESPI-1911-12-13; ESPI-1946

<u>See also these items elsewhere</u> (consult Author Index for location): HARR-1974a; HARR-1974b

BOWEN, J. Donald. "New Mexican Spanish Verb Forms." In Bills 1974, pp. 157-166.

    Brief mention of verb classifications and discussion of selected phonological and morphological aspects that make New Mexican Spanish a distinctive dialect. Bowen provides a quick overview of the verb inflectional system and then a description of the regular and irregular verb classes exemplified by the verbs found in the vocabulary of his dissertation (1952). [GB]

BRISK, María Estela. "The Spanish Syntax of the Pre-school Spanish American: The Case of New Mexican Five-year-old Children." PhD Diss., Univ. of New Mexico, 1972. x, 138 pp. [<u>DA</u> 34 (1973) 297-A.]

    This analysis of the speech of seven Spanish-English bilingual children, two from Albuquerque and five from the small town of Chililí, is intended to describe the extent and variety of Spanish syntax used by the pre-schooler. Although the analysis could be more rigorous and the writing and organization could stand improvement, this is a substantive pioneering effort in both child language and syntax in Southwest Spanish.

    The work contains seven chapters: Introduction (pp. 1-7), Theoretical Framework (8-18), Design and Methodology (19-32), Linguistic Maturity (33-39), Grammatical Analysis (40-85), Interference, Dialectal and Developmental Features (86-112), and Summary and Conclusions (113-132).

    Chaps. 5 and 6, as their length may indicate, are the most significant parts of this study for they are primarily concerned with the raw data elicited and tape-recorded. In the Grammatical Analysis chapter all of the structures occurring in the corpus are

taxonomically categorized and compared with the possibilities
permitted in standard Spanish. The simple sentence is treated in
some detail, covering the structure of the noun phrase, the
verb phrase (including tense and aspect), adverbials, negation,
and interrogation. Compound and complex sentences receive much
less attention because of their limited occurrence in the data.
In Chap. 6 the syntax deviations are considered under three very
broad categories: English interference (e.g., Yo está cinco),
dialectal structures (e.g., ¿Que no vistes bien?), and structures
not yet fully mastered (e.g., the subjunctive: Quiere que me como).
Noteworthy is the fact that exemplification is abundant in both
of these chapters.

In Chap. 4 Brisk provides the results of her measurement of
mean words per sentence (actually "T-unit") which seem to indicate
that the urban (Albuquerque) children are linguistically less
mature in Spanish than the rural (Chililí) children. The final
chapter provides a summary syntactic comparison of the performance
of her subjects and the Texas children studied by González 1970.
A brief examination of the verbal expressiveness of the urban and
rural groups is also contained in the final chapter.

Appendix I (133) contains an unimportant Spanish-Spanish
glossary of thirty entries. [GB]

BRISK, María Estela. [1974a]. "New Mexican Spanish Syntax of the
    Five-year-old." In Bills 1974, pp. 225-239.

This summary of the most significant linguistic points of
Brisk 1972 outlines the subject-selection and elicitation procedures; describes some of the salient developmental, interference,
and dialectal aspects of the children's speech; and comments on
urban-rural distinctions. [GB]

BRISK, María Estela. [1974b]. "A Preliminary Study of the
    Syntax of Five-year-old Spanish Speakers of New Mexico." In
    Spolsky and Bills 1974, pp. 69-78.

Moderately revised version of Brisk 1974a. [GB]

ESPINOSA, Aurelio Macedonio. "Studies in New Mexican Spanish.
    Part II: Morphology." RDR 3.251-286 (1911); 4.241-256 (1912);
    5.142-172 (1913).

See Espinosa 1946.

ESPINOSA, Aurelio Macedonio. Estudios sobre el español de Nuevo Méjico. Parte II: Morfología. Trans. and revised by Angel Rosenblat. BDH, No. 2 (Buenos Aires: Univ. de Buenos Aires, 1946). 394 pp. [Annot. Serís no. 15513; Solé 1970 no. 976. Rev. HLAS 12 (1946) no. 2323 (C. Kany). Also rev. RFE 30.176-177 (1946) (S. Gili Gaya); BBMP 22.393-394 (1946) (A. Zamora Vicente); RR 39.340-341 (1948) (T. Navarro Tomás); RF 43.424-427 (1951) (H. Meier).]

Pp. 1-102 of this volume are a translation, with some revisions, of Espinosa 1911a, 1912a and 1913a. Revisions are very minor, changes being made by both Rosenblat and Espinosa, with some minor shifting of pieces between Parts I and II. A summary of Espinosa 1934 and several extractions from Espinosa (1930b) are incorporated in the translation.

The brief introduction (3-4) mentions the major role in this morphology study assumed by phonetics and especially analogy. That is, this part is virtually as much concerned with phonetics and the phonetic form of lexical items as with morphology. Espinosa notes that problems of syntax and semantics are marginally raised--but very marginally.

The body of the text contains five chapters devoted to particular parts of speech: articles (4-9), nouns and adjectives (9-19), pronouns (19-39), particles (40-52), and verbs (53-102). The discussion throughout deals solely with nonstandard forms.

Chap. 1 is devoted exclusively to a detailed examination of the phonetic realization of definite and indefinite articles as pronounced in the stream of speech, especially in combination with prepositions. Chap. 2 is also primarily phonetic. The treatment of nouns is limited to gender changes and irregular plurals. A short discussion of adjectives focuses on gender, the use of rete- and its variants, and a nominal phrase type of adjective. Titles of address and numbers are also considered in this chapter. Chap. 3 deals in turn with personal, possessive, demonstrative, relative-interrogative, and indefinite pronouns. Again, the treatment is mostly phonetic, but with considerable discussion of new forms and the non-use of some standard forms. The "particles" treated in Chap. 4 are adverbs, conjunctions, prepositions, and interjections; emphasis is on nonstandard forms and phonetic realization.

Almost half of this study is given over to the verb (Chap. 5). Espinosa first discusses generalized modifications in stem form, endings, and accent, as well as general phonetic and analogical changes. The bulk of the chapter is then devoted to a detailed account of verb conjugation. Included are the two paradigms for regular verbs, 17 for vowel-final verb stems, eight for verbs with vowel alternations, and over a dozen for other irregular verbs. The chapter concludes with a discussion of five new verbal forms (meramentar, quése, ónde güeno, es fácil que, and esque and variants) and the form of verbal nouns and the use of several nominalizing suffixes.

Rosenblat's extensive footnotes to Espinosa's study are incorporated as a separate part of the volume and titled "Notas de morfología dialectal" (103-316). These superb notes, intended to "ampliar la documentación geográfica de un rasgo dialectal, . . . buscar sus antecedentes históricos y...tratar de explicarlo o de plantear el problema que suscita" (105), are divided into sections corresponding generally to Espinosa's sections.

This volume also contains two very useful indices for both volumes of the translated Studies: a word index (317-385) and a topical index (385-392).

In the preface (v-vii), Amado Alonso reaffirms that Espinosa's work guarantees that even as late as 1946 New Mexican Spanish is "la variedad regional del español más minuciosamente estudiada." (vi) This statement very likely remains true at present. [GB]

ROSENBLAT, Ángel. "Notas de morfología dialectal." BDH 2.103-316 (1946).
See Espinosa 1946.

3.5 SPANISH LEXICON (includes SEMANTICS)

Major Items: ESPI-1930b; GERR-1964; GROS-1935; KERC-1934; KERC-1967; KIDD-1951-52; SHOB/SING-1970; TIRE-1948a; TRUJ-1961

See also these items elsewhere (consult Author Index for location): BOGG-1954; DUNC-1956; MURP-RP-1972; EDMO-1952; EDMO-1957; ESPI-1913; MCSP-1934a; MCSP-1934b; ORNS-1951; TESC-1974a; TRAB/VALD-1937; YOUN-1971; YOUN-1973

APPLEGATE, Frank G. Native Tales of New Mexico. Philadelphia: Lippincott, 1932, 263 pp. [Rev. New Mexico 10.28 (1932) (J.B. Montgomery); NMQ 2.269-274 (1932).]

Posthumous collection of 22 narrations, some of which are claimed to be reworkings of authentic New Mexican Hispano folktales. The occasional Hispanisms used in these English-language tales are most often trivial but a given dialectal trait occasionally finds expression, as in the title of the story "Poco loco" ('a little crazy', pp. 139-149) where the suppression of the indefinite article (i.e., st. Sp. un poco loco) is in accordance with observed usage in New Mexico. Regrettably, one could form a rather voluminous disparatario from the prose of Applegate and his Anglo literary colleagues. In the book at hand I noticed rebosa for rebozo 'shawl' (p. 154), tortillo for tortilla (p. 158), manzano glossed as 'apple' rather than 'apple tree' (p. 27), and in Austin's preface descancio for descanso 'rest.' I suppose rebosa represents phonological [ribózə], a typical Anglophone rendering of rebozo. [JC]

ARELLANO, Estevan, ed. Entre verde y seco. San Anselmo, Calif.:
Centro de Comunicación [for the Academia de la Nueva Raza,
Dixon, New Mexico], 1972. 119 pp.

A hodge-podge of historical sketches, sayings, stories,
and corridos drawn from interviews conducted by the Academia de
la Nueva Raza. An attempt is made to present the contributions
as collected, but at times there are considerable revisions. The
informant sources are only occasionally noted and always with
insufficient detail; orthography generally reflects nonstandard
forms, though with just enough inconsistency to make one leary.
A glossary (pp. 108-114) contains some 225 regional variants,
usually phonological in nature, and some 60 "anglosismos, caló
y modismos;" each entry consists solely of the dialect form and
a standard Spanish gloss. [GB]

COLEMAN, William and Antonio Mondragón. Qué Pasó? An English-
Spanish Medical Dictionary with Vocabulary of Northern New
Mexico and Southern Colorado. Albuquerque: Univ. of New
Mexico Chicano Studies Program, 1974. iii, 33 pp.

A simple and not always careful listing of some 100 interview
phrases and some 500 vocabulary items. Despite the title description, the Spanish is generally standard Mexican Spanish (e.g.,
despertar, estómago, deletrear), with only a very few nonstandard
forms (e.g., jiel, mompes, muslo 'muscle,' atocar, los tonsils)
usually cited along with the standard form. [GB]

CROOK, Alice M. "Old-Time New Mexican Usages." In Dobie 1935,
pp. 184-189.

A folksy consideration of selected aspects of domestic life,
including cosmetics, marriage customs, household utensils, home
remedies, and foods. About 20 Spanish lexical items enter into
the discussion; some are explained in detail. The locale, presumably northern New Mexico, is not specified. [GB]

ESPINOSA, Aurelio Macedonio. [1930b]. "Apuntaciones para un
diccionario de nuevomejicanismos: algunas formas verbales
raras i curiosas." In Estudios eruditos in memoriam de Adolfo
Bonilla y San Martín (Madrid: Jaime Rates, 1930), Vol.
2.615-625. [Annot. Nichols no. 1142; Solé 1970 no. 975.]

This little article begins with the significant explanation
that the outbreak of World War I and the collapse of the RDR journal prevented the publication of the completed fourth part of his
masterwork, the vocabulary (also less clearly mentioned in Espinosa
1909a), and that "después, mi manuscrito ha sufrido tantos y tan
continuous cambios que la obra original es ya un Diccionario Nuevo-
mejicano que esperamos publicar algún día como obra separada"
(p. 2). This later publication did not occur and, lamentably,

the whereabouts of this manuscript seems to be unknown. However, Espinosa's statement should be considered in light of the fact that he directed the thesis by Gross 1935, a work that was concerned with tabulating the vocabulary cited in the Espinosa publications.

This paper discusses "la fonología, morfología y semántica de algunas formas verbales . . . sacadas de nuestro manuscrito" (2). In his accustomed scholarly philological-historical fashion, Espinosa considers in some detail 14 forms (with variants and derivatives): a redo vaya, cómo está muncho, desfondigarse, entengas, esmorecerse, esque, hallarse, meramente, ójala, ¿ónde güeno?, quése, refunfuñar, replantigarse, and ti albechu/yu bechu. [GB]

GERRITSEN, William D. "An English-Spanish Glossary of Basic Medical Terminology in the Dialect of Northern New Mexico." Santa Fe: Santa Fe County Health Department, 1964. 61 unnumbered pp.

This vocabulary of approximately 500 entries is similar in purpose and scope to the later compilation by Coleman and Mondragón 1974 but considerably more careful, reliable, and reflective of northern New Mexican Spanish. The English entries are given a simple Spanish gloss and part of speech designation; the article is cited with each noun, and each verb and adjective is provided with a brief sample sentence. All nonstandard forms are asterisked and followed by the Standard Spanish form in parentheses. These nonstandard forms amount to less than a third of the total; some are simply minor phonological deviations such as lastimao 'injured' and antiojos 'glasses' and others are common, but technically imprecise terms such as cortada instead of incisión for 'incision.' Anglicisms are strikingly infrequent-- for example the only glosses for 'appendix' and 'tonsils' are, resp., la tripita and the noteworthy las sanjinas. Preceding the glossary, a "Key to Pronunciation" provides an old-fashioned but surprisingly accurate explanation of letter values and accentuation that demonstrates the author's attentiveness to the local dialect. Although limited in linguistic expertise, this little pamphlet offers a reliable list of items easily overlooked in other works; part of its merit is the fact that it is a glossary of all relevant (not just quaint and curious) words. [GB]

GROSS, Stuart Murray. "A Vocabulary of New Mexican Spanish." MA Thesis, Stanford Univ., 1935. vi, 78 pp.

This thesis directed by A.M. Espinosa Sr. is useful but not very scholarly. The 78 numbered pages list the vocabulary; a brief introduction explains that this is a fairly exhaustive "dialectal" glossary of over 2,000 forms cited in twelve works by Espinosa (1910, 1911, 1911, 1912, 1913, 1914-15, 1930a, and seven others of folkloric content). G lists only those words "which differ in spelling by at least one letter from the accepted Modern Castilian orthography, not considering a change of accent or slight change in pronunciation, without resultant change in spelling, as sufficient basis for inclusion." (pp. i-ii) He claims to exclude (but in fact does not) forms that differ from Castilian only in such general ways as s for c, -au for -ado, etc.

Each entry contains the item in a dialectal-orthographic form (with an occasional phonetic diacritic), a minimal gloss in standard Spanish, and a reference to the page or paragraph of one Espinosa work in which it was encountered. Alternate forms, derived forms, and cross-references to other entries are cited with moderate frequency.

The vocabulary is divided into two parts. The first is an alphabetical list of "Words of Spanish Source including, also, a few derived from the Indian." (1-58) The second part lists "Words of English Source" (59-78) under the separate categories of nouns, English or German surnames, geographical names, adjectives, verbs, adverbs, and other words. Most of the English-derived forms are cited phonetically as well as orthographically; all but a few are from Espinosa 1914-15. [GB]

KERCHEVILLE, Francis M. "A Preliminary Glossary of New Mexican Spanish." UNMBLS 5:3.7-69 (1934). [Annot. Nichols no. 1144; Serís no. 15539; Solé 1970 no. 980. Rev. RHM 1.122 (1935) (J. Englekirk); Hispania 18.229-230 (1935) (J. Rael); Hispania 18.230-232 (1935) (E. Eyring and A. Rebolledo); HR 4.85-86 (1936) (A. Post).]

This unsophisticated but significant early lexicographical work (bound together with McSpadden 1934b) was compiled by Kercheville and his students at the Univ. of New Mexico from printed sources and conversations. The reader is told that each entry was verified for authentic New Mexican usage and that only those forms and uses not cited "in numerous standard dictionaries" are included. Each entry contains simply the form in Spanish orthography and a brief English gloss. Etymological or other explanatory notes are exceedingly rare. No grammatical information is given. There are occasional orthographical errors, but these are of little importance.

The glossary is presented in six parts: "Colloquialisms--Words of Peculiar or Local Usage" (13-29) with over 500 entries; "Words Which Suffer Phonetic Changes" (31-40) containing almost 300 forms, many of which are such widespread variants as acabao for acabado and agüela for abuela; "Archaic or Obsolete Words" (41-43) citing just 12 words; "Words of Indian Origin," (45-47) which lists only 13 forms and excludes Mexicanisms of Indian origin but fails to identify the source languages; "Mexicanisms Used in New Mexico" (49-56) with some 180 expressions; and "Hispanized English Words and Expressions" (57-68) listing perhaps 350 forms. This division into parts may serve some purpose, but many forms are listed in more than one part and there are numerous cases of erroneous assignment, e.g.: <u>vide</u> 'I saw' is listed as phonetic change rather than archaism while <u>onde</u> 'where,' <u>truje</u> 'I brought,' and <u>mesmo</u> 'same' are cited in both of these sections; <u>soportar</u> 'to aid politically' is entered as a colloquialism instead of as an Anglicism; etc. [GB]

KERCHEVILLE, Francis M. "A Preliminary Glossary of Southwestern and Rio Grande Spanish Including Semantic and Philological Peculiarities." Unpubl. ms., Kingsville: Texas A & I Univ., 1967. v, 71 pp. (Available at copying cost from the James Jernigan Library, Texas A & I Univ.) [Rev. HLAS 32 (1970) no. 3103 (D.L. Canfield).]

   This work is divided into two parts: "Section A. Upper Rio Grande Area: Southern Colorado and New Mexico" (pp. 1-56) and "Section B. Lower Rio Grande Area: Southern New Mexico, Southwest Texas, South Texas" (57-70). Except for very minor revisions Section A is identical to Kercheville 1934; additional entries, if any, are insignificant. Section B is a single list (without subparts) of almost 400 words, with the same minimal information for entries as in Section A. This section has more of a Pachuco orientation, though the words are not so identified. Again, the spelling is sometimes inconsistent and misleading. The work is notable for examples of popular usage, but the overall lack of care and documentation make it of little value to the linguist.
   The introduction to Section B contains the statement: "Work will be continued . . . leading to subsequent publication of a definitive Dictionary of Rio Grande Spanish . . . " (57) The status of such an endeavor is unknown, although it seems safe to assume that little additional was accomplished prior to Kercheville's death in 1971. [GB]

KIDDLE, Lawrence B. "Los nombres del pavo en el dialecto nuevomejicano." Hispania 24.213-216 (1941).

   This very brief preliminary report on the research that produced Kiddle 1951-52 lists 23 American Spanish words for 'turkey' and gives a short historical-descriptive commentary on the forms used in New Mexico. [GB]

KIDDLE, Lawrence B. "'Turkey' in New Mexican Spanish." RPh 5.190-197 (1951-52). [Annot. HIAS 18 (1952) no. 2343 (D. Wogan); Woodbridge p. 240.]

   This dialect geography study based on fieldwork in 1936-38 of nine words for 'turkey' remains highly valued as the sole work of its kind on any variety of U.S. Spanish. Following a brief description of New Mexico's populace there is a rather detailed historical account, documented with passages from various works written between 1540 and 1832, of the development of words for 'turkey' in the region. A discussion of the nine current forms (ganso, cócono, cócano, pavo, torque and its variants, gallina de la tierra, gallina de la sierra, guajolote, and güíjolo) cites the common broad phonetic forms heard, the geographical distribution of each term with comments on cooccurrence with other forms and any variations in meaning, and etymological comments. Two maps document the occurrences of the nine forms. Kiddle concludes that there are two major dialects of New Mexican Spanish, the northern characterized by the relic gallina de la tierra and the Anglicism torque and the southern distinguished by the Mexican terms guajolote and güíjolo. [GB]

*KIDDLE, Lawrence B. "Los nombres del pavo en el dialecto nuevomexicano." El Hispano [Albuquerque], Dec. 22, 1972.

We understand that this short newspaper article is a popularization of Kiddle 1941 and 1951-52. [GB]

RAEL, Juan B. "Cosa nada en el español nuevomejicano." MLN 49.31-32 (1934).

A short note on the apparently archaic use of nada as an adjective restricted to phrases of the form "no (verb) cosa nada." [GB]

RAEL, Juan B. [1939a] "Alternate Forms in Speech of the Individual." SPh 36.664-670 (1939).

A consideration of the usage in New Mexican Spanish, "by the same person, of two and sometimes even three alternate forms of the same word." (664) Rael presents numerous examples of forms such as decir/dicir, traje/truje, poseía/poseaba, and ample historical documentation. He generally adheres to the simple explanation of a confusion or non-awareness of the two alternating forms. [GB]

RAEL, Juan B. [1939b]. "Associative Interference in New Mexican Spanish." HR 7.324-336 (1939). [Annot. Nichols no. 1141; Serís no. 15519.] (Rpt. in HERN/etal-1975.

This study of perhaps 160 nonstandard lexical items whose deviances do not seem to be due to external influences is not very laudable in analysis but provides a handy list of vocabulary. The words are grouped according to the semantic process exemplified: Blending (in which the two words cited as the sources of the blends are often quite fanciful); Analogy, involving an addition or change of prefix or change of ending or stem (does not repeat those forms cited by Espinosa 1930a); Analogical Creation, in which the forms cited are limited almost entirely to examples of extention or reanalysis of suffixation processes; Ultracorrection, in which are noted a few forms with f instead of the expected j; Popular Etymology, with the two examples, solesía for celosía and cuerpo espín for puerco espín; and Malapropisms, a hodge-podge of words phonetically distinct from standard Spanish. Rael indicates with an asterisk all words that he believes to be of common use. For most words he cites a folktale reference from his collection (see Rael 1937). [GB]

ROMERO, Cecil V. [1928a]. "A Unique American Chronicle." El Palacio 24:9.154-165 (March 1928).

This romantic treatise on the New Mexican corruption of the language of Cervantes (documented with several archaisms on p. 155) discusses historical factors influencing New Mexican Spanish, citing the small influence of New Mexico Indian languages, some influence from Aztec (with comments on words for 'turkey' on p. 161), and the great influence of English (no examples). [GB]

ROMERO, Cecil V. [1928b]. "Notes on New Mexican Spanish." El Palacio 24:15.283-287 (April 1928).

A brief addendum to Romero 1928a specifying the only example known to the author of a possible Pueblo Indian (Keres) loanword in New Mexican Spanish: puya 'thorn.' [GB]

SHOBAN, Gloria and Pita Singer. "The Degeneration of the Spoken Language of San Miguel County." MA Thesis, New Mexico Highlands Univ., Las Vegas, 1970. v, 230 pp.

The researcher should not be tempted to ignore this item on the basis of the title or comments such as: "When two languages co-exist, each corrupts the other" (p. 1). This work is in reality a unique and very useful vocabulary study of the Spanish of this northern New Mexico region.

The motivation for the study and the procedures employed are set forth in two brief chapters: Introduction (1-14) and Design of Investigation (15-24). The stated purpose is to answer the question: "Has the spoken Spanish language of San Miguel County degenerated from one generation to the next?" (2) Lengthy (three-hour) tape-recorded interviews were held with 25 adults aged 45-55 and 25 high school students aged 17-19, all residents of the towns of Pecos and Las Vegas. One part of the interview was concerned with the elicitation of specific lexical items by means of pictures; the second part was devoted to "free" conversation. Although there were dreadful flaws in the interview methodology (e.g., the younger informants averaged ten months of formal study of Spanish and were selected by the principals of the schools; the interviewers used only English during the sessions), it is to the authors' credit that they state explicitly, though not always clearly, the procedures used.

The next three chapters, which present the results of the corpus analysis, provide a goldmine of information. Chap. 3

(25-101) lists every word elicited by the visual aids, grouped according to the standard expression sought in the interview. For each entry the number of responses from each group is noted. For each nonstandard entry a notation indicates the "error" type in a classificatory system that is too simplistic but still suited to the authors' attempt to achieve their purpose. This chapter presents over 1,500 forms, virtually all of them nominal expressions (each cited with the appropriate article).

Chap. 4 (102-164) lists all the nonstandard words (totaling over 1,200 entries) gleaned from the conversation part of the interviews. The listing is presented in groups according to word class (noun, adjective, adverb, conjunction, interjection, participle, preposition, pronoun, verb). For each entry the number of occurrences noted in the speech of the older and younger groups and the error type are noted.

Chap. 5 (165-173) simply presents for both groups examples of sentences illustrating "the most outstanding errors" noted in the free conversations.

The final chapter (174-180) very briefly contrasts the speech of the two groups on the basis of a tally of the various types of "errors" isolated in the vocabulary elicited by the visual aids (the complete list of error tabulations is contained in Appendix B, pp. 184-230). As one might expect, the degeneration of Spanish in the speech of the younger group is proved by these statistics. This chapter also includes occasional notes on general tendencies in phonology and morphology. [GB]

TIREMAN, Loyd Spencer [1948a]. Spanish Vocabulary of Four Native Spanish-speaking Pre-first-grade Children. Univ. of New Mexico Publications in Education, No. 2 (Albuquerque, Univ. of New Mexico Press, 1948). 64 pp.

This admirable dictionary of almost 3,500 words was compiled from the transcripts of interviews with four six-year-old Albuquerque children. The word list (pp. 13-64) presents the form in dialectal orthography; its part of speech; the number of children who used the word; the standard form, if different; and sometimes an indication that the entry is an Anglicism, archaism, New Mexicanism, "made-up" form, etc. The chief value of this work rests in the fact that it includes every word uttered by the children, not just the exotic and regional forms. The chief limitation on the value of the compilation is the fact that the interview sessions were recorded solely by hand with little regard for nuances of meaning. [GB]

TRAGER, George L. [1939a]. "'Cottonwood' = 'Tree': A Southwestern Linguistic Trait." IJAL 9.117-118 (1939). (Rpt. with slight revisions in Hymes 1964, pp. 467-468.)

In addition to brief comments on several Indian languages, Trager notes that in the Spanish of New Mexico and southern Colorado álamo refers to "any deciduous tree not specifically identified" while árbol means "fruit tree." [GB]

TRUJILLO, Luis M. "Diccionario del español del Valle de San Luis de Colorado y del norte de Nuevo México." MEd Thesis, Adams State College, Alamosa, Colorado, 1961. v, 41 pp. [Annot. Craddock 1973 p. 319.]

This list of some 1,200 words and phrases collected from conversations and from Rael 1939 may well be a useful lexical source, but the rigor of the study is decidedly unexceptional. The dictionary includes only forms "que no se encuentren registrados en él con una aceptación diferente" (iv). Each entry merely includes the form in dialectal orthography plus a minimal English gloss, and then indicates deviation by seven simplistic types: colloquialism, localism, phonetic deviation (in which case the standard Spanish form is also given), archaism, Hispanized English form, Anglicized Spanish form, and Mexicanism. "Phonetic deviation," often phonological deviations of wide diffusion, accounts for a large number of the entries. Grammatical information is virtually non-existent. [GB]

3.6 ONOMASTICS (includes TOPONYMY)

Major Items· (none)

See also these items elsewhere (consult Author Index for location):
(none)

AKIN, Johnnye. "The Anglicization of Hispanic Place Names in Colorado, U.S.A." In Proceedings of the Sixth International Congress of Phonetic Sciences Held at Prague, 7-13 September 1967, edited by Bohuslav Hála, Milan Romport and Přemysl Janota. Prague: Czech Academy of Sciences, 1970. Pp. 105-107. [TSBJr.]

The author states that the aim of his (her?) paper is "to investigate the approximately one hundred eighty Hispanic place names that remain [in Colorado] and to determine the extent of Anglicization used in the native culture." (p. 105) But Akin never tells us which "native culture" he is talking about, the Chicano or the Anglo; at first glance one assumes the former, but the many distortedly Anglicized examples presented on pp. 105-106 might well lead to the opposite conclusion. Akin's transcriptions are not always easy to follow since he nowhere defines the symbols used (although for the most part they are those of Lado, Fries et al.); at times he fails to comprehend that an "exception to a rule" (e.g., "Final e → /I - ∅/. Grande → /gráendI - ∅/ . . . . Exception: Santa Fe → /eI/" [106]) is actually nothing more than an illustration of a well-known rule of English phonotactics, i.e., that V́ does not produce "schwah" (ə or ɨ [Akin's I?]).

Akin notes that various words have undergone graphemic Anglicization (Aroya, Broncho, Fruita) and concludes that "Hispanic influence in Colorado is one of names rather than orthoepy." (ibid.) [RT]

CHÁVEZ, Fray Angélico. "New Names in New Mexico, 1820-1850."
El Palacio 64.291-318, 367-380 (1957). [Annot. Fody p. 534.]

An alphabetical listing with commentary of over 300 new family names gleaned from baptismal and marriage records. The historical data are of much interest as are the notes on the Spanish-influenced spelling of English names. [GB]

DAVIDSON, Levette J. and Olga Hazel Koehler. "The Naming of Colorado's Towns and Cities." AS 7.180-187 (1932).

This not very scholarly, popularistic treatment of place names in general includes a number of names derived from Spanish (especially on pp. 181-182). [GB]

PEARCE, Thomas Matthews. [1958a]. "The New Mexico Place Name Dictionary: A Polyglot in Six Languages." Names 6.217-225 (1958). [Annot. Fody p. 534.]

This witty and entertaining abstract of the conmingling of languages in place naming in New Mexico notes that some 45% of his dictionary names derive from Spanish, 45% from English, and 10% from four Native American language groups. Numerous illustrations of language inter-influences are cited and discussed. [GB]

PEARCE, Thomas Matthews. "Religious Place Names in New Mexico." Names 9.1-7 (1961). [Annot. Fody p. 534.]

A brief prosaic mention of numerous terms from many languages; Spanish religious names are of course prominent. [GB]

PEARCE, Thomas Matthews, ed. (assisted by Ina Sizer Cassidy and Helen S. Pearce). New Mexico Place Names: A Geographical Dictionary. Albuquerque: Univ. of New Mexico Press, 1965. xvi, 187 pp.

An alphabetical listing of some 5,000 primary entries (plus derived forms) of the most significant place names in the state. Although there is naturally a predominance of Spanish origin terms, Pearce provides minimal linguistic comments beyond translation of the Spanish term. This is a valuable and entertaining work of historical documentation but of little use to most linguists. [GB]

RICHIE, Eleanor L. "Spanish Place Names in Colorado." AS 10.88-92 (1935).

This crass and superficial article contrasts the good and bad pronunciation of Spanish place names in New Mexico and Colorado, respectively, and provides a sketch of the settlement of the two states as an explanation of these differences. An awful attempt at representing pronunciation by means of English orthography is aided by a concluding editorial note that attempts phonetic transcriptions of almost 50 of Richie's citations. [GB]

TRAGER, George L. "Some Spanish Place Names of Colorado." AS 10.203-207 (1935).

Intended to "record the pronunciation of a number of Colorado place names of Spanish origin in the mouths of native speakers of English," (203) this article cites over 50 place names (some of which are actually in New Mexico), providing careful phonetic transcriptions of variant pronunciations and commenting on whether the form represents spelling pronunciation, imitation of spoken Spanish, or a mixture of the two. [GB]

3.7 ENGLISH INFLUENCE ON SPANISH

Major Items: ESPI-1914-15; GARC-T-1939; MURP-RP-1972

See also these items elsewhere (consult Author Index for location):
BOWE-1972; BRIS-1973; BRIS-1974a; BRIS-1974b; ESPI-1913; GROS-1935; KERC-1934; PEÑU-1964

BOGGS, Ralph S. "Phonetics of Words Borrowed from English by New Mexican Spanish." In Homenaje a Fritz Krüger (Mendoza, Argentina: Univ. Nacional de Cuyo, 1954) vol. 2.305-312.

This poor paper discusses the phonetic adaptation of a number of English borrowings cited in term papers by two of Boggs' students (Enrique M. Armija and Sabine Ulibarrí) on the Spanish of San Miguel and Río Arriba counties in northern New Mexico. Boggs' apparent lack of familiarity with New Mexican Spanish makes the lexical information (i.e., the students' work) far more valuable than the phonological interpretation (i.e., Boggs' work, which though well organized is confusing; phonetic symbolization is often murky. In addition to the many lexemes cited in the phonological discussion, the article concludes with a list of twelve verbs borrowed from English that end in -ar and -ear/-iar. [GB]

DURAN, Felix Leroy. "A Compilation of Anglicisms in the Penasco Area." MA Thesis, New Mexico Highlands Univ., 1965. 57 pp.

This study aimed at getting to know the enemy the better to destroy him. Based on data gathered from students, the media and personal conversations, the list of Anglicisms (pp. 14-52) runs to some 800 entries cited simply in "phonemic" form with a minimal English gloss, e.g., /akčón/ 'action,' /ályibra/ 'algebra,' /baráieti/ 'variety.' These few examples should indicate the utter worthlessness of this work except, perhaps, as a vividly negative example of linguistic sophistication. [GB]

ESPINOSA, Aurelio Macedonio. "Studies in New Mexican Spanish. Part III: The English Elements." RDR 6.241-317 (1914-15). [Annot. Nichols no. 1133; Serís no. 15512. Rev. MLN 25.156-157 (1911) (C.C. Marden); RFE 5.195-198 (1918) (A. Castro, T. Navarro Tomás); HomMP 1.675 (1925) (L. Gauchet); Romania 42.462-463 (1913) (G. Millardet).]

This monograph-length study is perhaps the most rigorous work ever done on the influence of English on U.S. Spanish. Sociocultural background, phonology, morphology, and vocabulary are each examined with care and consummate skill in the four chapters of the article.

Chap. 1 provides a lucid overview of the "Origin, Character and Extent of the English Influence." (pp. 241-256) Espinosa's historical account of the sociological and political problems of

the English-Spanish contact situation is very nice, though brief.
He also discusses the channels of borrowing and the differential
usage of borrowings, speech mixture or code-switching, direct
translation from English in Spanish syntax and phraseology, and
loan translation of specialized terminology.

Chap. 2 "Phonology" (256-285) is more detailed than Chap. 5
of Espinosa (1909aa) in explaining the phonological adaptation of
English borrowings. Following a brief discussion of stress,
there is a careful and abundantly exemplified treatment of the
regular and exceptional adaptation of each English vowel and consonant in varied environments. Here and in Chap. 3 Espinosa makes
many comparative Spanish comments, especially on California Spanish
(primarily of Santa Barbara), for which numerous examples are
cited.

Chap. 3 "Morphology" (285-304) treats in order: nouns, adjectives, adverbs, exclamations, verbs, and the use of Spanish
derivational affixes with English borrowings. Chap. 4 "Vocabulary"
(304-317) provides a "fairly complete" list of some 350 hispanized,
non-derived, New Mexican Spanish words of English origin. The
entries give the borrowed form in dialect orthography and phonetically, the English word of origin, a separate gloss where the meaning is changed, cross-references to the textual discussion, and
derived forms. This vocabulary is listed in five groups: nouns
(over half of the forms, plus a sub-listing for surnames), adjectives, verbs, adverbs, and others. [GB]

ESPINOSA, Aurelio Macedonio. "Speech Mixture in New Mexico: The
Influence of the English Language on New Mexican Spanish." In
The Pacific Ocean in History: Papers and Addresses Presented
at the Panama-Pacific Historical Congress Held at San Francisco,
Berkeley and Palo Alto, California July 19-23, 1915, edited by
Henry Morse Stephens and Herbert E. Dolton. New York: Macmillan Co., 1917. Pp. 408-428.

An abbreviated version of Espinosa 1914a, containing virtually
all of the original Chap. 1 and the vocabulary of Chap. 4 reduced
to less than 300 entries citing solely the Spanish form and the
English word of origin. The phonology and morphology discussions
are entirely deleted except for a one-page note on vowels and
consonants. [GB]

GARCÍA, Trinidad. "A Vocabulary of New Mexican Spanish Words of
English Origin from Southwestern New Mexico." MA Thesis,
Stanford Univ., 1939. 96 pp. 1 map.

This noteworthy thesis, written under the direction of Aurelio
Espinosa Sr., is quite important because it deals with a regional
Spanish that has not otherwise been explored, the Spanish of the
Magdalena-Socorro region. It is also en exceptionally careful
work for an MA thesis. The listing contains 500 "basic words" and

135 derivatives and is limited to forms not included in Espinosa 1914a. Unfortunately, the method of collection is not stated.

The vocabulary is divided into two parts: "Entirely Hispanized" words (pp. 4-61) conforming fully to Spanish phonological structure (e.g., los apendesaidos) and "Semi-Hispanized" words (61-72) of incomplete adaptation that appear to be more recent borrowings and characteristic of the speech of bilinguals (e.g., los tónsols). Each entry is cited in orthographic form and in phonetic transcription and is exemplified by usage in a sentence. The English word from which the form is derived is noted, but no mention is made of the meaning of the Spanish word. Thus, for example, he states that apendesaidos derives from 'appendicitis' but fails to point out that its meaning, at least in the example sentence, is 'appendix.' Each noun is cited with its article, though gender is not specifically indicated. Derived forms of each entry, including the plural form of each singular noun and the conjugation type (either -ar or -iar) of each verb, are noted. Additional grammatical notes occur on occasion.

In the final chapter (73-96) the author examines the regular sound changes involved in the adaptation of English borrowings. He states 75 observations on adaptation, based on Espinosa (1914a), and provides ample exemplification for each tendency. These observations are grouped into sections dealing with stress, vowels, consonants, the inflection of nouns, adjectives, and verbs, and the formation of derivatives. [GB]

MURPHY, R. Paul. "Integration of English Lexicon in Albuquerque Spanish." PhD Diss., Univ. of New Mexico, 1972. vi, 150 pp. [DA 33 (1973) 3622-A.]

This extremely well-written work "is a preliminary investigation into the extent to which lexical items from English have become a firm part of the local Spanish of Albuquerque, New Mexico." (v) This is an earnest and unique study; unfortunately its data base is quite limited.

Most of the body of the dissertation is concerned with theoretical and methodological aspects of the synchronic description of borrowings. Chap. 4 "Interference, Integration, and Albuquerque Spanish" (66-111) reports on the study itself. A series of four tests were administered to a variety of Spanish speakers. In an "availability test" 55 informants listed (30 in writing and 25 orally) all the words they could think of within three minutes for each of ten semantic fields (clothing, furniture, food, house, school, body, transportation, animals, jobs, and games). All items, native or English borrowing, that were cited two or more times are listed by field and with the number of occurrences in Appendix A (132-137); every item elicited in the occupation domain is listed in Appendix B (138-140). Next, a "translatability test" elicited Spanish translations of 141 English words in the ten domains; the list of responses and frequencies is contained in Appendix C (141-147). In an "acceptability test" 22 informants were presented with 72 recorded sentences to be judged on a four-point scale of acceptability in Spanish. These sentences manipulated 17 lexical items in varied ways, including pronunciation, morphological form, and cooccurrence with other English forms in the same sentence. The 72 sentences and their acceptability ratings are cited on pp. 94-96, and careful consideration is given to interesting aspects of the test results. Finally, a brief and inconclusive "identification test" had informants listen to 20 recorded sentences and write down any non-Spanish words heard; the sentences and number of identifications for each English word are listed in Appendix E (149-150). In the final chapter the author devotes a number of pages (112-120) to contrasting the implications of his findings with the English borrowings cited by Hills 1906b, Espinosa (1914a, 1917a), and Kercheville 1934. [GB]

MURPHY, R. Paul. [1974a]. "The Extent of English Borrowing in Albuquerque English." In Bills 1974, pp. 107-118.

A critical discussion of the procedures used in Murphy 1972, exemplified by the availability, translatability, acceptability, and identification test scores for *suera*, *troca*, *torque*, and *sinque*, and ending with a consideration of the need for a much broader, more sociological approach to questions of linguistic-cultural integration. [GB]

MURPHY, R. Paul. [1974b]. "Interference, Integration, and the Verbal Repertoire." In Spolsky and Bills 1974, pp. 59-67.

A heavily revised version of Murphy 1974a retaining the central plan, ideas, and data. [GB]

TRAGER, George L. and Genevieve Valdez. "English Loans in Colorado Spanish." AS 12.34-44 (1937).

The authors' purpose is "to present a representative discussion of the English influence, in the form of direct and indirect loans, on the spoken Spanish of southern Colorado and northern New Mexico." (p. 34) To supplement Espinosa's phonetic description (1909b), they present a brief and solely suggestive description of the "modern phonemic" system, which among other things provides separate phonemic status for [b] and [β]. The stated pronunciations of consonant clusters like [ks] seem to indicate that they are based upon artificial speech (presumably that of Valdez). The remainder of the paper is concerned with listing and commenting on loanwords of three types. Listed are 48 direct loans, 13 Spanish words that show alteration in form or meaning due to the influence of a similar English word, and eight loan translations. Except for one verb, *guachar*, all entries are nouns. All forms in the first two groups are given in phonetic transcription. [GB]

3.8 SPANISH INFLUENCE ON ENGLISH

Major Items: HEFL-1941

See also these items elsewhere (consult Author Index for location):
 APPL-1932

BROPHY, Mrs. William A. [Kathleen McKee]. "The Language of the
 Santa Fe Trader." MA Thesis, Univ. of New Mexico, 1932.
 106 pp.

 Very similar in motivation and presentation to two other
theses directed by Thomas M. Pearce (Jenkins 1931 and Carlisle
1939), but considerably more coherent linguistically, this proposed "general survey of the language most commonly used on the
Santa Fe Trail" (p. 8) is devoted largely to a glossary (22-104)
of some 550 distinctive words collected from 11 memoir-type works.
Entries include the part of speech label, the language classification (slang, standard English, Spanish, [New] Mexican, etc.), and
the source work with a sample sentence. Brophy notes that the
vocabulary derives principally from four languages: American,
Spanish, Indian, and French. One short chapter (11-21) provides
an unsophisticated discussion of the flavor and function of the
words from the different languages; for Spanish she distinguishes
four kinds of words--standard Spanish, standard Spanish forms with
different meanings, Mexican/New Mexican, and Anglicisms, providing
a number of examples of each (16-20). [GB]

HEFLIN, Woodford A. "Characteristic Features of New Mexico English
 Between 1805 and 1890." PhD Diss., Univ. of Chicago, 1941.
 284 pp.

 The title notwithstanding, this dissertation is a vocabulary
of characteristic New Mexican words found in written sources
during the period indicated. The entries are modeled after those
of the Craigie/Hulbert 1938 ff., which Heflin meant to supplement
and complete with regard to the particular region and time that
interested him. A few spot checks, e.g.s.v. <u>caliche</u>, suggest
that his material was absorbed into Mathews 1951, though Heflin's
name does not appear in the bibliography of the <u>Dictionary of
Americanisms</u>.
 Hispanisms play a large part in this work and the author devotes
to them a good share of his introduction (pp. 1-33). In particular,
he attempts (pp. 9-10) to distinguish between Spanish loanwords
genuinely adopted into the English speech on New Mexico from mere
"occasionalisms" that crop up in the works of travelers, historians,
and novelists. Even after eliminating such spurious borrowings,
the number that remains strikes me as quite substantial. Another
useful feature of the introduction are the lists of sense groups
Heflin put together (pp. 18-31) so as to facilitate study of the
vocabulary relating to individual topics (foods, entertainment,
etc.). [JC]

KIMMERLE, Marjorie. "Bum, Poddy, or Penco." CQ 1.87-97 (1952).

Penco 'orphaned lamb', [píŋkou] in the local Anglo pronunciation, occurs only in the southern portion of Colorado, an area that ethnically and culturally once belonged to New Mexico. The term, no doubt related to the Mexican Spanish homonym meaning 'jade, nag,' is documented in New Mexican Spanish. The specific application to the 'orphaned lamb' seems to have occurred there. Further etymological connections are uncertain, though the Central American adj. penco 'stupid' may be involved. On pp. 89-90, the author apparently confused the word at issue with penca 'pulpy leaf,' which, semantically at least, shows no particular affinity to penco. [JC]

PEARCE, Thomas Matthews. "New Mexican Folk Etymologies." El Palacio 50:10.229-234 (Oct. 1943).

An outlandishly popular narrative discussion of six or seven place names and the forms gringo and greaser and their multilingual folk etymologies as reported in the region. [GB]

[anon.] "What Do We Speak?" El Palacio 13:10.130-131 (Nov. 15, 1922).

This popularizing, worthless article taken from the Albuquerque Herald deals with the use of Spanish and Native American words in the English of New Mexico. [GB]

3.8.1 ENGLISH OF THIS PARTICULAR HISPANIC GROUP

Major Items: GARC-Ri-1973

See also these items elsewhere (consult Author Index for location): GONZ-J-1972; TIRE-1948b; ZUNS-1935.

*ADKINS, Patricia G. "An Investigation of the Essentiality of Idioms and Figures of Speech in the Education of Bilingual Students in the Ninth Grade in Texas and New Mexico." PhD Diss., Univ. of Colorado, Boulder, 1966. 123 pp. [DA 28 (1967) 1142-A.]

From the abstract we learn that Adkins studied the degree to which "idioms and figures of speech" were comprehended by "Spanish-speaking bilingual students in ninth grade reading and social studies classes," and how this comprehension (or its lack) affected an understanding of the material's "context." Adkins concluded: "In the test for comprehension of total context in which idiomatic and figurative expressions occurred, the sign test indicated significantly that bilingual students do not understand materials in which idiomatic and figurative elements appear." She goes on to plan teaching methods of presumed remedial efficacy. [RT]

*GARCÍA, Ricardo L. "Identification and Comparison of Oral English Syntactic Patterns of Spanish-English Speaking Adolescent Hispanos." EdD Diss., Univ. of Denver, 1973. 140 pp. [DA 34 (1973) 3372-A.]

The abstract tells us that "this study was designed as an effort to help clarify the unresolved issue that Hispano bilingualism, per se, is detrimental to Hispano [English-language] syntactic language development," but the major focus of the study was to test the hypothesis that "the Hispano's oral English syntactic variations are related to his socio-economic status." To that end García examined the oral English syntax of lower and middle class Hispano adolescents (fifty-two Spanish-English bilinguals from two New Mexico high schools); unstructured speech was elicited through the description of five "action prints." Identification of the patterns revealed that all subjects used "the eleven syntax patterns basic to General American English regardless of socio-economic status." Low class students, however, used "a statistically significant higher percentage of Maze and Question patterns than the middle-class group," while the latter used a higher percentage of Sentence and Subordination patterns. Lower-class students thus "spoke a code that was restrictive: it was partially paratactic, partially void of subordinations, and laden with questions and mazes." In consequence "a relationship was found to exist between the Hispano's syntax patterns and his socio-economic status." With regard to the first of García's two issues, bilingualism cannot be said to hinder English competence since all middle-class subjects were bilinguals. [RT]

JOHNSON, Loaz W. "A Comparison of the Vocabularies of Anglo-American and Spanish-American High School Pupils." JEP 29. 135-144 (1938).

An early attempt at determining whether Chicano high school students (from Silver City, New Mexico) could recognize and identify as many words in English as their Anglo classmates could. The Inglis Test of English Vocabulary was used, along with several "teacher-made" exams designed to test for lexicon likely to be acquired in the classroom. Hispanos did less well than Anglos on the Inglis test but narrowed the gap on the tests of "classroom" vocabulary. Johnson's antediluvian explanations as to why the Hispanos lagged in English proficiency can only be termed typical of the times: "[The] Spanish-American is of a different race . . . And since he uses a different language early in life, his idioms of thought must necessarily be different." (p. 135) Apparently, Hispanos also bear the blame for the cultural apartheid of the day: "Their life habits . . . would naturally limit their contacts with the words which would be found in a general English vocabulary test." (141) [RT]

MURPHY, Marilyn. "The Effects of Modeling and Repetition Upon the
    Acquisition of Three Standard English Patterns by Spanish-
    speaking First-grade Children." PhD Diss., Univ. of New Mexico,
    1973. xiii, 229 pp. [DA 34 (1974) 6952-A.]

   This study of 15 Albuquerque children (including ten native
speakers of Spanish) with deficiencies in their command of English
was undertaken in order to (a) determine the effectiveness of
modeling and repetition in learning to use the possessive 's, ac-
companiment with, and instrumental with and (b) describe the
spontaneous English speech of the children. The latter is of possible linguistic interest not because of the analysis given, which
is exceedingly superficial and uninteresting, but because of the
vast amount of data presented (contained in two appendices, pp.
109-222). Murphy's statement that "there were only ten sentences
in the entire corpus which showed any resemblance to Spanish
structure" (91) is not to be believed. [GB]

SCHUPP, Ona E. "Oral and Written Language Errors of Sixth Grade
    Pupils." MA Thesis, Univ. of New Mexico, 1933. iv, 62 pp.

   This insignificant examination of the English of 290 Anglo and
131 Chicano children in Albuquerque simply provides gross tabulations of crude error categories ("spelling," "commas," "wrong
verb," "no such word," "John he," etc.). Oral errors are based
on the reports of teachers, written errors on three papers per
child. No specific language data are cited. Among Schupp's conclusions: the patterns of errors by Anglos and Chicanos are remarkably similar. [GB]

3.9 SPANISH INFLUENCE ON AMERINDIAN LANGUAGES

Major Items: DOZI-1956; ESPI-1932; MILL-1960; TRAG-1944

See also these items elsewhere (consult Author Index for location):
    (none)

DOZIER, Edward P. "Two Examples of Linguistic Acculturation: The
    Yaqui of Sonora and Arizona and the Tewa of New Mexico."
    Language 32.146-157 (1956). [Reprinted in Hymes 1964, pp.
    509-517.]

   A superb study of differential Spanish influence on Yaqui,
where there was a "permissive" Spanish contact and liberal borrowing, and Tewa, which experienced a "forced" contact and resisted
borrowing. Included is a list of Tewa words showing Spanish influence; most are new coinages that resulted from compounding or
meaning extension, but some 60 are Spanish loans (words for animals,
plants, religion, government, material items, time, and distance).
The use of Spanish names and the influence of Spanish on the structure of Tewa are also discussed very briefly. [GB]

ESPINOSA, Aurelio Macedonio. "El desarrollo de la palabra 'Castilla' en la lengua de los indios queres de Nuevo Méjico." RFE 19.261-277 (1932).

The purpose of this article is "sólo hacer algunas observaciones sobre las diversas y muy interesantes formas de una sola palabra...entre los indios queres de los pueblos de Acoma, Laguna, Paguate, Santo Domingo y Cochití." (p. 262) Espinosa notes that the borrowing of the word 'castilla,' used as a noun or adjective equivalent to standard 'castellano' or 'español,' was documented as early as 1610. He gives an exquisitely detailed phonetic description of all the forms and variants (total of 26) occurring in each pueblo. He then attempts historical explanations by detailing the phonetic changes involved, but these are marred by his lack of knowledge of the Indian languages concerned. His primary conclusion, however, is that the data provide "una prueba elocuente y definitiva de la pronunciación palatal lateral de la ll de los siglos en que los conquistadores españoles se establecieron en Nuevo Méjico." (276) [GB]

ESPINOSA, Aurelio Macedonio. "Miscellaneous Materials from the Pueblo Indians of New Mexico." PQ 21.121-127 (1942).

A brief listing of some Pueblo folkloric data (hymns, prayers, refrains, rhymes, tales) followed by minimal notes, some suggesting Spanish influence on topic and/or linguistic form. [GB]

ESPINOSA, Aurelio Macedonio. "Spanish Tradition Among the Pueblo Indians." In Estudios hispánicos: homenaje a Archer M. Huntington (Wellesley, Mass.: Wellesley College Spanish Dept., 1952), pp. 131-141.

General remarks intended to illustrate the range of Spanish influence on Pueblo language and culture. Specific examples of linguistic influence cited are: the Isleta Tiwa, San Juan Tewa, and Laguna Keres forms of 23 Spanish words (pp. 132-133), the days of the week in Taos Tiwa (133), several examples of religious (134) and administrative/political terms (141), discussion of the forms of Castilla (135). [GB]

MILLER, Wick R. "Spanish Loanwords in Acoma." IJAL 25.147-153 (1959); 26.41-49 (1960)

The first part of this careful and very well presented article describes the contact history of the region, outlines the phonemic systems of Acoma and New Mexican Spanish (based on Trager and Valdez 1937), describes in detail all generalizable substitution rules observable in the borrowings, and lists some 140 loanwords, each entered with an English equivalent, the Acoma form, a Spanish gloss, and sometimes with a specific New Mexican Spanish lexical item taken from Hills 1938 or Kercheville 1934.

The second part begins with special comments on irregularities in form or meaning among the listed borrowings and on 12 additional items that might be suspected to be of Spanish origin; both topics are amply supplemented with corresponding forms in four other Keresan languages and in Taos, Hopi, and Zuni. This is followed by a more detailed discussion of phonological substitution correspondences exhibited in the borrowings: multiple substitutions dependent on phonemic environment, the possibility of different periods of borrowing, diffusion by "interpueblo" borrowing, and the influence of dialect variation in New Mexican Spanish. Finally, there are remarks on the effect of Spanish loans on the Acoma phonemic system and discussion of other aspects of Spanish loanword integration. [GB]

SPENCER, Robert F. "Spanish Loan Words in Keresan." SWJA 3.130-146 (1947).

This sketchy "preliminary attempt...to consider the nature of linguistic borrowing" and the linguistic effects of culture contact (p. 130) is a perfunctory discussion of fully assimilated borrowings and relies heavily on the Taos work of Trager 1944. Following brief comments on the history of the Spanish-Keresan contact situation and on linguistic contrasts between the two languages, Spencer cites about 15 loan translations (all religious terms) and 100 borrowed words (religious, governmental, and material culture terms, names of plants and animals, and time words and numbers). In addition to these nouns, he notes the borrowing of two verbs, amar and pedir, and the use of hay 'there is, there are.' There is also a short discussion of phonological changes involved in adaptation of the borrowings (145-146). Spencer concludes that less than 5% of the Keresan words he has encountered are of Spanish origin. [GB]

TRAGER, George L. [1939b]. "The Days of the Week in the Language of Taos Pueblo, New Mexico." Language 15.51-55 (1939).

A rigorous, concentrated consideration of these seven Spanish loanwords, primarily with regard to phonological adaptations. [GB]

TRAGER, George L. "Spanish and English Loanwords in Taos." IJAL 10.144-160 (1944).

This superbly thoughtful and clear article describes 79 unimpeachably Spanish borrowings (distinguishing between oldest, more recent, and quite recent loans), as well as eight probable Spanish loanwords and 17 forms of English origin, mostly via New Mexican Spanish. These entries, almost all nouns, are presented with an English gloss, the Spanish word of origin and its meaning, and a phonemic transcription of the New Mexican Spanish form when distinct from the standard. Trager also discusses the regular and irregular patterns in the phonetic adaptation of the loans. [GB]

4. [CHICANOS:] ARIZONA

4.1 BIBLIOGRAPHY (nothing to report)

4.2 COMPREHENSIVE/GENERAL STUDIES; MISCELLANY; ANTHOLOGIES/ FESTSCHRIFTEN

Major Items: (none)

See also these items elsewhere (consult Author Index for location): (none)

ACOSTA, Vincent S. "Some Surviving Elements of Spanish Folklore in Arizona." MA Thesis, Univ. of Arizona, Tucson, 1951. 191 pp. [Annot. Woodbridge p. 241.]

Extensive collection (237 texts) of folkloric verse consisting principally of ballads (corridos) and occasional coplas (brief songs generally of a single stanza) and lullabies (canciones de cuna). The author has divided them according to their subject matter as follows: (1) traditional ballads (romances), (2) historical themes, (3) equestrian topics, (4) local events (esp. catastrophes such as train wrecks and earthquakes, but the depression of the 'thirties and World War II are also represented), (5) love poems and (6) social protest. Chapters III, IV and V respectively introduce prayers, coplas and lullabies. The last precedes a short section of "Conclusions;" various appendices ("Names of Informants," "Samples of Written [i.e., printed] corridos," "List of Recordings Made for this Thesis," "Glossary" and "Bibliography") conclude the work.
In his transcriptions the author used standard Spanish orthography; this practice probably masks a great deal of significant phonological detail. He underlines forms considered dialectal or substandard but rarely analyses them further. The commentary is sketchy and many verses in need of elucidation are passed over in silence. The glossary is too selective to be of great use to linguists. At one point Acosta frustrates in rather bizarre fashion the reader's desire to learn more about certain unusual words connected with horse racing. After describing an interview with one of the corridistas who agreed to explain a ballad on the horse El Merino (pp. 76-79), and presenting a list of forms Acosta specifically sought information about, the author blithely announces (p. 80), "The answers to these questions may be obtained by listening to the recordings that have been made" (and which are on file at the Music Division of the Library of Congress [p. 2]).
A trained linguist could glean considerable useful dialectal data from this collection, though he would doubtless want to obtain, if possible, copies of the recordings mentioned above. [JC]

DAVIS, Jack Emory. "Teaching Spanish in a Bilingual Area."
Hispania 40.206-207 (1957).

A mercifully brief note on the trials and tribulations suffered, and occasional blessings counted, in the author's attempts to teach good Spanish at the Univ. of Arizona. Davis provides modest exemplification of errors in phonology, grammar, Anglicisms, archaisms, and spelling. [GB]

MARTÍNEZ-BERNAL, Janet Ayers. "Children's Acquisition of Spanish and English Morphological Systems and Noun Phrases." PhD Diss., Georgetown Univ., 1972. ix, 301 pp. [DA 33 (1973) 3619-3620 3620-A.]

Primarily a bilingual replication and refinement of the testing procedures used by Berko and later researchers to determine the child's mastery of certain morphological and syntactic phenomena, this very good study is more valuable as a methodological experiment than as a description of child language. The subjects of the study were bilingual children in grades K-2 in Tucson.
The first five chapters provide an overview of the socioeducational situation in Tucson (including a language use survey of 247 families), a review of language testing literature, justification for the author's testing approach, an explanation of data-collection procedures, and composite demographic data on the home language, birthplace, and so forth of the subjects. The testing used real words, nonsense words, and visual aids to probe each child's dominance of selected aspects of morphology and noun phrase length and complexity in both Spanish and English. The morphological items treated are: noun plurals, diminutives, and various verb tense forms (including the subjunctive) in both languages; English comparative, superlative, and possessive forms and agentive -er; and Spanish -ero, -ería, and -or.
The composite results of the testing, based on percentage of correct responses, are presented in Chaps. 6-8. Each item is discussed separately and a superficial item analysis is given. Comparison is made with the findings of other researchers and between the older and younger children. Also presented are statistical correlations between the morphological and noun phrase tests, between the author's results and the results of other proficiency tests, and with the sociological variables of sex, age, and home language. These last correlations lead to a brief discussion of interlingual interference as a phenomenon, but here, as throughout this work, there is virtually no consideration of individual speech. [GB]

OLSTAD, Charles. "The Local Colloquial in the Classroom." In Turner 1973, pp. 51-66.

Although chiefly a discussion of the desirability of incorporating the local variety of Southwest Spanish into the classroom, Olstad does bring in examples of Southwest Spanish (pp. 57-65), presumably as spoken in southern Arizona, though this is never explicitly stated. Included are some thirty vocabulary items; several oft-cited verbs borrowed from English; brief comments on hiatus reduction, metathesis, and nonstandard verb forms; and one item of syntax: the use of hacer with an English verbal form where standard Spanish would permit a verb only. Discussion and grammatical explanations are simplistic. [GB]

POST, Anita Calneh. "The Spanish Dialect of Southern Arizona." MA Thesis, Univ. of Arizona, Tucson, 1917. iv, 51 pp.

This antiquated thesis is surely one of the sloppiest ever written. It was apparently copied from the grossest possible card file notes and its typing is as careless as its thought. Though a valuable work because of its early date, it must be used with great caution.

A two-page introduction specifies that the study is based on Post's own knowledge of the speech of southern Arizona (and northern Mexico), but the reader often wonders how much of the data is actually New Mexican Spanish from Hills 1906b and Espinosa 1909aa. The introduction also provides a short bibliography and such phonetic transcription notes as: "B = voiced nasal stop" (p. 2)!

A section on phonology (3-11) is a crude and often incomprehensible hodge-podge of observations on nonstandard pronunciations; this should be disregarded in favor of Post 1934. There follows the undoubtedly most important aspect of this work: three sections on vocabulary listing roughly 100 "Words of English Origin," (12-15) some 90 "Words of Nahuatl Origin," (16-20) and almost 500 "Spanish Words Used With a Change of Meaning, Form, Gender, or Accent." (21-39) Entries are limited to citation of the form and a minute English gloss; gender is usually cited for nouns.

A section on "Changes in Nouns, Pronouns, Adjectives, Verbs" (40-47) contains one page of common (largely phonological) deviations in part of speech and seven pages of conjugation paradigms for regular and irregular verbs. The thesis ends abruptly with a section misleadingly entitled "Syntax," which contains minimal remarks on English influence, "Indian Spanish," "illiterate" syntactic constructions, and an interesting list of some 45 idiomatic constructions. [GB]

4.2.1 SOCIOLINGUISTICS

Major Items: BARB-1952; BARK-G-1947a; BARK-G-1972; VOEG/etal-1967

See also these items elsewhere (consult Author Index for location):
(none)

BARBER, Carroll Gary. "Trilingualism in Pascua: The Social
    Functions of Language in an Arizona Yaqui Village." MA Thesis,
    Univ. of Arizona, Tucson, 1952. iv, 127 pp.

   An anthropological-linguistics study of the social domains of
Spanish, English, and Yaqui in the Yaqui Indian settlement of
Pascua in northwest Tucson. This early sociolinguistic endeavor,
modeled closely after the work of Barker 1947a and based on the
self-reports of 12 men between the ages of 19 and 31, contains no
primary linguistic data beyond scattered citation forms.
   The work is divided into five chapters: Introduction (pp. 1-
22), The Men and the Village (23-54), The Languages Spoken (55-81),
Languages in Action (82-114), and The Social Functions of Language
in Pascua (115-123). The third chapter provides a historical
sketch of the linguistic background of the Yaquis and a very general
discussion of the kinds of the three languages spoken. His comments on Spanish largely duplicate the differences cited by
Barker, although he tentatively argues against Barker's recognition
of a Yaqui dialect of Spanish, noting that "the only distinctive
features of the Spanish of Pascua appear to be in vocabulary." (72)
Chap. 4 discusses the "meaning" of each language to the informants:
how each language was learned, the situations in which each is
used (Spanish being associated with recreation, religion, external
friendly relations, and often internal informal relations), and
the men's attitudes toward each. The final chapter summarizes
the social functions of the languages and, on the basis of this,
hazards a few guesses about the linguistic future of Pascua. [GB]

BARBER, Carroll Gary. "Trilingualism in an Arizona Yaqui Village."
    In Turner 1973, pp. 295-318.

   A substantially abbreviated version of Barber 1952 with an
updated conclusion noting that Pascua has become even more trilingual and "will remain trilingual for considerably longer than
was anticipated twenty years ago." (p. 318) [GB]

BARKER, George C. [1947a]. "Social Functions of Language in a
    Mexican-American Community." PhD Diss., Univ. of Chicago,
    1947. v, 250 pp.

   This anthropologically oriented study of the Mexican Americans
of Tucson, Arizona, is readily the best treatment available of
the role of Southwest Spanish in a multilingual society. Based

primarily on a diary which Barker filled with impressionistic observations of twenty families while he lived in the community for eight months in 1945-46, this study examines the usage of Spanish and English from the viewpoint of the individual, the family, and the community.

In his general treatment of language usage in Chap. 4 he briefly discusses four major varieties of local Spanish: the southern Arizona, standard Mexican, Pachuco, and Yaqui dialects. He considers outstanding the following characteristics of southern Arizona Spanish: its archaisms (vinido, durmir); its English borrowings, called "pochismos" (several syntactic influences such as me agarró el chivo 'he got my goat'); the tendency to use tú displacing usted; and a pronounced "sonsonete" intonation (a totally unenlightening explanation so typical of comments on dialectal intonation). For the Pachuco dialect he briefly notes as characteristic its adaptations of English and Mexican slang vocabulary, "its use of a sonorous and pompous accent, its exclusive reliance on the formal verb forms [and] its use of gesture and signs to supplement its vocabulary."

Further information of a linguistic nature, including a few examples of the influence of Spanish on English, may be gleaned from the samples from his diary so liberally used to document usage trends in Chaps. 5 and 7. However, the reliability of these notations may be questioned since they were generally recorded not in situ, but at the end of the day.

Additional language raw data are contained in the two appendices of Pochismos (239-242) and Pachuco words (243-245). These limited glossaries are not very useful. The Pochismos list includes such widespread borrowings as beisbol, carro, and quequi, and even the not borrowed cerco 'fence.' Orthographical selections are careless, e.g., chain 'shine' versus shainar 'to shine,' suichi with u versus swera with w, and llaqui 'jack' instead of the more expected yaqui. Presumably quilta 'quilt' should be cuilta, as documented by Rael 1937 (149), but who knows? Such factors should influence anyone to ignore this work as a source of linguistic raw data, but its value as an overview of the sociolinguistic situation in Arizona can not be demeaned. [GB]

BARKER, George C. [1947b]. "Social Functions of Language in a Mexican American Community." Acta Americana 5.185-202 (1947). [Annot. HLAS 13 (1947) no. 1970 (C. Kany); Woodbridge p. 241.] (Rpt.: Bobbs-Merrill Reprint Series in the Social Sciences, A-5; also in HERN/etal-1975, pp. 170-182.

This article is a skillfully written summary of the main points of Barker's 1947 dissertation. No primary linguistic data are included, but brief mention is made of the four local varieties of Spanish (pp. 192-193). [GB]

BARKER, George C. "Growing Up in a Bilingual Community." The Kiva 17.17-32 (1951).

   This brief summary of Barker's dissertation (1947a) contains no primary linguistic data. [GB]

BARKER, George C. Social Functions of Language in a Mexican-American Community. Arizona Univ. Anthropological Papers, No. 22 (Tucson: Univ. of Arizona Press, 1972). v, 56 pp. (Introduction by Harry T. Getty.) [Rev. AA 76.457 (1974) (J. Hotchkiss); Bills 1974.]

   This publication of Barker's dissertation (1947a) has suffered rather extensive though generally good revision by an unnamed editor. Most of the primary language data have been edited out, although the dialect descriptions are retained in full (pp. 25-27). Gone are the Pachuco and Pochismos glossaries and virtually all excerpts from his diary. Indeed, the major change from the dissertation is the deletion of the original Chap. 5, the substance of which is condensed into three tables. [GB]

SERRANO, Rodolfo Gaitán. "Sociocultural Influences on the Development of Mexican American Language Styles." PhD Diss., Univ. of Arizona, Tucson, 1972. x, 114 pp. [DA 33 (1972) 1992-A.]

   Primarily concerned with procedures in identifying the language "style" of the bilingual individual in Tucson and the sociocultural influences on the development of this "style," this education dissertation provides very little direct linguistic information and is woefully lacking in linguistic sophistication.
   The first three chapters are the predictable Introduction, Review of the Literature, and Methods and Procedures, and the fifth and last chapter is the typical education-oriented Summary, Conclusions, and Recommendations. A short Chap. 4, "Presentation and Analysis of the Data" (56-85), provides the meat of the research. On the basis of interviews and conversations with 22 ninth-grade students and their parents, 18 language variables (such as number of nouns, number of clauses, identification of Pachuco terms, degree of bilingualism, and so forth) were selected for statistical analysis and resulted in the distinction of four "language-style groups;" one "style" for example is speech that exhibits good English grammar, good communication of ideas, coordinate bilingualism, extensive English vocabulary, and good standard Spanish. Differences between male and female performance, especially with regard to knowledge of Pocho and Pachuco terms, are discussed in some depth. [GB]

[anon. ed.] "Tucson: The Spanish Speaking People." The Kiva 17:1/2.entire issue (32 pp.) (Nov.-Dec. 1951).

This volume contains no significant linguistic information. Three brief articles are included: "People of the Old Pueblo" by Harry T. Getty (pp. 1-6), "Barriers to Mexican Integration in Tucson" by James E. Officer (7-16), and "Growing Up in a Bilingual Community" by George C. Barker (17-32). Officer concludes that "the greatest hindrance to complete cultural assimilation of Tucson's Mexicans is the language factor." (15) Barker's contribution is a very brief summary of his dissertation (1947a). [GB]

VOEGELIN, Carl F., Florence M. Voegelin and Noel W. Schutz, Jr. "The Language Situation in Arizona as Part of the Southwest Culture Area." In Hymes and Bittle 1967, pp. 403-451.

This comprehensive ethnolinguistic survey of the languages of Arizona (with some ranging into adjacent states) is eminently readable, quotable, and interesting, but often vague, careless, and bibliographically undocumented--"Our intention . . . is to give some indication of what can be done rather than to give conclusions of what has been done." (p. 404) With regard to Spanish, there is a sociolinguistic overview (411-414), some rather weak comments on Pachuco (441-442), and remarks here and there on the role of Spanish in different contact situations and the influence of Spanish on other languages, especially Native American languages. For all its lack of specificity and language data, this is certainly one of the best general language survey statements for the Southwest. [GB]

4.3 SPANISH PHONOLOGY (includes ORTHOGRAPHY)

Major Items: POST-1932; POST-1934

See also these items elsewhere (consult Author Index for location): LYNN-1940

BROWN, Dolores. "A Two-syllable Affective Affirmation in Spoken Spanish." In Ewton and Ornstein 1970, pp. 33-43.

This paper examines the rather frequent occurrence of the utterance "uh huh" in the Spanish speech of radio announcers and guests on Spanish language radio stations in Tucson, Arizona, and in Arizpe, Mexico. "Expressing comprehension, consent and encouragement on the part of the speaker, the utterance has two phonetic variants [mhm] [~h~]; four types of intonation pattern . . . ; a pitch interval of usually four half-tones;" and is usually stressed on the second syllable (pp. 42-43). Numerous conversational excerpts are cited, with each "uh huh" recorded phonetically on a musical scale. The author found no correlation of usage with sex, age, or education, and she doubts English influence because of the documentation for Arizpe. [GB]

MERZ, Geri W. "Speech Levels and Tucson Spanish Phonology." In Bills 1974, pp. 189-196.

This brief report on research in progress for the author's Univ. of Arizona dissertation reviews treatments of the isolation of speech "levels" or "styles," explains her interview techniques (with several sample protocols), and provides a tentative Labovian analysis of the phonological realizations of /s/ in three utterance speeds. [GB]

POST, Anita Calneh. "Southern Arizona Spanish." PhD Diss., Stanford Univ., 1932. vi, 79 pp.

This dissertation, written under the direction of A. M. Espinosa, Sr., was published with only slight modification as Post 1934. [GB]

POST, Anita Calneh. "Some Aspects of Arizona Spanish." Hispania 16.35-42 (1933). [Annot. Nichols no. 1139.] (Rpt. in HERN/etal-1975, pp. 30-36.

This short version of Post 1934 supplies a historical sketch of the region and the local Spanish, a cursory description of the nonstandard aspects of the phonology, and several brief stories and songs in dialectal orthography. [GB]

POST, Anita Calneh. "Southern Arizona Spanish Phonology." (Univ. of Arizona Humanities Bulletin, No. 1.) UAB 5:1.entire issue (vi, 57 pp.) (January 1934). [Annot. Nichols no. 1140; Serís no. 15529; Solé 1970 no. 963. Rev. BAAL 7-8.277-279 (1934) (E. F. Tiscornia); RFE 22.67-72 (1935) (A. Alonso).]

This publication of Post's dissertation (1932) deals with the Spanish of the extreme southern part of the state, primarily that of Yuma and Tucson. The study seems to be based largely on Post's personal acquaintance with the dialect, apparently gained mostly from her students. Although there are serious limitations to this work, the fact that it is the most complete phonological description of Arizona Spanish makes it an important contribution.

The body of the study contains an Introduction (pp. 3-12) and four chapters: Changes in Accentuation (13-14), Vowels (15-31), Consonants (32-44), and Phonetic Texts (45-50). The Introduction provides a historical sketch of the Spanish exploration and settlement of the area and some generalistic comments on the local Spanish: its close relationship to the Spanish of Sonora, Mexico; the negligible influence of Indian languages of the region; the influence of English; and the effect of heavy Mexican immigration and the teaching of standard Spanish in the schools.

The three chapters on phonology are closely patterned after Espinosa 1930a, although the description of the vowel sounds (15-17) seems to be most influenced by Navarro Tomás' Manual de pronunciación española. Indeed, such points as the identification of open variants of vowels before /x/ lead one to believe that the latter's influence was so great as to distort the description. The emphasis in this study is on the presentation of nonstandard aspects of the phonology, especially deviations in the phonological form of words. Historico-comparative documentation is usually attempted.

The final chapter contains five short tales in phonetic and dialect-orthographic transcription.

This work differs from the dissertation only in the addition of a Preface (iii), perhaps a few minor additions (only one was noticed), and some very slight typographical editing. One of the most notable defects in the editing is the often arbitrary addition of square brackets, presumably to make the work look more phonetically scientific. Unfortunateby, the dissertation is remarkable for the confusion of sounds and letters, and the addition of square brackets only compounds this confusion; §18 of the dissertation, for example, dealt with the conjunction y, whereas in this publication it deals with [y] (17). [GB]

4.4 SPANISH GRAMMAR (MORPHOLOGY AND SYNTAX)

Major Items: (none)

See also these items elsewhere (consult Author Index for location):
    MART-J-1972

4.5 SPANISH LEXICON (includes SEMANTICS)

Major Items: TREJ-1951

See also these items elsewhere (consult Author Index for location):
    POST-1917

MAYNES, J. Oscar, Jr. "A Comparison of Local Spanish and Standard Spanish Vocabulary." PhD Diss., Arizona State Univ., 1973. ix, 74 pp. [DA 34 (1974) 3841-A.]

Maynes initially assembled a list of 112 words from three texts (Barker 1950, Baker 1966 and Barker 1970) well known for the attention they direct to the oddities and non-standard aspects of some of the brands of Chicano Spanish. In nearly all instances the 112 were words the texts labelled as "different from" the corresponding standard items. Maynes attempted to learn whether second-generation Arizona-born Spanish-speakers would give "standard" or "non-standard" responses when questioned (chiefly by means of Wörter und Sache techniques such as the naming of pictured objects but also by translating short sentences from English). The initial list of 112 was administered to a pilot group of five 6-8 year olds, five junior high students, and five adults ("persons 25 years or older"), but was pared down to just 50 items since "over half of the items were difficult to elicit because they did not lend themselves to questions or pictures. For example, the occupation of Mayor is excellent because standard Spanish yields 'alcalde,' while local Spanish yields 'mayor.' However, it is difficult to use a question or a picture to elicit this desired response." (p. 28) Similarly the primary-schoolers were eliminated altogether because those used in the pilot study "had difficulty with directions and interpreting pictures. It was believed that these difficulties were caused by their limited age and experience." (ibid.) Maynes' final sample population consisted of forty 12-15-year olds and forty adults, randomly chosen.

The author sought to determine whether differences existed between (1) the native Spanish vocabulary of adolescents and adults, and (2) "local Spanish vocabulary spoken in Arizona" and the "standard Spanish vocabulary used in Junior High School Spanish programs." (35) The parameters of the latter are presumably to be determined by drawing up a conflation of lexical items found in representative texts used in the schools attended by the sample adolescents; thus a corpus of items common to several texts could be said to constitute the school-approved "standard," and if we resolutely overlook for the purposes of the moment the possibility that a given corpus of words common to first-year textbooks will not resemble in all points a given corpus from a putative frequency list of spoken Spanish, we would be able to agree that any deviation from the textbook vocabulary conflation could be said to constitute deviation from a "standard" Spanish, and would thus put our stamp of approval upon a project which sought to elicit "local" responses to the items in the conflation. However, Maynes' "Derived Word List of 50 Words" (31-33) thoughtfully tells which of the "five Spanish instructional programs chosen for this study" (Baker 1966 and four texts such as El Camino real and El español al día) contain which of the 50 words, and a close look at the list clearly demonstrates that it is largely an extract of Barker/Baker/Barker "oddities" and just incidentally a conflation of Standard Spanish à la junior high: of the 50 forms, 17 appear in Baker only and 7 others in Baker and but one of the junior high texts, while only 19 forms appear in any four or all five of the five texts. Not surprisingly most of the 24 "non-junior high" forms are words of relatively low frequency: agujero, ahogar, almohada, bomba, buey, ciencia, cohete, inspeccionar, manojo, saxófono, tigre, tropezar and others.

Given, then, the a priori and thus essentially fraudulent nature of Maynes' wordlist (designed as it is largely to elicit the very same small number of Variants that Barker/Baker/Barker have decreed as representative of "Southwest Spanish"), it is not hard to guess that the following would be one of Maynes' chief conclusions: "there is a significant difference between the local Spanish used in Arizona by Junior High aged children . . . and the Spanish used in Junior High Spanish programs." (37) Of the 2,000 responses possible the junior-highers gave but 452 "standard forms." While their elders did a bit better on the test (of the 2,000, some 583 were "correct"), Maynes concludes the same thing about them ("significant difference between the local Spanish" etc.), although the fact that adults gave 131 more standard responses than did adolescents "suggests that adults become more language conscience [sic!] with maturity and life experience." (44)

Tables 5 and 6 (pp. 40-41) list "local responses" used in place of standard nouns and verbs (other "parts of speech" were not tested with the exception of the preposition para); these déjà vu variants reflect time-honored phonological trends and indicate "that subjects tended to: change pronunciation, shift stress, 'hispanicize' English words, shorten words, interchange vowels, substitute consonants, delete consonants or vowels or both, and made-up [sic] words." (41) Maynes occasionally counts as deviant some forms which most works label standard or else regional (chiefly Mexican) such as elote 'maíz,' sacar brillo 'dar lustre, embolar.'

This ill-informed, badly conceived and mendaciously executed dissertation in "education, curriculum development" is solely of interest for the noticia that Arizona adult Spanish discards some of the "variants" (Maynes never says which ones) that adolescents employ. In all other respects the work is not only of no value whatsoever but can truthfully be labelled retrogressive to the degree that it has perpetuated well-known myths about "Tex-Mex," "border Spanish" and the like. [RT]

TREJO, Arnulfo D. "Vocablos y modismos del español de Arizona."
  MA Thesis, Univ. de las Américas (Mexico City College), México, D.F., 1951. v, 92 pp.

The great value of this work rests in the fact that it is the best lexical source available on the nonstandrd Spanish of the Tucson area. Our major criticism is that this is a work that has been forced into a chapter and section format with little apparent motivation. Fortunately, the data are made more useable by a glossary (85-92) that gives the page references for each of the approximately 700 words and phrases cited.

The thesis contains four chapters: El español de los estudiantes (4-31), El lenguaje familiar (32-56), Las jergas profesionales (57-69), and El argot (70-79). The purpose of each chapter is quite unclear and the prose exposition tying together the various sections and subsections falls apart after the first chapter. Each chapter generally considers three kinds of forms: Anglicisms, modifications in form and/or meaning of standard Spanish, and regionalisms. Pachuco forms are especially prevalent in Chaps. 1 and 4.

The entries are cited in dialectal orthographic form and are given a fairly careful Spanish gloss. Grammatical information is usually ignored, although in Chap. 1 gender is specified for all English-derived nouns and complete conjugations are provided for three types of verbs borrowed from English. Many entries contain minor comparative comments, largely with regard to Mexican Spanish, and all Anglicisms are cited with the English word of origin. Also included are occasional notes on such matters as phonetic form, social usage, and regional variation. [GB]

4.6 ONOMASTICS (includes TOPONYMY)

Major Items: (none)

See also these items elsewhere (consult Author Index for location): (none)

BARNES, Will[iam] C. Arizona Place Names. 2nd ed. (revised and edited by Byrd H. Granger) (1935; Tucson: Univ. of Arizona Press, 1960). xix, 519 pp.

Described by its author as the product of more than thirty years' research and based in no small measure on a direct knowledge of the territory gained from long experience in the U.S. Forest Service and the U.S. Geographic Board, this work lists, locates and relates the origin of close to 4,000 names of settlements, mountains, rivers, promontories, escarpments and the like. Perhaps 10 per cent of the names are Spanish-origin; of these some are prosaic though descriptive (Cerro Gordo, Mesa, Sierra de la Espuma) while others are innovative and even surprising (there is thus an Adonde, an Ajo, a Bolsa de Plata [supposedly after an early explorer's hyperbolic descriptions of the size of the silver nuggets to be gotten there], and even an Aztlan). Inevitably some of the Spanish forms are Anglicized or otherwise corrupted (Mesa Redondo, Arastra Gulch, Canelo). At times Barnes' etymologies are fanciful or folkish, as with "Cienega, The . . . Sp., 'A marsh, a swamp.' The word . . . really means 'hundred springs,' 'cien,' hundred; 'agua,' water or springs. It was generally pronounced 'Sinicky' or 'Senicky' by the uninformed." (Various errors of this sort are corrected in Granger's revision.) [RT]

GRANGER, Bryd H. Grand Canyon Place Names. Tucson: Univ. of Arizona Press, 1960. 26 pp. [Rev. Names 9.143 (1961) (T.M. Pearce); Fody p. 533.]

The entries contained in this slender pamphlet derive from Barnes/Granger 1960, shorn of much of the supporting material so generously provided in the larger work. Some Hispanic names occur, but almost all seem to be of quite recent origin; the author provides an interesting account of the various appellations given to the Colorado River since first discovered by the Spaniards in the 16th century. [JC]

4.7 ENGLISH INFLUENCE ON SPANISH

Major Items: (none)

See also these items elsewhere (consult Author Index for location):
    POST-1917; TREJ-1951

4.8 SPANISH INFLUENCE ON ENGLISH

Major Items: (none)

See also these items elsewhere (consult Author Index for location):
    (none)

LYNN, Klonda. "Gringoisms in Arizona." AS 25.234-236 (1950).

A careless note by Lynn and four of her students at the Univ. of Arizona, Tucson, describing the pronunciation of several Spanish forms used in English around the campus. Eleven deliberate mispronunciations (often for comic effect) and six imitation pronunciations are cited. [GB]

4.8.1 ENGLISH OF THIS PARTICULAR HISPANIC GROUP

Major Items: LYNN-1940

See also these items elsewhere (consult Author Index for location):
    (none)

LYNN, Klonda. "A Phonetic Analysis of the English Spoken by
    Mexican Children in the Elementary Schools of Arizona."
    PhD Diss., Louisiana State Univ., 1940. ix, 307 pp.

Although wordy and repetitive, extremely limited in its scope and data base, and quite dated methodologically and theoretically, this work merits recognition as a serious and significant early study of the phonetics of nonstandard Chicano English, a still little researched speech variety explicitly identified by Lynn as a viable dialect of English in Arizona.
    The parts of this study are as follows. The "Introduction" (pp. 2-13) explains methodology, procedures, and coverage. Chap. 1, "The Problem of Mexican-English," (15-27) elaborates on the historical background and the current educational situation of Arizona Mexican Americans. Chap. 2, "The Phonetic Structure of

Castilian Spanish," (29-72) a long and detailed phonetic description, is derived primarily from the work of Navarro Tomás. Chap. 3, "The Phonetic Structure of Mexican-Spanish," (74-85) based almost solely on Post 1934 and Espinosa 1930a but supplemented with a half-hour recording made by Lynn, simply notes differences between Southwest Spanish and Castilian Spanish. Chap. 4, "Analysis of Mexican-English Dialect," (87-187) is the core of the work. The brief "Conclusion" (189-192) is followed by three appendices (194-302) containing a short sample transcription of Arizona Spanish, over 100 pages of sample English transcriptions from the corpus, and a phonograph recording of the data collected from one informant.

The corpus for the English analysis was the recorded reading of an 81-word list and brief story by 150 Chicano children in grades 3-8 in 25 elementary schools scattered throughout Arizona. The analysis chapter describes in detail the standard English sound system, noting for each "phoneme" its differences from Spanish and any deviations found in the corpus and attempting to explain each deviation as interference from Spanish. A small section deals unexcitingly with phonotactic, stress, and intonation problems. This chapter concludes with a "Remedial Suggestions" section that is almost a parody of a rigid phonetics-based audio-lingual approach: the child will learn standard English through careful repetition exercises and correction of errors.

The analysis is generally quite precise and accurate, although a few gaffes occur, most notably with regard to the writing system, e.g.: "Since the Mexican child knows little about the Spanish spelling, he does not confuse the use of [a labiodental nasal] with the n spelling as in the phrase one visit. In a phrase such as from far away he uses the labio-dental [nasal] in the word from as readily as does any native English speaker." (112) Or again: "There is a confusion of the use of the sounds with the orthographic spelling as in the word jam... where the orthographic j is given the sound of [the semiconsonant] (j)." (189)

Lynn's analysis amounts primarily to a precise phonetic catalog of deviations attributable to Spanish influence; additional possibilities of analysis are largely unexplored. Frequency of deviations by grade are summarized in tabular form for only a very few phenomena, but it is noted in the Conclusion that there is no decrease "with the increased age and skill of the speaker." (190) Although a personal history questionnaire was administered to each child, one finds neither the results nor the correlations of these sociolinguistic data with linguistic performance. [GB]

LYNN, Klonda. "Bilingualism in the Southwest." QJS 31.175-180 (1945).

This essay on the need for phonetic studies of Southwest Spanish and English as a basis for improving the teaching of oral and written English provides brief comments (pp. 179-180) drawn from Lynn 1940 on phonetic interference causing confusion of two sounds, replacement of sounds, orthographic problems, elision, and stress misplacement. [GB]

*PIALORSI, Frank Paul. "The Production and Recognition of Grammatical and Ungrammatical English Word Sequences by Bilingual Children." PhD Diss., Univ. of Arizona, 1973. 119 pp. [<u>DA</u> 34 (1973) 2930-2931-A.]

Pialorsi's study sought to "measure the variance between the recognition and production of bilingual fourth graders, to what extent the first language (Spanish) interfered with the second (English), and which patterns might yet be unlearned by both native English speakers and non-native English speakers." (Abstract) An ancillary task was the determination of any differences between Spanish-mother-tongue children attending bilingual or English-monolingual schools. To these ends Pialorsi tested "ninety native Spanish-speaking fourth grade pupils who had participated three or more years in any of three bilingual programs or any of two non-bilingual programs" in Tucson and in the border community of Nogales, Arizona for (1) their ability to ascertain the "correctness" of 34 multiple-choice items couched in standard English or "Hispanized" English and (2) their aptitude for "producing" standard English sequences (in this case, their ability to <u>translate</u> into English "the correct items of Part I in their Spanish equivalents"). Part I was also administered to twenty English-mother-tongue children of the same age and economic background.

Results yield few surprises: "the native English-speaking groups differed from the five Spanish-speaking groups in their Recognition performances" in that they had "less difficulty in identifying the correct basic sentence types presented." While there were no significant performance differences among the five Chicano groups, it appeared that "the non-bilingual program subjects performed higher on the Recognition scale" but at par level on the translation test.

Personal communication from the author reveals that various representative responses (presumably from Part II of the test) are included in the dissertation. This work will therefore be of interest to students of Chicano childhood English. [RT]

VAN METRE, Patricia Downer. "Syntactic Characteristics of Selected Bilingual Children." PhD Diss., Univ. of Arizona, Tucson, 1972. xiv, 162 pp. [<u>DA</u> 33 (1973) 5160-5161-A.]

In this study 32 Spanish-English bilingual and English monolingual third grade students in Tucson were subjected to an attempted replication of Carol Chomsky's testing of the acquisition of "ask/tell," "promise/tell," "easy to see," and pronominalization in English. The author found good correlations with reading tests, with the age-grading and other findings of Chomsky and, very surprisingly, next to no difference between the performance of bilinguals and monolinguals. This work provides no language data other than a few sample protocols. [GB]

4.9 SPANISH INFLUENCE ON AMERINDIAN LANGUAGES

Major Items: JOHN-J-1943; LIND-1971

See also these items elsewhere (consult Author Index for location):
BARB-1952; MILL-1959-60

DOCKSTADER, Frederick J. "Spanish Loanwords in Hopi: A Preliminary Checklist." IJAL 21.157-159 (1955).

From a collection of 4,500 Hopi words, 66 are listed here as being of possible Spanish origin. The entries include only an English gloss and a Spanish source word. The author briefly comments on the Spanish-Hopi contact history and speculates that the borrowings took place at an early date (17th century) or else indirectly via Rio Grande Indians at a later time. [GB]

ESPINOSA, Aurelio Macedonio. "La palabra 'Castilla' en la lengua de los indios hopis de Arizona." RFE 22.298-300 (1935).

This brief supplement to Espinosa 1932c discusses two additional archaic forms that he found in the town of Oraibi. Again, his main point is that the occurrence of [l] in the borrowing shows that the ll of the 16th and 17th centuries was a lateral, probably something like [ly]. [GB]

GREENFELD, Philip J. "Playing Card Names in Western Apache." IJAL 37.195-196 (1971).

A very brief note citing some 15 Spanish borrowings in the White Mountain Apache dialect. [GB]

HOIJER, Harry. "Chiricahua Loan-words from Spanish." Language 15.110-115 (1939).

A documentation of the slight influence of Spanish on Chiricahua Apache despite 300 years of contact. Hoijer finds in his dictionary "but 19 words of indisputable Spanish origin;" (p. 110) these items, 17 of which are nouns, are listed in unadorned fashion with an English gloss and the Spanish sourceword. He discusses the major phonological substitutions involved in the complete adaptation of the Spanish forms and provides interesting comments on the adaptation of the adjectives rico and loco as Chiricahua verbs. [GB]

HOIJER, Harry. "Linguistic and Cultural Change." Language 24.335-345 (1948). (Reprinted in Hymes 1964, pp. 455-462.)

A general essay with only passing reference to the influence of Spanish on Chiricahua Apache and Navajo. [GB]

HYMES, Dell H. "The Supposed Spanish Loanword in Hopi for 'Jaybird.'" IJAL 22.186-187 (1956).

Convincingly refutes the claim of Dockstader (1955) that [ʔáʔa] 'jaybird' is the reflex of Spanish [gayo] or [gaya], on two counts: (1) that proto-(Aztec-)Tanoan "had a form with - ʔa for jay, and the Hopi form . . . must presumably be connected as a reduplication;" (186) and that a large number of Western North American languages have words for raven, jay or crow whose apparently onomatopoeic segmentals generally have in common the association of a back consonant (k, q, ʔ) with a low central vowel (a). [RT]

JOHNSON, Jean Bassett. "A Clear Case of Linguistic Acculturation." AmA 45.427-434 (1943).

This splendid brief consideration of the broad issues of linguistic acculturation presents data from the Yaqui language of Arizona and Mexico showing phonological, lexical, and morpho-syntactic borrowings from Spanish. The morpho-syntactic discussion is especially perceptive. The exemplification is quite reduced. [GB]

LINDENFELD, Jacqueline. "Semantic Categorization as a Deterrent to Grammatical Borrowing: A Yaqui Example." IJAL 37.6-14 (1971). [Abs. LLBA v-771].

This intriguing report examines the influence of Spanish on the Yaqui language of Arizona and Mexico with regard to comparative constructions. Three types of such constructions are cursorily described: Spanish, native Yaqui, and Spanish-influenced Yaqui. Most of the article is a probe of semantic reasons (utilizing a generative semantics/semantic feature approach) for the failure of Yaqui to borrow the comparative of inferiority. [GB]

PERRY, Edgar (Jaa Bilataha), Canyon Z. Quintero, Sr., Catherine D. Davenport and Corrine B. Perry. <u>Western Apache Dictionary</u>. Fort Apache, Arizona: White Mountain Apache Culture Center/ White Mountain Apache Tribe, 1972. xii, 135 pp.

Appendix 3 of this work contains a subsection listing without comment 22 "Words Derived from Spanish." (p. 122) [GB]

SPICER, Edward H. "Linguistic Aspects of Yaqui Acculturation." <u>AmA</u> 45.410-426 (1943).

This good but hesitant treatment of Spanish loanwords in Arizona Yaqui gives the typical historical sketch of the contact situation and considers three major groups of borrowings (household material objects, social organization, and ritual), cultural contexts in which about 65% of the vocabulary is derived from Spanish. Spicer also comments on the phonological and morphological adaptation of loans and their implications for establishing the time of introduction and on some semantic changes involved in borrowing. The examples scattered throughout the article are almost solely nouns, but several verb, adjective, and conjunction borrowings are noted. (p. 412) [GB]

TITIEV, Mischa. "Suggestions for the Further Study of Hopi." <u>IJAL</u> 12.89-91 (1946).

This minor note on the Hopi language mentions several loanwords, including three from Spanish (<u>lanza, carnero, caballo</u>). [GB]

5. [CHICANOS:] TEXAS

5.1 BIBLIOGRAPHY (nothing to report)

5.2 COMPREHENSIVE/GENERAL STUDIES; MISCELLANY; ANTHOLOGIES/ FESTSCHRIFTEN

Major Items: LANC-1969; REYN-1973; SANC-1972

See also these items elsewhere (consult Author Index for location): EVAN-1971; WHIT-1972

BLANCO, George M. "Teaching Spanish as a Standard Dialect in Grades 7-12: A Rationale for a Fundamental-Skills Approach." PhD Diss., Univ. of Texas, Austin, 1971. vi, 199 pp. [DA 32 (1972) 6259-A.]

This rather decent examination of the socio-culturo-linguistic aspects of teaching standard Spanish in Texas high schools is authored by an experienced administrator in the Texas Education Agency. Of greatest interest linguistically is Chap. 4, which presents "Some Elements of Texas Spanish and Exercises for Teaching Standard-dialect Equivalencies." (pp. 143-173) The language description in this chapter is not very substantive; the exercises are very audio-lingual in orientation. Blanco's bibliography (188-199) will be useful for the educator concerned with this problem. [GB]

CHILDERS, Jean. "Some Secondary Level Curriculum Considerations for Teaching Spanish to the Mexican American in Austin, Texas." MA Thesis, Univ. of Texas, Austin, 1971. v, 143 pp. [Available EDRS: ED 060 737; RIE 7:7.75 (July 1972).]

The purpose of this thesis is "to present curriculum considerations for the non-native who is interested in teaching [standard] Spanish to the Mexican American on a secondary level" (p. 2). The author considers classroom approaches and procedures and reviews available materials, especially Baker 1966, Barker 1970, and Arce et al. 1970. No linguistic raw data are provided other than a few examples on pp. 33-34 taken from Elías Olivares 1970. Appendix B (121-132) contains a noteworthy "Sample Questionnaire to determine Listening, Speaking, Reading, Writing, and Spelling Levels of Mexican American Students in Austin, Texas." [GB]

GARCÍA, Anita H. "Identification and Classification of Types of Common Deviations from Standard Spanish Made by Representative Native Speakers in South Texas." MA Thesis, Texas A & I Univ., Kingsville, 1969. 110 pp.

The title of this thesis effectively describes its contents. While rich in materials, García's work is haphazardly organized:

following a review of the literature (pp. 6-17) one finds a chapter on "Phonological and Orthographical Characteristics" whose largely unanalyzed entries are arranged, alphabetically, in three columns: "standard," "pronounced" and "written" (e.g., "leer/leyér/leyer"). Next García presents a chapter on "Morphological Characteristics" which deals with the lexicon, presented in word-list form. One finds first an embarassing <u>richesse</u> of Anglicisms (pp. 75-89, 307 entries), which are complemented (pp. 90-102) by 265 Mexicanisms, <u>pachuquismos</u> and ordinary phonological variants which García lumps together as "Other Barbarisms."

The raw material for this study was obtained from the author's high school Spanish classes in San Benito, Texas. [RT]

*GARCÍA, Fray Bartolomé. <u>Manual para administrar los santos sacramentos de penitencia, eucharistia, extrema-uncion, y matrimonio: dar gracias despues de comulgar, y ayudar a bien morir a los Indios de la Naciones: Pájalates, Orejones, Pacaos, Pacóas, Tilijayas, Alasapas, Pausanes, y otras muchas diferentes, que se hallan en las Missiones del Rio de San Antonio, y Rio Grande, pertenecientes â el Colegio de la Santissima Cruz de la Ciudad de Queretaro, como son: Los Pacuâches, Mescâles, Pampôpas, Tâcames, Chayopînes, Venados, Pamâques, y toda la Juventud de Pihuiques, Borrados, Sanipaos, y Manos de Perro. Compuesto por el P. Fr. Bartholome Garcia, Predicador Apostólico, y actual Missionero de la Mission de N.S.P.S. Francisco de dicho Colegio, y Rio de San Antonio, en la Provincia de Texas.</u> Impresso con las Licencias necessarias en la Imprenta de los Herederos de Dona Maria de Rivera, en la calle de San Bernardo, y esquina de la Plazuela de el Volador. Ano de 1760. [For locations and a résumé of contents v.s. Spell 1925-26.] [RT]

GILBERT, Glenn G., ed. <u>Texas Studies in Bilingualism: Spanish, French, German, Czech, Polish, and Norwegian in the Southwest, with a Concluding Chapter on Code-switching and Modes of Speaking in American Swedish.</u> Studia Linguistica Germanica, Herausgegeben von Ludwig Erich Schmitt und Stefan Sonderegger, 3 (Berlin: Walter de Gruyter, 1970). 223 pp. [Rev. Bills 1974 pp. 108-109.]

A collection of papers primarily describing individual languages in their bilingual contexts, but dealing very little with bilingualism per se. Annotated herein are the three articles dealing with Spanish: Coltharp 1970, Poulter 1970, and Sawyer 1970. [GB]

HATCHER, Mattie Austin. "Plan of Stephen F. Austin for an
   Institute of Modern Languages at San Felipe de Austin."
   THAQ 12.231-239 (1909).

   This descendant of Stephen Austin recounts a plan he presented
in 1831 or 1832 during his term of service as deputy for Texas in
the (Mexican) Congress of Coahuila and Texas. In those days Texas
seemed to be lacking in schools altogether, but Austin was especially atuned to the need for a school to teach Anglo colonists
Spanish. The following is part of the author's translation of
Austin's plan, first written in Spanish: "The colonies . . .
begin to find themselves in that advanced state which demands the
establishment of certain institutions . . . Among these, public
schools for the teaching of modern languages, and especially that
of Spanish, are of prime importance. These colonies are composed
of both foreigners and Mexicans; and the necessity for disseminating the national language [Spanish] among the former is evident.
They themselves are fully convinced of this necessity . . . "
(p. 235) [RT]

LANCE, Donald M., ed. (and chief contributor). A Brief Study of
   Spanish-English Bilingualism. (Final Report, Research
   Project ORR-Liberal Arts-15504.) Bethesda, Maryland: U.S.
   Dept. of HEW/EDRS, 1969. 104 pp. Available EDRS:ED 032 529.
   (Cf. Lance 1970 [rpt. 1972].) (The author's chapters 4 and
   5, "Dialectal and Nonstandard Forms in Texas Spanish" and
   "Spanish-English Code Switching" appear in revised form
   in HERN/etal-1975, pp. 37-51 and pp. 138-153.

   This important examination of the substance and the nuances
of language behavior within three generations of one Mexican-
American family in the east-central Texas city of Bryan is chiefly
the work of Prof. Lance but also contains work by two of his
graduate students.
   The first selection, "Discussion of Research Procedures and
General Observations Regarding Bilingualism," (pp. 1-16; Lance),
offers an anecdotal discussion of the research team's experiences
and points out the sociological implications of the various speaker-listener relationships involved; a handy summary of its findings is given on pp. 91-92 in Ch. 6, "Conclusions and Implications." (Lance) Selection no. 2 (Gail M. Smith, "Some Comments
on the English of Eight Bilinguals," 17-24) makes the claim that
"very little of [the non-standard English of the family's young
children] can be attributed to interference from Spanish," (17)
and that most mistakes are either the product of "arrested
language development" or are reflections of parental speech
patterns. Peripherically relevant to Mexican-American speech is
the third selection (by Barbara T. Ward) which reports on the
English errors of four students from the Dominican Republic and
compares these with the non-standard features of the English of
young Texas Chicano migrants, as reported by GONZ-1969-b.

It is in the fourth and fifth chapters, both by Lance ("Dialectal and Nonstandard Forms in Texas Spanish" and "The Mixing of English and Spanish") that we arrive at the heart of the work. Of the two, Ch.5 is the more original, as the other selection is essentially a digest of earlier findings on Texas Spanish variants, to which a list of forms elicited from Lance's informants is added. In the section on "mixing" (code-switching), Lance presents detailed evidence that "when Mexican-Americans mix English and Spanish together in the same sentence the result is not, as some have claimed, a creolized language but instead a very relaxed and arbitrary switching of codes, both of which are available for use at any time. The switching occurs not because the speaker does not know the right word but because the word that comes out is more readily available at the time of production." (93) [RT]

LANCE, Donald M. "The Codes of the Spanish-English Bilingual."
TESOLQ 4.343-351 (1970). [Abs. LLBA V-839] (Rpt. in Spolsky [1972], pp. 25-36.)

Here Lance gives a popularized encapsulation of the Bryan, Texas bilingualism-within-one-family project which he directed (v. s. LANC-1969) Much attention is paid to the history of each informant's linguistic development and considerable description is given of the difficulties attendant upon interviewing the family's children who, as English-dominants, refused to talk Spanish with Prof. Lance and were also reluctant to do so with the research team's bilingual Mexican-American secretary, who was a stranger to them. Lance draws the following conclusion: "In the case of the children . . . their contact with the surrounding community as a whole has apparently conditioned them to consider English as the appropriate medium of communication outside the immediate family environment, and any deviation from this expectation is so anomalous as to impede natural linguistic performance on their part." (p. 350) The educational implication of this is that "many school children with Spanish surnames have developed cultural orientations that do not fit neatly into stereotyped categories," and so "school populations in the Southwest simply are not globally differentiable . . . into two separate groups, the Mexican-American and the Anglo." (351) As a consequence, bilingual programs might not be favorably received by all Chicano youngsters, at least not at the outset. [RT]

[anon.] Los pastores: A Christmas Drama of Old Mexico. San Antonio: Treviño Brothers Printing Company, 1949. 168 pp.[TSBJr.]

This volume (available only from the Yale Univ. library) presents the five-part pastoral drama as remembered from a childhood in Mexico by one Leandro Granados, forty years a San Antonio resident when the unnamed editors of this volume helped him with the transcription, which in the original (Granados) version was an "amalgama of songs and dialogues, without unity and without dramatic interest [and written] in a very bad orthography. For instance, Hunibersario in the Preface . . . meant 'Aniversario' --Anniversary-- etc." (p. 2) The editors thus "have tried to amend the orthography, and to arrange the scenes in chronological order [but] have kept all the movements, scenes, words, songs, etc. intact." (ibid.) An English translation appears alongside the Spanish version, which is given without notes, commentary or glossary. Several pictures of San Antonio performances accompany the text. Editorial purification notwithstanding, occasional cacographs survive, e.g., "Adios, linda Paridita, dueña de mi corazón, de ti se aparta Gilita, héchale tu bendición," (69) and "Te ofresco Niñito / el rico collar, / y este rosarito / que acabo de rezar." (70) [RT]

LOWRIE, Samuel H. Culture Conflict in Texas, 1821-1835. New York: Columbia Univ. Press, 1932. 191 pp. [TSBJr.]

Written originally as a doctoral dissertation for Columbia, Lowrie's work is oriented chiefly towards history and sociology though language is discussed briefly: on pp. 120-121 we read that Anglo leader Stephen Austin "was very anxious that his younger brother learn to speak and write Spanish well, because, as he wrote him, all 'hopes of rising in this country depend on learning to speak and write the language correctly' [letter dated July 1832]." Austin was reputed to speak Spanish well himself, and as a result "was appealed to again and again for assistance in clearing up embarrassing situations in which Americans found themselves as a consequence on their inability to present their cases to the authorities." [RT]

MARROCCO, Mary Ann Wilkinson. "The Spanish of Corpus Christi, Texas." PhD Diss., Univ. of Illinois, Champaign-Urbana, 1972. 502 pp. [DA 34 (1973) 751-752-A.]

The author proposes a complete examination of the phonology, grammar and lexicon of the Spanish spoken in this South Texas city of 200,000 persons (roughly 45 per cent Mexican-American). She also attempts to investigate the theoretical problem of whether "Corpus Christi Spanish" is a separate dialect or whether it is identical to (and thus an extension of) an Hispanic dialect spoken elsewhere, most probably in Mexico.

Marrocco's dissertation is invaluable as a veritable course in Hispanic-American dialectology. Each of her three main chapters contains an average of fifty footnotes, most of which compare and contrast the "non-standard" features of Corpus Christi Spanish with similar or related deviances observed in all parts of Spanish America by most of the well-known Hispanic dialectologists.

As a theoretical construct and as a trustworthy examination of the Spanish of Corpus Christi, however, Marrocco's work is less than satisfactory. This is particularly apparent when one compares some of the generalizations appearing at the end of the three main chapters and again in Ch. 6 ("Conclusions," pp. 298-304) with the transcription of interviews which appears in Appendix A (311-480). One example: on p. 301 we read that "Among morphological features which have supplanted standard Spanish usage are the almost exclusive use of the masculine gender . . . " Turning to the chapter on morphology for confirmation of this rather eye-opening statement we find 23 examples of "feminine nouns with masculine article," (116) ten of which were uttered by informant number 3, Roberto, whom Marrocco describes as an adolescent whose attendance at an Anglo high school "has its consequences on his native tongue . . . His mother . . . is very conscious of Roberto's speaking substandard Spanish, and Roberto was not allowed to continue as my informant for that reason." (9) On the following page of the same chapter Marrocco states: "It is evident that different criteria are used in Corpus Christi to select the gender of a noun than those of Standard Spanish. For example: 1) -ción (or -sión) terminations are invariably masculine in Corpus Christi whereas they are feminine in Standard Spanish." (117) But a random check through two sets of three consecutive pages of Appendix A (informants 1, 324-326, and 4, 376-379) revealed seven examples of feminine -ción and only one example of the "invariably masculine" -ción.

Nor can one take Marrocco at her word in purely theoretical conclusions, especially when these are unsupported by any sociolinguistic or historical investigation, as is the case with her explanations of why Corpus Christi Spanish is not in full conformity with any one Mexican dialect. On p. 299 we are told that "The immigration from Mexico [to Corpus Christi] did not provide the necessary impetus for language change because the language already spoken in South Texas was so firmly established that it took precedence over that of the newly-arrived immigrants. So that the immigrant could adapt himself to his new environment, the replacement of the distinctive features of his dialect with those of the Corpus Christi dialect was necessary." On this same page, however, and by way of support for her theory, Marrocco adduces comments from Canfield 1968 (p. 72) which seem to contradict the foregoing: "Dr. Canfield asserts that 'Arizona, California, and Texas, if they resemble any other settlement, are reflections of an earlier type of Andalusian Spanish imported bodily from Mexico in more recent times. In a sense they are Spanish of 1850-1950 from Mexico, while New Mexico represents 1600-50 from Spain."

Marrocco's conclusion vis à vis phonology is that Corpus Christi Spanish is closest to "lowland" and even Caribbean dialects, but that by and large it forms part of that vague continuum known as "general rural Spanish." While the latter statement cannot be disputed in a study nearly all of whose informants are of lower class origins with no formal training in Spanish, it is still too early to accept the author at her word as to the representative nature of her phonological samples, since all that the 169 pages of transcript present are: individual interviews with three persons (two English-dominant adolescents and a widely-travelled high school Spanish teacher); a group conversation between four informants from the same family; and the speech of one television performer and the small collection of advertisers, musicians and talk-show participants who took part in a pair of his two-hour-long programs. [RT]

MAZEIKA, Edward John. "A Descriptive Analysis of the Language of a Bilingual Child." PhD Diss., Univ. of Rochester [New York], 1971. xi, 257 pp. [DA 32 (1971) 1497-A.]

Mazeika describes and then compares the English-Spanish language systems of a bilingual middle-class Mexican-American child of 26-31 months; he also compares both of these systems with the speech of a monolingual English-speaking child. His study is patterned after Ruth Weir's Language in the Crib (1962); it is with Weir's results that the comparisons are made. Mazeika thus seeks to determine whether these comparisons would reveal any degree of inter-lingual transfer within the bilingual child and also whether an examination of this sort would tell anything about the developmental nature of child language itself.

Among conclusions pertinent to Mexican-American child bilingualism: "the late development of the slit fricatives /θ, ð, v/ and the affricate /ǰ/ in [the child] Carlito's English may be a function of their absence in Mexican-Spanish phonology" (p. vii); "there is slight evidence that being bilingual may be beneficial when one can select words that are easier to articulate from either language and insert [them] in interchangeable slots," (ibid.) an example of this "advantage" being the child's systematic substitution of con for with in otherwise all-English sentences; that the English feature of vowel reduction under weak stress ("schwah") had phased itself out of the child's Spanish by age 30 months (p. 34); that the child's English and Spanish consonant systems likewise maintained their separate phonological integrities despite occasional intraphrasal code-switching; and that within the total recorded corpus "the proportion of Spanish vocabulary (35 per cent) to English (64) is very close to [the mother's] estimate of 40 per cent" as the amount of Spanish she spoke to her son. [RT]

*MC CLINTON, Johnnie W. "Effectiveness of a Bilingual Vocational-Technical Developmental Program." PhD, Univ. of Missouri, Columbia, 1972. 113 pp. [DA 34 (1973) 2307-2308-A.] Pages 103-134, previously copyrighted material [English version of the Stanford Achievement Test, High School Level, Forms X and W, 1965] not microfilmed at request of author. Available for consultation at the Univ. of Missouri Library at Columbia.

McClinton sought to evaluate the effectiveness of the program at the Harlingen (lower Rio Grande valley) Texas State Technical Institute campus "through achievement testing in both English and idiomatic Spanish languages." (Abstract) Among matters researched: "Do the Mexican-American students express their competencies better in 'Tex-Mex' [sic] than in English upon entering training?" To this end "the Numerical Competence, Reading and Technical Comprehension Tests of the Stanford Achievement Test . . . was translated into idiomatic Spanish" and then administered entering students. "The Mexican-American students began the training program expressing their numerical competencies equally well in both languages. In Reading and Technical Comprehension, they express themselves at a significantly higher level in English." Post-testing revealed some gain in Spanish "but the most gain was in English version tests." The conclusion is that "except for special cases, achievement testing should continue using standardized English version tests, since the Mexican-American student can express his competencies at least as well through written English as through written Spanish [understandably so, lacking previous training in the latter]." Those curious will want to consult this dissertation directly to learn the exact nature of the Spanish chosen to represent a sort of post-adolescent South Texas Chicano standard. [RT]

MELLENBRUCH, Julia Ida Klattenhoff. "Teaching Spanish to Spanish-speaking Students in Texas High Schools." MA Thesis, Univ. of Texas, Austin, 1954. v, 91 pp.

This sensitive but very bland and unimportant work discusses the inadequacies of Spanish-as-a-foreign-language materials (pp. 8-22) and offers proposals for materials and classroom techniques (23-82) couched in a mild prescriptivist tone. There are no language data other than minimal exemplification of two types of "errors": archaisms (21) and Anglicisms (44). A listing of grammatical items requiring instruction (75-78) indicates an awareness of typical problems but provides no explicit reference to the nonstandard language needing "correction." [GB]

MICHEL, Joseph. "A Pilot Project for Recording the Speech of the Five-Year Old Texas Spanish-English Pre-School Bilingual Child." FFLR 7.15-17, 20 (Fall 1969).

A very thorough summary of the fieldwork techniques used by Michel and four of his students at the Univ. of Texas-Austin in their attempt to elicit a corpus large enough to permit specific conclusions about pre-school Chicano language to be drawn. The researchers' thorough and candid descriptions allow future fieldworkers to profit greatly from the mistakes made; thus it is readily allowed that the children's interest flagged, that intimacy was hard to achieve ("Initially, the child was petrified" [p. 17]), and that many of the advantages of the at-home interviewing were cancelled by the inevitable distractions and background noises. Children were allowed to speak either language in the "dialog portion" of the interviews. Page 17 gives a very brief taxonomy of errors and general comments (the products of the initial analysis). For the most complete summary of the project's findings see Cornejo 1969. [RT]

MONTEMAYOR, Elsa Diana. "A Study of the Spanish Spoken by Certain Bilingual Students of Laredo, Texas." MA Thesis, Texas Woman's Univ., Denton, 1966. v, 106 pp.

Another attempt to demonstrate, by means of identifying various "non-standard dialectal elements" and then proving their contemporaneous usage elsewhere in the Hispanic world or their previous usage in medieval Spanish, that a particular brand of Texas Spanish "is not a 'border jargon,' but that it is basically the same as that spoken in Spain and other Spanish-speaking locales." (p. iii) To accomplish this, Montemayor took random notes on the Spanish of 300 Laredo highschoolers, presumably all students in her Spanish classes. She then compared her findings with those of other dialectologists, chiefly Aurelio Espinosa 1930a and 1946. Given Montemayor's focus and her frequent references to Espinosa, formal parallels with the later's work are inevitable: after a brief discussion of the ambient of the border city one finds a bulky chapter entitled "Dialect of Laredo" dealing chiefly with "Words Which Suffer Phonetic Changes," (21-48) such as prothesis, epenthesis, epithesis, apheresis, syncope, apocope, metathesis, dissimilation, etc. Following that are sections on archaisms, words of Indian origin, "Mexicanisms," Anglicisms, and "Pachuco."

In between prodigal references to other authors and other lands, one occasionally encounters information of a certain novelty, e.g., that "the word méndigo is a derogatory term" roughly synonymous with mean or lousy, with reference to persons. (p. 26) All in all, 162 words receive comment. [RT]

PEÑA, Albar Antonio. "A Comparative Study of Syntactical Structures of the Oral Language Status in Spanish and English of Disadvantaged First Grade Spanish-Speaking Children." PhD Diss., Univ. of Texas, Austin, 1967. ix, 142 pp. (Cooperative Research Project 2638, Part of the San Antonio Language Research Project, sponsored by the U.S. Office of Education and the College of Education, the Univ. of Texas, Austin.) [DA 28 (1968) 3903.]

One of the purposes of Peña's research was to ascertain the degree to which Anne Stemmler's Language Cognition Test (LCT) [Unpublished Research Edition, The Univ. of Texas, Austin, 1967, Mimeographed] would elicit statistically-significant samples of the Spanish and the English of six-year-old first-grade children living in poverty on the west side of San Antonio, Texas. Conceptual and methodological bases for the LCT derived from the findings of Bettelheim, Chomsky, Piaget, Reissman and Stockwell/Bowen/Martin; the analysis of the subjects' syntax follows the latter's model

(The Grammatical Structures of English and Spanish [1965]).
Basically the LCT elicits language by stimulating children to "tell everything they can" about objects, pictures, etc.

While Peña concludes that the LCT "did yield evidence of oral language judging by the considerable number of responses obtained in each linguistic category for each subject," (p. 108) and that in addition "it was possible to analyze and classify the responses according to their syntactical characteristics" by employing a sort of checklist (the "Linguistic Analysis Form") that synthesized Stockwell/Bowen/Martin, "the extremely fundamental nature of the basic sentences and the few transformations employed in the linguistic categories contained in the Linguistic Analysis Form did not, apparently, permit linguistic distinctions among the groups to be arrived at statistically." (ibid.) Also not found in Peña are any samples of either the children's English or their Spanish. This dissertation will thus be of slight interest to persons seeking information about Texas Chicano language; but lest this judgment sound overly harsh it is crucial to point out that Peña's chief concern was pedagogical and not linguistic. [RT]

RAMÍREZ, María Irene. "A Comparison of Three Methods of Teaching the Spanish-speaking Student." EdD Diss., East Texas State Univ., 1971. xiii, 75 pp. [DA 32 (1972) 5477-A.]

A simplistic study of the English language performance of 118 third grade children in four Laredo schools who had been and were being taught in three different programs: traditional, bilingual, and English as a second language. Group comparisons were merely based on results from the Comprehensive Test of Basic Skills, administered in the fall and again in the spring so as to measure improvement. The traditional method proved most effective in this naive experiment. No specific language data are included. [GB]

REYNA, José Reynaldo. "Mexico-American Prose Narrative in Texas: The Jest and the Anecdote." PhD Diss., Univ. of California, Los Angeles, 1973. viii, 294 pp. [DA 34 (1973) 3428-A.]

This valuable and pace-setting study represents the first (and to our knowledge the only) full-length analysis/anthology of Chicano jokes and longer "anecdotes." Reyna's 206 selections, recorded in 1969 and 1970 in Fort Worth, Corpus Christi, various small towns and ranch locations and representing the repertoires of thirteen males and six females who ranged in age from 15 to 84 (all Texas-born or long-time Texas residents) are classified according to such traditional categories as inter-sexual jest, perico jokes, blason populaire, lies and exaggerations, cleverness, numbskull jokes, and "jokes based on misunderstandings of language." The latter category is a critical one for what it reveals about the cultural circumstances of Texas Mexican-Americans who find themselves "in between" the worlds of the Anglo-American and the Mexican; thus many "language" tales involve an Anglo "portrayed as the immigrant who is unfamiliar with the language and customs of the native Texans and who commits the kinds of mistakes that any foreigner in a new country would commit," (p. 6) a reflection of the Tejano's view of Anglos as interlopers in an historically Hispanic province, while other jokes involve a "mexicano del otro lao" who commits lapses through ignorance of English ("But this does not necessarily reflect a willingness on the part of Mexican Americans to indulge in self-denigration, for one of the extremely important features of Mexican American culture is its bilingualism" [ibid.]).

Reyna notes certain trends among Tejano tale-telling: while the theme of Anglo-Chicano culture clash and especially "border conflict" was extremely popular in earlier decades, it is now being replaced by other themes (such as "language misunderstandings") which reflect in part the current "great preoccupation . . . with the struggle for cultural survival." (5) Other language jokes involving "solecisms, malapropisms, turns of phrases and double entendres" have always been enjoyed and do not usually depend upon ethnic themes for humor; "these are significant inasmuch as they are further indication of the importance of verbal expression in Mexican American culture, a feature which is not recognized by Anglo educators and social scientists." (7)

Language itself is examined briefly on pp. 12-15. Reyna's transcriptional style is conventionally Hispanic but allowance is made for dialectalisms (trajieron, güevo, 'tonces, li ice 'le dice,' and so forth); one regrets the author's decision not to include a lexicon, for although most Hispanists will have no trouble understanding nearly all of the material, comprehension will sometimes be stymied by words like guayacán and terremote (terremoto?). Some new information is given in this section: the special use of 'No, hombre' in a strictly affirmative sense equivalent to the English "I sure do!" (14)

This dissertation has made an invaluable contribution to our knowledge of the sociolinguistic circumstances of the Texas Chicano and constitutes "must" reading for all serious Hispanists. [RT]

ROOTS, Floy. "Methods and Materials for Teaching Spanish to Spanish-speaking Students in Texas High Schools." MA Thesis, Univ. of Texas, Austin, 1936. vi, 175 pp.

Basically an examination of the Spanish abilities of segregated classes of native Spanish- and English-speakers through a one-year course in San Benito, Texas, this thoughtful and studious work should be of special importance, not entirely historical, to the linguist concerned with this still unheeded educational problem. Dealt with in order are (a) an overview of the problem, with laudably careful pan-Southwest references and survey responses from various schools in the Rio Grande Valley, (b) the pretesting of the students at the beginning of the year, (c) a detailed discussion of the author's goals and curriculum plans, and (d) a comparison of the performances of the two groups that leads to the primary conclusion that a one-year course for Spanish speakers can be equivalent to a two-year course for speakers of English.

Although this work is most remarkable for these educational aspects, a modicum of linguistic data is also presented. A section (pp. 43-63) on the "Language Knowledge of the Spanish-speaking Pupils" has listed (in quite unsophisticated fashion) a variety of phonetic "errors," Anglicisms, deviant vocabulary, items nonstandard grammatical forms, and a few other aberrancies, including several examples of nonstandard English constructions.
[GB]

SÁNCHEZ, Rosaura. "Nuestra circunstancia lingüística." El Grito 6:1.45-74 (Fall 1972).

This satisfying and highly seminal article reports upon variation from standard norms in the Spanish written and spoken by 30 Mexican-American students at the University of Texas-Austin. The author, herself Chicano, argues strongly for Chicano retention of Spanish ("para sentir que lo nuestro tiene tanto valor como lo de cualquiera"--p. 46), and while she defends the right of each speaker to set essentially anarchic standards for individual or in-group speech, she nonetheless insists that "lo más factible sería aceptar el español standard ya existente de esta región, o sea el español standard del norte de México," (49) given the extreme unlikelihood that the various Chicano hablas populares (of which there are many, according to region, age, sex, social class or even political opinion; for a vivid exemplification of four of these ["un vato loco," "unas comadres," "una jovencita," "un Chicano militante"] see p. 48) will achieve the coherence or the force necessary to form a single standard dialect capable of winning recognition as such.

After relating the concepts "bilingualism" and "diglossia" to Chicano realities and then discussing the conceptual impoverishment of some sub-dialects (Sánchez's example: the extreme degree to which agarrar has displaced more than a dozen verbs meaning 'to take, get, achieve, embrace, detain, enjoy'), the author documents various phonetic changes typical of Texas Spanish and also found elsewhere (aphaeresis, sineresis, diphthong reduction, opening or closing of vowels, prothesis, metathesis, aspiration, lenition, simplification, etc.) and then presents what is probably her most neoteric material, an analysis of Texas verbal syntax (pp. 55-59): descriptively discussed are local tendencies to substitute progressive tenses for simple ones (both present and and imperfect), to limit the paratactic future to indications of probability (whereas futurity itself is usually expressed through ir plus infinitive), to eliminate the word-initial syllable of había in anterior past constructions and to produce bía or iba comido in consequence, and to substitute imperfect forms for conditional (a closely related matter is the dialects' fourfold handling

of "if-and-result" sentences: Si tuviera mil dólares yo fuera
a Europa/Si tuviera . . . yo iba/Si tenía . . . yo fuera/Si tenía
. . . yo iba [see pp. 58-59]). Texas subjunctive usage is on the
decline and thus increasingly at variance with pan-Hispanic norms:
while ojalá/ojalá y and other expressions of hoping invariably take
the subjunctive, "en frases introducidas por verbos de influencia
no hay uniformidad de uso [e.g., 'Quería que me paraba']," (58)
and the indicative is the rule after expressions of doubt or negation, as it likewise is (although to a lesser extent) in adverbial clauses. Sánchez's section on verbal morphology (59-62)
presents a wealth of dialectal detail which must be seen to be
appreciated. Also commented upon are pronominal usage (tú is crowd-
ing out Ud. especially among the young, while nosotros is even
used with sole reference to women), assignment of gender (usually
analogical ['la sistema'] and increasingly arbitrary) and patterns
of gender and number (frequent lack of concordance).

Sánchez's sections on English interference (65-70) and code-
switching (71-74) form articles unto themselves and can only be
recommended here; especially note-worthy (although perhaps debat-
able in some particulars) is her descriptive discussion of restrictions placed on switching. [RT]

SPELL, Lota M. "The First Text Book Used in Texas." SWHQ 29.
   289-295 (1925-26).

   Spell summarizes the contents of a small and rare volume,
printed in Mexico City in 1760, for whose full title v.s. GARC-B-
1760. In a footnote (p. 289) we learn that "a copy of this work
is in the Texas State Library, Austin, Texas. A reprint may be
found in the Boletín del Instituto Bibliográfico mexicano, número
10 (Mexico, 1910), 543-512 [sic]. It may also be found in the
fifth part of Nicolas Leon's Bibliografía Mexicana (Mexico, 1910)."
(ibid.) The work, intended to serve as a guide and handbook,
consists chiefly of questions "suitable for the missionary to use
in his daily work of civilizing and converting the natives of the
region;" (289-290) the text is arranged in parallel columns of
Spanish and "Indian" (in this case, the "Texas or Coahuiltecan
language," which seems to have served as a sort of lingua franca
for the circum-San Antonio region). The balance of Spell's
article details the types of questions priests were supposed to
ask in the confessional; among other things we learn that attempts
were made to uproot the peyote habit, and that "some of the dances
were sanctioned by the church, but of all forms of dancing the
mitote was in greatest disfavor [as] it figured in many drunken
revels." (293)

   García's handbook will be of interest for the information it
provides about the type of learned Spanish first brought to Texas.
[RT]

WOLFF DE PORRAS, Normina. "Anomalías lingüísticas en el español de un grupo de estudiantes bilingües." MA Thesis, Univ. of Texas, El Paso, 1971. 77 pp.

A short but well-handled study of the non-standard forms the author found in 43 short Spanish-language compositions written by bilingual Chicano students at the El Paso campus as part of a sociolinguistic study of southwestern bilingualism sponsored by Prof. Jacob Ornstein and others (see ORNS-v.d.). Wolff first lists and briefly discusses "morfología y gramática" (pp. 16-24) and then "variantes de orden lexical [sic, 'léxico']" (25-52); subsumed under the latter are "reducción de diptongos a una sola vocal," "metátesis," "la vocal $\underline{e}$ usada en lugar de la $\underline{i}$," etc., along with several sections cataloging the inevitable "English influences" and a rather long list of "confusiones ortográficas;" outstanding here are the interchanges of $\underline{s}$ $\underline{z}$ $\underline{c}$, $\underline{b}$ $\underline{v}$, $\underline{j}$ $\underline{g}$, and the like. Wolff's conclusions are thoughtful and reflect the ideas of Gumperz, Ornstein and others: while some of the variants are indubitably the products of English interference, others cannot be traced to English but appear rather to reflect "un simple control débil del idioma" (54) or else the special "norms" that bilingualism itself establishes. The greatest amount of "variety" turned up in the morphology of the verb. Lack of more than sketchy training in Spanish composition is reflected in the mediocre to low level of work produced by students whose command of spoken Spanish is relatively good. Wolff's thesis reproduces as "Apéndice 'A'" the "Sociolinguistic Background Questionnaire: A Measurement Instrument for the Study of Bilingualism" by Bonnie Brooks, Jacob Ornstein and others of the El Paso school. [RT]

5.2.1 SOCIOLINGUISTICS

Major Items: GARC-N-1971; JORD-R-1973; PATE-1971; PATE/KUVL-1973; SKRA-1967/70; THOM-1971

See also these items elsewhere (consult Author Index for location): GARC-M-1974; HENS-1974b; ORNS-1974; RAMI-K-197[1?]; RAMI-K-1973; SAWY-1957; SAWY-1959; SAWY-1964; SAWY-1969; and especially ROMA-1960

BLUM, Owen W. "Some Aspects of the Latin American Market of Austin, Texas, With Emphasis on the Radio as a Means of Reaching This Market." MA [MBA] Thesis, Univ. of Texas, Austin, 1952. x, 86 pp. [Annot. Sánchez/Putnam 1959 no. 726.]

While much of this thesis is concerned with the socioeconomic characteristics of the particular "market" (i.e., size of family, years of schooling, radio ownership, utilities in the home, buying power of the family, and the like), valuable information concerning station preferences (pp. 30-34), printed media readership (45-48) and "language preferences" (42-44) contributes much to our understanding of the sociolinguistic situation of Austin's Chicanos in the early 1950's. Most signs point to an overwhelming loyalty to Spanish: 96 per cent "listen regularly" and 89 per cent "listen most" to Austin's one Spanish-language (daytime) radio station, KTXN; at night 45 per cent "listen most" either to XEW (Mexico City) or to other Mexico stations despite less-than-perfect reception. A whopping 74 per cent "prefer Spanish-speaking programs in contrast to only 10 per cent who prefer English programming. Of those who prefer Spanish-speaking programs, 82 per cent of the Lower Class and 68 per cent of the Middle Class indicated their preference for the Spanish." (42) Spanish was spoken "most frequently" in the home by 78 per cent. Less loyalty was shown toward the Spanish-language press (see pp. 45-46), which in any event had to be imported from San Antonio (La Prensa) since Austin issued none. [RT]

*BRENNAN, James Edward. "A Study of the Channels of Communication Used By Spanish-named Residents of San Antonio, Texas." PhD Diss., Louisiana State Univ., Baton Rouge, 1968. 185 pp. [DA 29 (1969) 3245-A.]

From the dissertation's abstract we learn that radio, television, newspapers, and interpersonal relations were the most "preferred channels of communication" among an unstated number of San Antonio Chicanos, investigated as to where they obtained in-

formation concerning nine newsworthy topics such as the war in
Viet Nam, national/state/local politics, the 1968 San Antonio
Hemisfair, a strike by farm workers in the lower Texas Rio Grande
valley, etc. Television was regularly watched by 94.5 per cent,
radio regularly listened to by 75.5 per cent, and a newspaper
reportedly read each day by 71 per cent. While greater numbers
of respondents preferred the main Spanish-language radio station
(30.5) per cent) to the leading English-language one (13.5 per
cent), an overwhelming number chose English-language television
(61 per cent) over Spanish (12.5 per cent); readership of Spanish-
language newspapers appears not to have been included in the
sampling. Brennan states that "individuals using [the two
Spanish-language radio and television stations] were generally
less acculturated, older, less educated, and had lower incomes
than those using [the two English-language stations]." He reaches
the startling and, if true, depressing conclusion that "of all
respondents who spoke only Spanish in their homes, less than seven
per cent used any direct media other than relatives or friends or
neighbors" (i.e., interpersonal communications) to obtain news
information. [RT]

*DUNN, Edward Wesley, Jr. "A Factor Analysis of Communication
Habits and Attitudes Among Mexican Americans in Austin and
San Antonio, Texas." PhD Diss., Univ. of Texas, Austin, 1973.
230 pp. [DA 34 (1974) 6012-A.]

This is an attempt to define an "audience" in terms of cluster
of personal and social traits such as age, sex, educational level,
occupation and language habits, and also in terms of "such media
habits and preferences as time spent daily viewing television and
listening to radio, primary sources of news and information, newspaper reading preferences, and language preferences in radio
stations and television programs." (abs.) Dunn collected his data
through 1599 (!) individual field and telephone surveys and found
that despite various differences between the amount of Spanish-
language media available in each city (more in San Antonio than
in Austin), "the extracted factors showed substantial stability
across cities and survey types." He found three basic "clusters . .
readily identifiable across all four surveys": (1) "older respondents, who are housewives, call themselves 'Mexican' or 'mexicano', preferred to conduct the interview in Spanish," and preferred Spanish-language broadcast media; (2) "the contrasting, 'non-
traditional' cluster [which] includes younger, better educated
persons" who preferred English interviews and English mass media
and who "referred to themselves as 'Mexican American' or 'Chicano,'"
and (3), a group which Dunn calls "Radio Fans" who seemingly es-
caped socio-demographic characterization and whose sole unifying
trait was the one ear they apparently had cocked toward the crystal
set "between 10:00 AM and midnight." Another cluster consisted
of "housewives who preferred dramatic television programs and
Spanish-language radio stations." [RT]

GARCÍA, Nelda C. "Language Factors in the Employment of Bilingual
    Mexican-Americans: A Case Study Analysis." PhD Diss.,
    Michigan State Univ., East Lansing, 1971. xii, 329 pp. [DA
    32 (1972) 6681-A.]

This ambitious sociolinguistic study is described by its author as "a pilot investigation of the perceived English language performance of [45] employed bilingual Mexican-Americans" (abs.) working at white-collar jobs in the Texas cities of Beaumont, Brownsville, Corpus Christi, Dallas, Houston and San Antonio. By comparing self-perceptions, peer-worker perceptions and then employer-perceptions of the Mexican-American's English language abilities with parallel perceptions of the abilities of monolingual non-Mexican-Americans, García sought to determine "the importance of English language abilities for placement, adjustment, and advancement in white-collar occupations" and also to develop "comparative socioeconomic, educational, and employment background profiles of the two ethnic groups as well as a language profile of the bilingualism of the Mexican-Americans." (ibid.)

While sociolinguists may find some of García's data-gathering techniques overly impressionistic (see esp. her "Language Factors Rating Sheet" and the scoresheet for "Language Factors Relative to Employment Phases," Appendix B, (pp. 286-287), few will doubt the degree to which her conclusions conform to "known" reality: "the data from this study indicated that the perceived language performance abilities of both ethnic groups were relatively high, with Mexican-American subjects ranking somewhat lower . . . To a marked degree [they] were considered to speak English with Spanish accents, but the more critical factors . . . were vocabulary and fluency." (abs.) García also noted that "Spanish appeared to be used on the job without compensation or recognition of its skill and economic value." (ibid.)

Of particular interest is the section "Language Backgrounds" (145-161); there one learns that formal training in English has had little bearing on either frequency of English usage or on the ability to speak English, especially among older subjects. You can lead a horse to water . . . [RT]

JORDÁN DE CARO, Rosan. "Language Loyalty and Folklore Studies:
    The Mexican American." WF 31.77-86 (1973). [Abs. MLAAB/Ling
    1972.20 (no. 1766).]

An insightful look at the conflicting loyalties that form an integral part of the lives of urbanized Texas Chicanos. Jordán speaks of the "resistance on the part of many Mexican-Americans to learning and using English," especially in rural areas; "even in the cities, where almost all Mexican-Americans are bilingual, Spanish is tenaciously preserved within familial and societal circles, particularly among adults." (p. 78) There follows a lengthy anecdotal example of what seems to be a rule of thumb: if persons identifiably Mexican-American can function in Spanish

they are expected to do so in all "ethnic" situations. Jordán's story concerns one "Mary S., of Fort Worth, Texas," who came to prefer English (which she did not learn until age six) through strong identification with Anglo culture and values. Consequently as an adult she can recall no folktales, riddles or songs in Spanish from her childhood and "seems to be largely bored by and incredulous of the numerous superstitious beliefs shared by others of her family." (82) Nonetheless upon marrying and reaching adulthood she has found it essential to "revive" her Spanish and to <u>acquire</u> a knowledge of Raza folklore to participate fully in family and <u>barrio</u> life. But while her husband prefers Spanish, "her children speak only English," (81) and she continues to prefer English herself. "There are, however, some words and phrases which she seems to prefer to use in Spanish, even when she is speaking English, just as her husband's conversational Spanish is heavily loaded with English vocabulary and anglicisms." (ibid.) "Mary" relates two jokes concerning language use and describes her feelings toward "countrified" Chicanos.
[RT]

KUVLESKY, William P. and Victoria M. Patella. "Degree of Ethnicity and Aspirations for Upward Social Mobility Among Mexican American Youth." <u>JVocB</u> 13.231-244 (1971).

Although language is not discussed here per se, the degree of Spanish usage among 600 Laredo-area Chicano highschoolers (as measured in a 1967 study (see Kuvlesky 1973) was one of the factors by which the authors arrived at composite "mean ethnic identification scores" intended to indicate levels of in-group loyalty. It was concluded that "the results of this investigation did not support the hypothesis that degree of identification with the Mexican American subculture is inversely associated with the desire for upward inter-generational occupational mobility." (pp. 241-242) The authors wonder why their hypothesis failed, especially since their explanation "flies in the face of Rubel's (1966) observations and findings from Nall's (1961) earlier survey analysis, both of which involved populations similar to the one involved in this study." (242) Perhaps, they conclude, the particular indicators cast too wide a net to tap the critical aspects of language since "they simply refer to predominant use of one language vs. the other." (ibid.) So they suggest among other things that any future researcher who uses language to measure ethnicity "consider the qualitative nature of the language used--fluency, degree of accent, and breadth of vocabulary of English and/or Spanish." (ibid.).
[RT]

MADSEN, William. <u>Mexican-Americans of South Texas</u>. New York: Holt, Rinehart & Winston, 1964. xii, 112 pp.

Part of a series of "case studies in cultural anthropology," Madsen's work includes in passing a variety of in-group culture-related terms such as <u>empacho</u>, <u>susto</u>, <u>curandera</u>, <u>portador</u>, <u>mal de ojo</u>, etc., and often gives thorough explanations of their social context. At times Madsen's transcriptions are accurate, at times not ("'Madre Mio de Dios!' exclaimed Elsa"--p. 81). Language is never discussed as such but an analysis is made of its social aspects in the sub-section "The Language Barrier" (106-108). Some sample commentary: "For the Latin, Spanish is the primary symbol of loyalty to <u>La Raza</u>. The Mexican-American who speaks English in a gathering of conservative Latins is mocked and regarded as a traitor to <u>La Raza</u>. Among members of the lower class, such linguistic disloyalty is forgiven only when a man is drunk." (106)

In recent years Madsen's book has become a convenient target for militant criticism, of which the following is an example: "The author assumes a position of judging the Mexican-American on the basis of anthropological constructs which are sadly misused or perhaps over used or highly dramatized. . . . In detail and description, the observations are clearly transmitted, but the synthesis of these observations reflect [sic] an angry and intolerant individual whose thinking about differences is synonymous with inferior. . . . The book makes no constructive contributions but is an excellent example of psychological warfare on a minority group in the name of a superior culture." (Barrios 1971 p. 111) [RT]

MAHONEY, Mary Katherine. "Spanish and English Language Usage by Rural and Urban Spanish American Families in Two South Texas Counties." MA Thesis, Texas A & M Univ., College Station, 1967. viii, 69 pp.

Mahoney's thesis was directed by Prof. R.L. Skrabanek who evidently headed up the field project in San Antonio and (rural) Atascosa county which provided the data for Mahoney 1967 and, in turn, for the series of papers and publications by Skrabanek himself (1967 et seq.). Thus the scholar interested in all details of the project (research design, methodology, tables of statistics, full report of conclusions, etc.) will definitely want to consult Mahoney's well-written thesis, though this need not be done by the general reader already acquainted with Skrabanek 1967 et seq., since the overall conclusions are obviously identical. [RT]

MARTÍNEZ, Irma Herrera. "A Study of Parental Views Toward Spanish Instruction in Kindergarten Conducted at Ollie P. Storm Elementary School in San Antonio, Texas." MA Thesis, Univ. of Texas, Austin, 1972. ix, 92 pp.

To determine whether instruction in Spanish as well as in English would be viewed favorably by the parents of four-year-olds in a lower-income, solidly Mexican-American neighborhood on the West Side of San Antonio, Martínez sought out the reactions of 50 parents on a variety of educational issues and also compiled a sort of sociolinguistic profile of the interviews. The results (chiefly presented in Chs. 3, "Analysis of the Data," and Appendices A and B) demonstrate that although most homes are bilingual (to whatever degree), Spanish continues to be the preferred language, and that while support for bilingual schooling is strong, it is not universal. For example, 28 per cent "strongly agreed" with the statement that "kindergarten children who speak only Spanish at home should receive only English instruction," while 62 per cent "strongly disagreed." (p. 33) [RT]

MC CLENDON, Juliette J.C. "Spanish-Speaking Children of Big Spring: An Educational Challenge." PhD Diss., Univ. of Texas, 1964. 169 pp. [DA 25 (1965) 5282-5283-A.]

This pedagogically-oriented dissertation relies heavily on personal anecdotes and rarely on statistical support in its attempt to provide a general "picture" of Big Spring's Chicano youngsters, the families from which they come, and the schools which they attend. Its value, however, lies precisely in the richness of the anecdotes; one gleans much first-hand information about parental feelings toward bilingualism, Mexican-American Spanish, and educational policies in McClendon's petites histoires, especially Chs. 3 ("Case Histories of Some Spanish-speaking Children," pp. 28-39) and 6 ("Analysis of Psycholinguistic Factors," 68-113 but chiefly in the subsection entitled "The Mother Tongue," 92-113, where the author also gives bits and pieces of information about the morpho-phonology and lexicon of the local Spanish).

On p. 159 there appears a list of "variants used by Big Spring Spanish-speaking Children with Central Mexico equivalent[s]." Of the 89 words listed, 40 were found not to have been included in the Texas Spanish dictionary of Cerda et al. 1953. [RT]

MYCUE, Elena Inés de los Santos. "Testing in Spanish and the Subsequent Measurement of English Fluency." MA Thesis, Texas Women's Univ., Denton, 1968. v, 43 pp. [Available EDRS: ED 026 193.]

This modest work on testing, testers, and testees reports on a study of 48 five-year-old Mexican American bilinguals in two Fort Worth elementary schools. The children were divided into three groups--(1) response in English with an Anglo interviewer, (2) response in English with a Chicano interviewer, and (3) testing begun in Spanish and ending in English with a Chicano interviewer--and English fluency was measured by the children's telling of stories for each of five pictures. The results showed successively better performance by groups from (1) to (3). No language data are provided. [GB]

PATELLA, Victoria M. "A Study in the Validity of Language Usage as an Indicator of Ethnic Identification." MA Thesis, Texas A & M Univ., College Station, 1971. xii, 137 pp.

This important, well written thesis tested the hypothesis that relative use of Spanish vs. English is directly correlated with ethnic subculture identification. In effect Patella challenges language usage as an accurate measure of "ethnicity," and also seeks "to determine whether or not preference for the Spanish language implies rejection of the dominant culture in favor of the subculture." (p. 4) The object then is "first to examine those aspects of one bilingual subculture which differentiate it from the dominant culture, and second to discover which of those aspects, if any, are correlated with greater use of the mother tongue than of the second tongue, and which are not." (19) The "aspects" utilized are (1) family orientation characteristics (inter alia: parental birthplace, who is the chief bread-winner, does the mother work, relative education of parents, their marital status), and (2) aspirations for the "future family of procreation," (26) i.e., whether the subject wishes to continue "traditional" patterns. Specifically the hypothesis was that of the tested 596 male and female high school sophomores from five southwest and south Texas border counties of Chicano majority populations, those who came from "traditional Mexican-type" families (and who wanted that type of family for themselves) would also show the greatest loyalty to and use of the Spanish language.

"In general, the hypothesis was not supported" by the data. (71) But some indicators were exceptions to the general pattern and did support the hypothesis: (1) for both males and females, birthplace of parents (with those whose parents were both born in Mexico showing the greatest preference for Spanish and those whose parents were both born in the U.S. the least preference); (2) for males only, "ideal family size" and "employment of mother," with greatest Spanish preference expressed by males with non-working mothers and by males who desire large families; and (3) for females only, with those not desiring to work after marriage (and hence "most traditional") expressing strongest preference for Spanish.

Since the data tended to disprove the hypotheses but still failed to offer unequivocal support for any one conclusion, Patella conjectures that previous sociological descriptions of "traditional Mexican-American culture" may be off base, or that the index of language usage employed (that used by Joshua Fishman in the middle 1960's) is "too heavily weighted in favor of the speaking medium over the reading medium, with writing totally neglected," (76) no attention given to the "inner role" of language or to the relationship between content and medium, etc. "In summary, these conclusions point out that no sweeping generalization may be made concerning the validity, or lack of validity, of language usage as an indicator of ethnic identification." (86) [RT]

PATELLA, Victoria M. and William P. Kuvlesky. "Situational Variation in Language Patterns of Mexican-American Boys and Girls." SocSQ 53.855-864 (1973).

This seminal and carefully executed article complements Kuvlesky 1973 through its presentation of some of the same findings from the initial research project (see Patella 1971), although greater attention is paid here to the correlation of language usage to domain and to the degree that human gender influences language choice. (Only those findings not presented in Kuvlesky 1973 and Patella 1971 [see also Kuvlesky/Patella 1971] will be dealt with here.)

Male and Female adolescents were found to differ significantly in the use of Spanish according to interlocutor and domain: "Boys more often than girls spoke Spanish with their parents, with close friends in the neighborhood, and with close friends in school. . . In the neighborhood and in school, at least half of the girls used both languages equally as often in talking with friends. The boys behaved similarly in the school but used Spanish mostly in the neighborhood. Use of both languages was common for large proportions of both boys and girls in all three contexts considered and was the dominant pattern for girls outside the family." (p. 859) (Mass media consumption and general cross-sexual patterns are also discussed, as in Kuvlesky 1973.)

The authors conclude that while their other findings corroborate those of Grebler/Moore/Guzmán 1970 and provide "strong support for the assertion of Rubin that among bilingual people, use of one language versus the other is determined by the nature of the interaction situation," (863) none of those authors specifically dealt with sexual differentiation of usage, so this constitutes "the most significant of the findings here . . . Further research is needed to determine to what extent this is general among Mexican Americans and in other populations where bilingualism is a predominant behavioral pattern." (863) Why do females use more English than males? The authors guess that since much of the sociological literature on Chicanos indicates that "females are trained for obedience to authority, while males are groomed for independence," classroom efforts to "command obedience . . . may have much greater success with the females [who] may learn more English than the males . . . and thus their greater use of that language." (ibid.) They quickly note, though, that "it cannot be assumed here that amount of English used is directly related to level of fluency in the language. Males may know as much, or more English as [sic] females, but be using it selectively. The relationship between fluency and usage will have to be determined empirically, as will the question of relative fluency of males and females." (863-864) [RT]

RAMÍREZ, Karen G. "Bilingualism and Bilingual Programs in El Paso: Kindergarten and First Grade." MA Thesis, Univ. of Texas, El Paso, 1971. 153 pp. 1 map.

This thesis reports on a Spanish-English language proficiency survey of the 34 kindergartens and 48 first grades in the El Paso school district. The basis for the study was a form sent to all teachers asking them to evaluate each child on a five-point scale (only Spanish, mainly Spanish, equal proficiency, mainly English, and only English). The bulk of the thesis (pp. 37-153) is the presentation of the charts showing language dominance for the entire system, for eight regions, and for each school, with correlations showing experience in Head Start and Oral English programs, retentions in the same grade, and previous schooling. A fold-out map following p. 153 divides El Paso into "Language-Type Areas" with each region and school marked for four degrees of Spanish-speaking students (0-25%, 26-50%, 51-75%, and 76-100%). [GB]

RUBEL, Arthur J. Across the Tracks: Mexican Americans in a Texas City. Austin: Univ. of Texas Press, 1966. xxvii, 266 266 pp.

Of the Index'es ten references to "language" only four prove language-specific and all these pertain to language as an "issue": the refusal of the schools of "New Lots" (a small city in the border county of Hidalgo) to allow Spanish as a language of instruction or even as a second language at the elementary level (p. 44), the immediate and positive effect upon their candidacies brought about by politicians' repeating in Spanish a speech first given in English (130, 134), and the consequences of a Mexican-American's decision to foresake Spanish and use only English even among fellow ethnics: "Such an action immediately brands him a 'traitor,' one who has 'turned his back' on his traditional culture culture." (244) Rubel says that to date only a very few have taken this course; on the other hand, though, "no longer is the [total] rejection of English extolled as it was among many of the older generation" of Chicanos. (ibid.)

While both the prose and the sociology of Across the Tracks appear impeccable, the 150-entry "Glossary" (254-260) is riddled with rank errors in Spanish transcription (angel de la guarda, castigo de Díos, clase obrero, el mero palomilla, hay voy, jefe de la famitia, la lux mexicana, pelóns, peóns and a dozen others at least) and with untrustworthy definitions (muy feo 'embarrassment,' pescar brujos 'a technique for catching witches' are among the several citable). Perhaps ten per cent of the entries are Italian, a reflection of Rubel's comparison between Mexican and Mezzogiorno peasant cultures. [RT]

RUBEL, Arthur J. "Some Cultural Aspects of Learning English in
    Mexican-American Communities." In Schools in Transition:
    Essays in Comparative Education, edited by Andreas M. Kazamias
    and Erwin H. Epstein. Boston: Allyn Bacon, 1968. Pp. 370-382.
    [Annot. HLAS 30 (1968) no. 2645-a (D. L. Canfield); Fody pp.
    532-533.]

This is basically a discussion of negative Anglo attitudes
towards Chicano Spanish and its retention, and of Chicano attitudes towards these same concerns and toward the acquisition of
English; Rubel's empirical data derive chiefly from his research
in Hidalgo County, Texas (see Rubel 1966). After summing up the
history of these matters and delving briefly into educational,
demographic and economic questions, Rubel (who characterizes "the
striking determination of the Mexican-Americans to retain Spanish"
as an exemplification of "nativistic responses to acculturation
pressures" [p. 370]) states somewhat categorically that "relations
between Mexican-Americans and Anglos are premised upon an open-
class social system, the ideology of which stipulates that individuals be ranked according to achieved social and cultural
characteristics instead of ascribed racial traits. . . . It is
also assumed that the upwardly mobile Mexican-American strives
for complete assimilation . . . The most often utilized indicator
of whether a person is actively attempting to be assimilated is
whether or not he becomes a monolingual English-speaker, or remains a bilingual." (337-378) These remarks are balanced by
Rubel's admissions that "for the average Mexican-American, bilingualism represents a linguistic accomodation to the harsh
economic and social realities of an area in which most . . .
services and opportunities presume competence in English" and that
Spanish serves Chicanos as "a symbol of the continued existence
of their way of life." (378-379) LRTJ

SCOTT, Carmen Casillas. "Spanish Language Maintenance and
    Loyalty in El Paso-Juárez: A Sociolinguistic Study of the
    Contact Situation in a Highly Bilingual Area." MA Thesis,
    Univ. of Texas, El Paso, 1969. 67 pp.

For the most part this is an anecdotal interpretation of
factors favoring the likelihood that Spanish will long be heard
on the streets of El Paso. (One factor is clearly the "stone's-
throw" distance from Mexico's fourth largest city, Ciudad Juárez,
whose relatively high rate of unemployment drives thousands across
the border to El Paso.)
After an introductory history Scott discusses the roles played
by churches, schools, civic organizations, the labor force, mass
media, and the family in maintaining Spanish locally. The
Catholic Church enforces the use of Spanish in many parishes but
makes allowances for pro-English sentiment which often rears up,
says Scott, among Anglicized third- or fourth-generation El Paso
"Hispanos." Thirty priests were asked why they used Spanish in

sermons (Table I, p. 13): a plurality (33 per cent) did so to accomodate newly-arrived immigrants. Civic and political organiations encourage one language or the other according to attitudes toward acculturation; thus LULAC favors rapid acquisition of English whereas MACHO and NOMAS (local protest groups) find English at best a necessary evil. El Paso's schools were (as of writing) embroiled over the "no-Spanish" rule (quickly abandoned in 1969). Scott's chapter on "Mass Media" (45-54) promises much but delivers little, despite copious quotation (here as elsewhere from Joshua Fishman, Language Loyalty in the United States (1966): mentioned are the Spanish-language newspapers and magazines available in El Paso, the call letters of the eleven Juárez radio and two Juárez TV stations, etc., but not mentioned is the degree to which Juárez broadcasting is tuned in by El Pasoans. Scott's work is not without its statistics, though: the tendency for wealthier and hence more Anglo-acculturated Hispanos to abandon Spanish after several generations, even within the home, is documented on p. 59a: by the third generation the wealthiest of four sample groups "almost never" speaks Spanish to "siblings, friends, husband or wife, [or] own children" whereas the poorest group "frequently" speaks Spanish to friends "100 per cent" (?) of the time but "almost never" to husband or wife (?!); Scott sampled twenty families in all. [RT]

SKRABANEK, R.L. "The Use of English and Spanish by Spanish-Americans in Two South Texas Counties." Dallas: Proceedings, Southwestern Sociological Association Meeting, 1967 [mimeographed], pp. 189-194. Revised version printed as "Language Maintenance Among Mexican-Americans." IJCS 11.272-282 (1970); rpt. in Educating the Disadvantaged, vol. 4, edited by Russell C. Doll and Maxine Hawkins, New York: AMS Press, 1971, pp. 226-235. Slightly abridged version printed in Civil Rights Digest 4:2.18-24 (Spring 1971) and also in Language and Literature for Composition, edited by Sanford Radner and Susan Radner, New York: Thomas Y. Crowell, 1973, pp. 141-152. (All references below are to the 1970 article.)

The conclusions of this critical study are based upon data from interviews conducted in two contiguous South Texas locations--rural Atascosa county and the city of San Antonio. Children as well as adults from 544 households were researched as to "Spanish and English language usage in a variety of situations--in conversations with adults and with children in the home; while visiting friends, at work; at play; and at school;" (p. 275) preferred languages of news publications and mass media were also solicited, although less successfully, since the majority of rural households heads did not read a daily paper. Skrabanek's findings strongly support loyalty to Spanish: "not one person living in a Mexican-American home and old enough to talk was found who did not speak Spanish fluently, and an overwhelming majority speak

Spanish more fluently than English." (ibid.) Conversations at home are predominantly in Spanish regardless of generation: "Fewer than one half of either the younger or older children use mostly English when talking with adults or other children in their homes or when playing or visiting with friends. It is only when they are in school that a high proportion of the children use mostly English, and this is mainly because it is required of them by the school officials." (276) "Even while at work, English is the dominant language used by less than one half of the household heads." (275) Spanish-language radio is the rule, although "relatively high proportions of both rural and urban youngsters view television programs mostly in English and attend movies in English." (277) Skrabanek explains this extreme loyalty by citing socioeconomic factors and especially "ethnic factors" such as strong emotional attachment to Mexican-American culture on the one hand, "spatial isolation" from English-mother-tongue society on the other; the upshot is "social unity [which] contributes so strongly to a sense of social solidarity among Mexican-Americans that many who are able to speak English fluently nevertheless prefer to speak Spanish when they are with other bilingual persons." (280)

Skrabanek states (274) that his two study areas are representative of Chicano situations throughout the Southwest; for contrary findings see a study of Austin, Texas by Thompson (1972).

To a great extent Skrabanek's data and conclusions directly parallel those of the M.A. thesis of his student, Mary K. Mahoney; thus for a fuller presentation of much of the same material (clearly based on the same field project) the reader will want to consult Mahoney 1967. [RT]

THOMPSON, Roger M. "Language Loyalty in Austin, Texas: A Study of a Bilingual Neighborhood." PhD Diss., Univ. of Texas, Austin, 1971. xix, 132 pp. [DA 32 (1972) 6408-A.]

This extremely important and superbly written contribution to socio-linguistics is must reading for all who would claim to be knowledgeable in that field. Thompson's masterful discussion (pp. 1-19) of the theoretical aspects of language loyalty serves to introduce the specific problem at hand: whether Spanish is being dropped in favor of English as Texas Chicanos move from rural areas to cities. Austin is the case in point as its sizeable Spanish-surnamed population is largely the result of recent intra-Texas urbanization rather than immigration from Mexico.

Thompson first interviewed male heads of families in a randomly-selected ten per cent of Austin's barrio households to obtain estimates as to frequency of Spanish usage at home, with relatives and other adults, with subject's children, in the community, etc., and to obtain estimates of usage of other persons in the neighborhood. Data for these 136 subjects were analyzed against the variables of age, generation, place of birth, locality of childhood, education, and occupation. "Because location of childhood was found to be the most important variable, a second survey was

conducted with those heads of households who were raised in
Austin in order to validate the information supplied by the first
informant, and to control the location of childhood while examining the relation of the use of Spanish at work, occupational mobility," etc. (abs.) From the second survey Thompson again concluded that the location of childhood was the factor that most
determined loyalty to Spanish (and ability to handle Spanish
with greater fluency and in more domains? These topics are not
dealt with). "Adults who were raised in Austin use half Spanish
with fellow Mexican-Americans whereas those raised in rural areas
use only Spanish." (ibid.) In general terms such factors as age,
generation, occupation and level of education were not found significant. Other conclusions: types of English accent do not
reflect loyalties to Spanish, as "those who believe that occupational advancement depends on education and ability are adopting
Northern speech patterns" while those who feel it depends on
assimilation to regional norms adopt Texas patterns. "Generally,
the Austin second-generation family is not teaching Spanish to
its children. Instead, the parents expect the children to learn
Spanish from urban first-generation friends and associates;"
Thompson notes several cases of children who though exclusively
English-speaking in the home were observed speaking Spanish with
certain friends elsewhere. "Diglossia, which would prevent the
loss of Spanish, has not been established. The use of Spanish
depends not on social function but on the Spanish-speaking ability
of the person spoken to." (A new form of diglossia, perhaps?)
Thompson's overall conclusion is that "except for the constant
influx of rural Mexican-Americans, the use of Spanish would cease
within one more generation." See Skrabanek 1970 for findings which
reflect conditions in a different type of Texas city, San Antonio,
where the percentage of Chicanos is more than double Austin's.
[RT]

THOMPSON, Roger M. [1974a]. "The 1970 U.S. Census and Mexican
American Language Loyalty: A Case Study." In Bills 1974,
pp. 65-78.

Extracted from Thompson 1971, this superior paper probes his
Austin survey data to determine the correctness of the 1970 Census
implication that stable bilingualism has been established among
Mexican Americans. Although his correlations of the use of
Spanish with children and Mexican American friends with the variables of generation and age seem to support the Census data,
Thompson demonstrates that the crucial variable is whether childhood residence has been urban or rural. The trend among those
with an urban childhood apparently mirrors the trend of most immigrant groups: a shift to English as the mother tongue in the
third generation. This article contains no primary language
data. [GB]

THOMPSON, Roger M. [1974b]. "Mexican American Language Loyalty and the Validity of the 1970 Census." In Spolsky and Bills 1974, pp. 7-18.

Slightly revised version of Thompson 1974a. [GB]

5.2.2 TEXTBOOKS

Major Items: (none)

See also these items elsewhere (consult Author Index for location):

(none)

BUTLER, Susan Passmore. Usable Spanish. Dallas: Tardy Publishing Co., 1935. 47 pp. +.

This work "had its beginning in the classroom. Boys who were going directly from high school to the farm or shop, girls who would work in the five-and-ten, or in a restaurant, the son of a man in charge of relief . . . all wanted the Spanish that Mexicans use every day, all around us." (Foreword, n.p.) Thus the Spanish found in the dozen rather forcedly "conversational" chapters is intended to reflect rural Texas usage (exclusive employment of blanquíos for 'huevos,' monosyllabic maiz for 'maíz,' etc.) though in nearly all cases, verbal morphology is that of standard Spanish. Occasional expressions show English influence: "El Presidente de los Estados Unidos nos ha pagado no plantar los campos de algodón" (2), "Cuele la leche y póngala en el separador para remover la nata" (ibid.,--frequent instances of remover 'quitar' passim), the consistent use of "Venga otra vez" as an expression of leave-taking probably calqued from Texan "Y'all come back," etc. One is not sure whether the Anglicization is intentional or inadvertent, as footnotes are not provided and no other form of attention is drawn to local "peculiarities" beyond a 19-word lexicon of "Mexican Expressions Current in Texas" (p. 47). Some individual chapter titles: "La cocina y el comedor;" "Tienda de comestibles (víveres);" "La carnicería;" "Tienda de dimes (de variedades) (el Kres);" "El cuidado de los enfermos;" "La granja;" "El tribunal." [RT]

CRUZ-AEDO, Víctor, ed., et al. Español para alumnos hispanohablantes: Niveles I y II de secundaria. Texas Education Association Bull. No. 702 (Austin: T.E.A., 1970). vi, 197 pp.

This modestly self-proclaimed "bulletin," prepared from disparate materials by a committee of eleven Texas Spanish teachers (the majority Chicano), is actually a full-fledged course-of-study outline for teachers of Spanish-speaking Mexican-American junior high and high school Spanish students and (to some extent) a textbook for use by these same students. While much of the work naturally consists of the sort of pedagogical material that falls beyond our concern here, the inevitable corregenda will be of interest to linguists although of necessity the text is a distillation of previous findings and thus gives little that is new in the sections handling: nonstandard pronunciation (multiple and thus passim; see for example p. 46's "Ejercicios de pronunciación" intended to correct /h/ for /f/, /e/ for /i/ as in recebir, polecía, erroneous sineresis of such as planiar, golpiar, pior, etc.; see also Appendix C), verbal morphology (a long series of pattern drills on present subjunctives "podamos not puédanos, comamos not cómanos," etc. [53]); attention is also paid to "compraste not comprates/comprastes [p. 71]), and the like. With the onset of "Unidad III" (77) the correction of deviancy ceases and the work comes to resemble any other advanced-level high school Spanish textbook.

Of interest is the news that Texas Spanish lexicon varies regionally: the authors assert for example that in El Paso one says cinto but faja in Laredo, likewise EP balde, L cubeta, EP chavalo, L huerco, EP asadero/L asadera. Intonational differences exist as well: ¡Mira! '¡Qué barbaridad!' is [mira] in EP but [mira:] in Laredo. (12) [RT]

GALVÁN, Roberto A. and Damon Miller. "Student Study Guide for Contrastive Analysis of Regional and Standard Spanish." (U.S. Office of Education Grant No. OEG-0-9-530014-3480 [280], for the Bilingual Education Program, Harlandale-San Marcos-SWTSU Consortium.) San Marcos, Texas: Southwest Texas State Univ., 1972. 43 pp. Mimeographed (available upon request from the Dept. of Modern Languages, Southwest Texas State).

This "modular unit" is written for the classroom (in a somewhat catechismal fashion) and is meant for students of bilingual education who will need to know the differences between "Texas" Spanish and a purposefully standardized "universal" Spanish. The authors' statement of belief will probably anger conservatives and radicals alike: "The use of the Spanish vernacular as an expedient measure is valid [since 'on many occasions it may be the only tool of communication between the teacher and pupil . . . or among the pupils themselves'], but the universal dialect (the standard) should replace it as soon as it is feasible . . . " (p. 2) These concerns aside, though, the manual will be of value to linguists in need of a birds' eye view of Texas Spanish's salient features, phonological in the main but also morphological and semantic; for these the reader is directed to pp. 4, 10-11, 12 (a presentation of current Anglicisms), 13-17 (phonology), 27-30 (the various deviant forms used in context), and 33-36 (semantics). [RT]

5.3 SPANISH PHONOLOGY (includes ORTHOGRAPHY)

Major Items: CLEG-1969; POUL-1970

See also these items elsewhere (consult Author Index for location):

　　LOZA-1961; MONT-1966; PATT-1946; REYN-1945

*ÁLVAREZ, Salvador. "The Influence of Phonological Characteristics Upon Orthography in Mexican-American Second Graders." PhD Diss., Univ. of Texas, Austin, 1973. 222 pp. [DA 34 (1974) 5569-A.]

　　The study "attempted to ascertain the relationships that may exist between the way a child speaks and the way he spells in English and in Spanish." (abs.) A second and even more ambitious goal was "to determine the relationships that the variables of age, sex, home language, sibling placement, and type of instruction, bilingual or instruction in English only, have to speech and to spelling." The subjects were sixty-seven children from San Antonio and Corpus Christi, Texas; the San Antonio group received its schooling in English only. "Problem words" were elicited through repetition of twenty-five sentences in each language; each word contained at least one sound "which had been deviantly pronounced at least 10 per cent of the time by both samples combined." A spelling test containing fifteen of these words (why just fifteen?) was then administered to both groups in English, to the Corpus Christi group in Spanish as well.
　　The bilingually-educated children both spelled and pronounced English better than the others. Álvarez also found a definite relationship between standard pronunciation and correct spelling: "Correctly pronounced and spelled phonemes and graphemes were related over 56 per cent of the time for both samples." That this should be the case in Spanish will come as no surprise, since the Spanish language's degree of "fit" is among the world's highest; thus the spelling of the youngster who "incorrectly pronounces" peor as pior and mucho as muncho will probably reflect the sub-standard form, mutatis mutandis. English, however, is a language whose fit is much less perfect, and thus it is far less reasonable to expect that approximate standard English pronunciations will necessarily generate correct English orthography; this will be especially true of words with schwahs.
　　This thesis doubtless contains valuable data on its subjects' pronunciation. [RT]

BUSSEY, Jo Ann Keslar. "A Comparative Study of Phonological
    Variation Among First, Second and Third Grade Linguistically
    Different Children in Five San Antonio (Texas) Schools:
    1970." PhD Diss., Univ. of Texas, Austin, 1971. xi, 160 pp.
    [DA 32 (1972) 6675-6676-A.]

   Children in three predominantly Mexican-American and two predominantly black schools were asked to repeat sentences read to
them in both Spanish and English in order to determine the two
groups' respective phonological deficiencies in both languages.
It was also sought to determine which of these deficiencies
decreased or disappeared with age. From the resultant data Bussey
draws pedagogical conclusions. The linguist's attention is
directed to several sections of Ch. 3 ("Description of Research
Design, Procedures, and Data Analyses"), which are: "English
Variations Shared by Both Ethnic Groups," (p. 85) "English Variations of Spanish-surnamed Students," (86) and "Spanish Variations
of Spanish-surnamed Students" (88-89). [RT]

CLEGG, J. Halvor. "Fonética y fonología del español de Texas."
    PhD Diss., Univ. of Texas, Austin, 1969. viii, 88 pp. [DA
    30 (1969) 2989-A.] [Rev. Craddock 1973 pp. 317-318.]

   The goal of this discriptivist study was to unearth the allophones of Texas Spanish ("El aporte esencial . . . radica en la
minuciosa descripción de las realizaciones alofónicas y en el
estudio de su distribución"--p. 11). Apparently for this reason
the author has chosen to work "backwards" from a set of phonemes
established ab initio: "En. la presentación del análisis procedo
del fonema a la realización en virtud de que 1) la fonología
general del español estaba ya establecida, 2) se conocía cuáles
eran los fonemas del español de Texas gracias a estudios anteriores
[a statement much at variance with Clegg's earlier claim that
"la información que el dialectólogo puede tener sobre el español
de Texas es en extremo precaria"--p. 4], y 3) porque mi análisis
no arrojó diferencia alguna de sistema tan importante que hubiera
recomendado un orden inverso en la presentación." (10-11)
   Most notable among the discrepant allophonic phenomena is the
pharyngeal aspiration [h] with which /f/, /x/ and /s/ are each
realized in various environments. But as Craddock points out,
(317) Clegg "fails to note whether this apparent identity involves
phonemic overlapping or collapse;" indeed the possibility of
phonemic collapse, potentially quite relevant to any discussion
of Texas Spanish phonology, is nowhere examined. Now lack of
speculation on these matters is a likely product of Clegg's exclusive concern with phonetic detail. But in view of this concern
it is curious that the phonetic analysis was undertaken without
benefit of spectrograph. Also notably absent is any investigation
of allophonic frequency, and as a consequence Clegg's assertion
that he is seeking out the linguistic norms of Texas Spanish

("[Vamos] por lo tanto, del sistema a la lengua en busca de una norma"--11) necessarily rests on impressionistic bases. [RT]

EVANS, Phyllis Joyce Howell. "Word-Pair Discrimination and Imitation Abilities of Pre-School Economically-Disadvantaged Native-Spanish-Speaking Children." PhD Diss., Univ. of Texas, Austin, 1971. xiii, 172 pp. [DA 33 (1972) 636-A.]

Evans' work reached a number of noteworthy conclusions. It examined the word-pair discrimination and imitation abilities, in both Spanish and English, of forty children between the ages of 5 and 6; 20 of them were upper-middle-class whites from Austin and 20 were poverty-level Mexican-Americans from the Lower Rio Grande Valley. Ultimately Evans's goal was to test the validity of two contrasting theoretical explanations of "Chicano deficiencies in English and Spanish," the "linguistic theory" and the "social-factor theory;" the former holds that inter-lingual phonological differences create interference in learning a second language among proficient speakers of a first language, while the latter postulates that "among the economically-disadvantaged, auditory discrimination deficits develop within the child which depress phonological abilities, and implies that the deficits would be equally applicable to both languages [our emphasis]." (p. iv)
Evans's findings prove the social-factor theory wrong: "Analysis of total score performance revealed no significant differences between the two groups on the four tasks." (v) Even more startling is the following: while the Anglos evinced noticeable difficulty with twelve English words, the Hispanos only stumbled over seven Spanish words, and thus "The Spanish-speakers were more proficient in their native language than were the English-speakers, which was also reflected in the inferential analyses." (vi)
Evans notes, however, that the Spanish-speakers showed a slight tendency toward lower performance on word-discrimination (as opposed to word imitation). But a critical examination of some of her word pairs gives us clues as to why this was so. Two of Evans's "minimal pairs" involved supposed "dialectal contrasts" between /v/ and /b/, /č/ and /š/, which "native Spanish-speakers" told her were common in the Valley; "consequently, bamos/vamos [and also mucho/mušo] were included as a word-pair, recognizing that the meaning of the words is identical." (48) It is not surprising then that the majority of children "corrected" [vamos] to [bamos] when asked to repeat the first form, or that most of them discerned "no difference" between the two forms when asked to ascertain distinction. Elsewhere Evans shows similar lack of familiarity with Spanish dialectology, as when she exhibits surprise at the frequency of muncho; (116) that her doctoral committee would have benefitted from the presence of a Hispanist is shown by the following: "the native-Spanish-speakers who had assisted with Spanish item selection considered [muncho] a severe mis-pronunciation of the word mucho which occurs in the McAllen area." (ibid.) [RT]

GONZÁLEZ, Gustavo. *The Phonology of Corpus Christi Spanish.*
Austin: Southwest Educational Development Laboratory, 1969.
12 pp.

This concise and easily-consultable presentation of the phonology of Corpus Christi six-year-olds is based on materials the author assembled for his Master's Thesis (see González 1968). In his discussion of phonemes and allophones (pp. 3-4) González notes that the distribution of the allophones of /b/ differs slightly from standard Spanish: [b] occurred consistently only after nasals, whereas in all other environments, labio-dental [v] varied freely with [β]; sporadic free variations of [s̃] with [ĉ] were also reported.

The rest of the study concentrates on "deviations in pronunciation which did not involve allophonic variations," and presents such familiar traits as reduction of consonant clusters, insertions of vowels or consonants, deletions of syllables, alternations of vowels in unstressed syllables, and so forth. He theorizes that the various deviancies are "traces of baby speech [whose presence is] due in part to lack of correction of speech patterns on the part of parents," (12) although he admits that this is hypothetical. [RT]

HAYES, Alice Frazer. "Acoustic Vowel Charts: Spanish Vowels of One Idiolect." MA Thesis, Univ. of Texas, Austin, 1961. vii, 37 pp.

Using the voice of San Antonio-born fellow linguist Anthony G. Lozano as the a source, Mrs. Hayes repeats an experiment done earlier by Daniel Cárdenas and described in his "Acoustic Vowel Loops of Two Spanish Idiolects," *Phonetica* 5.9-34 (1960). But replication of Cárdenas's procedures was not total; by altering them, Hayes feels that "the acoustic charts presented in this paper give a better picture of Spanish vowels in various environments than [do these] worked out by Cárdenas." (p. 1) Hayes's improvement consists of a more minute measurement of the lines produced on the spectrograms; thus her range of frequencies "is more easily visualized on a formant chart on which the frequency of each vowel is charted every 2 centiseconds." (4) [RT]

POULTER, Virgil L. "Comparison of Voiceless Stops in the English and Spanish of Bilingual Natives of Fort Worth-Dallas." In Gilbert 1970, pp. 42-49.

A very meticulous study of the phonetic realization of /p t k/ in both the languages of eight bilingual Chicano college students (ages 18 to 25) who were born in north Texas and had spoken both languages at least from the age of six. Poulter ascertained and then detailed the three consonants' realizations in nearly all environments in both languages (initial, medial, before and after stress, in combination with each other, before laterals, nasals and voiceless spirants, etc.) but did not examine word-final realizations in English. His data reveal the important general conclusion that neither language influences the students' pronunciations of the other; such lack of interference is noteworthy in view of Poulter's method of data collection, which required informants "to read two lists of words selected to elicit" the phones, to translate phrases from English into Spanish and to complete Spanish sentences guaranteed to produce desired phonations. (p. 44) Only two of the informants showed English-influenced Spanish: "one informant pronounced bilabials with strong aspiration when they occurred medially before stress as in Japón [ha'pʰon] . . . but with weak or no aspiration when these stops were initial . . . The other case was one whose bilabials were strongly aspirated in all positions in both English and Spanish" (45)-- an instance of articulatory pathology or of 'unnatural speech,' perhaps? [RT]

POULTER, Virgil L. "A Phonological Study of the [Spanish] Speech of Mexican-American College Students Native to Fort Worth-Dallas." PhD Diss., Louisiana State Univ., 1973. xi, 188 pp. [DA 35 (1974) 1082-A.]

This dissertation claims to investigate selected aspects of Chicano phonation according to the post-Bloomfieldian canons of Charles Hockett and Kenneth Pike.

All of Poulter's informants (11 of each sex) were college students or graduates ranging in age from 18 to 36 and native to the Dallas-Fort Worth metropolitan area; in most cases their Spanish was self-described as "inferior" and used as a second language. Poulter's manner of gathering data appears eclectic and is not fully described in any case (see pp. 31-32); it was based in part on Tomás Navarro Tomás's Cuestionario lingüístico hispanoamericano, in part on the Wörter und Sache guides of Einar Haugen's The Norwegian Language in America, but in the main "the organization of the questionnaire followed substantially the one designed by Lurline Coltharp [1965] and used in a study of the criminal argot of El Paso, Texas." Indeed, Poulter's failure to employ one single questionnaire ultimately capable of eliciting the same corpus of sound sequences from all informants is responsible for several of the work's major failings.

Poulter taped the interviews, transcribed the tapes and transferred his utterances (discrete lexemes for the most part but sometimes full phrases as well) "to data processing work sheets wherein the phonetic symbols were replaced by symbols available to computer components." (32) Poulter's own transcription was checked independently "by a graduate research assistant who was trained in phonetics and who had no background in Spanish." Resultant differences of opinion were then reconciled; no machine analysis was employed.

The local phonology as presented in Ch. 4 (35-53) does not vary from what those acquainted with structuralist studies of Western Hemisphere Spanish have come to expect: 5 vowel phonemes /a e i o u/ and 18 consonant phonemes /p t k b d g č f w s y x m n ñ l r R/. Nearly all of the more salient allophonic features of this particular dialect are ascribable to English influence: a tendency to schwa unstressed vowels, a certain "free variational" aspiration of non-syllable-final voiceless stops, and the occasional intromission of English retroflex [ɹ].

The presentation of certain aspects of the phonology, however, not only leaves much to be desired from the standpoint of any methodological canon but actually fails to provide the sort of basic information which readers must be given to understand how the dialect handles certain "problems." Poulter's treatment of /i/ and /y/, /u/ and /w/ is one case in point; his description of /r/ and /R/ is another. In the section on "allophones" he assigns [y] first to /i/ and then to /y/ ("voiced palatal slit fricative"); thus while /i/ > [y] "in unstressed syllable in the environments: CVV /iglésia/, VVV /réies/, CVV /límpia/, CVV̆ /leksión/," (36) "/y/ has the allophones: [y] in all environments: /yérba/, /káye/" (40) as well as "[ž] as a free variant occurring medially: [ladrížo]." (ibid.) Readers shaken by the arbitrariness of /réies/ on the one hand and /káye/ on the other will be further jolted by Poulter's handling of "vowel sequences" (43-44): "/iá/," for example, gives "[iá], [yá]: [vaskiár], [byáxe]," and /ia/ >[ia] and [ya] in turn, as in [límpia] but then [médya]. One is frankly at a loss as to how to interpret this: as a "sequence" of discrete or else unitary syllabic units, perhaps along the lines of Poulter's adjacent examples in which /ío/ and /ía/ give the well-known "Mexican Spanish" distinctions of either [frío] or [fríyo], [tía] or [tíya], etc.?

In the Abstract (p. xi) one is intrigued to learn that single-tap [r] and multiple-tap [R] are both shared by phonemes /r/ and /R/ and that /r/ gives [ɹ] as well. But intrigue is met by disappointment and even mystification when one reads (40-41) that "/r/ has the allophones: [r] in initial, medial, and final positions and occurs in all environments . . . [ɹ] is a free variant occuring in all environments . . . [and] [R] is a free variant occurring initially and finally . . . /R/ contrasts with /r/ only in the environment VCV and has the variants: [R] . . . [r]." Now if the local dialect's treatment of /R/-/r/ is approaching phonemic collapse, then why not say so? If, conversely, one discerns a series of trends revealing incipient collapse in part but retention of largely-standard /R/-/r/ distinctions in the main, then Poulter would have done well to document this by extracting all pertinent examples from his bulky, computer-produced and alphabetically-arranged corpus (pp. 62-178).

Students willing to trust Poulter's phonetic interpretations and who furthermore have the time and patience to examine the corpus on their own will doubtless retrieve some information on the pronunciation of northern Texas Spanish as recorded in this dissertation. [RT]

*SÁNCHEZ, George I. and Charles L. Eastlack. Say It the Spanish Way. Austin: The Good Neighbor Commission of Texas, 1960. __?__ pp.

Owned by no library (including all the obvious ones in Texas itself), this item was formerly distributed gratis by the Commission but is now unavailable as the supply is exhausted (according to information received from the Commission). [RT]

5.4 SPANISH GRAMMAR (MORPHOLOGY AND SYNTAX)

Major Items: GONZ-Gu-1968; GONZ-Gu-1970; GONZ-Gu-1974; HENS-1973;

SAID-1970

See also these items elsewhere (consult Author Index for location):

HENS-1974b; SIMO-1945; WOLF-1971

GARCÍA, Maryellen. "Para-pa Usage in United States Spanish." Paper presented at the Texas Symposium on Romance Linguistics, Austin, March 1974. 13 pp. ms. (Will appear in the proceedings of the symposium, to be published by Georgetown Univ. School of Languages and Linguistics.)

A semi-sociolinguistic study of the use of para and pa based on a taped acceptability test given to 77 Chicanos, mostly from El Paso, and 77 Mexicans, mostly from Ciudad Juárez. The analysis of the responses discusses: the extent to which the reduction of para to pa is categorical in Chicano Spanish; differences in the usage of the two forms in Chicano and Mexican Spanish; the adverbial uses of para-pa that are semantically unique to Chicano Spanish; and the use of para-pa as a directional preposition replacing a. This laudable report is flawed only by the limitations of the testing instrument. [GB]

GONZÁLEZ, Gustavo. "A Linguistic Profile of the Spanish-speaking First-grader in Corpus Christi." MA Thesis, Univ. of Texas, Austin, 1968. 83 pp.

This unusually well-written thesis presents an exhaustive, skillful analysis of the Spanish syntax and morphology of thirteen youngsters; it attempts to determine "the level of linguistic competence of the Mexican-American child when he enters the first grade" (p. 1) and investigates whether he has "internalized the

basic structures of his native language, or if he actually speaks
an unintelligible mixture popularly known as 'Tex-Mex.'" (ibid.)
After transcribing each child's hour-long unstructured conversational interview González gathers an inventory of syntactic structures
(Ch. 2), verbs (Ch. 3), types of transformations, tenses, and
grammatical "variants from standard forms" (Chs. 4, 5 and 6, resp.)
Stockwell/Bowen/Martin's The Grammatical Structures of English and
Spanish (1965) is the point of departure; all material is matched
with Spanish features as that volume presents them.

González concludes (p. 82) that the children's syntactic
patterns "are largely the same as those of normal adult Spanish"
and that "although there is influence from English, this influence
is minimal." The not-insubstantial number of "variants" in Ch. 6
might give partial lie to these claims, but as the author seems
to admit, many of the deviant patterns may be remnants of baby-
talk; to this end he suggests extensive testing of "monolingual
Spanish children from Mexico to determine which of these areas of
deviation may be due to the age of the child and which may be due
to the particular dialect and/or socio-economic class of the
child." (ibid.) [RT]

GONZÁLEZ, Gustavo. "The Acquisition of Spanish Grammar by Native
    Spanish Speakers." PhD Diss., Univ. of Texas, Austin, 1970.
    vii, 178 pp. [DA 31 (1971) 6033-A.]

González proposed to determine developmental sequences in the
speech of native Spanish-speaking children of the Lower Rio Grande
Valley of Texas, and also to examine "which syntactic structures
are characteristic of each age level and what the range of language variability is" for each group. (p. 2) The ages studied
range from two to five; examination proceded an on "apparent time"
basis, i.e., instead of following the development of the same
informants from age to age, four different children were interviewed for each of the six-month intervals studied. To obviate
possible effects of poverty on language behavior only middle- and
lower-middle-class children were studied; interviews were likewise
limited to children with active knowledge of Spanish. Each child
was given two hours of interviews, both conversational and guided.

Findings are organized chronologically: "Each chapter
[presents] the syntactic structures found in that age group, a
discussion of the development of certain grammatical features of
interest, and a look at the deviations encountered at the age
level under study." (p. 8) González also presents the relative
frequency of occurrence of all significant syntactic patterns and
examines other grammatical items such as verb tenses, negation,
interrogatives, possessives and so forth. In Ch. 10 ("Summary and
Conclusions") we learn that the perfect tenses are the last to
appear, negation through no is established at age 2.6 and expands
to other negatives later, sentences progress from simple to complex
to compound, etc.; González also repeats an earlier claim (1968):

"our study provides emphatic proof that the Mexican American child['s grammar] . . . is probably as purely Spanish as that found anywhere in the Spanish-speaking world." (167)

While the foregoing must be approached with caution, given the author's careful pre-selection of informants, this superbly-written work is still obligatory reading for all students of child language and Texas Spanish grammar. [RT]

GONZÁLEZ, Gustavo. "The Acquisition of Questions in Texas Spanish." In Bills 1974, pp. 251 266.

This superb "apparent time" study of the development of interrogatives between the ages of two and five is based on the speech of 27 middle-class informants (three at each of nine age levels) from the Lower Rio Grande Valley (see also González 1970 et seq.). For each age level the findings are presented together with explanations of the emergence of varied types of yes-no, information, and tag questions, comments on deviations and discrepancies between competence and performance, and ample examples. González concludes that questions are learned in the order: yes-no, information, tag, and that the three basic types are fully acquired by age 3.3. His findings are briefly compared with findings on the acquisition of questions by English speakers. [GB]

HENSEY, Fritz G. "Grammatical Variables in Southwestern American Spanish." Linguistics 108.5-26 (July 1973).

Hensey presents and then analyzes a series of deviant or nonstandard Spanish constructions from a corpus of short essays written for the most part by Mexican-American students at the University of Texas-El Paso. The goal is to discover "grammatical variables pertinent to the Spanish of El Paso;" (p. 6) a taxonomy of perhaps one hundred clearly variant forms is presented on pp. 8-13 under the following major headings: deviations in the noun and verb phrases and deviations involving transformations; among the latter we find reflexivization, concord, sentence embedding, mode selection, word order, passivization, etc.

While "no attempt is made to account for deviations in terms of Anglicisms, regionalisms, and the like," (8) the majority of the variants are obviously the product of English influence, whether directly so, as "calques"--quisiera ser una profesora / después de graduación / "*los que hablan un (i.e., un sólo [sic, 'solo']) idioma," (ibid.) / otro pasatiempo es viendo a las muchachas (nine instances of gerunds used as nouns)/ no me gustó que hacían / hay mucho que ver y divertirse con / la gente son muy cariñosas / me enamoré con esa ciudad--or else indirectly, as manifestations of increasing disregard for distinctions which Spanish makes but which English does not (or vice versa): un persona bondadosa / prefieren a los que no son chicanos (seven eschewals of obligatory subjunctive) / esposa y hijos / no nomás quiero ser profesora pero también quisiera / quieren que les enseñara / cuando tuve siete años vivía, etc. Still other variants are indeed "regionalisms" and are readily classifiable as such: la clima/la programa, sépamos/dígamos/téngamos, etc. However, Hensey's detailed analysis of a limited number of variants (pp. 14-25) is careful to focus upon "the mechanism involved in the deviation" (8) and thus manages to avoid the question of "origin" in all but two instances, and then grudgingly ("Deviations [which involve] using a gerund instead of an infinitive or a relative clause, are probably instances of syntactic interference from English" [21]). In some cases, presentations of the deviation's mechanism are brilliant tours de force, but unnecessarily so, since a brief analysis of Spanish usage as contrasted with English would have sufficed (see for example the explanation of the superfluous indefinite article on p. 15); in other cases (generally those which do not involve Anglicization) both length and attention to mechanism are fully justified, as in Hensey's fine analysis of ill-placed determiners (e.g., los tesoros famosos [preliminary theoretical considerations on pp. 12-14, specific examination p. 16]).

Since according to Hensey "the very fact of undertaking so-called Mexican-Americanist research is a sociopolitical act," one presumes he went to such lengths not to ascribe variance to English influence in order that the following conclusion could be reached (p. 24): "these deviations . . . are mostly low-level problems [and] do not tend to affect the higher levels of syntax but seem to confine themselves to lexicon, phonology, and transformational rules." Thus "the corpus provided no solid evidence for breakdown of basic sentence structure." The superficial reader of Hensey, then, is apt to conclude that the students' Spanish is almost free of English influence since even its "variants are not tagged as calques of English. Such is not the case. (Possibly Hensey could have lent weight to his argument by telling what percentage the variants formed of corpus word totals, T-group totals, or whatever.) [RT]

PATTERSON, Maurine. "Some Dialectal Tendencies in Popular Spanish in San Antonio [Texas]." MA Thesis, Texas State College for Women [Texas Women's Univ.], Denton, 1946. 120 pp.

Limited though it is to an exegesis of "variant forms," Patterson's study nonetheless represents the first serious attempt to examine the Spanish language of Texas and furthermore is the first scholarly work to espouse a viewpoint which for its time was clearly avant-garde, namely, that "the type of Spanish spoken in San Antonio is not a 'so-called jargon,' but that most of the dialectal forms found [there] have their counterparts" in medieval, peninsular or Western Hemisphere Spanish. (p. iii)

The work's material was abstracted "from the Spanish of the 1,000 Latin-American students enrolled in Spanish classes at [San Antonio Vocational and Technical High School] during 1940-1946," (7) initially from sporadic jottings-down of "interesting dialectal tendencies" found in oral recitations and subsequently through the administration of a questionnaire listing 155 of these variants (the students were asked to mark "only the terms which they themselves used" [ibid.]). Patterson classifies her findings rather broadly as "archaisms," "vulgarisms," "Mexicanisms" and "Anglicisms;" the first category lumps morphology with phonology in commentary on verbal, nominal and adjectival variants such as semos, traiba, truje, divertoso, fierro, etc., while the second category deals almost exclusively with phonology ("destruction of hiatus to form diphthong," "synalepha," "alphaeresis [sic]," "addition of consonants," "metathesis" and the like). Most of the "-isms" are well-known specimens by now, although Patterson's comments on "suffix le [ándale/pásale/córrele]" and siempre 'todavía' still bear consultation. Her analytical modus operandi is to demonstrate her forms' antiquity or ubiquity and to explicate their particular deviation(s) by citing pertinent passages from Aurelio Espinosa Sr., Ramón Menéndez Pidal et al. [RT]

PEÑA, Albar Antonio. "Spanish-Speakers." In Reading for the Disadvantaged: Problems of Linguistically Different Learners, edited by Thomas D. Horn. New York et elibi: Harcourt, Brace & World, Inc., 1970. Pp. 157-160 (part of Ch. 7, "Language Characteristics of Specific Groups").

The bulk of this is a summary of the author's doctoral dissertation (1967), a study of the basic sentence patterns and transformations that poverty-level bilingual San Antonio first-graders possess in both their languages. While "the findings suggest that their [Spanish] is more developed than most educators would expect," it was clear that even though the children's grammatical constructions were complete, "the noun and verb slots were often filled with words borrowed from English or English words they had hispanicized." (p. 158) The children were also prone to fill English sentence noun slots with Spanish, e.g., "This is a lápiz." (159)

Brief, subsequent sections discuss "dialect" and "effective teaching methods;" in the first of these Peña mootly posits mainland Puerto Rican Spanish as more corrupted than Chicano Spanish, and goes on to state that "under the present conditions, the Cubans now residing in the United States probably find themselves in the same situation as the Puerto Ricans." (159-160) Mexican-Americans "have been able to maintain control of their dialect because of their proximity to Mexico." (159) [RT]

REYNOLDS, Selma Fay. "Some Aspects of Spanish as Spoken and
Written by Spanish-Speaking Students of a Junior High School
in [Corpus Christi,] Texas." MA Thesis, Texas Women's Univ.,
Denton, 1945. vii, 107 pp.

Resembles substantively the descriptivist work done at the
same university by Patterson (1946) in that it presents a catalogue
of "deviations from the literary norm" extracted (in this case)
from the compositions of sixty 12 and 13 year-olds and from
several dozen "conversations" between groups of those same children
and the author. Like Patterson, Reynolds compares her findings
to commentary on identical phenomena by Aurelio Espinosa, Ramón
Menéndez Pidal and others. Her chapter on "phonological changes"
discusses vowels (tonic and otherwise), then consonants (initial,
intervocalic, loss and interchangeability of fricatives, various
combinations, etc.). Linguists will find little here they have
not found elsewhere, but Reynolds' work is nevertheless valuable
as an early attestation to the very same low-level rule differences now being "discovered" by persons new to the field; see esp.
pp. 60-64 for pre-scientific though telling discussions of such
things as the abolished distinction between the second and third
conjugations, the leftward placement of stress in most first-
person present-tense plural verb forms and the near-exclusive use
of /nos/ as marker for these. Like all variants produced only in
the writing of persons not overly familiar with the orthographic
conventions of their "first" language, Reynolds' composition-
derived material will have to be taken at less than face value for
the most part, although from time to time the forms do appear to
mirror variant pronunciations and even offer up new keys to old
problem areas ("A very original solution to the ['ll'/'y'] problem
was the spelling of the word allá in the phrase 'a pasar la noche
a hiá'"..p. 38).

Another very noteworthy feature is the author's Bildungsphilo-
sophie: "Linguistic needs of these children who speak Spanish on
entering Spanish classes are naturally different from those of
their classmates who do not. This study has grown out of the
investigator's increasing sense of their need for instruction
partly corrective in nature and partly aimed toward growth in
power of linguistic expression beyond that possible to English-
speaking students. Such a program, while it may include the aims
set up for non-Spanish-speaking students, cannot be limited to
them only." (pp. 2-3) Nihil nŏvum . . . ? [RT]

SAID, Sally Eugenia Sneed. "A Descriptive Model of Austin Spanish
Syntax." MA Thesis, Univ. of Texas, Austin, 1970. viii, 62 pp.

Using Chomsky's Aspects (1965) as a model and Stockwell/Bowen/
Martin (1965) as the Spanish grammar referent, Said has analyzed
transformationally the corpus collected by Lucía Elías Olivares
1970 from ten adolescent informants bilingual in Spanish and
English. Each interview ran 25 minutes. Only verbal fragments

were analyzed. As one of Said's goals was the reconstruction of developmental processes, care was taken to determine "stages" in a string's progress to its final form: Ch. 3 shows, for example, "the probability of occurrence of fourteen one-string transformations, and resulting conditional probability for combining a particular sentence pattern in Stage One with a particular transformation in Stage Two." (pp. 3-4) Ch. 5 presents as the Model a summation of patterns, transformations and probabilities. The many references to "probability" indicate the degree to which this competent thesis bristles with the sort of statistics that would surely permit "definitive conclusions about sex and age differences" (50) had the sample's size been greater (it averaged 50 utterances per informant). [RT]

5.5 SPANISH LEXICON (includes SEMANTICS)

Major Items: BAUG-1933; CERD/etal-1953; CORN-1969; FODY-1969; GALV-1955; HARR-1967; ROMA-1960

See also these items elsewhere (consult Author Index for location):

CRUZ-1970; GONZ-Gu-1968; GONZ-Gu-1970; HERN-1970; JANU-1970; KERC-1967; MCCL-1964; PATT-1946; RAMI-K-197[1?]; RAMI-K-1973; RUBE-1966

BAUGH, Lila. "A Study of Pre-school Vocabulary of Spanish-speaking Children." MA Thesis, Univ. of Texas, Austin, 1933. 129 pp.

Ostensibly an attempt to establish the "mental equipment" that Texas Chicano youngsters bring to school at age six, Baugh actually produces a rather accurate statement of childhood Spanish lexical norms, and in that sense has written a guide which other researchers would do well to consult for purposes of comparison. Although at first glance B's method of collection appears suspect, and for the usual reasons (i.e., an unconscious "predetermining" of findings through reliance on set topics and a limited series of visual aids), an examination of her Vocabulary (pp. 38-129) shows clear transcendence of expected findings. That the children (all from the Kingsville area and all Spanish-monolingual) give every appearance of possessing a rich active vocabulary is demonstrated by B's comparison of her own items with those from three very disparate lists: M. Buchanan's literature-based Graded Spanish Word Book (1927), and two lists drawn up by the National Society for the Study of Education of "the commonest words in the spoken vocabulary of [English-monolingual] children up to and including six years of age." (p. 35) Not only does Baugh conclude that her youngsters "know many Spanish words that have no English equivalents in the two [English] word lists," (54) but that many of their Spanish words "have a wide range of usefulness," (56) since more than half of them appear in the Buchanan list. [RT]

CARROW, Elizabeth [Sister Mary Arthur]. "Comprehension of English and Spanish by Preschool Mexican-American Children." MLJ 55.299-306 (1971). [Abs. LLBA V-1546.]

Following an unfortunate allegation that "investigations involving direct study of oral language performance of Mexican-American children are practically non-existent," (p. 300) Carrow presents the findings from her study of the auditory comprehension of Spanish and English of 99 Houston-area poverty-level Chicano youngsters ages 3.10 to 6.9. Each child was administered Carrow's own (1969) Auditory Test for Language Comprehension which "consists of a set of 114 plates, each of which contains three [drawings] which represent referential categories that can be signaled by form classes and function words, morphological constructions, grammatical categories and syntactic structure." (ibid.) Subjects were tested first in the language in which they appeared least fluent (after such was ascertained through introductory unstructured conversation). Carrow then chronicles words understood and the percentages of children who understand them at the various age levels; thus "in rank order, the nouns understood by most children in both languages were 'boy' ('muchacho'), 'mother' ('mamá'), 'girl' ('muchacha'), 'shoe' ('zapato'), and 'baby' ('bebé')." (302) Among the Spanish words least understood were such non-urban or else cold-climate nouns as abrigo, árbol, rancho, pescado; other specific findings appear on pp. 301-303. Among the general conclusions: young Chicanos are linguistically "a very heterogeneous group [since] at each age level among these children, there is wide variation in the combinations in which the two languages are known."(303) Though of the pre-Schoolers tested "the greater proportion understand English better than Spanish," "in general both languages improve as the children become older." (ibid.) Specific areas of difficulty in both languages were pronouns, use of negatives, and the ability to handle "tense markers--with the exception of the present progre sive, adjectives, prepositions and plurals [?]." (ibid.) [RT]

CARROW, Elizabeth [Sister Mary Arthur]. "Auditory Comprehension of English by Monolingual and Bilingual Preschool Children." JSHR 15.407-412 (1972). [Abs. LLBA 6.7206324; MLAAb/Ling 1972.24 (no. 2054).]

Carrow has singled out the thirty most thoroughly bilingual of 99 previously interviewed children (see Carrow 1971) for further testing and for explicit comparison with English-monolingual children from the same chronological, socioeconomic and regional backgrounds. Test procedures resembled those employed in the earlier experiments results from the present one led themselves to a variety of interpretations: while "the mean number of correct responses for monolingual children, 94.50 (out of 114) and for bilingual, 88.66, were significantly different" (p. 409) and

"bilingual children made a greater number of errors than did
monolingual children in all areas except verbs, plurality as
signaled by 'is' and 'are,' and verb tense," (410) it was also
learned that "the bilingual children in the six-year age group
performed slightly better than monolingual children" vis à vis
correct responses given; thus it is that Carrow can claim in the
same paragraph that "the results of this study support earlier
findings about the language comprehension (hearing vocabulary)
of bilingual Mexican-American children [reference here is to Carrow
1955]," and that "there is a tendency for the language comprehension gap to narrow at the age level of five years, 10 months,
to six years, nine months." (411) (Further testing of the same
two groups of children as they advanced in years might possibly
have revealed a continuation of the narrow gap.) The remainder
of this article attempts to explain the bilinguals' posited
developmental retardation in terms of structural dissimilarities
between English and Spanish. [RT]

CASTILLO NÁJERA, Francisco. "Breves consideraciones sobre el español que se habla en Méjico." RHM 2.157-169 (Jan. 1936).
  [Annot. Nichols no. 911.]

Although the greater part of this article limits itself to
describing in general terms the phonology, morphology, lexicon,
etc., of the Spanish of Mexico, a small section (167-169), devoted
to Anglicisms, includes words which the author indicates are
commonly used in San Antonio, Texas, where Castillo served as
Mexican consul for several years. The material is presented by
topic; the following citation is typical: "La taberna, aristo-
cratizada, resulta salón; las bebidas son drinques, la tienda
común es una chopa, y el expendio de abarrotes se rebaja hasta
convertirse en grocería." [RT]

CERDA, Gilberto, Berta Cabeza and Julieta Farias. Vocabulario
  español de Texas. (University of Texas Hispanic Studies, No.
  5) Austin: Univ. of Texas Press, 1953. vii, 347 pp. (Reprinted, Austin: Univ. of Texas Press, 1970.) [Annot. HLAS
  19 (1957) no. 4518 (D. Wogan); Serís no. 15552; Solé no. 993.
  Rev. Hispania 36.419 (1953) (D. Walsh); NRFH 10.214-219 (1956)
  (P. Boyd-Bowman); Thesaurus 26.1-4 (1971) (R. Galván).] (The
  Vocabulario represents a synthesis of three Master's theses
  written by the authors of the published volume and directed
  by Prof. M. Romera-Navarro at the University of Texas: Berta
  Cabaza, "The Spanish Language in Texas. No. 2: Cameron and
  Willacy Counties," 1950, 183 pp.; Gilberto Cerda, "The Spanish
  Language in Texas. No. 1: Val Verde, Edwards, and Kinney
  Counties," 1950, 305 pp.; and María Julieta Farias, "The
  Spanish Language in Texas. No. 3: Duval, Webb and Zapata
  Counties," 1950, 122 pp.)

To date this is the only published full-length dictionary of any dialect of Mexican-American Spanish (in this case, the speech of eight of the twelve southern-most Texas Chicano-majority counties).

Faithfully following the lamentable tendency of many Hispanic regionalist lexicographers to limit their lexicons to lists of "voces no registradas en el Diccionario Académico o registradas en él con una acepción diferente" (p. iii), Cerda et al. draw harsh criticism from Boyd-Bowman 1956, who notes that the dictionary "consigna, sin más criterio que [el de reunir palabras no registradas por la Academia] . . . y sin estudio alguno, un caudal de palabras, ordenadas alfabéticamente, en que se mezclan variantes fonéticas muy ordinarias (maistro, tiatro, ajuera, usté ...), vulgarismos y arcaísmos demasiado conocidos (muncho, mesmo, lamber, caiba, haiga, ansí ...), americanismos (boleto, ahorita, mayoreo, puro, frijol ...) y muchos mexicanismos, anglicismos y regionalismos sin clasificar." (214) Both Boyd-Bowman and Galván have noted the dictionary's failure to accompany entries with historical interpretation. Galván takes the work to task for not providing even the briefest of usage labels (e.g., no assigning of "pachuco" to words which clearly deserve that label). Perhaps the severest criticism both reviewers make is that because the Vocabulario lists definitions for words whose relation to the Texas entries is solely homophonous and thus strictly coincidental, it therefore includes a vast quantity of useless information which adds nothing but bulk; one of the very many examples of this is the Anglicism chara < charter 'código fundamental de una ciudad, estado o sociedad,' on which are wasted ten lines annotating the homonym chara 'pollo de la avestruz,' 'la oca puesta a helar,' 'la sopa ... hecha de granos de cebada tostada,' etc. Galván points out the work's frequent failure to mark Anglicisms as such; he also criticizes its "falta total de metas y de conclusions"; (4) nowhere does Cerda explain the methods employed to collect the corpus--whether with a questionnaire, through free conversation, from the mass media, etc.

It is Boyd-Bowman's judgment that "todo el material nuevo hubiera formado un bonito artículo de unas treinta páginas;" (215) to this end he himself does the user of the Vocabulario a considerable service by extracting a largely complete "selection" of what he finds to be its three groups of "palabras interesantes"; Mexicanisms, Anglicisms and regionalisms. Footnote 5 lists the first of these, footnotes 6-8 and also pp. 216-218 the second two groups. He notes that "las páginas 247 a 335 del Vocabulario contienen una lista de modismos, locuciones y refranes, corrientes muchos de ellos . . . en otras partes de América y en España [que está] bien hecha y de alguna utilidad;" (218) far less complimentary is his opinion of the work's final section, "Hispanismos que usa la gente de habla inglesa" (337-347): "está tan infelizmente concebida que lo más caritativo sería no hablar de ella." [RT]

CERVANTES, Alfonso. "A Selected Vocabulary of Anglicisms Used by the Spanish-speaking First Grade Students of the Elementary Schools of Del Río, Texas." MA Thesis, Southwest Texas State Univ., San Marcos, 1973. vi, 68 pp.

This thesis's general outline closely resembles that of the other half-dozen lexical studies of Texas Spanish directed by Prof. Roberto Glaván; for more specific comments on the general type see Frausto 1969. Cervantes, an evaluator for the Del Río bilingual education program, has taken his entries largely from the natural speech of four different schools' first-grade Chicanos, 40 per cent of whom are Spanish-dominant (according to results obtained from Peabody Picture Vocabulary testing) and 25 per cent "bilingual" (balanced?). Additional information was obtained extramurally from the same general group of informants. Several sets of parents were also interviewed in an approximate attempt to determine English influence on the local adult Spanish; C found that parents often used Anglicisms which had not yet become part of their children's vocabulary. He also surveyed the local Spanish-language broadcast media (including stations transmitting from neighboring Ciudad Acuña, México) to ascertain English influence.

C found that the bilingual school is beginning to have a limited "ameliorative" effect on the subjects' Spanish: "The same child will generally use the correct Spanish term when he is aware that the teacher or teacher's aide is paying attention to him in the classroom but will revert to the corresponding Anglicism when he is out in the school yard." (p. 66) Many of the forms C records are well-known to Anglicismologists; among the new and variant: a min 'quiero decir' (used almost interjectively), chanza used phrase-initially and adverbially ('Chanza que vaya a las vistas el sábado'). [RT]

CORNEJO, Ricardo J. "Bilingualism: Study of the Lexicon of the Five-year-old Spanish-speaking Children of Texas." PhD Diss., Univ. of Texas, Austin, 1969. 228 pp. [DA 30 (1970) 1544-A.]

This dissertation was the "pilot" of what was intended to be a much larger Bilingual Research Project embracing the entire Southwest, sponsored by the University of Texas' Foreign Language Education Center and chiefly supported by the Southwest Educational Development Laboratory of Austin (see Michel 1969). Cornejo's purpose was to record and examine the speech of five-year-old Mexican-American children from rural and urban, border and interior Texas, in order to determine how well they knew Spanish, English or both, so as to ascertain the children's linguistic background upon entering school. C's work focuses largely on the children's lexicon; the bulk of the dissertation (pp. 62-153) is a composite lexical count of the recorded speech. Small subsequent sections analyze the lexemes phonologically and morphologically; also present are the inevitable lists of "Structural and Lexical Interference from English to Spanish," "Mexicanisms,"

"Archaisms in Spanish," "Metathesis" and so forth. From the description (pp. 52-60) the interviewing procedure appears highly structured; much use was made of visual materials and directed dialogs to elicit speech. Ideally, each of the 24 children was interviewed for 15 minutes in English and 15 minutes in Spanish, but no child was forced to speak one language exclusively if there was disinclination to do so.

C's conclusions (185-192) indicate that the Spanish of young Texas Chicanos will decay or disappear unless schools make efforts to preserve it: "The majority of the children expressed themselves better in English than in Spanish;" "Spanish structure and phonology are influenced by English" and "there is significant interference from English to Spanish." "Serious deficiencies were found in the articulation of common Spanish words," most of which could be categorized as "baby talk" (examples p. 187 and elsewhere). By the same token the schools must play a role in illustrating the children's English, but while "interference from Spanish to English is highly significant at the phonological level, it is minor at the lexical and grammatical levels." [RT]

ELÍAS OLIVARES, Lucía E. "Study of the Oral Spanish Vocabulary of Ten High-school Mexican-American Students in Austin, Texas." MA Thesis, Univ. of Texas, Austin, 1970. 110 pp.

Like Cornejo 1969, Elías Olivares is chiefly concerned with establishing a composite count of lexical items by means of half-hour-long interviews with local Mexican-American youth. But since the greater maturity of her subjects enabled E to utilize a less highly-structured interview technique, it is possible to conjecture that her findings are nearly as comprehensive as Cornejo's, differences in academic degree notwithstanding. Still, E's lexicon is somewhat skewed in favor of "household" words, a probable result of the questions which made up the "daily routine interview" format adhered to. Following the item count E analyzes the more salient lexemes in time-honored fashion: Mexicanisms, "regionalisms," "obsolete words," English borrowings and influences, etc. [RT]

FODY III, Michael. "A Glossary of Non-standard Spanish Words and Idioms Found in Selected Newspapers of South Texas During 1968." MA Thesis, Southern Illinois Univ., Carbondale, 1969. xxxvii, 154 pp. [Annot. Fody p. 536.]

As Fody points out, "there is a very strong Anglicizing process constantly taking place" in South Texas among Mexican-Americans (p. x), loyalty to the Spanish language and the values of Mexican culture notwithstanding. Thus it is no surprise that Anglicisms constitute the largest single category of "non-standard" words which Fody skillfully culls from the Spanish-language press of Corpus Christi, McAllen, Laredo and Brownsville and (to a lesser extent) Harlingen, Kingsville and elsewhere. Other categories are, invariably, "Mexicanisms," archaisms, and miscellaneous neologisms. Annotations or incidental cacographs are also frequent. It is understandable that Fody has been able to assemble a very large corpus (433 entries, pp. 1-149), given his definition of a non-standard Spanish word as "one which does not appear in the Real Academia Española's <u>Diccionario</u> [1956]." (p. iii) Fody also compares many entries to listings in Santamaría (<u>Diccionario de mexicanismos</u>, 1959), the Velázquez Spanish-English dictionary (1943), and the 1964 <u>Pequeño Larousse ilustrado</u>. One of the thesis's noteworthy features is a long list of the "nicknames" Chicanos and Anglos apply to themselves and to each other (Tables 3 and 4, pp. xviii-xix). [RT]

FRAUSTO, Manuel H. "Vocabulario español de San Marcos, Texas."
    MA Thesis, Southwest Texas State Univ., San Marcos, 1969. vi, 55 pp.

    Chronologically the first of the seven MA theses on regional aspects of Texas Spanish lexicon directed at SW Texas State by Roberto Galván (see also Cervantes 1973, García 1972, Luna 1970, Marambio 1970, Ramón 1974, and Reséndez 1970), Frausto's "Vocabulario" is in most ways typical of the general type and will therefore be described in detail, thus obviating the need to discuss parallel features in the other six theses.
    Frausto's work records, defines, categorizes and then sets in context all "variant" lexemes its author noted in use among several generations of Spanish speakers in the Texas city of San Marcos. By "variant" Frausto means all forms not listed in the eighteenth edition of the Royal Academy dictionary (1956), or which though listed are found there "en sentido distinto, . . . con distinto o con igual sentido, pero con designación geográfica, con distinto o con igual sentido, pero como voz anticuada, arcaica o jergal." (p. iv) Occasional use of other works of value to regionalists is made throughout the lexicon (divided into two parts: the "vocabulario" [i.e., the listing of single words], pp. 14-46, and the "expresiones," 47-52): Santamaría, Cerda et al., Malaret, etc. Prior to the lexicon itself, F offers the reader some "Breves apuntes históricos" on the history of San Marcos (pp. 1-8), epsecially as it focusses on the city's Mexican-American population. F also speculates on the way the various tides of migration have influenced the local Spanish and demonstrates that Spanish has been spoken without interruption in San Marcos since the beginning of the 1800's. The "Método" by which collected his data is examined on pp. 10-12: initial investigation found the author "[recorriendo] las calles de San Marcos con lápiz y tarjeta en mano, listo para apuntar palabras que pareciesen regionales." (11) During later stages Frausto conducted individual interviews in order to collect specific <u>Wörter und Sache</u> information ("Nombre Ud. las prendas de vestir que usan usted y su familia, incluyendo desde el niño recién nacido hasta el abuelo" [12], etc.).

F's essentially morphophonological conclusiones (8-10) are thorough and well-handled, though they offer the reader little that is new: One learns that the local habla is characterized phonologically by prothesis (destornudar), epenthesis (aigre), apocope (pa 'para'), metathesis (estógamo), confusion as to unstressed vowel quality (difícil), etc., etc.; that a good part of the local lexicon is "Mexican;" and that, above all, English has left its mark: baquiar 'apoyar,' bendéi 'tira que sirve para curbrir heridas pequeñas,' bil 'cuenta,' bísquete 'bizcocho, panecillo,' and many more. For these reasons much of this will leave the reader with a strong sense of déjà vu; of greater interest are the expresiones found in the lexicon's second section; here one encounters a wide variety of idioms expressing drunkenness, "crazy" behavior, alacrity, anger, and the like, as well as various colorful items of reasonable novelty, of which the following complete entry is an example:

ESTAR A UNA Y UN PEDAZO. estar escaso de dinero: Cuando no tenía trabajo, estábamos a una y un pedazo. / to be short of money: When I did not have a job, we were short of money.

As individual contributions the seven Southwest Texas State theses are perhaps best viewed as competently-executed trabajos de iniciación which reflect the skilled guidance and also the special research interests of their director, Prof. Galván. As a unified whole, however, the theses make a singularly important contribution to what we know about the lexicon of Texas Spanish. [RT]

GALVÁN, Roberto A. "Un estudio geográfico de algunos vocablos usados por los habitantes de habla española de San Antonio, Texas." MA Thesis, Univ. of Texas, Austin, 1949. iv, 142 pp.

In the first of his many writings on Texas Spanish lexicon, Galván sets out to "catalogar un vocabulario que deje ver los elementos que constituyen el habla de los habitantes hispanoparlantes de San Antonio, Texas, dando, a la vez, alguna idea de la distribución geográfica de este léxico entre los países de habla española." (p. iii) The 599 items Galván includes are divided into three categories: "Vocablos de San Antonio usados en toda la América Latina o en la mayor parte de [ella] y en otros países hispano-parlantes," "Vocablos . . . usados en algunos países de la América Latina y en otras partes del mundo hispanoparlante," and "Vocablos del habla pachuca en San Antonio con su distribución geográfica;" this latter category's list is especially extensive and rivals in scope the works of George Barker (v.d.), to which it is demonstrably superior in method. That Galván has put much effort into determing whether a lexical item is "universal" or else "essentially local" (nowhere does Galván claim, as do so many others, that he has listed items found "only" in the given region) can be appreciated by examining the contents of his 92-item bibliography (134-141).

In the introduction (1-22) Galván offers sociolinguistic information on the various levels of San Antonio Spanish and on the social class and age group to which each corresponds. There the reader also learns, almost in passing, that Galván, himself a native of San Antonio, spent nearly two years in lexical fieldwork, roaming the city and jotting down words. Much was jotted, for Galván admits to "3115 palabras coleccionadas" (p. 4); it appears, though, that only the most "unusual" ones made their way into Galván's thesis and also into his PhD dissertation (1955), which in most respects is a continuation and an amplification of his MA work. [RT]

GALVÁN, Roberto A. "El dialecto español de San Antonio, Texas."
PhD Diss., Tulane Univ., New Orleans, 1955. 315 pp. (Tulane Abstracts, Series 55, no. 14, p. 90.) [Annot. Fody pp. 535-536.]

This is a continuation of the lexicon begun with Galván's MA thesis, and thus the reader will note many parallels between the two works: concern for establishing geographical distribution of words, interest in determining which San Antonio terms are "local" (of the 920 items Galván lists, 220 are adjudged peculiar to San Antonio, but the great majority of these are Anglicisms or else figurative or extended meanings of words documented elsewhere), etc. The difference between the two lies in the dissertation's considerably greater amplitude of scope: whereas the commentary accompanying the typical entry in Galván 1949 had chiefly to do with geographical distribution, its counterpart in Galván 1955 presents all the information one would normally expect to find in an encyclopedic or historical dictionary. The typical entry consists of: "(1) la palabra; su ortografía, su acento prosódico y sus variantes colocadas . . . después del vocablo principal; (2) la parte de la oración; (3) la etimología [origen semántico, origen de los derivados, etc.] . . . ; (4) la significación de la palabra en San Antonio" and its level of social usage (e.g., lower class, pachuco) along with various other usage indicators such as jergal, vulgar, arcaico; and (5) geographical distribution. Considerable attention is paid to this last section, and Galván appears to have run the gamut of regionalist dictionaries (see the Bibliografía, 300-314) in his search for a word's extension; in turn, each variant is treated exhaustively (place used, author in which cited, part of speech, meaning, usage labels, derivatives and alternate forms, etc.); Galván's concern with these matters often causes entries to run for pages and pages.

Galván indicates that no attempt was made to include "ejemplos del español general, por componerse éste de voces castizas;" (14) this is to be regretted, since the presence of a particular "castizo" form is often of as much interest as the occurrence of a form judged "unusual."

Among Galván's conclusions is that San Antonio Spanish generally continues to form part of "universal Spanish"; "la mayor parte de las palabras ['regionales'] han adquerido su sentido regional a través de las mismas causas que han ocasionado los provincialismos de otras zonas lingüísticas." (27) Among typical causes for variation one finds reduction or amplification of meaning. Attention is also paid (in the Introduction, esp. pp. 27-28) to the logic behind the semantic peculiarity of various pachuco interjections such as <u>calentadoras</u> 'cállese' ("el fenómeno consiste en escoger alguna voz que empiece con la primera letra o sílaba de la palabra cuya significación se desea emplear") (27).

Considerations of space prevent further examination of this important study. A comparison between it and Cerda 1953, however, proves most instructive and also brings one to regret that the fortuitous timing of the inferior Cerda dictionary apparently forestalled Galván's attempts to put his own work into print. [RT]

GALVÁN, Roberto A. "'Chichecano,' neologismo jergal." <u>Hispania</u> 53.86-88 (1970). [Annot. <u>HLAS</u> 32 (1970) no. 3080 (Canfield).]

An extremely thorough analysis of the etymology and semasiology of the word <u>chichecano</u>, and of the geographical distribution throughout Hispanic America of its component parts, which are <u>chiche</u> '<u>teta</u>' and <u>chicano</u> 'méxico-americano.' "El <u>chichecano</u> es, pues, el <u>chicano</u> que vive de la <u>chiche</u>, es decir, el estadounidense de origen mejicano que disfruta de una sinecura. . . [Se] trata de establecer una analogía entre el <u>chichecano</u> y el bebé que vive de las chiches (los pechos) de la madre sin más esfuerzo que el de aspirar su alimento." (87) The word appears to have been born in San Antonio in 1968 at the Kelly Air Force Base. [RT]

GALVÁN, Roberto A. "More on 'Frito' as an English Loan-Word in Mexican Spanish." <u>Hispania</u> 54.511-512 (1971)

The title of Galván's carefully-documented article is misleading: its reference is to a short piece by Charles Olstad ("'Frito': An English Loan-Word in Mexican Spanish," <u>Hispania</u> 53.88-90), whose article Galván uses largely as a point of departure to comment upon three instances of Spanish > English > Spanish reborrowing found <u>in Texas</u>. These are: <u>rancho</u> 'choza, etc.' > <u>ranch</u> 'large stock-raising concern' > <u>rancho</u> 'hacienda, finca grande;' also <u>cucaracha</u> > <u>cockroach</u> > <u>roche/rocho/rucho</u>; also <u>vainilla</u> > <u>vanilla</u> > <u>vanela/vanila</u>. Galván also takes Olstad to task for having failed to use some of the more obvious reference works such as Ricardo Alfaro, <u>Diccionario de anglicismos</u>, 2nd ed. (1964) where Olstad (had he checked) would have found other instances of the same phenomenon, such as <u>cafetería</u>. [RT]

GARCÍA, Lucy. "Vocabulario selecto del español de Brownsville, Texas." MA Thesis, Southwest Texas State Univ., San Marcos, 1972. 64 pp.

This Master's Thesis was directed by Roberto Galván and closely resembles the work of Frausto 1969, both in terms of its organization and its conclusions, presented as a "lexicon" (pp. 12-61). Of special note is the chronological catholicity of García's informants, who number 15 and who represent all the ages of man, from two informants who are seven to two in their seventies. [RT]

HARRISON, Helene W. "A Methodological Study in Eliciting Linguistic Data from Mexican-American Bilinguals." PhD Diss., Univ. of Texas, Austin, 1967. 119 pp. [DA 28 (1969) 4157-A.]

In an effort to determine whether an educationally, socially and sexually variegated group of 96 Mexican-Americans from central Texas provided a greater number of responses to 25 sensitive and 25 non-sensitive catchwords in Spanish than they did in English, Harrison reaches a number of conclusions regarding various methods of data elicitation which need not concern us here. For the linguist, the main value of her dissertation lies in the impressive number of colloquialisms and slang terms elicited. An alphabetical list of these is found at the end of the work (pp. 104-119); the terms are also arranged in a valuable frequency list ("Appendix C: Table of Responses in Chronological Order," 53-86). The "questionnaire" used to elicit responses appears on pp. 48-51; a typical lead-in phrase and a few of the responses to it: "40. a person who always complains / persona que siempre se queja -- [responses:] quejador, llorón, renegador, disgustado, repelón, fregón, calambre, chinga mucho, malcontento, adolorido, ¡como jode!. dolores, soflamero [etc., etc.]" Among other "sensitive" descriptions for which Harrison obtained interesting responses: "un immigrante [sic] de México que viene a los Estados Unidos sin papeles ni permiso," "un hombre casado que siempre coquetea o sale con otras mujeres," "un latino que adopta las maneras de los anglos," "una persona que siempre bebe mucho alcohol." [RT]

HENSEY, Fritz G. [1974b]. "Two Current Trends in Sociolinguistic Research." In Hoffer and Ornstein 1974, pp. 5-11.

Following a discussion of "sociological" versus "anthropological" research on the sociology of language, Hensey mentions his own study of the grammatical variables of El Paso Chicanos (HENS-1973) and briefly mentions three: adjective placement (an aberrant number of adjectives preceding the nouns they modify), infinitives with gerund complements (empecé yendo 'empecé a ir'), and indicatives where standard Spanish demands subjunctives ('no hay nadie que entiende'). H suggests that future studies of Mexican-

American lexicon "attempt to account for the distribution of a small number of socially important words or expressions that occur in two or more variants" (7) rather than aiming to produce "exhaustive" compilations of dictionary size and sort. [RT]

IVEY, Alfred Joe. "A Study of the Vocabulary of Newspapers Printed in the Spanish Language in Texas." MA Thesis, Univ. of Texas, Austin, 1927. iii, 137 pp.

This early work lists the 1,500 most frequently used words in a total of 42 issues of four newspapers from San Antonio, Brownsville, Laredo and El Paso, respectively, and also from six issues of the New York-based La Prensa, for "purposes of comparison" (although no significant frequency differences were found between New York and Texas). The words themselves are presented in frequency groups of twenty (pp. 33-107) and are unaccompanied by contextual citations or by any other form of annotation. Definite articles (grouped as a single entry) appear most frequently, followed by the function words que, de, a, en, and y, the indefinite articles, and the verbs ser and estar which are likewise grouped as single entities, no distinction being made as to tense or person. After drawing various pedagogically-oriented conclusions (Ch. 5), Ivey presents a brief lexicon of "some of the more interesting 'border Spanish' words, as they are called by Texas authorities on Spanish," (122) including many sports Anglicisms. [RT]

KELLY, George W. and Rex R. Kelly. Farm and Ranch Spanish. N.pl.: Authors, 1960. xv, 241 pp. (Mimeographed and bound. Loc.: Univ. of Texas, Austin, Library.) (Cf. Rex Kelly 1938.)

A curious presentation in "phrase-book" fashion of all the terms and sentences a rancher will theoretically need to know to communicate with his "Mexican" help, this work's topically-arranged tripartite division ("Ranch Section," "Farm Section" and "Grammer [sic] Section") includes chapters on "The pastures and the pens," "Today we round up goats," "Drenching and marking sheep," irrigation, picking cotton, beets, tomatoes, lettuce and so forth. Along the way the authors drop various mind-blowing hints on morphosyntaxis ("Remember that you can accomplish most of your work by using the present tense. The average Mexican laborer knows only the present and past verb forms"--p. 3) and lexicon ("There are many names in English that the Mexican does not have the equivalent in Spanish [sic], for example: They say . . . jeepe [pron.?] for jeep, trucke [?] for truck, and others that have been listed in other chapters"--62-63). But in other chapters the authors consistently use camioneta for truck and never employ the forms troca/troque one expects to find in Texas Spanish. Despite the Introduction's disclaimer that "many of the words [the Mexicans] use have been made without any thought of Spanish foundation," (iii) nearly all the items in the bilingual Vocabularies (187-241) can be found in any pocket dictionary, although from time to time one runs across an item of interest such as regación 'riego' and repolla 'repollo.' [RT]

KELLY, Rex R. "Vocabulary as Used on the Mexican Border." MA Thesis, Baylor Univ., 1938. 39 pp.

This is a very pre-scientific piece of work which faithfully reflects the epoch's linguistic prejudices (Kelly speaks of a separate "Texas-Mexican language" among border-dwellers and then opines that "many of the words that they use have been made without any thought of Spanish foundation, but rather for the purpose of realistic description"). (p. 3) It is nevertheless a valuable sourcework as an early attestation to the presence of a wide variety of archaisms, ruralisms, Anglicisms and "Mexicanisms" in the Spanish of Texas. Kelly's wordlist is divided into chapters on animals, foods, people (e.g., the interesting gavialobo 'shrewd person'), underworld and sporting terms, and the like. On p. 3 he claims that "there can be no bibliography for this thesis," and indeed none is provided (although he refers often to "the Spanish dictionary"); Kelly would have done well to consult the works of Joaquín García Icazbalceta, Darío Rubio and Augusto Malaret, to name just a few available at the time. [RT]

LEÓN, Aurelio de. Barbarismos comunes en México. 2 vols. (vol. 1: México D.F.: Imprenta Mundial, 1936. 80 pp., supl.; vol. 2: México D.F.: 1937. 92 pp.) [Annot. HLAS 3 (1937) no. 3442 (Wright); Nichols no. 953.]

De León's alphabetical listings consign words to the following (often redundant) categories: anglicismos, barbarismos, cursilerías, palabras extranjeras, voces forenses, voces usadas en el norte de la República, provincialismos, and tejanismos. Part One contains 329 words, Part Two about 200 more. Most of the tejanismos are English loanwords; some samples: "aplicación.--Tejanismo en lugar de 'petición,' 'solicitud,' 'memorial,' etc.." "chainero.--Tej. Se usa esta palabra en la frontera del norte y en Tejas, en vez de 'limpiabotas' o del barbarismo nacional: 'bolero.'" "pompa.--Enorme barbarismo inventado por los tejanos, con lo que quieren significar 'bomba' con 'b,' refiriéndose a las de automóvil generalmente. Está tomada del inglés: 'pump.' En realidad 'pompa' quiere decir fausto, vanidad, grandeza, etc. . . ." [RT]

LUNA, Juanita J. "A Selected Vocabulary of the Spanish Spoken in Sabinal, Texas." MA Thesis, Southwest Texas State Univ., San Marcos, 1970. 101 pp.

This work was directed by Prof. Roberto Galván and closely resembles the theses of other Galván students in its organization (introduction to the locality, then a bi-partite lexicon giving individual words and then "phrases and sayings," a section of conclusions, etc.); for further comments on the general type see Frausto 1969. Luna's lexicon (pp. 16-93) is fairly extensive and contains various items of interest such as the unusual spelling pronunciation <u>desplogiar</u> (< to unplug, e.g., 'Por favor, desplogea la cuerda de la plancha'), the possibly ultra-corrected <u>desvolver</u> 'devolver,' and the likely phonological collapse of /r̄/ to /r/ in several words (e.g., <u>eror</u> 'error'). [RT]

MARAMBIO, Juan. "Vocabulario español de Temple, Texas." MA Thesis, Southwest Texas State Univ., San Marcos, 1970. 110 pp.

This is another in a series of MA theses on the "regionalisms" and the Anglicisms of local Texas Spanish directed by Prof. Roberto Galván; see my discussion of Frausto 1969 for a description of the general type. Marambio's work is typical of the rest, although noteworthy for the conclusion it reaches regarding English influence on "Temple Spanish": "El hispanoparlante de Temple usa hasta un cincuenta por ciento de anglicismos en su conversación diaria;" (p. 12) unfortunately Marambio does not provide <u>in situ</u> citations of what would certainly be an astonishing form of idiolect. But perhaps the author meant to refer not to Anglicisms but to the frequent code switching which would produce sentences that alternated evenly between Spanish and English. [RT]

MAY, Darlene Rae. "Notas sobre el tex-mex." <u>ICCNC</u> 70.17-19 (Nov. 1, 1966).

This is a popularized summary of some of the features of Texas Spanish together with a relation of the history of Hispanic settlements and populations in Texas. Most of May's linguistic information is excerpted from the dissertation of Sawyer 1957: May repeats Sawyer's conclusions about Texas Chicano English phonology and also her information on the extent to which "los latinos evitaban palabras españolas comúnmente usadas por los anglos." (18) It would appear that May has taken her information on the lexicon of Texas Spanish (and on the Hispanisms in Texas English) from Cerda et al. 1953, although this source is not cited. One is surprised that the article bears the title it does since the term "Tex-Mex" figures among May's list of words with which Anglos insult Chicanos in San Antonio, the others being "<u>greasers, wetbacks, brownies, pepper bellies, bean bandits</u> y <u>peons</u>." (19) [RT]

MC KEE, Okla Markham. "Five Hundred Non-dictionary Words Found in the El Paso-Juárez Press." MA Thesis, Texas Western College [Univ. of Texas-El Paso], 1955. 75 pp. [Annot. Fody p. 538.]

This is one of the very few studies of the lexicon of the Mexican-American press, although strictly speaking McKee's survey of several Ciudad Juárez newspapers alongside the El Paso publications inevitably weakens that claim, as does the fact that she often fails to cite the periodical in which the entries were published.

Through cross-references with the Royal Academy dictionary and other well-known sources, the study examines "Form (new formations, suffixation, new verbs, orthographic changes, abbreviations and shortened expressions, borrowed words, change of form and/or usage) and Meaning (unlisted meanings, mistranslations, substitutions of English usage via translation)." (Fody) Though rich in lexical materials the work is poorly organized and quite difficult to consult. Its 150-some Anglicisms, for example, are largely concentrated on pp. 29-34 ("Borrowed Words"), but also appear on pp. 23 ff., 55 ff., and elsewhere passim. Her categorization scheme, as spelled out by Fody supra, is simultaneously overladen with fine distinctions and underendowed with a clear understanding of the processes of neologization. Nevertheless the work contains many items that are not recorded elsewhere, along with various amusing examples of picardía mexicana. [RT]

RAMÓN, Simón René. "Vocabulario selecto del español regional de Del Río, Texas." MA Thesis, Southwest Texas State Univ., San Marcos, 1974. vii, 70 pp.

Identical in format and modus operandi to Frausto 1969 (q.v.) and the other theses on Texas Spanish lexicon directed by Roberto Galván, Ramón's work is the product of interviews with four separate generations of Del Ríoans (14 informants ages ten to seventy-one). Many words also found in Frausto et al. are included here too, though "covert" terms stand out more in Ramón than elsewhere, e.g., crema, feme, flor and joto ('homosexual'). Also of interest: the radical-changing Anglicism deservar ('Desiervo un premio'), huesito 'trabajo de poca duración,' the curious puertamonera 'portamoneda,' the "rhotacism" of sarsa 'salsa.' [RT]

RESÉNDEZ, Víctor. "Vocabulario español de Seguín, Texas." MA Thesis, Southwest Texas State Univ., San Marcos, 1970. v, 81 pp.

This thesis conforms in outline and methodology to the theses of Frausto 1969 and others. Reséndez's fifteen informants ranged in age from 11 to 64; all were native to the small central Texas city of Seguin (38 per cent Mexican-American). The alphabetized lexicon contains nearly 500 items; many of them duplicate the findings of Frausto and others, but various entries are original and of more than passing interest: the well-assimilated noun <u>alcaserse</u> 'Alka-Seltzer,' <u>camañuelas</u> (cf. the DRAE's second definition of <u>cabañuelas</u>) 'temporada del año, comúnmente en enero, cuando hay cambio frecuente de tiempo seco a lluvioso ([vocablo] usado más por la gente anciana)," (p. 17) lengthy and revealing discussions of the folk-terms <u>empacharse</u>, (<u>La</u>) <u>llorona</u>, (<u>mal de</u>) <u>ojo</u>, etc. Items designating sicknesses, animals and typical Chicano foods appear frequently. Little-known idioms such as <u>meter chango</u> 'salir de cita con la esposa o amante de otro' and <u>sacar la garra</u> 'hablar mal de una persona cuando no está presente' appear in the separate section (74-79) of "Expresiones." [RT]

ROMANO-V., Ocatvio Ignacio. "Donship in a Mexican-American Community in Texas." <u>AmA</u> 62.966-976 (1960). [Annot. <u>HLAS</u> 24 (1962) no. 4776 (Wogan).]

This fascinating article tells most of what there is to know about the use of the term <u>don</u> in a small Hidalgo County border town, "Frontera," an estimated 95 per cent of whose 50 households "were composed of refugees from the civil strife which blanketed Mexico at the turn of the century." (p. 966) From Romano's careful descriptions the town appears traditionalist and <u>envidia</u>-ridden to a fault and thus would seem as good a place as any to observe donship patterns at their most explicit.

"When a man has been granted the respect term <u>don</u> it then becomes a part of his name, as in Don Pedro. The use is always with the given name, never with the surname," (967 [also subsequent quotes unless specified]) since to apply <u>don</u> to the surname "is generally considered a base insult. Furthermore, it is never used alone, nor is it ever combined with a descriptive term." Other stipulations: <u>don</u> must not be used with reference to a member of one's own family for in such cases kinship terms or given names take precedence. "Neither does a man use the term when referring to himself, such as in signing his name to a letter or a document" since this would display excessive self-importance. One always addresses a <u>don</u> as <u>usted</u>, while a <u>don</u> "has the prerogative to speak to younger men, and those not called <u>don</u>, with the familiar <u>tú</u>." "When one <u>don</u> addresses another, the prevailing rules apply and the term is used;" from this one infers that two dons speak to each other as <u>usted</u> although Romano does not make this explicit. There are two classes of <u>don</u> in "Frontera": those to whom the term is "granted on the basis of traditional usages and categories" such as local wealthy businessmen, the Mexican consul, "individuals in relatively high political office, <u>curanderos</u> or folk-healers, and very old men" and those who have "achieved" donship as reward for "having met the prevailing conditions of Frontera life in a particular fashion and exhibiting particular behavior characteristics," which chiefly involve a combination of keeping a constantly saved face and achieving "withdrawal" from most community affairs by getting others to do one's bidding. These and other strictly anthropological concerns take up much of the remainder of the article, though additional linguistic information is also found, e.g., in order to "achieve" donship (and in general to avoid being the town's laughing-stock) a man must "learn to cope with the daily onslaughts of verbal dueling [which] consists of a complex use of everyday words as metaphors which contain insinuations, innuendos, and outright accusations of effeminacy and lack of courage. For example, seemingly innocent remarks which contain the word leche . . . may constitute a veiled reference to sperm. Words such as 'key,' 'whip,' or 'walnut' may refer to male genitalia. A statement with the word 'eye' may refer to the anus, as might the word 'pocket.'" (972) [RT]

SHARP, John M. "The Origin of Some Non-standard Lexical Items in the Spanish of El Paso." In Ewton and Ornstein 1970, pp. 207-232. [Rev. Craddock 1973 p. 324.]

Sharp attempts to briefly "identify the origins of a representative sample of non-standard words and phrases observed in the speech of college-age individuals in El Paso" during the 1950's (p. 209). Three types of words are considered: "English loan-words," with 28 entries; "Mexican Spanish words, altered semantically and/or morphologically,," with 84 entries; and "Archaisms from the rogues' jargon ('germanía') of Spain," with five entries. The listing cites simply the orthographic form of the item, a brief English gloss, a curt, often highly speculative note on the word's origin, and frequently a sentence or two exemplifying the use of the item in context. There are no grammatical notes and few attempts at documentation. Words generally labeled "Pachuco" are prevalent but not so indicated. A final list contains 17 "Words and phrases of uncertain origin," mostly pachuquismos. [RT]

SIMÓN, Alphonse, O.M.I. Pastoral Spanish. San Antonio: Standard Printing Company, 1945. xxii, 511 pp.

Sponsored by the archdiocesis of San Antonio, Fr. Simón's book seeks not only to offer a complete "guide" to the sort of Spanish that priests might need but to provide a summary of Spanish grammar as well; both sections appear designed for the non-native. While the traditionalistic survey of grammar (pp. 1-88) offers nothing of interest to students of regional speech, there is much for the researcher in Simón's lengthy "Book Two" (89-352), which contains "conversations" that priests are expected to have with parishioners concerning baptism, marriage, confirmation, confession, extreme unction, death, and the like. Though the severely homiletic nature of the conversations is often reflected in their rather formal prose style, Simón conscientiously inserts popular phraseology throughout, at times as the "sole likely" expression and at times as an alternate mode. For example the section on how the priest should handle "Godparents Not Married By the Church" (104-111) contains such Mexicanisms as más a menudo, se me hace que, la mera verdad, demasiado 'mucho,' amancebado--"Aquellos que no quieren casarse por la Iglesia . . . viven en concubinato (viven amancebados), y dan escándalo a los demás fieles" (107); all variants are italicized or capitalized and are then explicated in the "grammatical notes" sections which follow the conversations. Some of these notes are unsophisticated, prolix, or else of interest solely to the neophyte student, but others are helpful to linguistis and are sometimes of more than routine interest, for example, the news (in the section "Confession of a Pious Soul") that some parishioners use vos; thus a woman addresses her confessor with: "Por estos pecados, y por los que ahora no me recuerdo [italicized as regional in the text], le pido a mi Dios perdón y a VOS [caps.], Padre, absolución y penitencia." (171) Simón comments (172) that vos "is more formal and respectful than tú and less formal than Ud. It is now used mostly to address God. Sometimes it is used when addressing others, for instance, priests, as in this example. Another example: Vos, Clara, sois virtuosa."

Both the "Foreword" by the archbishop of San Antonio and the "Introduction" by the author espouse Chicanophile attitudes surely advanced for their time.

The work continues with a third "Book" which explains the catechism and also reflects local speech somewhat, especially in the children's responses and questions; Simón concludes with an "ecclesiastical vocabulary," a grammatical index and a homiletic index. [RT]

TESCHNER, Richard V. [1974a]. "Preparing a Regional Lexicon: One Interim Solution to the Problem That Is Southwestern Spanish Lexicography." In Bills 1974, pp. 207-221.

A lucid and thoughtful explanation of the multitude of problems encountered and the decisions made by Teschner and Roberto A. Galván in their endeavors to compile a dictionary of Texas Spanish. The article deals with a consideration of the purpose of a "regional" dictionary and the problems of selectivity and interpretation of sources (63 cited), especially with regard to infant speech items, Anglicisms (including a notable section on the meaning of patrás), and orthography. This paper also includes brief comments on the difficulty of undertaking a more general dictionary of Chicano Spanish with special reference to the problems created by the Spanish of northern New Mexico. [GB]

TESCHNER, Richard V. [1974b]. "Problems of Southwestern Spanish Lexicography." In Spolsky and Bills (1974), pp. 41-51.

Slightly revised and abbreviated version of Teschner 1974a. [GB]

WARD, Hortense Warner. "Ear Marks." PTFS 19.106-116 (1944).
[Annot. Woodbridge p. 238.]

Curious exposition of Spanish ear-mark terminology (with appropriate illustrations) recorded by the Nueces County, Texas clerk beginning in 1847. The author provides skillful translations that assist greatly in understanding this peculiar jargon. Chuso 'point' (cf. the diagram on p. 112) has nothing to do with la lechuza 'the owl,' but doubtless corresponds to Am. Sp. chuzo 'beak (of a bird).' There seem to be a number of misprints or erroneous readings in the transcriptions (115: lade for lado; 116: des for dos); some dialectal traits are also in evidence (116: avujero for agujero). [JC]

5.6 ONOMASTICS (includes TOPONYMY)

Major Items: (none)

See also these items elsewhere (consult Author Index for location):
    (none)

ANDERSON, John Q. "Texas Stream Names." In A Good Tale and a Bonnie Tune, edited by M.C. Boatwright, W.M. Hudson and A. Maxwell. Publications of the Texas Folklore Society No. 32 (Dallas: Southern Methodist Univ. Press, 1964). Pp. 112-147.

Pp. 128-131 include a list of nearly 200 stream names from Spanish (some attributions are doubtful). Unfortunately, the author provides little help to the linguist, since he fails to indicate the local English and Spanish pronunciations of the names, or to the historian, since his sources (official county maps and correspondence with librarians, newspaper editors, postmasters and other allegedly knowledgeable individuals) are exclusively contemporary (with the exception of secondary historical works). He made no attempt to delve into primary sources such as county land office records, surveyors' logs, early newspapers, Spanish and Mexican governmental and private documents, personal memoirs, i.e., every type of material that one would naturally ferret out in attempting to date the first appearance and establish the origin of place names of any sort. He even neglects to inform the reader of the location of the streams, so any scholar wishing to do more than scratch the surface of this genuinely engrossing topic will have to do Anderson's work over again. [JC]

COLTHARP, Lurline H. "Bilingual Onomastics: A Case Study." In Turner 1973, pp. 131-140.

An examination of the twin influences of English and Spanish on the naming of streets in El Paso, Texas and an illustration of some of the problems bilingual nomenclature creates. El Paso streets are named for people, places, plants, trees, minerals, etc. Six of the streets bear the names of presidents of Mexico;

one is even named for Porfirio Díaz. In an effort to avoid problems of bilingual translation the local planning board directs that no name in one language shall duplicate a name in the other. Miscellaneous goofs occur in Spanish names, apparently not prevented by legislators less than familiar with the language: there is thus a "Monte Cito Street" and a "La Guna Avenue." [RT]

GILPIN, George H. "Street Names in San Antonio: Signposts to History." Names 18.191-200 (1970).

Street names of Spanish/Mexican origin as well as those of French, German and Anglo-Saxon background are discussed and many historical anecdotes are related. Inevitably San Antonio's oldest names are eighteenth century and Hispanic, but the practice of using Spanish names did not stop with the Texan secession: nearly all "west side" east-west streets were named for Mexican towns (Mérida, Saltillo, etc.) and to their north are streets commemorating prominent colonial settlers, e.g., Salinas, Pérez, Menchaca, Delgado, etc. While an abundance of documentation attests to the diligence of the author's research, the fashion in which he cites the "original Spanish names" of today's hybrid designations can only be said to reveal a lack of familiarity with Spanish, e.g., Dolorosa Street < *Calle de Dolorosa (clearly < Calle de la Dolorosa), *Calle de Real, *Calle de Presidio, and also the following: "One example of the Anglicizing of an original Spanish name is King Philip V Street . . . obviously named Calle de Rey Philip [sic] for the illustrious Spanish king." (p. 194) [RT]

WATERS, Lena W. "Mexican Geographical Names from the Old Tales and Chronicles of Early Explorers." MA Thesis, Baylor Univ., Waco, Texas, 1948. vi, 55 pp.

Passing references to early South Texas place names are found throughout this non-circulating item (partial copies are purchaseable from the parent library), but chiefly in Ch. 7, "The Conquest of Nueva Galicia." [RT]

5.7 ENGLISH INFLUENCE ON SPANISH

Major Items: LOZA-1961

See also these items elsewhere (consult Author Index for location):
    [All items in Sec. 5.5, supra.]

LOZANO, Anthony Girard. "Intercambio de español e inglés en San Antonio, Texas." Archivum 11.111-138 (1961). [Rev. Craddock 1973 p. 317.]

This valuable study measures the degree of phonetic adaptation to Spanish of various English forms which Lozano deliberately elicited from four Spanish-dominant San Antonio Chicanos. The 155 forms were all recorded earlier by Cerda et al. (1953) and could thus be presumed familiar.

Lozano's article is helpful in that it examplifies, "in the field," many of the specific problems which Spanish-dominants face in the pronunciation of English; scholars interested in the theoretical issues anent "integration vs. interference" will also want to check Lozano's findings. Craddock, however, has judged the work as "plagued with some rather elementary misconceptions," and asserts that some of Lozano's conclusions are misleading since he included as phonetic adaptations various Spanish words substituted for the English such as [garáhe] qua hypothetical reflex of [gəráǰ] and not (as is much more likely) as either a spelling pronunciation of the English form garage or else a slightly modified variant of the standard Spanish garaje [garáxe]. Among other examples of misinterpretation are [grádo] as the supposed reflex of [gréid], etc.

San Antonio English was an "r-less dialect" until quite recently, and Lozano's data confirm this, i.e., the reflex of ruler is rula, that of scooter is escura, and so forth. [RT]

5.8 SPANISH INFLUENCE ON ENGLISH

Major Items: ATWO-1962; TALL-1896

See also these items elsewhere (consult Author Index for location):

CERD/etal-1953; SAWY-1957; SAWY-1964

ATWOOD, E. Bagby. "A Preliminary Report on Texas Word Geography." Orbis 2.61-66 (1953).

   The author includes a brief discussion (pp. 64 ff.) of Spanish loan words in Texas English (mott 'clump [of trees]' < mata 'bush, shrub', pilon 'an extra gift with a purchase, something extra'). The distribution of pilon vis-à-vis lagniappe 'id.' is plotted on a map (p. 65). His informants are "native, elderly member[s] of [their] home communit[ies];" he notes that some forms (acequia 'irrigation ditch,' olla 'earthen jug,' partera 'midwife') occur only near the Mexican frontier. Atwood occasionally indicates pronunciation (olla [ójə]) but more consistency in the regard would have been advisable. [JC]

ATWOOD, E. Bagby. The Regional Vocabulary of Texas. Austin: Univ. of Texas Press, 1962. 273 pp. [Annot. Fody 534-535; HLAS 26 (1964) no. 1307 (D. Wogan). Rev. Language 40.296-298 (1964) (C. Reed).]

   This monograph embodies the results of the dialect survey which, the title notwithstanding, includes Oklahoma, Southern Arkansas, Louisiana and Southern New Mexico and is described in Atwood's "Preliminary Report" (1953). It contains chapters on (I) demography (figure 5 [p. 13] indicates the percentage by county of the "Latin" population) and economy, (II) methodology, (III) a "Topical Survey of the Vocabulary" where frequency, vitality and areal distribution of the informants' responses are assessed, (IV) "Geographical Aspects of Usage", (V) "Dialect Mixture and Meaning", (VI) "Obsolescence and Replacement", (VII) "Lexicographical pilón", a discussion of various Spanish loanwords in Texas English, and, finally, (VIII) the dialect atlas of 125 maps. There is also an appendix concerning computer analysis of linguistic data; a word index that includes brief glosses completes the volume.
   Probably in no other work on U.S. English does one find such careful and detailed work on Spanish loanwords as in the volume under discussion. This follows from the author's belief that "most of the distinctively Southwestern words are of Spanish origin" (91). Of particular importance to students of S.W. Spanish are Chap. III, pp. 91-94 ("Southwestern Words"), pp. 109 ff. ("terms from the cattle country, specifically those of Spanish origin, do not show the same decline in frequency as the terms from the farm vocabulary"), Chap. VII, and maps 2 (resaca,

vaquero), 3 (llano, pelado), 4 (acequia, toro), 5 (chaparral),
6 (mott < mata), 7 (reata, hacienda), 8 (mesquital, bosque,
partera, potro, bosal), 14 (olla), 15 (arroyo), 17 (frijoles),
18 (pilón), 19-20 (corral), 21 (mesa), 22 (remuda), 23 (morral),
24 (wrangler < caballerango), 26 (tank), 27 (hackamore), 28
(bronc[o]), 29 (cinch), 30 (canyon), 31 (lariat, lasso), 33 (burro),
35 (chaps), 36 (hoosegow), 37 (pinto), while maps 116 ff. present
isoglosses purporting to demonstrate the easternmost boundary of
a good number of these same Hispanisms.

The chief shortcoming, and I believe a very serious one, of
Atwood's work is the failure to determine the pronunciation of
informants' responses; this is especially awkward in the case of
Spanish loanwords whose phonological transformation in passing
from Spanish to English is drastic and for that very reason intensely interesting. Note for example, the rendering "sakey"
(p. 91), i.e., [séjki], for acequia. But for Atwood, phonetics
"is hardly necessary for observation of vocabulary" (p. 31), a
claim difficult to comprehend in a self-confessed disciple of
Gilliéron. [JC]

BIERSCHWALE, Margaret. "English of the Texas Range." MA Thesis,
    Columbia Univ., 1920. 28 pp.

This surprisingly brief essay, based to a large extent on the
author's personal experience, is slipshod and unscholarly, but
nevertheless contains some items of interest. Typographical errors
are so numerous one would have to seek independent verification
for any form mentioned. Hispanisms are discussed in particular
on pp. 7-10; among the more unusual words I note gaucho (possibly gancho?) 'branding iron' (p. 8; wanting in Mathews 1951 but
cf. Salado Alvarez 1924, p. 79), caberos 'halter,' a variant of
cabestro (p. 9, listed by Mathews but not documented), and chicherones 'cracklings' < Sp. chicharrones. (p. 11) There is a
brief handwritten phonetic transcription of cowboy speech on p. 28.
[JC]

BRADDY, Haldeen. "Cowboy Lingo of the Texas Big Bend." DN 6.617-
    621 (1937).

Toward the end of her narrative presentation of the lore and
the lexicon of the West Texas borderland cowboy, Prof. Braddy
mentions six Spanish loans common to the parlance: segundo "often
used instead of foreman, who is second in command to the rancher;"
cocenero "cook" (no figured pronunciation given); Sancho as "a
favorite name for a pet lamb or kid;" riata, lazo ("wherever writers
of Western thrillers found the corrupt lassoo for 'lasso,' it
certainly was not West of the Pecos") and dally man ("instead of
saying 'give it a turn,' the Mexicans say da le vuelta [sic]; and
the Texans have compromised by calling this type [of functionary]
a dally man") (all p. 621). [RT]

HEARD, Betty R. "A Phonological Analysis of the Speech of Hays
    County, Texas." PhD Diss., Louisiana State Univ., Baton
    Rouge, 1969. 308 pp. [DA 30 (1969) 1546-A.]

    The author ran across a few Hispanisms of limited currency
in the course of her work: for example, grullo 'ash-colored
(horse)', (p. 106) caliche 'poor soil that supports little or no
vegetation' (Sp. 'flake or crust of lime') = dobie/dogie hills,
(p. 109) and [sIn'dɛr], (p. 111) a response offered by one informant as a synonym of 'valley, gulch or wash' (< Sp. sendero
'path', note her explanation [p. 282]: "place where you cut out
an opening"). Heard had the industry and good judgment to include
in extenso her field notes (pp. 165-296) so that one can, with a
certain degree of patience, verify the exact pronunciation of each
word discussed, e.g., on p. 280, caliche is rendered as [kə'liči].
I should point out that Spanish-speaking bilinguals were excluded
from the survey. [JC]

NORMAN, Arthur M.A. "A Southeast Texas Dialect Study." Orbis
    5.61-79 (1956).

    This is a summary of the author's identically-entitled doctoral
dissertation (PhD, Univ. of Texas, Austin, 1955, 930 pp.), written
under the supervision of Prof. E. Bagby Atwood. Of Atwood's Texas
English Hispanisms "only norther, lariat and corral are in common
use" (73) in the four-county area surround Beaumont, Texas.
Norman's informants numbered twelve of whom none were Chicano;
indeed the area appeared to have few if any Hispanic residents,
according to Norman's calculations. [RT]

SOCRATES, Hyacinth (pseud?). "Southwestern Slang." TOM 3.125-131
    (1869).

    A folksy, anecdotal presentation of words and sayings peculiar
to Texas more than a century ago. Among many other things, four
English Hispanisms are mentioned: cabestros (not discussed), corral
(used as a verb, 'to round up [cattle]'), quirt (type of horsewhip),
and mezquite. [RT]

TALLICHET, H. [Part] I: "A Contribution Towards a Vocabulary of
    Spanish and Mexican Words Used in Texas." DN 1.185-196 (1896);
    II: "Addenda to the Vocabulary of Spanish and Mexican Words
    Used in Texas." DN 1.243-253; III: "A Vocabulary of Spanish
    and Mexican Words Used in Texas--Additions and Corrections."
    DN 1.324-326.

    These three complementary pieces list nearly 400 forms which
entered (to a greater or lesser extent) the English of "surveyors,
cattlemen, prospectors, land agents, and old settlers on the
border" who used them "as they would words already naturalized in

English," (p. 185) although therein lies a rub, as the author's attempts at figured English pronunciations are infrequent and generally pre-scientific; thus <u>caballada</u> is "generally pronounced <u>cavyyard</u> by Americans. The forms <u>cavallad, caballad, cavallard</u> . . . are the more common in Texas." (188) But as Tallichet admits, phonetic adaptations "vary almost infinitely according to place and person, this being especially the case with words frequently used in writing or printing, when most Americans pronounce them as if they were English, while the original pronunciation persists with occasional variations among others." (186) In general Tallichet's definitions have stood the test of time although inevitably some etymologies fare less well (see for example <u>belduque</u>, for which one Captain John Bourke, who helped out with pp. 243-253, suggests "handsome duke"). At the end of each part the editors of <u>DN</u> add minor comments on meaning and etymology. [RT]

WOODBRIDGE, Hensley C. "A Handful of Western Americanisms." <u>AS</u> 33.140-142 (1958).

A concise, well-handled study of 35 "Americanisms that are not included in the [Mitford Mathews <u>Dictionary of Americanisms</u>, 1951] and several terms that do appear therein "but for which earlier evidence is offered." (p. 140) The 35 were taken from a GPO <u>Report on the Productions of Agriculture as Returned at the Tenth Census (June 1, 1880)</u>; Woodbridge is the first scholar to examine this document. About half the forms are of Spanish origin and most are orthographically unassimilated and appear, furthermore, in italics or within quotes in the Report (e.g., a typical entry containing several forms: "BARADULCIA, n. 'Farther South, along the Mexican border, in Kinney and Maverick counties, occurs the prairie grass, which is cut for hay to supply the government posts, and other plants of special value to stock are found, as the 'juahia,' the 'sotal,' the 'nopal,' cactus, the 'saladio,' the 'baradulcia' or greasewood . . . . ") (ibid.) Most of the Hispanisms were cited as peculiar to Texas. [RT]

5.8.1 ENGLISH OF THIS PARTICULAR HISPANIC GROUP

<u>Major Items</u>: BENI-1970; HEIL-1966; HOFF-1974; NATA-1969; SAWY-1957

<u>See also these items elsewhere</u> (consult Author Index for location):

ADKI-1966; BUSS-1971; CARR-1971; CARR-1972; LANC-1969; MYCU-1968; and especially POUL-1970

BAXLEY, Dan Michael. "The Utility of 45 Phonic Generalizations as Applied to Oral Vocabularies of Economically Limited Spanish Surname Children." EdD Diss., Arizona State Univ., 1972. xiii, 158 pp. [<u>DA</u> 33 (1972) 1309-A.]

Baxley is a reading specialist who is firmly convinced (as are most American educators, to judge from the battery of citations in Ch. 2, "Review of the Related Literature") that "the importance of phonics in early reading instruction could not even be considered controversial." (p. 15) Phonics (for those unaware of the exact parameters of the term) is "the application of sounds to written symbols;" (5) as specifically applied to education the discipline attempts to establish "generalizations" about relationships between English graphemes and sounds; given the arbitrary and chaotic nature of the English spelling system this is no mean task, but it is clearly a crucial one if children are to be taught to read. Proponents of phonics, however, labor under a series of very unfortunate misconceptions about the scientific representation of sound; at least this is the impression received from Baxley's own chart of "phonic equivalencies" (p. 50), of which the following are illustrative: "short vowels" <u>a</u> as in <u>a</u>dd, <u>a</u> as in <u>a</u>ccount, <u>e</u> as in <u>e</u>nd, <u>e</u> as in sil<u>e</u>nt, <u>i</u> as in <u>i</u>ll, <u>i</u> as in char<u>i</u>ty, <u>o</u> as in <u>o</u>dd, <u>o</u> as in s<u>o</u>ft, <u>o</u> as in c<u>o</u>nnect, and "long vowels" <u>e</u> as in <u>e</u>ve, <u>e</u> as in <u>e</u>vent, etc., etc. The redundancy of the symbolism is as evident as is the ignorance of such things as the presence of schwa vowels in all but the most highly contrived or <u>largo</u> forms of spoken English. In similar fashion the terms "long" and "short" should be limited to denoting, popularly, the features Tense and Lax.

Given the pre-scientific nature of "phonics" as a form of phonological analysis, it is necessary to disallow the possibility that Baxley's otherwise lucid work can have much to say to linguists about the English pronunciation of his target population. But other considerations vitiate its usefulness too. Baxley's corpus was simply extracted from the English lexicon of five-year-old Texas Chicanos as recorded by Cornejo 1969; it was not, however, from Cornejo's tapes but from his printed pages that Baxley took the words, thus completely disallowing the possibility that any "variant" pronunciations (of which there surely were many) would serve as relevant input. The "derived word list of 716 words" was then transcribed "using the 1961 edition of the Webster's new Collegiate Dictionary [!] . . . as the authority"

for pronunciation and even for phonetic transcription. (49) The
results of this are worse than useless, as can be seen by the
following examples from p. 132 of Baxley: "peanut /p ee -n u t/,
pear /p aer/, people /p ee -p le/, picture /p i k -t uer/, popcorn
/p o p - k orn/."
    The end goal of Baxley's exercise was to refine the conclusions
of one T. Clymer ("The Utility of Phonic Generalizations in the
Primary Grades," Reading T 16.252-258 [1963]); for the most part
Baxley substantiated Clymer.
    It has already been demonstrated that this work has nothing
to offer the linguist, its tantalizing title notwithstanding.
There is nothing here for the educator either, given the author's
reliance on English orthography as his sole source of information
about the way Chicano children pronounce English. [RT]

BEBERFALL, Lester. "Some Linguistic Problems of the Spanish-
    speaking People of Texas." MLJ 41.87-90 (1958). [Annot.
    Fody p. 535.]

    A quick discussion of the errors some South Texas Chicanos
make when speaking English. The work focuses chiefly on phonology
(the confusion between /š/ and /č/, for example) but also mentions
varius syntactical hypercorrections, tense usages and so forth.
The author taught for several years at Pan American Univ. in the
lower Rio Grande Valley. [RT]

BENÍTEZ, Carrahlee. "A Study of Some Non-standard English
    Features in the Speech of Seventh-grade Mexican-Americans
    Enrolled in a Remedial Reading Program in an Urban Community
    of South Texas." MA Thesis, Texas A & I Univ., Kingsville,
    1970. iv, 82 pp.

    This is a well-written structuralist analysis of the "deviant
features" observed in the speech of 19 young Kingsville Chicanos
(14 male and 5 female), all Spanish-English bilingual. Benítez's
models for what constitutes standard English are those presented
in Mary Finocchiaro, English as a Second Language (New York, 1964)
and Politzer and Bartley, Standard English and Non-standard
Dialects: Phonology and Morphology (Stanford, Calif., 1969).
She limits her investigation to features generally considered
troublesome for Chicanos; her study transcends Politzer/Bartley's
in that it tests for suprasegmentals and syntactical usage as
well as for morphophonology; similarly, "Politzer listed and described fundamental lists of possible variants; this study tests
students to see to what extent they are variants." (p. 11) Thus
percentages of variance are given throughout.
    Of the 14 phonemes studied 10 were consonants: v θ ð ŋ y z
š ž č ǰ, and four were vowels (all [+ high], both tense and lax);
one questions the failure to test for vowel neutralization in
absence of stress and also for the production of two other vowels

lacking in Spanish, /ʌ/ and /ae/. Phonation was often elicited through the reading of various clipped sentences of a very 'Enry 'Iggins hue, e.g., "The thief said 'thank you.' And took a bath. There were three thick inches of ice. . . . Look at Luke. I found some boots. . . . There are zebras in the zoo. I see the fuzz." (70) Benítez found that "the two phonemes most frequently 'missed' were /ĉ/ and /š/ with a total of 102 and 95 deviations respectively. The two least . . . were /y/ and /z/ with only three deviations each." (27) As for intonation the students had most trouble with tag questions of the "He didn't go, did he?" sort. Morphologically trickiest was the production of final -ed in verbs (a 50 per cent deviation), followed by the irregular forms of plurals (42.6), past tenses (40.3), the proper distribution of /s/ in the present tense (30.9), plural morphemes in nouns (29.4) and the non-periphrastic possessive markers (5 per cent). In syntactical (and lexical) variation one finds many old friends which reflect a variety of influences (copula deletion, "it's a ___ here" for "there's a ___ here," possible negative transfers from Spanish ["that looks something else"]), as well as several newcomers such as "He's long hair" for "He has long hair," the probable product of a misa plied deletion ("He's [got] long hair"). In many instances Benítez lists as deviations forms which enjoy considerable popularity among large numbers of monolingual American English-speakers as well, such as "he got vs. he has," (49-50), "there is vs. there are," (48), "double negatives," (51), etc. [RT]

DILLON, David Andrew. "An Analysis of the Written Syntactic Maturity in English of Mexican-American Migrant Students." MA Thesis, Southwest Texas State Univ., San Marcos, 1972. ix, 104 pp.

This study applies the methodology of Kellogg W. Hunt (<u>Grammatical Structures Written at Three Grade Levels</u>, 1965) and Roy C. O'Donnell et al., (<u>Syntax of Kindergarten and Elementary School Children: A Transformational Approach</u>, 1967) to a corpus of compositions by Chicano youngsters in a South Texas community. Dillon's hypothesis was that there would be "a significant difference between the syntactic embeddings used by fourth, sixth and eighth grade Mexican-American migrant students as indicated by the quantitative measures of syntactic maturity, namely, clause length, T-unit length, and clauses per T-unit, that were applied to the students' writings;" (pp. 3-4) for Dillon (as for Hunt) a T-unit is a "minimal terminable unit, [i.e.,] one main clause with all the subordinate clauses attached to it." (6)

Among the conclusions: while there was an apparent lack of growth between grades four and six, there was a good deal of it between grades six and eight (thanks perhaps to the number of students who had dropped out of school by grade eight?). A possible though somewhat overgeneralizing explanantion, given the fact that Dillon's students were all migrants and thus impoverished (cf.

Ri.GARC-1973, Ro.GARC-1973): "it may be that Spanish-speaking
children between fourth and sixth grades are still at the stage
of collecting various elements of English syntax in little bits
and pieces" (88) and their ability to develope and consolidate
may thus be retarded. There is more: "in the measure of average
clause length, the migrant students not only scored generally
lower than the monolingual children of the other studies [Hunt's
middle-class white students in Florida] but also showed less growth.
Thus [the migrants] are falling farther behind in syntactic
development rather than catching up to their Anglo counterparts."
(89) For one refutation of the theory that bilingualism per se
causes retardation see, again, Ricardo García 1973. [RT]

*FISHER, Alan Thomas. "English Proficiency of Beginning Elementary
    Spanish-Speaking Students." PhD Diss., Univ. of Houston,
    1973. 61 pp. [DA 34 (1974) 5652-B.]

    (From the Abstract:) "The purpose of this study was to provide
more extensive normative data, reliability data and data which
would allow a judgement to be made about the minimum level of
English proficiency required for predicting adequate performance
in kindergarten and the first grade using the Children's English
Proficiency Test (CEPT) (Webster, 1971)." To that end 219 Corpus
Christi Mexican-American beginning elementary-level students from
all socioeconomic levels were tested. Fisher attempted "to create
an age scale and to identify difference in English proficiency
among different educational groups," i.e., those who had attended
kindergarten and those who had not. Perhaps predictably the
combination of these two goals prevented the establishment of an
"age scale" (developmental ranking) but did prove the superior
performance of the group that had had kindergarten training.
Language-specific concerns are not mentioned further in the
Abstract and given the brevity of the work it is not likely that
many samples of the children's English are included. [RT]

*GONZÁLEZ, Gustavo. [1973b]. "The English of Spanish-Speaking
    Migrants in Texas." (Unpublished) Paper Presented at the
    Mexican-American Studies Center, Univ. of Texas, Austin, 1973.
    (Encapsulated in Matluck/Mace 1973, q.v.)

HEILER[-SAAVEDRA], Barbara. "An Investigation of the Causes of
    Primary Stress Mislocation in the English Speech of Bilingual
    Mexican-American Students." MA Thesis, Univ. of Texas, El
    Paso, 1966. 118 pp.

    This fastidiously researched study proposed to determine whether
Spanish-mother-tongue bilingual El Paso fourteen-year-olds committed errors in English stress placement through application of
Spanish stress rules or for putative "other" reasons. Some 75
cognates (such as verbs <u>accept</u>, <u>invite</u>, <u>invent</u>, <u>interrupt</u>, <u>operate</u>;

homographic noun/verb pairs insult/insult, conduct/conduct; nouns family, history, victory, mystery, education, operation, division; adjectives horrible, impossible, etc.) were elicited through rapid "fill-in-the-blank" questioning; the author also investigated the way the students would handle "non-permitted endings," i.e., word-final consonant clusters such as /nt ns t ts nts/ to learn if these would be rendered as in English, resyllabified through vowel insertion, or else reduced.

Amply documented conclusions were that in general the 20 ninth-graders "did not stress by analogy with the Spanish cognate." (p. 80) Though the location of major (primary) stress was sometimes varied in different inflected forms of the verb, variance was not ascribed to analogy with cognates but rather "to confusion between primary and secondary stress" through less-than-perfect control of a peculiarly English phenomenon (some examples: [ăpə̆rĕy̆t] rather than [ăpə̆rĕy̆t], [gră dž̆uwĕy̆t ə d] for [gră dž̆uwĕy̆təd]). Informants generally contrasted the noun-verb homographs as in standard educated English and "did not generally resyllabify non-permitted endings," preferring instead (when not following the standard) to reduce the consonant clusters. [RT]

HOFFER, Bates. "Bilingual Language Development and Bilingual Education." In Hoffer and Ornstein 1974, pp. 81-90.

Parts of this well-researched article make important contributions to what we know about child language development. Hoffer has investigated Spanish-monolingual or -dominant, English monolingual or -dominant, and balanced or "proficient" bilinguals from San Antonio-area schools through modifications of tests developed by Carol Chomsky (Acquisition of Syntax in Children 5 to 10, 1970), with emphasis upon performance in two syntactic areas, "easy to see/Eager to see," and "ask/tell." Data from the first test show that "the control group of monolingual English speakers acquired this syntax by age 8; the [Mexican-American] bilinguals were 50 per cent wrong [at age 8] and were at age 10 before learning was complete." (82) Of the five progressively more difficult-to-handle levels of ask/tell, the middle "stage C" is reached by monolinguals at age 8 and by bilinguals a year later while the final stage ("E") is reached at 10 by monolinguals but not until 12 (if then) by bilinguals. "By taking the bilinguals and subgrouping them by sociological factors, a further pattern emerges. Upper middle class bilinguals reach stage D by age 10 while lower mid reach Stage D at age 12. . . . Also, the urban bilinguals as a group reach Stage E by age 11, while the rural reach Stage E after age 12." (84)

Subsequently Hoffer analyzes levels of syntactic difficulty in one particular textbook used in Texas and concludes that its material is far too difficult for all but Spanish monolinguals and proficient bilinguals. [RT]

JACKSON, Lucile Prim. "An Analysis of the Language Difficulties of the Spanish-speaking Children of the Bowie High School, El Paso, Texas." MA Thesis, Univ. of Texas, Austin, 1938. xi, 170 pp.

The author's purpose is "to identify and record extensive examples of the major varieties of the typical language difficulties to be overcome in the understanding and use of English by the Spanish-speaking high school pupils" that she dealt with during 1935-36. (p. 161) The study is an analysis of a mass of data on "pronunciation, confused diction, and sentence structure errors." Chap. 3 (66-160) presents the results of the classification and includes massive exemplification. [GB]

NATALICIO, Eleanor Diana S. "Formation of the Plural in English: A Study of Native Speakers of English and Native Speakers of Spanish." PhD Diss., Univ. of Texas, 1969. 181 pp. [DA 30 (1970) 2993-A.]

This extremely careful and conscientious study sought to establish "what differences, if any, are manifest in the sequence of acquisition of noun plurals by native as opposed to non-native speakers of English." (p. 32) The salient conclusion is that native speakers of English improve markedly from grades 1 through 10 in their control of the morphological process in question while native speakers of Spanish fail to improve as rapidly: "by the tenth grade, their level of performance regarding plural formation is significantly inferior to that of their N[ative] E[nglish] S[peaker] counterparts." (109) Theoretically interesting is her observation (pp. 151 ff.) that the concept of "negative transfer," espoused, among others, by Stockwell and Bowen 1965, seems quite irrelevant to the situation she was analysing. Her bilingual subjects did not introduce Spanish patterns or rules into their formation of English plurals.
Unfortunately it is not possible to discover in specific terms just what particular deviations were involved in individual cases, since basically the tabulations reflect only correct and incorrect responses. The author's field notes might reveal among 10th-graders the existence of a "Chicano English" norm that holds their allegiance (perhaps tacit or unconscious), a fact that might help account for their partial lag in mastering the exact English pattern for forming plurals. [JC]

SAWYER, Janet Beck Moseley. "A Dialect Study of San Antonio, Texas: A Bilingual Community." PhD Diss., Univ. of Texas, Austin, 1957. vi, 323 pp. [DA 18 (1958) 586.] [Annot. Fody pp. 539-540. Rev. Craddock 1973, p. 316.]

This is a study of the English lexicon and pronunciation of seven monolingual Anglo English speakers and seven Mexican-Americans whose Spanish-English bilinguality ranged from near-perfectly balanced to largely Spanish-monolingual (i.e., English understood but poorly spoken). Following closely the methods and the checklists of Hans Kurath as revised and expanded upon by E. Bagby Atwood (Sawyer's adviser), Sawyer reaches various conclusions about the phonological and especially lexical sources of "San Antonio English;" only information that pertains to the language and the sociolinguistics of San Antonio (SA) Chicanos will be summarized here.

Pp. 10-14 recall twentieth-century Mexican migrations to SA and describe contemporary (1950's) conditions and social relationships; stressed here is the perceived existence of Anglo discrimination against Chicanos and of the cultural barriers separating the groups. Pp. 25-30 contain capsule biographies of the seven "Latin" informants who ranged in are from 74 to 21; five are life-long SA residents. Ch. 2's substantial sec. B (71-100) presents a descriptive model of the phonology (Sawyer follows Harold King, "Outline of Mexican Spanish Phonology," 1952); as expected, an informant whose English is least proficient shows the most (and the most predictable) Spanish influence: in vowels, for example, a failure to distinguish consistently between /īy/ and /ĭ/, /ēy/ and /Ē/, /ūw/ and /ŭ/, /ōw/ and /ɔ/; lack of stable /ae/, absence of /ʌ/, etc. Sawyer intelligently notes that only "the most truly bilingual speakers" (75) employ regional or Southern/South Midland phonetic features such as /ĭ/ for /ĕ/ in pen, ten, fence, /ēy/ for /ae/ in can't, etc. English consonantal production again varied as per speaker competency, though "not even the best bilinguals always use the phone [z]" (91) as distinct from [s] in pairs such as raise ≠ race. One important finding is the near-universal tendency to shift the strong stress to the right in such noun-noun compounds as cherry tree, hang over, storage room, hot cakes, etc.: not /hát kéyks/ (standard English) but /hàt kéyks/. Further information on suprasegmentals was not given since "the worksheets do not afford a great deal of material on stress, intonation and juncture." (100)

"Lexical Pecularities of the Latins" as well as, once again, the social/cultural situation are examined in Ch. 3, pp. 125-145; this section's new information is twofold: (1) "the old words, which are the intimate reflection of tradition and regional culture, are for the most part absent from" the Chicano English lexicon, (128) (the generally absent terms such as lightning bug, laying hen, grub worms, dish rag, pully bone, snap beans, blinky, etc. are listed on pp. 129-133); and (2) "the English of the Latins reflects their cultural situation . . . also in their rejection of words borrowed from Spanish" (133) (i.e., some of Sawyer's seven informants not only assign Anglicized pronunciations to Spanish-origin proper names they need to use when speaking English but also reject occasional Anglicized words of Spanish origin such as corral, morral, lariat, cinch et al.; for the 31 words see pp. 135-143).

A summation and restatement of much of the above is given on pp. 182-188. Ch. 6 (189-314), "Inventory of the Worksheets," contains occasional informant-provided Spanish substitutes for Kurath list items such as cottage cheese (queso fresco) (a very brief list of "English Terms That Are Used in Spanish" appeared earlier [144-145]); an embarrassing itemization of Anglo insult names for Chicanos and vice versa on pp. 283-285 (among these: pilaus < pelados, bean bandits, pepper bellies for Chicanos, cuadrito and cabeza cuadrada for Anglos [but especially for those of German descent]); and passing annotations of Chicano English verbal morphology (e.g., sweat [292]; says one informant: "'I don't know how to handle [the simple past tense of] sweat, so I get out of it by going into Spanish'") which are also included in among the general discussion of verbal morphology in the misnamed Ch. 4, "Inflextional [sic] Forms of Anglo Speech in San Antonio," 165-177. [RT]

SAWYER, Janet Beck Moseley. "Aloofness from Spanish Influence in Texas English." Word 15.270-281 (1959). (Rpt. as "The Speech of San Antonio, Texas," in A Various Language: Perspectives on American Dialects, edited by Juanita V. Williamson and Virginia M. Burke. New York: Holt, Rinehart and Winston, 1971. Pp. 570-582.) [Annot. HLAS 23 (1961) no. 4473 (D. Wogan); Fody p. 540.]

Sawyer rejects the possibility that the peculiarities of San Antonio Anglo English can be attributed to some sort of Spanish "substratum" influence and goes on to comment that indeed, those few elements of Spanish lexicon which still form part of the local English are remnants of an earlier, nineteenth century period of borrowing, since by the 1950's the local Spanish and its speakers had sunk to a level of lower prestige due to animosities between the now-dominant Anglos and the Chicanos, etc., and that as a consequence Spanish-to-English borrowing has ceased. Also presented is information abstracted from Sawyer 1957 on "Latin English Phonology" and "Grammar and Lexicon of Anglo and Latin English in San Antonio." [RT]

SAWYER, Janet Beck Moseley. "Social Aspects of Bilingualism in San Antonio, Texas." PADS 41:1.7-15 (1964). (Rpt. in Readings in American Dialectology, edited by Harold B. Allen and Gary N. Underwood. New York: Appleton-Century-Crofts, 1971. Pp. 375-381. Also in Language: Introductory Readings, edited by Virginia P. Clark, P.A. Eschholz and A.F. Rosa. New York: St. Martin's Press, 1972. Pp. 430-437.)

Encapsulates information from Sawyer 1957 concerning San Antonio Chicano English phonology and lexicon; mentions that certain Hispanisms in English connected strictly with ranch life are retained only in the vocabulary of older Anglo informants; gives a run down on the language characteristics and the socioeconomic status of her study's Chicano informants (Sawyer 1957); and repeats the information that "if a Spanish word could be avoided in English, the bilinguals would not use it at all. . . . This was in direct contrast to the freedom with which all the Latin informants used English words in Spanish . . . " (p. 13) [RT]

SAWYER, Janet Beck Moseley. "Spanish-English Bilingualism in San Antonio, Texas." In Gilbert 1969, pp. 18-51. (Rpt. in HERN/etal-1975, pp. 77-98.

Much of what appeared in Sawyer 1964 and 1959 (and which first saw the light in Sawyer 1957) is repeated or reworked here: the history of Anglo-Chicano relations, capsule biographies of informants, comparisons between Anglo and Chicano English phonology and verbal morphology, a listing of Latin lexical peculiarities, etc. What is new is Sawyer's assertion that there is no such thing as a Mexican-American English dialect, at least not in San Antonio; these statements are made in refutation of William Stewart's remarks to the contrary. Sawyer says: "The English spoken by the bilingual informants was simply an imperfect state in the mastery of English. . . . [The] relatively unskilled bilinguals . . . did not pass on their imperfect English to their children. . . . It was clear that the linguistic norm was not the English of their relatives or neighbors, but rather that of the members of the prestige, English-speaking community. From generation to generation, the second language was in a fluid state, becoming more and more expert." (p. 19) [RT]

TEEL, Tommy Lou. "A Sociolinguistic Study of Spanish Linguistic Interference and Nonstandard Grammatical Phenomena in the Written English of Selected Mexican-American Bilinguals." MA Thesis, Univ. of Texas, El Paso, 1971. 116 pp.

Following her largely derivative descriptions of "related research," "general ethnolinguistic background" and "the Southwest as a sociolinguistic area," author Teel presents examples of Spanish interference in English (and/or deviant but not necessarily Spanish-influenced English) which appeared in the one-page compositions of fifty-five bilingual Mexican-American students at the University of Texas-El Paso. Teel's work is part of Prof. Jacob Ornstein's on-going SSSB project (see also Scott 1969, Wolff de Porras 1971, and Ornstein v.d.); Teel's conclusions (pp. 43-61) nicely complement the findings of Wolff de Porras, who pinpointed deviancies in Spanish-Language compositions. High-frequency nonstandard grammatical phenomena as unearthed by Teel are: omission of articles and their unnecessary inclusion, omission of pluralization markers, omission of the /ed/ marker of simple regular past tense (the single most troublesome goof--14 instances in all), prepositional misuses (especially involving 'on,' 'in'), and various "lexico-grammatical and syntactical phenomena" (p. 61) such as numerical and time expression errors, confusion of close equivalents such as 'see' for 'watch,' 'win' for 'beat, defeat,' 'say' for 'tell,' and the like. [RT]

WILLCOTT, Paul. "Differences in English Dictation Response by Spanish Speakers and by English Speakers." In Bills 1974, pp. 309-315.

This report on a simple dictation experiment indicates that spelling errors may be correlated with phonological confusion. Results of the test showed that the disparity in spelling performance of Spanish speakers and native English speakers was greater for "focal errors" (spellings reflecting phonological distinctions not found in Spanish) than for other errors. [GB]

5.10 CODE-SWITCHING

Major Items: (none)

See also these items elsewhere (consult Author Index for location):

MARA-1970; and especially LANC-1969

6. [CHICANOS:] CALIFORNIA

6.1 BIBLIOGRAPHY (nothing to report)

6.2 COMPREHENSIVE/GENERAL STUDIES; MISCELLANY; ANTHOLOGIES/ FESTSCHRIFTEN

Major Items: BLAN-A-1971

See also these items elsewhere (consult Author Index for location):

(none)

BLANCO, Antonio. La lengua española en la historia de California. Madrid: Cultura Hispánica, 1971. 829 pp.

In one of the most voluminous studies ever attempted on any variety of U.S. Spanish, Blanco offers his readers a socio-historical introduction (Chaps. II-IV), a vocabulary of "Californianismos" stemming largely from unpublished sources housed in the Bancroft collection of the University of California (Chap. V), a history of California Spanish to the end of the 19th century (Chap. VI), an account of Hispanisms absorbed into English, especially those dealing with mining technology (Chaps. VII-VIII), and two essays on contemporary California Spanish concerning loan verbs (Chap. IX) and pachuco (Chap. X). The body of the the text concludes with a homily on the need for intelligent bilingual education in California (Chap. XI). A thick batch of apendices contains excerpts from memoirs written during the gold rush days of California, an annotated edition of Father Florencio Ibáñez' Pastorela, and, finally, documents of a socio-economic character, with numerous graphs.

No doubt the abundance of material here printed is meant to answer the requirements of those in the Spanish-speaking world who lack any familiarity with the topic. On this side of the Atlantic, it may strike more than one reader as rather overstuffed. While the author does indeed provide a great deal of interesting and useful data, especially of a lexical nature, he all but buries it in some of the most punishing verbosity it has ever been my misfortune to wade through.

The usefulness of the most original portion of the book (Chap. V) is limited by the failure to make allusions fully retrievable; the sources are given, but very often without any indication of page or folio. The analysis of the language reflected in documents of the early period (up to 1823) suffers from an apparent lack of training in structural and historical linguistics; far too much importance is attributed to mere cacographic variants (boeyes, p. 294, is certainly no more than a hypercorrect spelling;

compare norueste [p. 291] for noroeste). Finally, the author's
unrepentant purism will no doubt excite the annoyance of some
readers (p. 257).

On balance, however, I must admit that the book is a veritable gold mine, though extracting the ore is sometimes difficult.
Blanco observes intelligently and sensitively this particular
corner of the erstwhile dominions of Spain. [JC]

RIZZO, Gino L. "Lingua e costumi spagnoli in California ad un
    secolo dall'occupazione statunitense." QuadIb 17.24-30
    (1955). [Annot. Fody p. 533.]

The pleasant description of certain cultural vestiges left
in California by the declining Californios contains very little
of interest to the linguist. The author records the text of
several songs and sayings which betray more or less standard
Spanish diction. [JC]

WILLIAMS, Stanley T. The Spanish Background of American Literature.
    2 vols. New Haven, Conn.: Yale Univ. Press, 1955. xxvii,
    441 pp. [TSBJr.]

The first of Williams' two hefty volumes (parts one and two)
discusses "the origins and beginning of Spanish culture in America" and "Spanish and Spanish-American Culture in the United States
during the nineteenth and twentieth centuries (1800-1950)." The
second volume (parts three and four) contains sections on each of
the major interpreters in American literature of Spanish and
Spanish-American culture: Washington Irving, George Ticknor,
William Prescott, William Cullen Bryant, Henry Wadsworth Longfellow
et al.

In part II, ch. 5, Williams speaks at some length of the influence exerted by California's Spanish and Mexican traditions
upon nineteenth-century American novelists Bret Harte and Helen
Hunt Jackson; the latter's "sentimentalized social document [and]
layman's poetic version of ancient California," Ramona, is discussed on pp. 230-232. Clearly the section of Williams' work
that will most interest students of U.S. Spanish language is
volume two's chapter on Bret Harte, (208-239) of whom Williams
says: "Among the experimenters in fiction and travel literature
in the Southwest and West, only he . . . rose above the common-
place, the sensational, the subliterary." (208) Harte arrived
in California in 1854 at the age of 17 and was immediately "taken"
by California's Hispanic culture. His writings reflect his
enthusiasm: "At least sixty-two of [Harte's 243 tales], including
the novels, reflect Spanish influence, and of these some twenty-
seven are primarily Spanish in materials and backgrounds . . .
Altogether Harte created some 108 characters, Spanish, Spanish-
American, or Mexican. A dozen or so of the poems are entirely
Spanish in subject." (222) On pp. 228-229 Williams quotes a
sample from one of Harte's frequent attempts to recreate "the im-

perfect English spoken in California in his time by persons of Spanish or Mexican extraction. Hearing this mongrel speech daily, he strove to capture its sounds precisely; he wrote 'lofe' for 'love' or 'mooch' for 'much.' Sometimes on the lips of his heroines, so conventionalized, with fans in their hands, roses in their hair, and nothing in their heads, the result is hardly more than baby talk. Realism is lost in a deadening verbal accuracy. In the later stories, such as 'Chu Chu,' this dialect is more convincing." (229) [RT]

6.2.1 SOCIOLINGUISTICS

Major Items: BREK-1973; COHE-1973

See also these items elsewhere (consult Author Index for location):

CLAR-1959/70

*ADORNO, William. "The Attitudes of Selected Mexican and Mexican-American Parents in Regards to Bilingual/Bicultural Education." PhD Diss., United States International Univ., San Diego, Calif., 1973. 225 pp. [DA 34 (1973) 1574-A.]

The abstract states that the study sought insights into "parent understanding of the main component of bilingual education, . . . their attitudes relative to the use of Spanish as a medium of instruction, [and] their perceptions as to the importance of their children learning the English and Spanish languages and knowing about the cultures of the United States and Mexico." Seventy-five parents from San Diego, Santa Ana and Oakland were involved. With regard to language usage attitudes the study found that the parents "were seeing the importance of English for their children from the framework of practical or pragmatic considerations, whereas they were seeing the importance of Spanish . . . from the framework of idealistic or personal considerations." Other study findings pertain specifically to education. [RT]

*BREKKE, Alice M. "Evaluational Reactions of Adolescent and Pre-adolescent Mexican-American and Anglo-American Students to Selected Samples of Spoken English." PhD Diss., Univ. of Minnesota, Minneapolis, 1973. 136 pp. [DA 34 (1973) 2153-2154-A.]

Brekke's work reproduces the study by Wallace Lambert et al. in Montreal ("Judging Personality Through Speech: A French-Canadian Example," The Journal of Communication 16.305-321 [1966]); Brekke is the first to apply an experiment of this sort to the perception (by 131 Anglo-American and 131 Mexican-American youngsters attending school in Riverside, California, equally divided

as to sex and subdivided into two chronological categories: mean
age of 10.6 and mean age of 16.3) of what the author defines as
"a variety of spoken English, 'Mexican-American English.'"
Listeners heard recordings of four one-minute conversational-
style speech samples, two "Anglo-American [standard educated
northern?] English" (AAE) and two "Mexican-American English" (MAE);
all four speakers were adult Mexican-American males. The listeners
were asked to judge each speaker's ethnic background and education-
al/occupational level, and to evaluate speech and speaker characteristics on various semantic differential scales. The results
parallel those of Lambert: "subjects consistently distinguished
speakers of MAE and AAE and judged the educational/occupational
level of speakers of AAE higher than that of speakers of MAE. . . . "
It is noteworthy that preadolescents "rated AAE speakers significantly less correct, less acceptable, and less valuable than did
adolescents [and also] rated MAE speakers significantly more
correct, more acceptable, and more valuable than did adolescents."
While ethnicity of subjects made no difference in the evaluation
of speakers of AAE, Mexican-Americans predictably rated speakers
of MAE "significantly more confident, happier, more successful,
kinder, more dependable, and more handsome" than did Anglo-American
subjects. No differences were reported according to sex. [RT]

COHEN, Andrew David. "A Sociolinguistic Approach to Bilingual
    Education: The Measurement of Language Use and Attitudes
    Toward Language in School and Community, with Special Reference
    to the Mexican American Community of Redwood City, California."
    MA Thesis, Stanford Univ., 1970. iii, 64 pp. [Available
    EDRS: ED 043 007.]

This paper is a sort of dissertation proposal or progress report for the research leading to Cohen 1973. It is primarily a
review of the literature with preliminary remarks on the sociolinguistic situation in Redwood City, deviant linguistic forms,
and measurement instruments. [GB]

COHEN, Andrew David. "Innovative Education for La Raza: A Socio-
    linguistic Assessment of a Bilingual Education Program in
    California." Ph.D. Diss., Stanford Univ., 1973. xv, 334 pp.
    [DA 33 (1973) 6582-6583-A.]

Although devoid of primary linguistic data, this is a
thorough and meticulous piece of language sociology research. The
study is a multifaceted comparison of 90 Mexican-American children
in grades K-2, half in a bilingual education program and half in a
traditional classroom. Pretested in the fall of 1970 and post-
tested in the spring of 1972, the children are compared with regard
to proficiency in both Spanish and English, usage of the two languages outside the school, performance in mathematics, and attitudes
toward language, culture, and school. Cohen found that the bilingual education group at the end of the study was just as profi-

cient in English, somewhat more proficient in Spanish, generally used more Spanish, performed as well or better in math, showed no difference in attitude toward the two languages or Anglo culture, and had a more positive attitude toward Mexican American culture and school. This careful and judicious argument for the efficacy of bilingual education merits scrutiny by all interested in Spanish educational linguistics. [GB]

CURRIE, Mona Boyd. "Problems of Teaching Spanish to Spanish-speaking Students in California." MA Thesis, The Claremont Graduate School, Claremont, Calif., 1950. vii, 145 pp.

This work contains no primary linguistic data, but it does present valuable information on attitudes toward Spanish. The study is concerned with the need to provide special high school instruction in Spanish for native speakers and is based on questionnaire responses from 98 teachers and 772 Spanish-speaking students. In addition to consideration of general foreign language teaching methodology and available materials for Spanish, the study treats in detail the student responses about student/parent nationality, occupation, literacy, objectives in studying Spanish, ability in Spanish, and attitudes toward special instruction, as well as the teacher responses on the social behavior of the Spanish-speaking student and the need for special instruction. [GB]

LANE, James Alfred. "A Descriptive Study of Spanish Language Television Station KMEX and the Spanish-Speaking Audience of Los Angeles." MA Thesis, Univ. of California, Los Angeles, 1966. ix, 183 pp.

An exhaustive survey of the Chicano "market" of California (and, in particular, the Greater Los Angeles area) in terms of buying habits, living conditions and especially media preferences and listening patterns, this well-written thesis is also a careful description of the type and content of the programming of KMEX, a UHF station founded in 1962. Lane finds that KMEX is heavily dependent on videotape imports from Mexico, largely concentrates on "entertainment," and presents public service broadcasting almost as an afterthought, though a "learn English" program and a show entitled "Conozcan sus escuelas" were regular features. Lane's reportage reflects conditions upon the eve of the Chicano political activism of the late sixties, and can thus serve as a baseline study for examinations of more contemporary programming. [RT]

PEÑALOSA, Fernando and Edward C. McDonagh. "Social Mobility in
a Mexican-American Community [in Pomona]." SFor 44.498-505 (1966).

Nothing on language per se, but occasional sociolinguistic
commentary draws one's attention to this seminal article. For
example the researchers found that "use of the English rather
than the Spanish language in the interview was found to be significantly associated with upward mobility;" (p. 503) apparently it
was the interviewee who was allowed to determine language of
interview, although bilingual versions of the interview schedule
were readily at hand and the interviews themselves were conducted
by Peñalosa and not McDonagh. (Of the 147 interviews held in
1960 and 1961, 104 were conducted in English and 43 in Spanish.)
It was learned that upward mobility did not go hand in hand with
deethnicization: "Rather, as Mexicans go up and out of the strictly
Mexican-American colonia they remain loyal to the Mexican identification. There is the development or retention perhaps of
ethnocentrism . . . " (504) [RT]

SKOCZYLAS, Rudolph V. "An Evaluation of Some Cognitive and Affective Aspects of a Spanish-English Bilingual Education Program."
PhD Diss., Univ. of New Mexico, 1972. xii, 168 pp. [DA 33
(1973) 5711-A.]

There are no primary language data in this pleasant sociolinguistic study intended to determine the effect of bilingual
education on children in the Santa Clara Valley of northern
California. The results of the author's experiment showed that
the experimental group (children who had had two years of bilingual
instruction) performed as well as or better than the control group
on all measures (command of English, command of Spanish, intellectual functioning, self-image, and so forth) except mathematics.
Chap. 3 (pp. 62-78) provides a good sociolinguistic overview of
the community studied, including the results of a small English-
Spanish language use survey of the adults. [GB]

6.3 SPANISH PHONOLOGY (includes ORTHOGRAPHY)

Major Items: PHIL-1967

See also these items elsewhere (consult Author Index for location):

(none)

LAWSON, Jack. "Bobby and John: A Study of the Spanish of Two American Boys of Mexican Descent." MA Thesis, Fresno State Univ., Fresno, Calif., 1969, 97 pp.

Fifteen minutes of tape-recorded conversations have here generated nearly 100 pages of analysis; I hope that doesn't represent a trend. The author's observations are frequently naive and largely uncontrolled by any expertise in the field of Hispanic (esp. Southwest U.S.) dialectology. Nevertheless, the raw data he has gathered are of interest, ranging from dialect words (cobete = cubeta 'bucket,' apá = papá 'daddy,' amá = mamá 'mommy'), verb forms (ta = está, hició = hizo), and characteristic phonological traits (nojotros = nosotros, collapse of the rr/r contrast in favor of the latter), to individual forms probably attributable to child language (ponién = también 'also,' ará = verdad 'isn't that so?'). Very laudable was Lawson's decision to list all utterances he failed to understand, rather than passing over them in silence. It should be noted that his informants' family were compara ively recent "in-migrants" from Texas, to use Beltramo's (1972) apposite term. [JC]

PHILLIPS, Robert N., Jr. "Los Angeles Spanish: A Descriptive Analysis." PhD Diss., Univ. of Wisconsin, Madison, 1967. 718 pp. [DA 28 (1968) 2667.] [Rev. Craddock 1973 pp. 482-484.]

This is one of the most thorough-going accounts of any species of U.S. Spanish, especially since it includes such a large section devoted to syntax (pp. 384-617). The author also treats phonology (with spectrographic analyses), morphology and "bilingual phenomena," (pp. 618-645) concluding with a lengthy lexicon. The work shows Phillips to be a skilled field worker and descriptive analyst; he is somewhat weaker when attempting historical and comparative explanations.

A laudable innovation he has introduced is the marking of each utterance by a code that identifies in very broad terms the sex, age, predominant language and social status of each informant. While the grid he used was probably too widely gauged to reveal hitherto unsuspected sociolinguistic correlations, it nevertheless represents an effort that should be made in all descriptive studies.

His categorization of loanwords, blends and loanshifts (pp. 620 ff.) must be read in the light of Beltramo's excellent discussion of the subject (1972); for further criticism of details see my critique mentioned in the heading of this item. [JC]

PHILLIPS, Robert N., Jr. "The Influence of English on the /v/ in Los Angeles Spanish." In Ewton and Ornstein 1972, pp. 201-212.

This article reworks the corresponding portion of his dissertation (1967, pp. 67-73). His main conclusions, i.e., that /v/ is less common among older speakers and those whose predominant language is Spanish, and that the distribution of stop vs. fricative allophones ([b] vs. [ƀ] or [v]) is less "neat and nice" than in the standard language, are not surprising. The methodology used in attempting to discover sociolinguistic correlates (sex, age, language use and social class) would be more convincing had it revealed unexpected or unanticipated correlations.

Nowadays one should not remain content to plot allophonic distribution against the narrow phonetic criteria Phillips uses. The frequency of fricativization among voiced stops between words might depend, for instance, on whether or not the two words in question descend from the same immediately superior syntactic node: estos vinos vs. a las dos vino el muchacho.

While Phillips is certainly right in attributing /v/ in Los Angeles Spanish to English influence, it is odd that he overlooks the possibility that the same lnaguage may be responsible for the appearance of the stop [b] between vowels in words like globo 'baloon' and automóvil. [JC]

6.4 SPANISH GRAMMAR (MORPHOLOGY AND SYNTAX)

Major Items: (none)

See also these items elsewhere (consult Author Index for location):

GING-1974; LAWS-1969; and especially PHIL-1967

VALLS, Dolores L. "Linguistic Description of Samples of Oral Spanish Spoken by California High School Students of Mexican Background." MA Thesis, Sacramento State Univ., Sacramento, Calif., 1971. 59 pp.

The author had the novel idea of subjecting the utterances of the corpus she gathered to an immediate constituent analysis in the hope of thereby isolating characteristic deviations from standard Spanish. Unfortunately, the small size of the corpus to say nothing of the narrow topics of conversation contained in it failed to provide sufficient raw data for such an undertaking to be illuminating. Hence her observations tend to be as atomistic and ad hoc as those of the other purely descriptive accounts that abound in this field. The chief defect that I noted was her consistent inability to distinguish between what was accidentally absent from her corpus and what may have been genuinely absent from the speech of her informants.

Writers of theses like the one under discussion would do well to remember that perhaps the most significant contribution they can make as beginners is to set down for posterity careful and complete transcriptions of the material they collect. This allows subsequent researchers to make use of their efforts for all sorts of linguistic investigations that the original field worker has no way of anticipating. Valls' work affords no such basis for further study. [JC]

6.5 SPANISH LEXICON (includes SEMANTICS)

Major Items: (none)

See also these items elsewhere (consult Author Index for location):

LAWS-1969; and especially PHIL-1967

CLARK, Margaret. Health in the Mexican-American Culture. 2nd ed. (1959; Berkeley: Univ. of California Press, 1970.) xiv, 253 pp.

This book seeks to present sociocultural information useful to health practitioners, welfare workers and others and does not pretend to be a language study; it nevertheless contains much valuable sociolinguistic information on the few pages that deal with language (53-59; see also "Literacy," 59-61). Especially interesting are the attitudes of the "older generation" in the San José, California barrio Clark studied: most parents wanted their children to speak both Spanish and English well, and often punished youngsters for failing to speak Spanish to their elders. Local Mexican-American politicians and would-be community leaders are shunned if they do not speak Spanish. For the residents of "Sal si puedes" the language is a symbol "of their existence as a community of people with a proud history and time-honored traditions." (56) A certain schizoglossia is evident: while recent Mexican immigrants speak disparagingly of the local "bracero Spanish," Mexican-Americans often claim they are unable to understand "many of the expressions" the foreign-born use. Brief examples of intra-sentential code-switching are given. On pp. 241-244 Clark provides a well-handled glossary of common Mexican Spanish folk terms, expressions of sickness, etc. [RT]

STEWART, George R. "Two Spanish Word Lists from California in 1857." AS 16.260-269 (1941). [Annot. Woodbridge p. 242.]

Two commentaries accompany these lists (designed to acquaint newcomers with necessary and useful phrases for dealing with the Hispanic population): the anonymous author's and Stewart's. The former provides interesting notes on meaning and usage as of 1857 while the latter adds erudite observations of a historical and comparative nature. In all, a fascinating glimpse into a period when English speakers seem to have felt the pressure to adapt even more than the Californios. Stewart adds some unusual Hispanisms not included in the two lists: pungle 'to pay up' < póngale 'place your bet! (in monte)' and mahaly 'squaw' < mujer 'woman.' [JC]

6.6 ONOMASTICS (includes TOPONYMY)

Major Items: BRIG-1967/71; GUDD-1949/69

See also these items elsewhere (consult Author Index for location):

(none)

BRIGHT, Elizabeth S. A Word Geography of California and Nevada. Univ. of California Publications in Linguistics, No. 69 (Berkeley and Los Angeles: Univ. of California Press, 1971). ix, 228 pp. (This is a revised version of the author's identically-entitled PhD Diss., Univ. of California, Berkeley, 1967. 355 pp. [DA 29 (1968) 244-A.])

This very impressive work is a traditional dialect geography study based on data from 300 interviews presented in the field records of the Linguistic Atlas of the Pacific Coast. The book devotes a special section (pp. 100-108) to the 48 borrowings from Spanish the Atlas elicited; generally relating to ranching, topography, and family-social relations, these words are crudely grouped into 38 "Spanish" forms (i.e., altered to some greater extent). Two maps show the percentages of occurrence of the Spanish borrowings in the two states while a third map illustrates the distribution of "Spanish" rodéo vs. "Americanized" ródeo. One fails to see why the author considers [láe-soU] (lasso) more "Americanized" than the typical pronunciation of arroyo: [ərɔ́yə]. In this connection we note that pronunciation is only infrequently given.
The curious form sanky 'ditch' may be more than an Americanization of Sp. zanja; the -k- suggests a blend with the Sp. synonym acequia, documented as [séIki] in the Southwest. A couple of etymological blunders are present: pinto is from Sp. pinto 'id.,' not pintado 'painted,' nor is pachuco (ultimately and most probably a hypocoristic derivative of the name of the city of El Paso) related to pechuga (p. 103). [GB/JC]

GUDDE, Erwin G. <u>California Place Names: The Origin and Etymology of Current Geographical Names</u>. 3rd ed. (1949; Berkeley and Los Angeles: University of California Press, 1969). xxi, 416 pp. [Rev. <u>JAF</u> 63.121-122 (1950) (R. Heizer); <u>RPh</u> 8.68-69 (1954-55) (Y.Malkiel); <u>AS</u> 35.210-211 (1960) (K. Malone); <u>Names</u> 12.58-64 (1964) (E. W. McMullen).]

The virtues of Gudde's superb reference work are sufficiently well-known as to excuse detailed analysis here. Hundreds of Hispanic names populate the pages of the work, each carefully traced in historical and linguistic terms to its first application to a geographic feature in California. In the third edition and index of obsolete names was added (pp. 403-416). [JC]

MORENO, H.M. <u>Dictionary of Spanish-Named California Cities and Towns</u>. San Luis Obispo, Calif.: Author, 1916. 95 pp.

The dictionary alluded to in the title is but a small portion of the whole (pp. 11-26), where a selection of Spanish words occurring in California place names are matched with glosses from Velázquez' venerable lexicon. The remainder takes up the origin of the name of the state (pp. 27-33), reprints two items on the names of the cities and counties of California (pp. 35-91) from the <u>California Blue Book or State Roster</u>, and concludes with an exhortation to all Californians to resist the sinister efforts of the U.S. Post Office and the railroads to corrupt the state's euphonious place names (pp. 93-95) by accepting, for example, the vernacular abbreviation of <u>San Buenaventura</u> into <u>Ventura</u>. In sum, a small piece of bibliographical refuse that must forever clutter compilations like ours. [JC]

SÁNCHEZ, Nellie Van de Grift. <u>Spanish and Indian Place Names of California: Their Meaning and Their Romance</u>. 3rd ed. (1914; San Francisco: A.M. Robertson, 1930). 446 pp.

While the scholarly content, such as it is, of this attractive book has been superseded by Gudde 1949, it retains some interest for the numerous anecdotes and photographs that adorn its pages. The presentation proceeds by geographic areas ("In and About San Diego," "Los Angeles and her Neighbors," etc.) with a full alphabetical index (pp. 347-446) that includes numerous items not discussed in the body of the work. [JC]

SHAFER, Robert. "The Pronunciation of Spanish Place Names in California." <u>AS</u> 17.239-246 (1942). [Annot. Woodbridge p. 243.]

Based on his long acquaintance with the area and the corroboration of others, the author lists the phonetic norm for 165 names, giving alternate forms where it was difficult to ascertain the norm. This list is followed by cursory comments summarizing the interesting patterns of phonological adaptations. The pronunciation in

the vast majority of cases is based on the spelling, not the
Spanish pronunciation, but Shafer steadfastly refuses to mention this general rule. [GB]

6.7 ENGLISH INFLUENCE ON SPANISH

Major Items: BELT-1972

See also these items elsewhere (consult Author Index for location):

   AMSD-1969; ESPI-1914-15; GING-1974; PHIL-1972

BELTRAMO, Anthony Fred. "Lexical and Morphological Aspects of
   Linguistic Acculturation by Mexican Americans of San José,
   California." PhD Diss., Stanford Univ., 1972. 331 pp. [DA
   33 (1973) 4379-4380-A.]

   The basis of this extremely competent and well organized description of the lexical impact of English on the Spanish of San
José is a "Glossary of Borrowings" (pp. 197-304); but it is very
far from a mere word list. The introductory material, in particular Chap. 3 ("Classification and Analysis of Borrowings"), deserves to be included among the standard readings on the subject
of lexical interference. Beltramo, besides applying skilfully the
well known criteria developed by Haugen, pays close attention to
phonological and morphological aspects of borrowing; I find especially noteworthy and unusual his comments on derivational
morphology (pp. 106 ff.).
   The bulk of the Spanish-speaking population of San José are
"in-migrants" from southwest Texas, rather than direct immigrants
from Mexico. Spanish monolingualism is declining while English
monolingualism is increasing, and the massive infusion of English
lexical material is simply a response to evident environmental
exigencies. The patterns of adaptation are quite similar to
those observed elsewhere, but few accounts have been carried out
with the care and good sense that Beltramo reveals. I would like
to single out for praise his paragraphs on "Loan Homonyms" (pp.
122-125) where an eminently sensible distinction is drawn between
coincidental homonyms and loanshifts: "Since however, there is
no common semantic ground between these two words, we do not say
that Spanish carpeta ['letter file'] was either extended in meaning' or 'shifted in context' to acquire the meaning 'carpet'.
Carpeta 'carpet' is simply a different word, adapted in the same
manner as cuilta 'quilt'." [JC]

CHACÓN, Estelle. "Pochismos." El Grito 3:1.34-35 (Fall 1969).

Impassioned defense of pochismos, a label that for Chacón seems to include code-switching as well as strictly lexical substitution and interchange. I imagine that by now most knowledgeable people would accept her contention that pochismos add "spice, stimulus, color [and] drama" to the language of Chicanos, whose particular variety of Spanish must be considered as legitimate a form of linguistic communication as any other. I note the author uses the word piquete 'spice' (standard 'sharp jab') in reference to one's diction (cf. 'alcoholic beverage secretly added to a non-alcoholic refreshment,' 'indirect caustic or witty remark,' Santamaría 1959, p. 860). [JC]

DÍAS, Rosario Simón. "A Vocabulary of California Spanish Words of English Origin Used by the First Generation Spaniards of California." MA Thesis, Stanford Univ., 1941. 131 pp.

This glossary includes only loanwords detected in the speech of Spanish-speaking immigrants dwelling in central California. If I understand the brief, vague indications provided in the opening chapter, we are probably dealing with Spaniards and not, for instance, Mexicans or persons of Mexican descent; no hint is otherwise given as to the provenience, occupations, social status, etc., of the author's informants. The loanwords are carefully transcribed and may serve as useful primary data for further study, but Días' own analysis (pp. 100 ff.) is entirely worthless, since it reveals such poor understanding of English phonology and Spanish derivational patterns. In addition, certain important facets of Spanish, esp. dialectal, phonology were apparently beyond the ken of the author.

Despite the intentional limitation to loanwords, an occasional loanblend crops up, unbeknownst to Días: [čampeón] is Sp. campeón blended, of course, with Eng. champion; [engančá] (f. sg.) indeed reflects Eng. engaged but it seems likely that Sp. enganchar 'to hook' is also involved, perhaps as a jocose calque on Eng. hooked 'hopelessly compromised to matrimony.'

Plomero 'plumber' (p. 77), lit. 'lead worker' occurs in any dictionary of standard Spanish, though cañero may be the more common term. In any case the phonological shape of the word requires at the very least the assumption of blending with plomo 'lead', particularly in view of the form pláma 'plumber' recorded on p. 76. It is quite absurd to allege that plomero is derived from plomería (p. 77)

One last point: both -ear and -ar are productive verb-forming suffixes in Spanish, so the claim that, for instance, scrape is first "Hispanized" as escrepe then derived with the suffix -ar to form the verb escrepear (pp. 125 ff.), must be disregarded. [JC]

6.8 SPANISH INFLUENCE ON ENGLISH

Major Items: (none)

See also these items elsewhere (consult Author Index for location):

BRIG-1967/71; SHAF-1942; STEW-1941

BEELER, Madison S. "The Californian Oronym and Toponym Montara."
RPh 20.35-39 (1966-67).

The author conjectures Sp. montera *'place where wild game abounds, where hunting is good' as the source of Montara [mantɛ́rə]. The semantic reconstruction is based on the related derivatives montero 'huntsman' and montería 'hunting' ← monte 'forest, wood; mountain.' [JC]

GRANT, Rena V. "The Localized Vocabulary of California Verse."
CFQ 1.253-290 (1942). [Annot. Woodbridge p. 243.]

Of the ca. 200 words (including spelling or possible pronunciation variants) listed in the Glossary (pp. 268-289), 37 per cent are of Spanish origin, many familiar and easily identifiable as "Westernisms": adios, adobe/dobe, arroyo, barranca, bronco, buckaroo/buckeroo/bucharo, burro, etc. Each entry is defined and then cited in context, hence dated; in the case of five of the Hispanisms the time of first appearance antedates the one given in Craigie 1941. Grant also marks several forms as "foreign terms [usually Spanish] anglicized at an early date, which have since dropped out of common usage. They appear nowadays almost exclusively in 'local color verse.'" (260) Indeed, in her search for first appearances and an adequate corpus the author deserves full credit for much patient wading through the "regional" poetry and prose of long un-read authors such as Joaquín Miller, Badger Clark, H.H. Knibbs, S.D. Hubbell and others, the progenitors of volumes entitled Sun and Saddle Leather, Riders of the Stars, Satin Slippers, Songs of the Lost Frontier, and Scrap Book of Specimens of My Verse, by one J.A. Swett, of which the following in situ citation (from the poem "Vaquearo [sic] Life [1857]") bears vivid witness: "We give the hours to mirth and dance / In the señorita's love-lit glance." (286) As Grant notes several times in her long preamble to the Glossary, the flood of Hispanisms surely proves how much the Anglo newcomers stood to benefit from the already-established Hispanic population in matters of mining, farming, livestock raising and herding, etc. A typology of "Western" (including Spanish-origin) vocabulary is attempted on pp. 259-260 and again on p. 262. [RT]

HAMILTON, Marian. "California Gold-Rush English." <u>AS</u> 7.423-433 (1932).

This inane prose listing of vocabulary items, all tranquilly cited without glosses, contains several dozen Spanish borrowings a few of which are even explicitly noted as deriving from Spanish (p. 432)! [GB]

SHULMAN, David. "Some Californian Contributions to the American Vocabulary." <u>AS</u> 24.264-267 (1949). [Annot. Woodbridge no. 242.]

A straightforward citation of 42 lexical items either not listed in the <u>Dictionary of American English</u> or listed there with a later date than Shulman documents. The entries simply give a sample sentence from a 19th century Gold-rush literary work without even a gloss. About one-half of the entries are of Spanish origin. [GB]

SHULMAN, David. "Spanish Words in American English." <u>AS</u> 30.227-231 (1955).

Identical in purpose and form to Shulman 1949, but with definitions this time, this little note presents 64 words of Spanish origin encountered in mid-19th century English-language writings. [GB]

6.8.1 ENGLISH OF THIS PARTICULAR HISPANIC GROUP

<u>Major Items</u>: AMSD-1969; BROU-1972; POLI/RAMI-1973; WILLA-1971

<u>See also these items elsewhere</u> (consult Author Index for location):

 (none)

*AMSDEN, Constance E. "A Study of the Syntax of the Oral English Used by Thirty Selected Mexican-American Children Three to Five Years Old in a Preschool Setting." PhD Diss., Claremont Graduate School, Claremont, Calif., 1969. 197 pp. [<u>DA</u> 31 (1970) 49-50-A.]

The abstract of this seminal dissertation is well-written and, as a résumé of contents, extremely thorough; it appears one need not consult the work itself unless details are desired. Amsden attempted to determine which syntactical patterns the children used and how Spanish influenced their English syntax, and strove "to develop hypothesis about various aspects of the oral language development of Mexican-American preschoolers." (abs.) The subjects

all lived "in a low socio-economic Spanish-English-speaking
community and [attended] an East Los Angeles preschool."
Throughout the schoolday, tape recordings were made of the
children's spontaneous speech. Language samples "selected at
random" were analyzed according to four measures: basic structure, complexity, variety, and variation from standard English.

Amsden's conclusions are largely pessimistic; in general "the
children's language appears to be forceful, full of imperatives
and interjections, but lacking in qualifiers and evidences of
subordination." When compared with other groups of children of
the same age it was found that these youngsters overused imperatives and underused interrogatives. The complexity level of
their language was low: "only one-sixth of their T-units included phrases; only 3 per cent included subordinate clauses.
Adverbial constructions were rarely used." While "several variety
measures developed for the study increased significantly from age
three to four," thus indicating achievement of greater flexibility,
"the number of verbal variations and the total number of variations
from standard English increased" during the same period of time,
in seeming proportion to the use of greater variety. Although
Amsden claims that it was "acceptable" to use both Spanish and
English in the preschool, "only a small percentage (less than 10
per cent) of the children's T-units were in Spanish. However,
the influence of their linguistic [home] environment was evident
in the frequent transfer of Spanish words into the English language stream, the formation of 'Spanglish' words and awkward word
arrangement." [RT]

*BROUSSARD' Neonetta Cabrera. "The Spelling Errors of Mexican-American High School Students Tested at UCLA." MA Thesis,
Univ. of California, Los Angeles, 1972. ix, 112 pp. [Abs.
UCLAW/TECL 6.94 (1972).]

In the abstract of this very impressive-looking thesis
Broussard states she will determine which "sounds in American
English are commonly misspelled by Mexican-American high school
students and what spelling patterns are giving [them] special problems." The corpus for the study consisted of essays written by
each of 487 applicants to UCLA's High Potential Program during
1969-70. To determine the trouble zones Broussard drew up frequency charts for all the phonemes and all the graphemes employed
in all 487 essays (!). The result was "a list of the first ten
most frequently misspelled vowel sounds and a list of the first
ten most frequently misspelled consonant sounds." These lists
were then compared with simlarly-derived lists from other studies
of English grapheme-phoneme correspondences, and a set of four
"categories" was established: spelling patterns with high English
occurrence and high percentage of misspelling; patterns with high
occurrence and low misspelling; low occurrence and high misspelling;
and low occurrence and low misspelling. "A detailed listing of all

the spelling patterns for each category together with an alphabetical list of words representing each pattern is provided in the Appendix." [RT]

METCALF, Allan A. "Mexican-American English in Southern California." WR 9.13-21 (1972). [Abs. MLAAb/Ling 1972.61 (no. 7996).]

From his tapes of three dozen free-conversational interviews in the Riverside area the author concludes that while many California Chicanos "are native speakers of a legitimate Spanish-influenced dialect of American English," (abs.) grammatical and lexical differences between this dialect and local varieties of Anglo English are minimal and the chief distinctiveness is phonological. At times the phonology reflects Spanish influence and at other times a hypercorrection of patterns the speakers perceive to be Spanish-influenced. Intonation often includes separate peaks of loudness and pitch change within a phrase; of probable Spanish genesis is what Metcalf has found to be a "less rapid falling off of pitch and loudness at the end of a declarative sentence than in Anglo dialects." (ibid.) Metcalf also gives random though insightful information about language use (pp. 14-15) and notes that the only group of Riverside Chicanos likely to speak a brand of English markedly influenced by Spanish are the first generation immigrants from Mexico. [RT]

METCALF, Allan A. [1974a]. "The Study (Or, Non-study) of California Chicano English." In Bills 1974, pp. 97-106.

Because of the lack of objective linguistic research on the English variety typical of many Southwest Mexican Americans, this short and not very substantive article merits acclaim as an initial step toward remedying the situation. Intended primarily to stress the need for more research in this field, the paper cites only a few intriguing examples of this supposed dialect: the use of plate versus dish, wash the dishes versus do the dishes, couch versus sofa, [sy] versus [s], and stress placement on rodeo. [GB]

METCALF, Allan A. [1974b]. "The Study of California Chicano English." In Spolsky and Bills 1974, pp. 53-58.

A somewhat shortened version of Metcalf 1974a. [GB]

POLITZER, Robert L. and Arnulfo G. Ramírez. An Error Analysis of the Spoken English of Mexican-American Pupils in a Bilingual School and a Monolingual School. Research and Development Memorandum No. 103 (Stanford: Stanford Univ. Center for Research and Development in Teaching, 1973). 36 pp. Rpt. in LL 23.39-62 (1973) and also available through EDRS (ED 073 879).

    This important study provides crucial information for scholars interested in language acquisition as well as for students of Chicano English. The authors sampled 61 children attending a monolingual (English-language) school and 59 attending a bilingual school in Redwood City, California; the two schools' programs are examined intensively by Andrew Cohen (1970, 1973). The children were shown a silent movie and asked to tell a story. Their answers, recorded and transcribed, were analyzed for deviations from "standard English;" these were described and then categorized into errors in morphology, syntax, and vocabulary, and were counted as to relative frequency so as to determine (1) major sources of variant patterns, and (2) whether bilingually-schooled children performed at the same level as monolingually-schooled ones. Major findings were "(1) that deviations apparently were the result of the expected Spanish interference, the improper application of standard English rules, and the influence of nonstandard English dialects and (2) that children in the bilingual school did not differ significantly from those in the monolingual school with respect to frequency of deviations from standard English." (from Preface, EDRS [n.pag.])
    Spanish intrusion, while not the sole cause of error, plays a considerable role and seems to be the major cause of deviation "in the following examples: the use of the simple verb form for the past tense of regular verbs (evidently due to misinterpretation of final consonant clusters), nominalization by using the infinitive rather than the gerund, uncertainty in the use of subject pronouns, the use of the definite article for the possessive, confusion in the use of prepositions (especially in the use of in, on, etc.), uncertainty in the use of to in verb + verb constructions, confusion in word order (object-subject-verb construction)." (ibid., pp. 25-26) The authors concluded that errors from other sources (chiefly through misapplication of English rules) are best described as "developmental" and thus typical of the mistakes that any learner of a second language would commit: "Both the 'regularization' by adding -ed and the substitution of the simple non-past ('present') occurred with great frequency: He fall in the water, He came and bring it in the house . . . He putted the cookie there . . ." (p. 5) It is noteworthy that while the children "had probably had little if any contact with speakers of Black English," (8) omission of the copula BE was not uncommon and must thus be ascribed to other causes. [RT]

SPECTOR, Sima. "Patterns of Difficulty in English in Bilingual
    Mexican-American Children." MA Thesis, Sacramento [Calif.]
    State Univ., 1972. iii, 34 pp.

   Spector's work could well have been titled "Variance from
Standard English among Bilingual and English-Monolingual Mexican-
American Children," for that is what it investigates, using the
grammatical Closure Subtest of the Illinois Test of Psycholinguistic Abilities and the Michigan Oral Language Productive Test.
Tested were 15 bilingual and 15 monolingual first and second grade
poverty-level Sacramento children. Spector found that both groups
were equally deficient; this lead her to conclude (as have many
others) that not bilingualism but low socioeconomic status or the
cultural bias of the testing instruments engender low performance.
"Types of Nonstandard Forms" are presented and levels of frequency
are indicated for these on pp. 16-19; the categories that elicited
"more of a variety of nonstandard types than others" were past
participles, past tenses and partitive pronouns ("double negatives"
substituted for standard any, etc.); reflexive pronouns were also
problematic. [RT]

TURNEY, Douglas. "The Mexican Accent." AS 4.434-439 (1928-29)

   A naive, cute, popular, ambling discussion of "accent" focusing on the pronunciation of English by California Spanish speakers.
[GB]

VÁZQUEZ ARJONA, Carlos. "Spanish and Spanish-American Influences
    on Bret Harte." RHisp 76.573-621 (1929). (Cf. Williams 1955.)

   In his discussion of "Spanish Characters: Other Types" (A.IV)
Vázquez speaks of Enríquez Saltello (?), the hero of Harte's The
Devotion of Enríquez, and of the "amusing" way in which Saltello
employs the English language; a tiresome example of this is
quoted: "As to thees women and their little game, believe me my
friend, your old oncle 'Enry is not in it. No; he will ever take
a back seat when lofe is around. For why? Regard me here! . . .
[etc.]" (p. 592) The rest of Vázquez's article mentions Spanish
art, architecture, horsemanship, love and diversions, but not
language; the "Spanish Vocabulary" which accompanies Harte's
Gabriel Conroy, vol. 2, is apparently reproduced in its brief
entirety (pp. 617-621); there is nothing here that any general
dictionary would not give, with the possible exception of semi-
cuaca 'dance of Moorish origin.' [RT]

WILLARD, Caroline Corser. "A Linguistic Analysis of Written
   Compositions by Mexican-American Students on College English
   Placement Examinations." MA Thesis, Univ. of Texas, Austin,
   1971. 117 pp.

   This important and well written work was born out of frustration: at the time the author was an English teacher at a community college, and the research thus engendered sought "to discover how the writing of a group of [100] Mexican-American high school and college students from Bakersfield, California differs from standard formal written English and from the writing of a control group of [50] (presumably) monolingual English-speaking Anglo-American students of the same geographical area." (p. 14) While rightly convinced that it was necessary "to compare the Mexican-American students' writing with that of the other students," (15) since not all Chicano deviancies are peculiar to "Chicano English" alone, Willard nonetheless seeks to establish Spanish-based sources of error wherever possible, as she concluded initially that Spanish structures prompted many of them, if only through the indirect influence of "barrio English," as in the case of those students whose knowledge of Spanish was minimal or even non-existent (though the author made no attempt to determine dominance configurations or to survey "languages spoken" among her Chicanos). Stockwell/Bowen (1965) and Stockwell/Bowen/Martin (1965) were the models for the necessary contrastive analysis. While Spanish patterns indeed lie behind many deviancies, others are more readily classed as developmental mistakes typically made by persons who are still "experimenting with" a second language and thus cannot be attributed directly to Spanish.
   Willard's conclusions are not comforting: "with the exception of be, nouns, articles, and personal pronouns, all of the Mexican-American totals [of significant deviations] were at least twice as large as those of the Anglo students. Mexican-American deviations with auxiliary verbs other than be, other verbs, prepositions, and word choice were three times greater than Anglo deviations in the same categories. And there was a difference of more than twenty percent between the two student groups for initial consonants and syllables and idioms, since no Anglo students had any deviations of these two types." (105-106) Greatest difficulty occured with verbal suffixes and final consonant patterns in English and Spanish" (106) is to blame here. Function words and especially prepositions constituted another main problem area. Additional information as to which forms were problematic was deduced from substitutions or omissions. [RT]

6.9 SPANISH INFLUENCE ON AMERINDIAN LANGUAGES

Major Items: BRIG-1960a; SAWY-JO-1964a; SHIP-1962

See also these items elsewhere (consult Author Index for location):

(none)

BEELER, Madison S. "Inyo." Names 20.56-59 (1972). [Abs. MLAAbs/ Ling 1972.32 (no. 2519).]

Beeler suggests that the etymon of the California toponym Inyo may be, prosaically enough, no more than a native adaptation of Sp. indio 'Indian.' Along the way, he convincingly demonstrates the legendary character of the hitherto accepted source (cf. Gudde 1949). [JC]

BRIGHT, William. [1960a]. "Animals of Acculturation in the California Indian Languages." UCPL 4:4.215-246 (1960). [Rev. RPh 14.360-(1960-61) (Y. Malkiel).]

A masterful short monograph summarizing the words employed for 16 typical European domestic animals (horse, mare, colt, donkey, mule, cow, bull, calf, sheep, goat, pig, cat, chicken, rooster, turkey, dog) in all indigenous California languages for which he could find data. For each animal the words are listed in groups according to etymology or etymological process: outright borrowings, extensions of native words, new descriptive coinages, and unknown origin. Spanish is, of course, the dominant source of borrowings. In the conclusion (pp. 32-34), Bright discusses some implications to be drawn about early California Spanish, differences in Spanish contact suggested by accomodation of borrowings, and resistance to English borrowings due to sociocultural differences between the nature of English- and Spanish-speaking contacss with the Indians. Four linguistic geography maps display the most generalized source-terms for horse, cow, cat, and dog. [GB]

BRIGHT, William and Elizabeth S. Bright. "Spanish Words in Patwin." RPh 13:2.161-164 (1959).

The Patwin tribe of the lower Sacramento Valley is among the most northern of Californian tribes whose language was influenced by Spanish. This article considers some phonological and semantic aspects of this influence. The discussion of the phonological changes involved in borrowing includes a nice, though token, mention of dialect variants in Spanish. The semantic aspect treats categories of meaning (mainly domestic animals, cultivated plants, and new artifacts), semantic shift, the occurrence of Spanish and Patwin synonyms, and problems of etymology. [GB]

MC LENDON, Sally. "Spanish Words in Eastern Pomo." RPh 23.39-53 (1969).

A tidy examination of Spanish linguistic influence, both direct and indirect (through other Indian languages), on this northern California tribe that first came into ready contact with Spanish speakers in 1836. The phonological adaptation of Spanish borrowings is considered in some detail and the semantic categories of the loans are briefly considered. The article concludes with a list of 150 Spanish words and their reflexes in Eastern Pomo, as well as Wappo, Lake Miwok, and Southern Pomo. [GB]

SAWYER, Jesse O. [1964b]. "Wappo Words form Spanish." In Studies in Californian Linguistics, edited by William Bright. UCPL No. 34 (Berkeley: Univ. of California Press, 1964), pp. 163-169.

This list of some 200 lexical items of Spanish origin (much greater than the number of English origin) is based on data collected from one of the last two or three speakers of Wappo, a language of inland northern California. Each entry gives the Wappo form, an English gloss, the Spanish etymon, the Southern Pomo form when distinct, and where possible an indication of the probability that the borrowing came directly from Spanish or through Southern Pomo. There are also minor comments on the phonological adaptation of borrowings and comparisons with the Spanish borrowings in Southern Pomo. [GB]

SAWYER, Jesse O. [1964a]. "The Implications of Spanish /r/ and /rr/ in Wappo History." RPh 18.165-177 (1964).

This excellent, detailed study of some 90 Spanish loans containing /r, r̄/ and their three types of reflexes draws on phonological and semantic clues to reconstruct three periods of borrowing of Spanish words: early borrowing from other Indian languages, direct borrowing after the arrival of the Spanish, and direct borrowing after the establishment of the northernmost Spanish settlement. The article contains a historical sketch and notes on the phonological adaptation of borrowings (and some irregularities), the semantic domains of borrowed words (plants, animals, new artifacts, etc.), and words from Central American Indian languages and from Mexican Spanish. [GB]

SHIPLEY, William. "Review of <u>Bilingualism in the Americas</u> by E. Haugen." <u>RPh</u> 13.84-86 (1959).

Very brief comments to supplement the reviewed book's treatment of aspects of Maidu-English bilingualism. A mention is made of some non-contact borrowings from Spanish into Maidu and the curious results of these. [GB]

SHIPLEY, William. "Spanish Elements in the Indigenous Languages of Central California." <u>RPh</u> 16.1-21 (1962).

This substantive but poorly written article carefully examines the Spanish borrowings in 12 languages of the Great Central Valley. Shipley discusses the possible role of Mexican Spanish, the semantic domains of the borrowings (almost entirely food, animals and European artifacts), the diffusion of the borrowings throughout the area, and the phonological adaptation of the loans. This last is a meticulous analysis of consonant, consonant cluster, and vowel correspondences, from which he deduces for example that /x/ and /ĩ/ were pronounced [h] and [y] at the time of borrowing. Other processes treated are metathesis, vowel loss, change, and addition, initial syllable loss, and article and plural incorporation. The study concludes with a list of some 150 Spanish words with their reflexes in the various languages and English glosses of the reflexes where distinct in meaning from the Spanish sourceword. [GB]

6.10 CODE-SWITCHING

<u>Major Items</u>: GUMP/HERN-1972; MCME-1973

<u>See also these items elsewhere</u> (consult Author Index for location):

AMSD-1969; CHAC-1969

GINGRÀS, Rosario C. "Problems in the Description of Spanish-English Intrasentential Code-Switching." In Bills 1974, pp. 167-174.

A limited attempt to explain code-switching as syntactically rule-governed behavior (in generative-transformational terms), this article is of interest primarily because of the display of acceptability (grammaticality) judgments of varied code-switched sentences made by Chicano as well as non-Chicano Spanish speakers; the judgments strongly support the concept of rule-governed code-switching. Also intriguing is the author's attempt to distinguish lexicalization of English forms, bilingual interference (a performance factor), and code-switching (a competence phenomenon). The attempted explanation merely scratches the surface of this exceedingly complex topic. [GB]

GUMPERZ, John J. and Eduardo Hernández-Chávez. "Bilingualism, Bidialectalism, and Classroom Interaction," in <u>Functions of Language in the Classroom</u> (New York and London: Teachers College Press, 1972), pp. 85-108. ˙This article amalgamates two earlier papers: Gumperz, "Verbal Strategies in Multilingual Communication," <u>MSLL</u> 23.129-143 (plus discussion, 143-147) (1970) [Abs. <u>LLBA</u> V-815] = Working Paper No. 36, Language-Behavior Research Laboratory [University of California, Berkeley], (1970), and Gumperz and Hernández-Chávez, "Cognitive Aspects of Bilingual Communication," in <u>Language Use and Social Change</u>, edited by W.H. Witeley (New York and London: Oxford Univ. Press, 1970), pp. 111-125 = Working Paper No. 28, Language-Behavior Research Laboratory (1969). [Rev. Craddock 1973 pp. 481-482.] ("Cognitive Aspects..." also rpt. in HERN/etal-1975, pp. 154-163.

Perhaps the most astute paper on code-switching that has come to the attention of this writer. The authors attempt to demonstrate the connotative function of the phenomenon in question by noting how the shift to Spanish in an English context "signal[s] a change in interpersonal relationship in the direction of greater informality or personal warmth" (p. 89). Another useful comparison they make is to the literary device called <u>foregrounding</u>, which involves the use of words charged with "a host of culturally specific associations, attitudes and values" (p. 99); code-switching serves a like purpose. The paper includes numerous illustrative texts that reveal effectively the importance of code-switching in the stylistic repertoire of bilingual speakers. [JC]

MC MENAMIN, Jerry. "Rapid Code Switching Among Chicano Bilinguals." <u>Orbis</u> 22.474-487 (1973)

Ambitious as to its attempted conclusions about code-switching from lengthy but un-taped interviews with 15 Chicanos of all ages and both sexes residing in California's Pájaro Valley (near Monterrey), this article is nonetheless valuable for what it adds to our knowledge of an as-yet badly understood phenomenon.
McMenamin, who attempted to "test the seemingly random variation of Chicano code switching by correlating features of language choice and switching to some socioeconomic and cultural characteristics [of the informants and their milieu]," (474) "timed the informant's total speaking time with a stopwatch to arrive at an average 'switches per hour' basis" (476) for correlational purposes, and reached many conclusions thereby, inter alia: "It is evident that, in speaking Spanish, the younger and older groups were more likely to switch to English, and the middle age group was less likely. In speaking English, only older persons switched to Spanish... Older, first and second generation Chicanos ["generation" = "degree of removal from Mexico"?] definitely switch more overall than do younger ones." (478) Texas-born informants

switched the most and "persons born in Mexico switched least" (thanks perhaps to an insufficient knowledge of English?). Switching is claimed to be largely characteristic of informal, unguarded and spontaneous conversation because few switches to Spanish appeared in the six English sentences that seven informants were asked to translate. Perhaps M's most seminal conclusion is that "those who said they spoke Spanish best also switched most; those who spoke English best switched least;" (479) from Table I (477) we learn that self-evaluated Spanish-dominants switched from Spanish to English an average of 44 times per hour, from English to Spanish an average of 22, whereas avowed English dominants averaged 21 Spanish-to-English switches and only one E-to-S switch per hour.

But the problem of the direction of the switch is a murky one, and largely muddies theoretical waters throughout: thus one is rather mystified to learn that "the other 60 per cent did not switch once to Spanish while speaking English, even though close to half of each conversation was in English;" (480) M himself confesses to the unresolved nature of the question of "direction" on p. 481.

"Relation of Situation to Language Choice and Switching" and "Reasons for Switching" (chiefly verifications of the Gumperz/Hernández-Chávez point [1970 et seq.] that code alternation is used as a strategy in communication) complete the analysis. [RT]

7. [CHICANOS:] ELSEWHERE (MIDWEST, PACIFIC NORTHWEST, ETC.)

7.1 BIBLIOGRAPHY (nothing to report)

7.2 COMPREHENSIVE/GENERAL STUDIES [etc.] (nothing to report)

7.2.1 SOCIOLINGUISTICS

Major Items: HUMP-1943-44; MACE-1971

See also these items elsewhere (consult Author Index for location):

(none)

HUMPHREY, Norman D. "The Education and Language of Detroit Mexicans." JES 17.534-542 (1943-44).

An important (if largely anecdotal) discussion of language-use attitudes among first- and second-generation Mexicans and Mexican-Americans in Detroit. Humphrey is remarkably perceptive and much of what he has to say about these matters is as valid now as when it was written. Among his conclusions (all based on interviews with and observations of perhaps twenty subjects, whose words are quoted frequently in footnotes): while illiteracy in both languages is not uncommon, Detroit Mexicans nevertheless "feel a need for literacy in Spanish, and since they fear that their children will be educated only in English, they sporadically attempt to educate themselves and their offspring in Spanish." (p. 535) To that end various Spanish-literacy programs were inaugurated throughout the 1930's, with mixed success. In general "it appears that the more Mexican schooling to which a migrant had been subjected, the greater the probability of a linguistic adjustment [to English]." (539) Some members of the immigrant generation learn very little English because they actively resist English ("Language itself constitutes a value for the mother tongue is an aspect of culture shot through with ethnocentrism" [538]); it is not until they "have reconciled themselves to living out their lives in the United States" (537) that the barriers fall and knowledge of English increases. Economic as well as psychological factors have a hand in these decisions: "an increasing facility in the use of English, at least for the lower economic levels of Detroit Mexicans, dates from the beginning of relief recipience," (538) a crucial consideration in Depression times.
    The rest of the article deals with educational consequences and "remedies" which some readers will reject as overly assimilationist, though the author shrewdly notes that some resistance to schooling has stemmed from immigrant parents' shock upon discovering what their children are being taught about Mexican culture and especially U.S.-Mexican relations in the nineteenth century. [RT]

MACE, Betty J. "A Linguistic Profile of Children Entering Seattle
    Public School Kindergartens in September, 1971, and Implica-
    tions for Instruction." MA Thesis, Univ. of Texas, Austin,
    1972. ix, 172 pp.

   An important study of the language background(s) and English
abilities of selected five-year-olds from Seattle's major bilingual
ethnic communities (Chinese, Philippine, "Spanish" [Central and
South American as well as Mexican and Chicano], Japanese and
German; the Chinese were the largest group and the Hispanos the
third-largest). From questionnaire surveys of parents, home interviews and a series of oral language tests the following conclusions were reached (concerning Spanish/English bilinguals [pp. 142-
144]): the majority of the children were U.S.-born as were the
majority of their parents; "however, the foreign born parents (29
per cent) reflect thirteen countries of origin." "English is
the first language of the majority (58 per cent)" and Spanish "is
the primary language of communication in only a small number (24
per cent) of the families." Loyalty to Spanish is maintained,
though, since English "is spoken almost exclusively in the homes
of slightly less than one-half (45 per cent) of the children."
All but one child surveyed had "some facility" in Spanish; 97 per
cent spoke English "fluently." Results from the <u>Michigan Oral
Language Productive Test--Structured Response</u> show that young
Hispanos "are only slightly less proficient in English than are
their monolingual English-speaking peers," who were also tested.
Analysis indicted the following needs and/or deficiencies in
English: formation and use of the past participle, extension and
refinement of the use of comparison, acquisition of the full
morphological rules governing inflection, reinforcement in the
use of affirmative noun determiners following negated main verb,
and irregular plural forms. [RT]

MYERS, Gail Eldridge. "A Study of the Channels of Communication
    Used by One Hundred Spanish-Named Residents of Denver,
    Colorado." PhD Diss., Univ. of Denver, 1959. xii, 249 pp.
    [Not in <u>DA</u>.]

   Of some value to persons interested in specific information
about the media subscribed to by Denver Hispanos in the late
1950's, this dissertation focusses largely on the ways that persons of various social classes obtain information on national/inter-
national, civic, and in-group (ethnic) happenings. The weekly
<u>El Sol</u> is described in detail on pp. 107-108, the largely-Spanish
radio station KFSC on 128-130. All direct interviews were conducted by Ms. Myers and a Chicano colleague; the two sets of
findings were then compared to determine whether response differed
according to the ethnic background of the interviewer. Not surprisingly the informants reported many more specific charges of
anti-Mexican-American Anglo media bias to the Chicano interviewer
than to Ms. Myers. However, more informants claimed primary

allegiance to Spanish-language media in Ms. Myers' interviews than in the Chicano's: of the 28 responding to Myers, 6 reported they used "only KFSC" for national/international reportage while none of the 23 responding to the Chicano reported KFSC as their sole source for non-local news. [RT]

7.4 SPANISH GRAMMAR (MORPHOLOGY AND SYNTAX)

Major Items: TORO-1972

See also these items elsewhere (consult Author Index for location):

LOZA-1974

TORONTO, Allen Sharp. "A Developmental Spanish Language Analysis Procedure for Spanish-Speaking Children." PhD Diss., Northwestern Univ., 1972. xi, 326 pp. [DA 33 (1973) 5051-B.]

Asserting that the "study of the acquisition of Spanish grammar by native Spanish speakers has been greatly neglected by language researchers," (p. 278) and that furthermore the extant information "is of little use to the language pathologist interested in identifying language deficiencies in Spanish-speaking children," (ibid.) Toronto sought to fill the void "by proposing developmental hierarchies of Spanish syntax and providing a tentative set of norms which were determined by a scoring system similar to the Developmental Sentence Scoring procedure (DSS)" (278-279) of Lee and Canter (1971) and Koenigsknecht and Lee (1971) of Northwestern Univ. The DSS "is a technique which assigns weighted scores to proposed developmental hierarchies of eight grammatical categories from a sample of 50 sentences obtained from a child's spontaneous speech [but using 'fixed stimulus materials' such as pictures, toys, etc.--281] in conversation with an adult. In addition to measuring syntactic complexity, the DSS measures increase in length of children's utterances with increasing age." (279) To accomplish this, Toronto and his team of assistants analyzed results from the speech of 48 Spanish-dominant or Spanish-monolingual Mexican-American children, two boys and two girls falling within each three-month age interval between ages 3.0 and 5.11, all from lower- or working-class families residing in the same Chicago barrio studied by Teschner (1972). Six grammatical categories were used for construction of the hierarchies: indefinite pronouns, personal pronouns, "primary verbs, secondary verbs [after the transformational analysis of David Wolfe (1966 PhD Diss.) and others], conjunctions, and interrogative words. Negation and pluralization were taken into account within each category." (280) Special attention was paid to the acquisition of verbal morphology; here Toronto acknowledges his debt to Gustavo González (1970). Adjectives, adverbs and articles were not examined.

Much of this well-written work discusses methodological or statistical questions which cannot be treated here. Among the conclusions of greater interest to linguists: "Scores for individual scoring categories generally increased with increasing age, except for those of interrogative words and sentence point, which decreased with age." (282) The following is the "over-all rank order of discriminating categories from most discriminating to the least: 1) primary verbs, 2) secondary verbs, 3) conjunctions, and 4) personal pronouns. The scoring category of indefinite pronouns had discriminating power only between the two older age groups, while interrogative words and sentence point categories were not significant in discriminating between any of the successive age groups." (ibid.) No significant sex- or test administrator-based differences were noted.

While on the whole the work impressed the present reviewer (who is nevertheless an admitted neophyte in the field of speech pathology) as fully competent, Hispanists will note with dismay a certain tendency to mistranscribe or even misinterpret Spanish. Orthographic accents and tildes are not always where they should be (see for example pp. 113-115). One finds some statements dubious--"Expressions such as Es que (It's that), which are complete sentences, . . . " (115)-- and others erroneous, at least from the standpoint of twentieth-century Spanish: "The use of the subjunctive is complicated by its three tenses: present, past and future." (260) Especially vexing is Toronto's Appendix A, "Glossary of Spanish Words and Phrases," (294-302) in which the author translates "only what he feels the reader needs to know concerning the Spanish words and phrases" (295) that appear in the text. The 90-some entries include conjugated verbs that are sometimes handled strangely: era for example is glossed "I, he, she, it was, you were" but Espero que venga is "I hope that he comes [why not 'you, she, it' as well?]." (297) Object pronouns and possessives are similarly underglossed. The typically Mexican phrase anda buscando is badly rendered as "He, she, you or it walks looking" (296; see also 262). One becomes wary of Toronto's insistence as to the exclusively Mexican background of his informants when one reads that "common statements [were, inter alia] El va a subir y manejar la guagua," (210) although if Toronto's claim is true then guagua in Mexican mouths is a noteworthy piece of evidence that some "dialect mixing" is afoot in zones where Chicanos live alongside Puerto Ricans (as in the neighborhood under study).

These minor criticisms, though, while pointing out the need for Hispanists on doctoral committees which deal with Spanish language, are not meant to detract from the generally high quality of this important contribution. [RT]

7.7 ENGLISH INFUENCE ON SPANISH

Major Items: TESC-1972; TSUZ-1963/71

See also these items elsewhere (consult Author Index for location):

(none)

BECK, Mary Margaret. "The English Influence on the Spanish Spoken in Bowling Green, Ohio." MA Thesis, Bowling Green State Univ., 1970. iv, 75 pp.

A tidy and competent structuralist treatment of Anglic incursions (chiefly lexical) into the Spanish of the Texas- and Mexico-born migrant workers recently settled in this northwestern Ohio community. In all, 25 persons were interviewed. Comparisons were sometimes made between local variants and "the standard Spanish found in the Diccionario de la Real Academia Española" (p. 1) but for the most part Beck patterns her analysis after the works of Tsuzaki 1963, Kreidler 1958 and especially Phillips 1967; the section on phonology is effectively handled (see pp. 29-37), and Beck wisely avoids drawing sweeping conclusions from her necessarily limited corpus: "Even though there were nearly as many Spanish phonological influences on English as there were [English on Spanish], those influences did not seem to be systematic nor fully predictable [since] they varied within one person's speech and from one person's to another's." (43-44) Thus the same informant who produced /keyk/ 'cake' subsequently gave /estéy/ 'steak.' [RT]

GRAHAM, Robert Somerville. "Spanish-Language Radio in Northern Colorado." AS 37.207-211 (1962). [Annot. HLAS 25 (1963) no. 3923 (D. Wogan); Craddock 1973 p. 319.]

This little note on the Spanish heard on a radio station in Denver is of little linguistic value. Graham states that the Spanish used is "not essentially different" from Mexican Spanish except for English inroads. The bulk of the article discusses some of the English words and phrases heard. [GB]

MARAVILLA, Frederick R. "Los anglicismos en el español de Indiana Harbor, Indiana." MA Paper, Univ. of Chicago, 1955. 40 pp. (On file, Office of the Chairman of the Dept. of Romance Languages, Univ. of Chicago. Circulates with permission of the author and the Department.)

This is probably the first study done of Chicano Spanish in an area not part of the greater Southwest. It lists close to 450 examples of English lexical influence on the Spanish spoken in

the "Indiana Harbor" neighborhood of the industrial city of East
Chicago, where the author was born and raised. Each entry is
defined, etymologized and then cited in context. While a healthy
share of entries inevitably has to do with the city's chief industry, steel-making (e.g., blasfones < blast furnace, clobarra <
clawbar), other entries, especially those which are not nouns,
come as surprises, e.g., api (< up, 'el niño quiere api'),
charapiarse (< to shut up, '¡Charápese, muchacho!'), esbera (< it's
better, 'si no viene, esbera para mí'), etc. Following its lexicon the paper discusses the morphophonological changes which the
loanwords undergo. [RT]

TESCHNER, Richard V. "Anglicisms in Spanish: A Cross-Referenced
    Guide to Previous Findings, together with English Lexical
    Influence on Chicago Mexican Spanish." PhD Diss., Univ. of
    Wisconsin, Madison, 1972. 1251 pp. [DA 33 (1973) 3625-A.]

    In reality this work represents a merger of two distinct though
relatable topics which could (and ought to) have constituted two
separate dissertations. As it was Teschner's conclusion that
nearly all discussions of Spanish Anglicisms present their findings in isolation and thus do not cross-reference them to the
material of others, he attempted to collate "all previous Anglicism research . . . into one single dictionary" (abs.) in the
dissertation's third chapter (pp. 130-1036) after having discussed
earlier "The Origins of the Spanish Anglicism" (Ch. 1) and "A
Chronology of Anglicism Reportage" (Ch. 2, which also includes a
synopsis of U.S. Spanish studies, all incorporated into the present Bibliography). Each dictionary entry is accompanied by the
available source-author information, i.e., definitions, etyma,
examples of usage, extent and social level of circulation and
usage, etc.
    Pertinent to the examination of United States Spanish is the
lexicon which Teschner incorporated into the conflation of second-
ary-source material; this lexicon consists of 1,017 Anglicisms
used by the 30 Spanish-mother-tongue Chicago residents (28
Chicanos or Mexicans and 2 Puerto Ricans) volunteering for a total
of 60 hours of free-conversational interviews, as well as the
findings from an equal number of hours spent monitoring Chicago
Spanish-language radio and television programs. Copious examples
of informant or mass media usage illustrate each of the 1,017
entries. Several subchapters following the "dictionary" discuss
a variety of instances in which English influenced Chicago Spanish
syntax; Chs. 4 and 5 present, respectively, "A Statistical Analysis
of the Types of Borrowing: A Variety of Comparisons Between the
Chicago Corpus and Other Sources [chiefly Einar Haugen, The Norwegian Language in America]" and "Inducements to Borrowing: The
Environments of Borrowing" (among the "inducements" were: previous intromission of a borrowed word, code-switching to anticipate borrowing, quotation of something said originally in English,
direct or [as in the mass media] simultaneous translation from

English, humorous effect and emphasis [categories amply commented upon by Haugen], inadequate or non-existent standard Spanish equivalent, etc., etc.).

Teschner's dictionary included material from 77 secondary sources, and it is here that the author must be taken to task rather severely, for his claim to having included "all previous material" on Spanish Anglicisms has had to be revised substantively in light of subsequent findings (see R.V. Teschner, "A Critical Annotated Bibliography of Anglicisms in Spanish," Hispania 57.631-678 [1974]). But an even more serious charge is that of the 77 sources, 32 deal solely with United States (usually Mexican-American) Spanish, the remainder with "south-of-the-border" Anglicization or else Spanish-American cum US Spanish Anglicisms; thus the reader is presented neither with a study that focusses on US Spanish nor with one that directs itself entirely southward. To facilitate comparison between what may well be two different "types" of English influence, Teschner would have done well to segregate US Anglicisms from the others. [RT]

TSUZAKI, Stanley M. "English Influences in the Phonology and Morphology of the Spanish Spoken in the Mexican Colony in Detroit, Michigan." PhD Diss., Univ. of Michigan, Ann Arbor, 1963. vii, 117 pp. [DA 24 (1963) 2471-A.] (Reprinted with minor revisions as English Influence on Mexican Spanish in Detroit. The Hague: Mouton & Co., 1971. 92 pp. [Rev. Thesaurus 29.197-201 (1974) (M. Fontanella de Weinberg).]) All page references are to the dissertation.

This structuralist study of two "languages in contact" examines the incursions of locally dominant English into immigrant Spanish in the manner of Einar Haugen, Uriel Weinreich and others. Tsuzaki employed a questionnaire designed by his thesis director (see Kreidler 1957) to elicit English-influenced speech from 30 informants, the majority born in Mexico and ranging from Spanish- to English-dominant; some interviews included free conversation as well. The bulk of Tsuzaki's own findings appear in chapters 4 ("Phonological Influences," pp. 58-70) and 5, the misnamed "Morphological Influences" (71-83) which handles lexical borrowings and sense loans. Chs. 1, 2 and 3 represent "Introduction," "The Mexican Colony in Detroit" and "Outline of Mexican Spanish [phonology]."

Tsuzaki's discussion of phonological influences is noteworthy in that it represents a thoughtful edging away from the cases vides explanation of intrusive phonemes that dominated the thinking of the times. After deriving "an inventory of established English phonological influences" from the 45 loanwords common to more than one informant (the intrusive phonemes are /ǰ š/, the clusters /st sk ts ks gs nk tb td nw/ along with certain otherwise allowed Spanish combinations not found in Spanish in certain environments such as /nĉ/ word-final), the author admits difficulty in attempting to explain "the relative ease of borrowing new clusters as compared with new combinations" (66) and hazards the guess that "rather than purely structural factors, considerations like frequency of occurrence, degree of bilinguality, and psychological appeal and need are probably involved." (ibid.) However, Tsuzaki's treatment of English lexical intrusiveness, and especially his understanding of what is shift and what importation, is nearly always attuned to purely formal considerations ("The rule of thumb followed was that if there was a word in Spanish in exactly the same phonemic shape as the loan, the latter was to be classified as a [loan shift] rather than a [loanword]"--18), and thus of the 16 "established loanshifts" on p. 78, five are probably phonological replicas of English forms and not sense shifts of words already present in the informants' lexicons, e.g., chansa, galón, marqueta (can we logically accept a "shift" from 'cake of crude wax' > 'market' in the same way we can accept carro 'cart' > 'automobile'?), pinta 'pint' and gira 'heater.' More examples of "shifts" that are probably loanwords are found at the end of Appendix C (111-113); among the more noteworthy are guía 'gearshift,' crismas 'Christmas,' lina ("coarse wool > Lerner Shops"), pene 'penny' and troque 'truck.'

In fairness, though, such mechanistic methods of classification reigned unchallenged until several years after the completion of Tsuzaki 1963 and even continued to inform similar studies in the following decade (e.g., Teschner 1972), long after they should have done so. [RT]

7.8.1 ENGLISH OF THIS PARTICULAR HISPANIC GROUP

Major Items: (none)

See also these items elsewhere (consult Author Index for location):

MACE-1972

ALLRED, Forrest Rich. "Errors in Oral English Usage of Mexican-American Pupils With a Spanish Language Background in Grade III in the State of Colorado." EdD Diss., Univ. of Northern Colorado, Greeley, 1970. xii, 265 pp. [DA 31 (1971) 4028-A.]

This and four other dissertations from the Univ. of Northern Colorado (Frydendall 1972, Hicks 1970, Pauls 1970, and Roberts 1970) assess the English of Mexican Americans in grades 2-6 in precise duplication of five dissertations on Anglo English done at Colorado State College (Fort Collins) in 1963. The five studies are virtually identical in methodology and procedure; each analysis is based on six minutes of recorded speech by a group of four students at 45 schools having more than 100 Spanish-surnamed pupils. Analysis is very crude, dealing with such things as gross counts of "errors," grammatical types of errors, frequency of errors, errors per 1,000 words, and so forth. No attempt is made to provide an explanation of errors. This set of studies is practically worthless as linguistic analysis, although the appendices do cite numerous interesting examples from the corpora. [GB]

FRYDENDALL, Dennis Joe. "Errors in Oral English Usage of Mexican-American Pupils With a Spanish Language Background in Grade IV in the State of Colorado." EdD Diss., Univ. of Northern Colorado, Greeley, 1972. xiii, 216 pp. [DA 33 (1972) 551-A.]

See Allred 1970.

HICKS, Jerral Robert. "Errors in Oral English Usage of Mexican-American Pupils With a Spanish Language Background in Grade II in the State of Colorado." EdD Diss., Univ. of Northern Colorado, Greelye, 1970, xii, 229 pp. [DA 31 (1971) 3778-3779-A.]

See Allred 1970.

PAULS, Leo Wayne. "Errors in Oral English Usage of Mexican-American Pupils With a Spanish Language Background in Grade V in the State of Colorado." EdD Diss., Univ. of Northern Colorado, Greeley, 1970. xii, 227 pp. [DA 31 (1971) 6477-6478-A.]

See Allred 1970.

ROBERTS, Neil Alden. "Errors in Oral English Usage of Mexican-American Pupils With a Spanish Language Background in Grade IV in the State of Colorado." EdD Di s., Univ. of Northern Colorado, Greeley, 1970. xi, 192 pp. [DA 31 (1971) 4020-A.]

See Allred 1970.

7.9 SPANISH INFLUENCE ON AMERINDIAN LANGUAGES

Major Items: (none)

See also these items elsewhere (consult Author Index for location):

(none)

CASAGRANDE, Joseph B. "Comanche Linguistic Acculturation." IJAL 20.140-151, 217-237 (1954); 21.8-25 (1955).

Throughout this superbly rigorous study of the influence of English and (to a far lesser extent) Spanish on Comanche there are scattered references to Spanish, but the main discussion of Spanish influence is in the second part (228-233), where the author gives a "virtually complete" list of 18 Spanish loanwords, plus seven derived forms and 15 place or personal names, and discusses the usage of these borrowings and how they reflect the historical contact situation. [GB]

8. [CHICANOS:] PACHUCO/CALO STUDIES

8.1 BIBLIOGRAPHY (nothing to report)

8.2 COMPREHENSIVE/GENERAL STUDIES; MISCELLANY; ANTHOLOGIES/ FESTSCHRIFTEN

<u>Major Items</u>: BARK-G-1950

<u>See also these items elsewhere</u> (consult Author Index for location):

COLT-1964; COLT-1965; WAGN-153-54

BARKER, George C. "Pachuco: An American Spanish Argot and Its Social Functions in Tucson, Arizona." <u>UAB</u> 21.entire issue (38 pp.) (Jan. 1950). (Published simultaneously with identical title, etc., in: <u>UASSB</u> 18.entire issue [Jan. 1950].) (Rpt., unrevised, with identical title, etc., Tucson: Univ. of Arizona Press, 1958, 1970 [46 pp.]. Note: the 1958 edition, paid for by Barker's parents as a memorial upon his death that year, differs from the 1950 edition only in the addition of a photo of Barker and a short biographical sketch by Harry T. Getty. The 1970 printing lacks only the photo. Page references below are to the 1970 reprint.)

This monograph is intended to explore the "origin and nature" of Pachuco and its social usage and meaning; its primary significance is the fact that it is the earliest substantial treatment of Pachuco. Barker begins with a discussion (pp. 13-16) of the four Tucson Spanish dialects, a very slight revision of his dissertation statement (1947a). In treating The Structure of Pachuco (16-21) he states that its syntax is most like the southern Arizona dialect, except for its use of the <u>usted</u> verb form only and its distinctive and frequently employed sentential interjections, for which several examples are given (17). The rest of the discussion of Pachuco structure considers five classes of words and expressions: (a) English forms that have been Hispanized (<u>birria</u> 'beer') or translated (<u>agarrar patada</u> 'to get a kick out of'), (b) New Mexican Spanish forms cited by Kercheville 1934 (<u>entabicar</u> 'to put in jail'), (c) colloquial Mexican Spanish expressions adapted in form and/or meaning (<u>chanate</u> 'blackbird' > 'Negro,' <u>andar aguetando</u> [sic] > <u>andar huitado</u>), (d) standard Spanish words adapted in form and/or meaning (<u>al alba</u> 'at dawn' > 'sharp, smart,' <u>Arizona</u> > <u>araisa</u>), and (e) forms of "undetermined" origin (<u>bola</u> 'shoe shine').

The Origin and Spread of Pachuco is considered briefly (21-24). He suggests its development in the El Paso region in the early 1930's, even though he has evidence that it already existed in Tucson as of 1933. On pp. 25-33 he deals with the usage and function of Pachuco, describing each of his fifteen young male informants and their attitudes toward Pachuco.

The monograph concludes with the text of a staged dialogue (34-35), the texts of several popular Pachuco songs (35-40), A Glossary of Common Pachuco Words (40-43), Some Common Pochismos Used in Tucson 1945-48 (44-45), and a selected bibliography (46). The two glossaries are slightly improved from the lists in his dissertation--e.g., lida 'guitar' is now lira, cerco has been deleted (but sopa 'soup' is included!)--though spelling inconsistencies, here and throughout, are still abundant. The Pachuco glossary is greatly expanded. [GB]

WEBB, John T. "Investigation Problems in Southwest Spanish Caló." In Bills 1974, pp. 145-153.

This extremely scholarly short essay on the diachronic and synchronic problems and pitfalls awaiting the researcher attempting to describe "Pachuco" speech discusses the practical problem of data collection and informants, the historicity problem of Spanish caló, and the analysis problem probingly illustrated with several examples that have misled other investigators (e.g., ¿jamás caliche?, buri, guachar). [GB]

8.2.1 SOCIOLINGUISTICS

Major Items: (none)

See also these items elsewhere (consult Author Index for location):

ALVA-1967; BARK-G-1947b; BARK-G-1972; HELL-1967

GRIFFITH, Beatrice. [1947a]. "The Pachuco Patois." CG 7.77-84 (Summer 1947).

Reprinted in Griffith 1948.

GRIFFITH, Beatrice. [1947b]. "Who Are the Pachucos?" The Pacific Spectator 1.352-360 (Summer 1947).

This descriptive sociological overview incorporated in Griffith 1948a, provides no language data. [GB]

GRIFFITH, Beatrice. [1948a]. *American Me*. Boston: Houghton Mifflin, 1948. x, 341 pp. (2nd printing: New York: Pennant Books, 1954. 3rd printing: Westport, Conn.: Greenwood Press, 1973.) [Annot. Woodbridge pp. 243-244.] (Cf. Wagner 1953-54.)

This empathetic though treacly collection of 13 fictionalized autobiographical tales, each followed by a historical-sociological homily-essay placing the topic in the broader Mexican-American perspective, describes the life and times of the Los Angeles Pachuco in the 1940's. Aside from scattered lexical items cited in the text, this volume contains two parts specifically dealing with language. First, a brief commentary on the "Pachuco patois" (pp. 55-60 [13-19 of the 1954 edition], a reprint of Griffith 1947) provides a shallow discussion of the origins, social role, and creative aspects of Pachuco speech and the "language block" and "sense of poetry" displayed alike by Mexican-American children. One example: "The word 'jale' means both 'to work' and 'to make love' . . . , on the premise that love is work." (57) Second, a glossary of Spanish and Pachuco terms used (310-318 [155-166 of the 1954 edition]) contains over 300 entries, almost two-thirds marked as Pachuco forms, giving simply an English gloss and (for Pachuco items) a crude comment on derivation or usage. Like the essay, this glossary does have some interest but it is certainly not a work of scholarship.

(There was separate publication of several of the stories [four in *CG* in 1947 and 1948; one in *Seventeen*] and of one other essay [*The Pacific Spectator* 1.352-360 (1947)].) [GB]

8.5 SPANISH LEXICON (includes SEMANTICS)

<u>Major Items</u>: COLT-1964; COLT-1965; GAAR-1944; JANU-1970; KATZ-1974; RAMI-K-197[1?]; RAMI-K-1973; TREJ-1968; WAGN-1953-54

<u>See also these items elsewhere</u> (consult Author Index for location):

BARK-G-1947a; GONZ-N-1967/69; GRIF-1947a; GRIF-1948a; KEEV/etal-1945; ORNS-1951; ORNS-1971a; ORNS-1972b; PEON-1966; SHAR-1970; TREJ-1951; and especially GALV-1949 and GALV-1955

ALVAREZ, George R. "Calo: The 'Other' Spanish." *ETC.* 24.7-13 (1967).

This simplistic article attempts to provide a socio-psychological explanation of the role of Pachuco as the third "language" of the Mexican-American. The reader gets the impression that the definition of "Mexican-American" is something like "a male ghetto gang member who speaks Pachuco." Here is an example of the author's linguistic sophistication: "The combination of phonemes and morphemes that comprise its principal terms are such that its utterance necessitates a low, harsh, and sometimes shrill elocution. It is predominantly a 'snarl' language; it implies an uncompromising attitude of anger, sarcasm, cynicism, and undifferentiated rebellion." (p. 9) The author's concluding hypothesis is that "extensive use of Calo by the Mexican American warps his social perceptions." (12) Two dozen or so examples of Pachuco words and phrases are cited. [GB]

BOGGS, Ralph S. "Términos del lenguaje popular y caló de la capital de México." BFUCh 8.34-43 (1954-55).

Presents and discusses the uses and the origins of two dozen terms collected in 1938 from "un ratero de la capital, quien me dio la mayor parte de las palabras aquí citadas, con su significado." (p. 35) Boggs' discussions of forms such as abuja, baisa, cacle, cantón, chantar and so forth will be of interest (albeit dated) to students of caló. Nothing else here on Chicano Spanish per se. [RT]

BRADDY, Haldeen. "The Pachucos and Their Argot." SFQ 24.255-271 (1960).

This article paints a particularly harsh and bitter picture of the Pachuco juvenile delinquent in El Paso and draws the novel conclusion that the single example of "any positive contributions to culture" made by the Pachuco is the coinage of new lexical items. A glossary of roughly 250 "fresh entries" (forms not found in Cerda et al.1953) concludes the article (264-271). Speculative comments on the historical origin of many of the terms are included. [GB]

COLTHARP, Lurline H. "The Influence of English on the 'Language' of the Tirilones." PhD Diss., Univ. of Texas, Austin, 1964. vi, 345 pp.

See Coltharp 1965 (p. 249 of this Bibliography).

COLTHARP, Lurline H. The Tongue of the Tirilones: A Linguistic
Study of a Criminal Argot. Alabama Linguistic and Philo-
logical Series, No. 7 (University, Alabama: Univ. of Alabama
Press, 1965). vi, 313 pp. [Annot. Solé 1970 no. 999; Fody
p. 535. Rev. HLAS 28 (1966) no. 1535 (D.L. Canfield);
Craddock 1973 pp. 322-324; IJAL 32.297-301 (1966) (D.W. Mauer);
RPh 21.110-113 (1967) (W.C. Sinclair); BHS 44.137-138 (1967)
(K. Whinnom).]

   This book is Coltharp's dissertation (1964) with a few very
minor revisions; aside from the title the most notable revision
is the deletion of the multitude of examples in Appendix II,
"Symbols" (indeed, pagination of the two works is identical up
to this point). This study of Pachuco speech of South El Paso,
based on field work done in 1962-63, is the most substantive
study of this language variety, especially with regard to vocabulary. In fact, the vocabulary included herein is one of the
best lexicographical analyses of any single brand of United States
Spanish. The prose exposition, however, is often poor, and makes
the interpretation of some details quite unclear.
   Chap. 1, "Anthropological Background," (pp. 1-34) provides a
fair ethnographic description of the area and its inhabitants.
Coltharp's interpretation of the value system of the young gang
members who served as her informants makes delightful reading.
A brief section on language (30-33) examines the role of Pachuco
as the third speech form of the community. Chap. 2, "Methods,"
(35-47) is a minutely detailed description of the author's initial
sampling, elaboration of the phonology questionnaire, procedures
in eliciting vocabulary, perusal of published materials, and
card file system. Chap. 3, "Informants," (48-55) is a most unclear statement on the 47 informants and how they were used.
Background information on the informants is extremely limited;
age, for examples, is cited for only a few of them.

   Chap. 4, "Phonology," (56-73) is a phonetic analysis of the
tape-recorded responses of six informants to a 197-item, largely
fill-in-the-blank questionnaire based on items selected from
Navarro Tomás' Cuestionario lingüístico hispanoamericano. This
is a generally careful examination of each informant's pronunciation of each special word elicited, but Coltarp seems to have followed too closely Navarro Tomás' suggestions of possible variations
and failed to sufficiently explore variations of more interest
in the Spanish of this region. In addition, the elicitation procedures were apparently not highly successful in obtaining natural
speech (and exactly how the questionnaire was administered is
never made clear).
   In Chap. 5, "Characteristics of the Caló," (74-90) Coltharp
first considers the problem of how to label Pachuco in both
Spanish and English, settling on the terms caló and "argot" respectively. She also discusses Pachuco lexicon, touching briefly
on how coinages are made from Spanish, Engish, or both, the

rapidity of change in lexical usage and variations in pronunciation and meaning, and works on Southwest and Mexican Spanish that she consulted in search of similar lexical items.

Up to this point the study would have to be judged as mediocre, but Chap. 6, "Vocabulary," (91-282) makes the work an invaluable classic. The listing includes approximately 750 entries, inclusion being limited to those forms that (a) were confirmed by at least two informants and (b) were not cited with the same form or meaning in the Diccionario of the Real Academia Española. Each entry is cited in orthographic form and is marked for part of speech (but no other grammatical information is given); whether it occurs in the Academy dictionary and if so whether it differs in form or meaning; the informants who approved it; a brief gloss, with an occasional comment on usage variations, other explanations, and cross-references to other items; and whether or not the form was found with the same definition in each of seven other studies: Braddy 1960, McKee 1955, Barker 1950, Cerda et al. 1953, Santamaría's Diccionario General de Americanismos and Diccionario de Mejicanismos, and the Academy dictionary.

The phonology questionnaire is included as Appendix I (283-303). Appendix II (304-308) is an explanation of phonetic symbols employed. [GB]

COLTHARP, Lurline H. [1970a]. "Invitation to the Dance: Spanish in the El Paso Underworld." In Gilbert 1970, pp. 7-17.

Two and a half pages of a conversation (with English translation) between a prostitute and her neighbor forms the basis for this short discussion of South El Paso Pachuco. She lists some thirty lexical forms already included in Coltharp 1965 and thirteen new expressions in the same format. She also comments briefly on the sociocultural situation and the influence of English lexicon on Pachuco. [GB]

COLTHARP, Lurline H. [1970b]. "Some Additions: Lexicon of The Tongue of the Tirilones." In Ewton and Ornstein 1970, pp. 67-78.

This poorly written article provides additional lexical data from the speech of two new informants to supplement the listings in Coltharp 1965. Sixteen new words are cited in accord with the 1965 format. A number of new meanings or derived forms for items previously listed are briefly mentioned in discussing the problems encountered by the lexicographer. [GB]

FRENK ALATORRE, Margit. "Designaciones de rasgos físicos personales en el habla de la Ciudad de México." NRFH 7.134-156 (1953).

Valuable to the student of U.S. Spanish largely for the paragraph it devotes (p. 150) to the etymology of the word pachuco (Frenk asserts that it derives from El Paso as a "deformación pintoresca . . . con apoyo en Pachuca, ciudad mexicana, capital del Estado de Hidalgo"). A substantive description of the Pachuco's sartorial habits is also provided. [RT]

GAARDER, A. Bruce. "Notes on Some Spanish Terms in the Southwest." Hispania 27.330-334 (1944). [Annot. Woodbridge p. 239.]

Primarily a short (but decent) vocabulary list of some 130 Pachuco words and phrases with definitions in standard Spanish. The article also contains a brief Pachuco Spanish text that was elicited from a Tucson tirilí; checking of the text with an El Paso pachuco, a Los Angeles cholo, and a New Mexican manito Gaarder found "close agreement on the meanings of the words." (331) [GB]

GALVÁN, Roberto A. "Más observaciones sobre el argot de Barranquilla." Hispania 49.483-485 (1966). [Annot. HLAS 30 (1968) no. 2569 (D. L. Canfield).]

This critical response to an earlier article on "exclusively Colombian" argot documents the wider use of a number of forms, a half dozen used in Southwest Spanish. He also cites an additional five or six forms illustrating substitution by similar sound sequences, e.g., simón for sí. [GB]

GONZÁLEZ, Rafael Jesús. "Pachuco: The Birth of a Creole Language." AQ 23.343-356 (1967).

This generalistic historico-sociological essay on the Pachucos and their speech contains a number of words cited as typically Pachuco to illustrate the origins of this particular code: four words from Mexican Caló, ten from New Mexican Spanish, 24 borrowings from English, eight Spanish words influenced by English in meaning, six Spanish words with new meanings, ten Spanish expressions "derived from metaphor or image," and seven "invented" forms. Documentation of the claim that Pachuco is becoming a creole language is notably lacking. [GB]

GRIFFITH, Beatrice. [1948b]. "Fingertip Coats Are the Style." CG 8.61-67 (Spring 1948).

This Pachuco-theme short story, reprinted in Griffith 1948, is followed by a short glossary of 15 expressions, mostly Pachuco. [GB]

HERNÁNDEZ, José Gonzales. Chicano Dictionary: Means of Communication in the Chicano Community. San José, Calif.: Author, 1970. vi, 48 pp.

This exceedingly amateurish glossary of Texas Pachuco terms is divided into three parts: a Spanish-English section (pp. 1-24) with some 450 entries; a section on "Words That Have a Phrase Meaning," (25-28) which duplicates some 50 forms cited in the previous section; and an English-Spanish part (29-48) with some 400 entries. The work suffers from a lack of sophistication in Spanish, English, and linguistics. No grammatical information is included in the glossary. The Pachuco items are cited in an inconsistent and illiterate orthography, e.g., aguitado for agüitado, borlo 'dance' versus vorlotiar 'to dance,' cilo for kilo or quilo lleleda for (one supposes) hielera, wadaches for huaraches. English glosses are colloquial and careless, e.g., "Bárbaro Untolerable, to much"; "Chiguawa Golly"; "Panocha Vigina"; "Puerta When a girl is sitting improperly and a man in front is getting an eye's full, door." Although the dictionary emphasizes strictly Pachuco terms, it also contains many standard forms (e.g., amargo 'sour') and common phonological variants of the standard form (e.g., aigre 'air'). Perhaps the greatest value of this work is its liberal sprinkling of obscene and off-color terms that seldom appear in print elsewhere. [GB]

JANUARY, William Spence, Jr. "The Chicano Dialect of the Mexican-American Communities of Dallas and Fort Worth." MA Thesis, Texas Christian Univ., 1970. iv, 245 pp.

This wordy and repetitive study of nonstandard Spanish vocabulary attempts (a) to determine the currency in the Dallas-Fort Worth area of the lexical items contained in Coltharp 1965, (b) to provide new items not noted by Coltharp, and (c) to document the usage of these items in three age groups. The attempt is well-intended and noteworthy, though flawed by procedural matters and the size of the sampling.

Following a sketch of the historical and sociocultural background and the nature of language variation in the first three chapters, Chap. 4 and the first part of Chap. 5 purport to explain, without success, the author's methodology. The main body of the vocabulary was apparently checked with 31 informants on the basis of their ability to translate the term into English. It appears that for the age-groups distinctions only 12 informants were used, four in each of three generations.

The lexicon is presented in three different chapters. Chap. 5 lists 317 forms elicited from at least 75% of the informants in one generation and 112 entries from at least 50% of one generation. All entries are cited in dialectal orthography with a brief English gloss, an indication of the part of speech, whether it differs from the standard in form or meaning, and whether it is found in Coltharp 1965. The first group also specifies whether the form was found in any of five other dictionaries, tells which informants provided the documentation, and gives variations in meaning and an occasional simplistic comparative-historical comment. Chap. 6 provides brief and vague remarks on the meanings of some 50 taboo words that were checked separately, while Chap. 7 contains 97 criminal (narcotic) argot items that were elicited from four special informants.

A final chapter spews out an array of statistics on the "Distribution of Vocabulary by Age Groups" which provide interesting implications (if one keeps in mind the limitations on the study's reliability) as to which terms are stable, dying out, increasing in usage, and so forth. [GB]

KATZ, Linda Fine. "The Evolution of the Pachuco Language and Culture." MA Thesis, Univ., of California, Los Angeles, 1974. viii, 183 pp.

This exploratory venture into the lexicon of ex-Pachucos and semi-Pachucos of the Los Angeles area is romantic and often gushing, but certainly serious and even valuable. The early parts of the work provide a loose characterization of the author's 15 informants (ranging in age from the mid-20's to the mid-40's), a crude historical-sociological survey of the Pachuco gang phenomenon, and comments on the history and social functions of Pachuco speech. Chap. 2 also discusses and exemplifies the varied origins of Pachuco lexicon (from English, standard Spanish, colloquial Spanish, Mexican Spanish, New Mexican Spanish, and general caló/germanía) and the abundance of synonymous terms (e.g., for 'girl,' 'police,' 'marijuana,' etc.).

The most significant parts of this thesis are the last two chapters. Chap. 3 (pp. 59-142) superficially explores the retention of lexicon. From Barker 1950, Braddy 1960, and Griffith 1948, 159 words were selected and presented to 13 informants for judgments of current usage; the responses are roughly grouped into six categories ranging from "still used with the same meaning" (50% of the words) to "totally unknown" (16%). The bulk of the chapter is a word-list that cites grammatical classification, the source work and its definition, the current meaning and usage attested by the informants, and historical comments with bibliographical references. Chap. 4 presents an original short story, "La vida de un bato-loco" (145-153), followed by a glossary of about 140 previously documented and 40 new items presented in the Chap. 3 dictionary format. [GB]

RAMÍREZ, Karen G. "Original Research for 'Lexical Usage of and
    Attitude Toward Southwest Spanish in the Ysleta, Texas,
    Area.'" Incidental paper, Univ. of Texas, El Paso, 197[1?].
    84 pp. (Owned and circulated by the Univ. of Texas-El Paso
    Library.)

   This paper presents a range of background and statistical
data supplementing Ramírez 1973. The three questionnaires (personal data, test sentences, and questions to accompany the test
sentences) are cited in full. Following a summary of the findings
on those forms which showed 100% agreement by the informants, the
complete recognition and acceptability data are presented in separate sections for the three age groups; this listing (pp. 10-35)
includes each word the informants recognized with the percentage
of citations as "proper/acceptable/slang" and "chosen/used/heard."
The remainder of the paper is devoted to a detailed description
of each informant and his responses to each question. [GB]

RAMÍREZ, Karen G. "Lexical Usage of and Attitude Toward Southwest
    Spanish in the Ysleta, Texas, Area." Hispania 56.308-315
    (1973). (Cf. Ramírez 197[1?].)

   "The purpose of this study is to attempt to determine the
extent of the use of Tirilongo, an informal code of Southwest
Spanish (also called Tirilí, Tirilón, Bato, Pachuco, etc.), in the
Ysleta area of El Paso." (p. 308) A 25-sentence fill-in-the-
blank questionnaire was constructed and administered to 15 informants of three age groups to elicit selected "slang" words from
Coltharp 1965 and to determine the informants' recognition and
acceptance of standard and nonstandard lexical items. Each sentence and all the completion items suggested by the informants are
listed with comments on their status: "proper," "acceptable," or
"slang." Three tables provide information contrasting the three
age groups with regard to those items cited as first choice,
those considered standard or proper, and those that were known.
This compact study's lucid interpretation of the linguistic ambience and the roles of Spanish and Pachuco in El Paso is a
laudable examination of the role of attitude in language change.
The details given in Ramírez 197[1?] make a valuable supplement
to this report. [GB]

SUÁREZ, Mario. "Kid Zopilote." AQ 3.130-137 (1947). "Southside
    Run." AQ 4.362-368 (1948). "Maestría." AQ 4.368-373 (1948).

   These three short stories on Pachuco themes contain a few examples of Spanish phrases, including code-switching (as well as
one Spanish phrase spoken by a Chinese!). [GB]

TREJO, Arnulfo D. "Una contribución al estudio del léxico de la delincuencia en México." PhD Diss. ("Thesis para optar el grado de Doctor en Letras"), Univ. Nacional Autónoma de México, 1959. xiii, 215 pp. (Cf. Trejo 1968)

This work is primarily a lexicon divided into four parts—thievery, fighting, civil authority, and prison—of criminal argot employed in Mexico City. Wider occurrence of each entry is noted by simple documentation only; for Southwest Spanish reference is infrequently made to Barker 1950, Cerda et al. 1953, Espinosa 1946, Gaarder 1944, Griffith 1948, Kercheville 1934, and Wagner 1953-4. Trejo 1959 will be difficult for most researchers to acquire, but no matter: all of its material has been incorporated into the wider-scoped Trejo 1968. [GB]

TREJO, Arnulfo D. Diccionario etimológico latinoamericano del léxico de la delincuencia. México, D.F.: UTEHA, 1968, xli, 226 pp. [Rev. HLAS 32 (1970) no. 3015 (D.L. Canfield); Craddock 1973 p. 324.]

This excellent study of the lexicon of thieves' argot in Ibero-America is based primarily on Mexican caliche, Peruvian replana, Argentine lunfardo, Chilean coa, Brazilian gíria, and Southwest Pachuco speech. The references to Pachuco are not overly frequent and are documented with reference to such works as Barker 1950, Cerda et al. 1953, Coltharp 1965, Espinosa 1946, Kercheville 1934, and Wagner 1953-54.

The list contains almost 1,000 entries (a few of them duplications) personally known to Trejo. The entries are divided into 15 semantic groups, dealing primarily with thievery, fighting, civil authority, and sex (drug terminology is not included). Each entry contains the form and its cross-reference number, a generally careful etymological explanation showing the form's origin (usually peninsular), a brief indication of grammatical function, the meanings known to the author (with corroborative documentation), the different meanings cited by others, and often an illustrative sentence taken from a literary work or from actual speech. The word index (pp. 211-226) is useful and there is a rather lengthy bibliography (197-210). This book is an indispensable reference for anyone working in Pachuco. [GB]

WAGNER, Max Leopold. "Ein Mexikanisch-amerikanischer Argot: das Pachuco." RJB 6.237-266 (1953-54). [Annot. Fody p. 533. Rev. HLAS 21 (1959) no. 3671 (D. Wogan).]

Although drawing exclusively from previously published data on Pachuco and Southwest Spanish, this superb but oft-ignored article is a valuable piece of scholarship in its own right. It is intended primarily to correct the historical-comparative deficiencies in the vocabularies of Barker 1950, Gaarder 1944, and Griffith 1948-1973. The substance of the article is a listing (pp. 246-266) of all argot forms cited by those authors--some 250 main entries, plus derivatives--with rather extensive documentation to demonstrate the slang (and often standard Spanish) parallels throughout Latin America and Spain as well as in New Mexico and Texas. Some historical documentation is also included.

As an introduction to this argot list Wagner provides a cursory description of the Pachuco gang phenomenon and of other aspects of Pachuco speech: the strong influence of English, the use of abbreviated forms and new derivations, and so forth. This overview is also based solely on the work of others and is thereby limited in value, but it does constitute a good résumé. [GB]

8.7 ENGLISH INFLUENCE ON SPANISH

Major Items: (none)

See also these items elsewhere (consult Author Index for location): BARK-G-1947a; BARK-G-1950; COLT-1964; COLT-1965; COLT-1970a

8.8 SPANISH INFLUENCE ON ENGLISH

Major Items: (none)

See also these items elsewhere (consult Author Index for location):

(none)

BRADDY, Haldeen. "Narcotic Argot Along the Mexican Border." AS 30.84-90 (1955).

This discussion of vocabulary used by drug addicts in El Paso, Texas, lists 83 terms not previously appearing in publications on narcotic speech; some 17 of these lexical items are Spanish or of possible Spanish origin. [GB]

BRADDY, Haldeen. "Smugglers' Argot in the Southwest." AS 31.96-101 (1956).

This general discussion of narcotics vocabulary in El Paso contains about ten lexical items from Spanish that were not noted in Braddy 1955. [GB]

DE LANNOY, William C. and Elizabeth Masterson. "Teen-age Hophead Jargon." AS 27.23-31 (1952).

This list of English narcotic vocabulary contains four or five loans from Spanish, but none of them is marked as such. [GB]

8.10 CODE-SWITCHING

Major Items: (none)

See also these items elsewhere (consult Author Index for location);

SUAR-1947-48

9. SECTION 9 (PUERTO RICANS ON THE U. S. MAINLAND)

9.1 BIBLIOGRAPHY

Major Items: (none)

See also these items elsewhere (consult Author Index for location):

(none)

CORDASCO, Francesco, Eugene Bucchioni and Diego Castellanos.
Puerto Ricans on the United States Mainland: A Bibliography of Reports, Texts, Critical Studies and Related Materials.
Totowa, New Jersey: Rowman and Littlefield, 1972. xiv, 146 pp. [Rev. RIR 3.406-408 (1974) (C. Gauld).]

The majority of this highly professional bibliography's 754 items are annotated, at times extensively. Reviews of major items are usually cited but major items are infrequent, since the greater part of Cordasco's items have appeared only in serial publications or else as privately-printed "reports" by labor organizations, community service groups, and the like; of course it is to the author's credit that he has managed to locate this material at all.
The book is divided into six sections: I. General Bibliographies, II. The Island Experience, III. The Migration to the Mainland, IV. The Mainland Experience, V. The Mainland Experience: Education, and VI. The Mainland Experience: The Social Context. Section II is necessarily quite selective and could well have been omitted. Cordasco's readable "Foreword" (pp. ix-xiv) serves as a general introduction to the Puerto Rican experience; for an excellent, evocative description of the myriad problems associated with mainland Puerto Rican Spanish monolingualism or inadequate bilingualism see Diego Castellano's "Introduction" (1-19).
One notes with regret that this otherwise excellent bibliography, which focuses with such acuity on the literature of social problems, welfare, labor, acculturation, etc., offers little of interest to linguists; teachers will also be rather disappointed by Cordasco's coverage of bilingual education. While it is true that publication on the language(s) of mainland Puerto Ricans has hardly been voluminous, Cordasco has nevertheless given short shrift to what there is. One notes for example that only six lines of type are devoted to the numerous publications of Joshua Fishman and associates (see below, sec. 9.2.1); Cordasco mentions (no. 525) Language Loyalty in the United States, a work which pays only passing attention to Puerto Rican Spanish, and goes on to list Fishman's massive, pioneering Bilingualism in the Barrio project (no. 526) inaccurately and without annotation. None of the many articles which derived from the Project's preliminary report is mentioned. And while Cordasco delves exhaustively into educational materials from the 1950's and the early 1960's, he fails to include much of the growing literature on East Coast Puerto Rican bilingual

education regularly annotated or listed in Research in Education and elsewhere. [RT]

DOSSICK, Jesse J. "Doctoral Research on Puerto Rico and Puerto Ricans." New York: School of Education, New York Univ., [n.d.]. 34 pp.

An unannotated list of some 320 dissertations from mainland universities dealing primarily with island Puerto Ricans. The list is arranged in groups according to doctoral fields; some 20 entries are cited under "Language" and "Language in Education." [GB]

VIVÓ, Paquita, ed. The Puerto Ricans: An Annotated Bibliography. New York and London: R.R. Bowker Co., 1973. 299 pp. [Rev. Américas 26:9.37 (Sept. 1974) (F. Hebblethwaite).]

Vivó's bibliography was sponsored by the Puerto Rican Research and Resources Center, Inc., in turn part of the mainland "Universidad Boricua" with headquarters in Washington D.C. and a branch in New York City. More than 2,600 entries appear, some annotated. Materials are arranged according to size and publication type: part I includes "books, pamphlets and dissertations," II "government documents," III "periodical literature," and IV "audiovisual materials." Part I's "Language" subsection (pp. 103-108) includes 41 items, only 3 of which deal with mainland PRSp; a glance at the only two language-related keywords in the subject index uncovers 25 items that pertain to "bilingualism" (9 relate to the mainland and 3 of these are annotated) and 63 to "language" (including all of pp. 103-108); few of the last category relate to the mainland either. There is little here for the student of U.S. Spanish in this otherwise excellent and attractive bibliography. [RT]

9.2 COMPREHENSIVE/GENERAL STUDIES; MISCELLANY; ANTHOLOGIES/ FESTSCHRIFTEN

Major Items: ANAS/JESU-1953

See also these items elsewhere (consult Author Index for location):

HAMC-1971; KREI-1957; MART-A-1970; MENC-1919/36;

ANASTASI, Anne and Cruz de Jesús. "Language Development and Nonverbal IQ of Puerto Rican Preschool Children in New York City." JASP 48.357-366 (1953). [Annot. Cordasco 1972 no. 489.]

The authors engaged 50 Spanish-dominant Puerto Rican five-year-olds (25 of each sex) in generally unstructured Spanish conversation in order to determine the degree to which their speech showed syntactical maturity, especially as compared with the recorded English speech of similar numbers of black and white lower-class New York five-year-olds. (Anastasi and de Jesús also sought to determine comparative nonverbal IQ's by means of "draw-a-man" tests, but these findings do not concern us here.) The results were very "surprising," especially in light of the almost universally poor scholastic performance of young Puerto Ricans in the English-monolingual schools of the day: "Although the Puerto Rican sample was inferior to the Negro and white samples in educational and occupational level of parents, the Puerto Rican children . . . excelled both white and Negro groups in mean sentence length and in maturity of sentence structure." (p. 365) The authors suggest the greater amount of adult contact in the Puerto Rican home environment (the one positive effect of over-crowded slum apartments) as a possible explanation of this superiority. It was noted in passing that although all children were allowed to use English if they wished, the language samples obtained "were almost wholly Spanish, only about 2 per cent of the individual words and about 1 per cent of the sentences being English." (362) At this preschool age "the Puerto Rican child is predominantly Spanish-speaking and has not yet been exposed to the sharp linguistic bifurcation brought on by monolingual English schooling." (358) But a certain amount of intrasentential code-switching was observed, especially among boys; the authors note that mixed sentences reflect "the beginning of a trend which becomes more marked in older Puerto Ricans." (362) [RT]

FERNÁNDEZ, Micho. "El Barrio Diccionario: Spanglish Made Easy." New York 5:32.46, 48 (Aug. 7, 1972).

A brief, breezy but well-informed account of certain features of "New York Spanglish," chiefly lexical and grammatical English influence along the lines of vacunar la carpeta 'limpiar la alfombra con el aspirador,' llamar para atrás 'volver a llamar por teléfono,' etc. A "Glossary of Spanglish Terms" appears on p. 48 and includes la rufa, la fensa, el toquen, braun, el raincoat, etc., as well as a few forms which are not Anglicisms at all (la estufa, el elevador). Fernández gives valuable information on the by-now-famous "Spanglish battle" between the New School for Social Research and some very irate Puerto Rican leaders who deeply resented the bastardization implicit in the very name of the "new language." [RT]

[FISHMAN, Joshua A. [1969c.] "Puerto Rican Intellectuals in New York: Some Intragroup and Intergroup Contrasts." CJBS 1.215-226 (1969).] V.s. FISHM-1968/71 ("Project-based Materials Not Included in BB, 1971").

[FISHMAN, Joshua A. and Heriberto Casiano. "Puerto Ricans in Our Press." 1969.] V.s. FISHM-1968/71, Ch. 2.

GALÍNDEZ SUÁREZ, Jesús de. Puerto Rico en Nueva York: sociología de una inmigración. Buenos Aires: Editorial Tiempo Contemporáneo, 1969. 106 pp.

Chiefly a popularized narration of life in East Harlem and elsewhere throughout Puerto Rican New York, Galíndez concentrates on religious practices, popular diversions, personal histories, socio-geographical descriptions, etc., and mentions language only twice: on p. 76 (three Anglicisms are cited and the following comment is made: "[En cuanto a] ese nuevo lenguaje, híbrido de español y americano . . . los puristas alzan el grito hasta el cielo, con razón; pero ¿quién será capaz de ponerle el cascabel al gato? ¿Quién podrá introducir el Diccionario de la Academia . . . entre la gente que acude a la Marqueta?"), and on pp. 79-80, where the author notes the first generation's fear of speaking an "incorrect" English and the bilingual second generation's "superiority complex" which results from knowing English. [RT]

*GOSNELL, Patria Arán. "The Puerto Ricans in New York City." PhD Diss., New York Univ., 1945. viii, 639 pp. (All New York Univ. School of Education dissertations are now purchasable through Xerox University Microfilms of Ann Arbor, Michigan, including those which, like Gosnell 1945, were not initially copyrighted with XUM and thus not abstracted in DA. Because XUM now handles this item it can no longer be borrowed from libraries at New York Univ.)

From the chapter and sub-section headings in the Table of Contents it is clear that Gosnell gives an impressive encapsulation of Puerto Rican history, culture, socioeconomics, etc. But "language" receives rather short shrift, and as pertains to continental Puerto Ricans is mentioned only once, in Ch. 15, "Acculturation," in the subsection "Uses of Spanish in New York City" (pp. 474-475). Such paucity of treatment did not encourage us to acquire this item. [RT]

HOUCK, Helen Phipps. "[Review of] 'Lo español [en los Estados Unidos],' <u>Revista bimestre cubana</u>, Nov.-Dic., 1938, pp. 165-184." <u>Hispania</u> 22.325-328 (Oct. 1939).

This is partly a review of a speech given Aug. 8, 1937 in Havana by one Herminio Portell Vila and subsequently printed in the Cuban journal cited. On p. 326 the reviewer makes reference to "Pablo de Torriente Brau's unfinished study of New York Spanish [which] lists such amazing innovations as 'El grosero acaba de traer las groserías.'" It appears this study has remained unfinished since no source lists it. On the same page Houck speaks of "Puerto Ricans to the number of 200,000 [who] have emigrated to the United States but have remained aliens, as is evident from the Spanish-speaking section of New York." [RT]

JESÚS, Cruz de. "A Study of Language Development and Goodenough IQ of Puerto Rican Preschool Children in New York City." MA Thesis, Fordham Univ., 1952. vi, 60 pp. (Cf. Anastasi and Jesús 1953.)

This is the thesis by Jesús, directed by Anastasi, which forms the base of both persons' 1953 article on New York Puerto Rican child language. The article is a digest of the thesis, whose structural organization it preserves and whose findings it repeats; thus there is no need to consult the thesis separately. [RT]

LABOV, William, Paul Cohen, Clarence Robins and John Lewis. <u>A Study of the Non-standard English of Negro and Puerto Rican Speakers in New York City</u>. 2 vols. (Cooperative Research Project No. 3288, Office of Education, U.S. Dept. of HEW.) Bethesda, Maryland: U.S. Dept. of HEW/EDRS, 1968. 375/356 pp. Available EDRS: ED 028 424.

Sec. 1.0.1 (vol. 1, pp. 2-3) is entitled "The relation of Negro to Puerto Rican and other Spanish-speaking groups." Here Labov notes that "in every Negro adolescent group studied, there are some speakers with Spanish-language background who have become integrated into the group . . . In this study, we will be concentrating exclusively upon those factors which are common to the Negro groups and the Spanish-background individuals associated with them; we will not be dealing with the major part of the Spanish-speaking population which is isolated from the Negro population." If anything the remark understates the aplicability of this <u>caveat</u> to the report itself: a careful check reveals that only one <u>small</u> section ("Puerto Rican Responses to the SR [Subjective Reaction] Test," pp. 257-258, vol. 2) is specifically concerned with Puerto Ricans; likewise one discovers that just one of the Harlem gangs from which linguistic and sociological information was elicited had even a single Puerto Rican member and that no effort was made to contrast his English with the others). In this sense, then,

Labov's title misleads. But while there is almost nothing here for the student of Puerto Rican speech, this excellent study is nonetheless of primary value for the information it provides on lower-class black language and value systems. [RT]

*LEACH, John Nathaniel. "Cultural Factors Affecting the Adjustment of Puerto Rican Children to Schooling in Hartford, Connecticut." PhD Diss., Univ. of Connecticut, 1971. 109 pp. [DA 32 (1971) 2308-A.]

Of passing interest to linguists, this work focussed on the degree to which "regional" differences affect "adjustment to schooling;" specifically the study compared students from Puerto Rican "coastal areas" (thereby lumping together persons from metropolitan San Juan and remote-rural Boquerón, Palmas Altas, Yabucoa and similar aldeas) with those from the island's "hill country." For example, Leach tested whether "the hill people make better progress than the coastal people in learning to read English." He found that they did not. One also learns (without quite seeing the point of the whole exercise) that the two "groups" did not differ significantly in any other realms, either, e.g., grade point average, tardiness, rule-breaking, math achievement, etc.

LEWIS, Oscar. La Vida: A Puerto Rican Family in the Culture of Poverty--San Juan and New York. New York: Random House, 1965. lx, 669 pp. (Spanish translation of the Introduction and the Author's Commentaries [passim] by José Luis González, La Vida: una familia puertorriqueña en la cultura de la pobreza: San Juan y Nueva York. México, D.F.: Editorial Joaquín Mortiz, S.A., 1969. lvii, 646 pp.)

The Spanish version is a word for word transcription of the original taped interviews. Linguists will consequently prefer it to the "original" 1965 version (in English translation, but not always faithful and sometimes abridged, presumably for stylistic purposes), although for most research one would definitely want to use the tapes themselves since any "orthographic" transcription inevitably reflects actual phonation to a limited extent only: while some consonants are transcribed a lo boricua to give the dialogues a certain sabor popular, e.g., "ehta pelsona," the majority appear as they would in "standard" Spanish, clearly so as not to tire the reader and to avoid distracting from the work's contents. Attitudes toward language as expressed infrequently by "Fernanda" and her relatives are scattered throughout the work's multiple autobiographical recitations; neither edition contains an index so one must read the text to locate references to language. The following paragraph, a sample of Lewis 1969's transcriptional style, is also one of the more vivid expostulations on language attitudes and usage (as expressed by "Felícita," the thirty-ish daughter of "Fernanda"): [p. 316]

"¡Lo que yo le haría a la gente que se las echa hablando inglés!
Si yo por lo menos fuera cinco o diez minutos la gobernadora de
Puerto Rico o la alcaldesa de Nueva Yor, yo cogería un revólver y
le entraba a tirar a tos los puertorriqueños que se les ha olvidao
el español. Eso de los puertorriqueños hablando inglés es una poca-
vergüenza porque nosotros los latinos allá debemos de hablar el
propio latino de nosotros, por lo menos el castellano. --
Hay muchas pelsonas como los teenagers, que se les está olvidando
el español para venir a hablar inglés que casi no entienden lo que
están diciendo. Ponen un disco en inglés y dicen: --¡Ave María,
qué chévere, qué chévere!-- Y uno les pregunta qué es lo que dice
ese disco y entonces se quedan callaos. Lo único que saben decir
es el nombre del artista. Yo hablo inglés cuando me toca con cual-
quier americano, pero eso de yo olvidar mi lenguaje, no. Nunca.
Los latinos debemos hablar nuestro idioma en la casa. Los que no
lo hablan no pueden querer a su propio padre y a su propia madre.
Si quieren olvidar su idioma no deben llamarse puertorriqueños."

The 1969 edition contains a useful "Glosario" of the Puerto
Rican "regionalisms" (pp. 641-644) and Anglicisms (644-646) which
appear in the text. Occasional noteworthy variant surface forms
will be noted, e.g. bugarrón 'hombre aficionado a los homosexuales'
(cf. DRAE bujarrón). [RT]

OLIVA, Félix S. Nueva York para el perfecto turista. Barcelona:
    Ediciones Marte, 1970. 298 pp.

The eighth chapter is entitled "El idioma español en Nueva
York," but only a very small part of it has to do with that topic.
On pp. 250-252 the author deals conversationally with "el español
hablado," and on p. 252 with "el español escrito." The first of
these mentions a few common New York Puerto Rican Anglicisms (estar
supuesto a, llamar atrás [sic, 'patrás']) and speaks of "ese
cariño y lealtad tradicional que profesa [la comunidad puertorri-
queña] hacia el idioma español." The second section deals briefly
but critically with New York's leading Spanish language daily.
[RT]

REYNOLDS, John J. and Thomas D. Houchin. A Directory for Spanish-
    speaking New York. New York and Chicago: Quadrangle Books
    [for the New York Times Co.], 1971. ix, 340 pp. [TSBJr.]

While not directly pertinent to New York Spanish per se, and
quite properly conceived as a "handbook" for persons in need of
Spanish-speaking services in the metropolis, the Directory will
nonetheless serve the scholarly public as a handy guide to "where
to hear" New York Spanish spoken and, indubitably, as a vivid
testimony to the massive extent to which New York has become a
Spanish-speaking city. This "guía bilingüe para vivir, visitar,
trabajar, comprar, vender, estudiar y festejar a sus amistades en
la colonia puertorriqueña, la cubana y las otras hispanas de

Nueva York" (back cover) contains "seis mil datos ordenados alfabéticamente en 106 categorías" and claims to be "el primer gran directorio clasificado de empresas comercíales, tiendas, servicios, iglesias, escuelas, abogados, médicos, farmacias, restaurantes, oficinas gubernamentales, organizaciones cívicas, periódicos, revistas, radio y TV, etc., sirviendo [sic] a los dos millones de residentes de habla española en el área metropolitana," (ibid.) which includes northern New Jersey and a part of Connecticut as well. Pp. 243-244 list no fewer than 17 radio and television stations which broadcast partly or exclusively in Spanish; pp. 202-210 list more than one hundred periodicals, everything from Escándalo and Pica-pica to the Reportero industrial. There is even a substantial list of "Fortune Tellers (including Curanderas, Adivinas, etc.)" (pp. 122-125). [RT]

RIBES TOVAR, Federico. El libro puertorriqueño de Nueva York/Handbook of the Puerto Rican Community. New York and San Juan: Plus Ultra Eeucational Publishers, Inc., 1970. 496 pp.

Despite small sections on language-related issues ("Deficient Knowledge of English" [p. 68], "Bilingualism and 'Bi-culturalism'" [79-80]) there is really next to nothing on language/linguistics in this otherwise worthy volume, the first of its kind to present a fully Puerto Rican view of the life and times of la colonia boricua in New York City. The book has eight sections and is written in both Spanish and English consistently throughout; while the level of prose is high and even "literary" at times, occasional "Anglicisms in Spanish" and "Hispanisms in English" do appear, but most of these would appear to result from translation and it is thus unlikely that they are "mirrors of" popular speech (for the most part the quality of the prose is such that one has a hard time determining which of the two versions constituted the original). Section titles and sub-titles reveal topical orientation: "The Puerto Rican Migrant's Contribution to the Life of New York City" [24-26], "Analysis of the Educational Process in New York" [sec. 2, pp. 61-94], "New York Politics and the Puerto Ricans" [155-182], "Cultural Panorama" [sec. 5, pp. 183-198; inter alia: "The Problem of the Uprooted Literary People"]. [RT]

SOTO, Pedro Juan. Spiks: Grabado en linoleum de Lorenzo Homar, Carlos Raquel Rivera y Rafael Tufiño, impresos directamente del original. México D.F.: Los Presentes, 1956. 109 pp.

This fictionalized account of the lives of half a dozen New York Puerto Ricans faithfully reproduces the local Spanish habla through frequent "phonetic" transcriptions, e.g., ehtoh papeleh, tú sabeh, and the like. But Soto's goal was art, not linguistics, thus no glossary appears and the more regional words and phrases are nowhere "explained." A valuable secondary source nonetheless. [RT]

VARO, Carlos. <u>Consideraciones antropológicas y políticas en torno a la enseñanza del 'Spanglish' en Nueva York</u>. Río Piedras, Puerto Rico: Ediciones Librería Internacional, 1971. 127 pp.

Taking as its point of departure the by-now famous New School for Social Research course on New York City "Spanglish," this militant work eventually discusses the course (and the phenomenon itself) after more than a hundred pages of history, sociology and protest (some chapter titles: "Puerto Rico, Fortaleza Militar Norteamericana;" "Integridad Social y Cultural, Tartamudez Expresiva;" "La Colonia es Castrante por Esencia"). The author, a Spaniard, contrasts U.S. absorption of European immigrants with the Puerto Rican's resistance to assimilation: "El puertorriqueño se niega a esa absorción. Instalado en un deficiente bilingüismo, ese 'spanglish' ejemplifica su dolorosa ambigüedad cultural, no solo lingüística." (p. 109) For Varo, Spanglish is a "jerga llena de barbarismos, un español escuálido hasta la depauperación total en sus recursos expresivos léxicos, sintácticos, propio de gentes sin cultura;" (110) therefore "el aparentemente inofensivo curso de la New School for Social Research es un insulto más, gratuito, a la comunidad puertorriqueña." (ibid.) But on the other hand the jargon "no hace sino exasperar algunas de las tendencias del español actual en Puerto Rico" and is hardly a "mixed language" since not only has it preserved an entirely Spanish structure but "aun el puertorriqueño de la más baja condición cultural no sólo entiende sino que envidia las formas más correctas del español." (111) A half-dozen well-known examples of Anglicization appear on pp. 110-111; two "classroom dialogues" (119-121) composed by the street-wise adolescent who instructed the course are vivid reflections of Spanish Harlem's depressing milieu and serve to illustrate Varo's asserverations of <u>depauperación</u> and the like. They are also fully beyond the level of beginning Spanish students, the group for which the course was intended in the first place. [RT]

9.2.1 SOCIOLINGUISIICS

Major Items: FISHM/1968-71; HERM-1971; LEAV-1969; MA/HERA-1968/71/72; RAMO-I-1972

See also these items elsewhere (consult Author Index for location): CRAI-1969; and especially WOLFR/etal-1971 and WOLFR-1973

[BERNEY, Tomi D. and Robert L. Cooper. "Semantic Independence and Degree of Bilingualism in Two Communities." 1968; 1969; (with J.A. Fishman) 1969.] V.s. FISHM-1968/71, Ch. 12.

CHENAULT, Lawrence R. The Puerto Rican Migrant in New York City. 2nd printing (1938; New York: Russell and Russell, 1970 [with a Foreword by Francesco Cordasco]). 190 pp. +.

    References to "language" in this classic work on New York's earlier Puerto Rican settlement are scattered and few, but do provide occasional commentary of great value. On pp. 144-145 (tucked away in a subsection on "The Need for Vocational Training") we learn that "Puerto Ricans, except for the student group in colleges, cling strongly to their own language. Many of them give as the main reason for this the pride in their own language and customs which they profess to have to such a marked degree. Their indifference toward the learning of English is probably to be explained by earlier association with the language on the island.[16] [Fn. 16 in part: 'In seeking an explanation for (this antipathy) the author has most often received the reply that they "just do not like English" or that they "do not like the sound of the language."'] Many Puerto Ricans resent [the attempt to teach them English] as an encroachment upon their own language and culture. English in their minds is associated with the coming of the sugar interests which bought their lands, and with a culture which many of them do not understand." Other, briefer references to language usage and attitudes are found on pp. 44, 77, 96 and 150.
    Cordasco's "Foreword" was written especially for the 1970 edition, it points out the continued timeliness of Chenault's observations and also brings the reader up to date on the major works in the field (chiefly sociological) which have been written since Chenault first appeared. [RT]

[COOPER, Robert L. "Two Contextualized Measures of Degree of Bilingualism." 1968; 1969.] V.s. FISHM-1968/71, Ch. 12.

[COOPER, Robert L. "Theme Address Session 4: 'How Can We Measure the Roles Which a Bilingual's Languages Play in His Everyday Behaviour?.'" In Description and Measurement of Bilingualism . . . , 1969, pp. 192-208.] V.s. FISHM-1968/71, ("Project-based Publications Not Included in BB 1971").

[COOPER, Robert L., Barbara Fowles and Abraham Givner. "Listening Comprehension in a Bilingual Community." 1968; 1969.] V.s. FISHM-1968/71, Ch. 13.

[COOPER, Robert L. and Lawrence Greenfield. [1968/69a]. "Language Use in a Bilingual Community." 1968; 1969.] V.s. FISHM-1968/71, Ch. 12.

[COOPER, Robert L. and Lawrence Greenfield. [1968/69b]. "Word Frequency Estimation as a Measure of Bilingualism." 1968; 1969.] V.s. FISHM-1968/71, Ch. 12.

[EDELMAN, Martin. "The Contextualization of Schoolchildren's Bilingualism." 1968; (with R.L. Cooper and J.A. Fishman) 1969.] V.s. FISHM-1968/71, Ch. 12.

[FERTIG, Sheldon and Joshua A. Fishman. "Some Measures of the Interaction Between Language, Domain and Semantic Dimensions in Bilinguals." MLJ 53.244-249 (1969).] V.s. FISHM-1968/71 ("Project-based Publications Not Included in BB 1971").

[FINDLING, Joav. "Bilingual Need Affiliation and Future Orientation in Extragroup and Intragroup Domains." 1969.] V.s. FISHM-1968/71, Ch. 14.

<u>FISHMAN, Joshua A. et al. 1968/71 and v.d.: "Bilingualism in the Barrio" Project.</u>

Not just several, but vast numbers of publications have resulted from what Craddock (1973 p. 307) has described as "the most ambitious project in recent years concerning any variety of U.S. Spanish," an effort employing linguists, psychologists and sociologists whose overall goal was the complete description of all aspects of Spanish-English bilingualism as practiced by several hundred Puerto Rican residents of Jersey City, New Jersey, across the Hudson River from Manhattan Island. Fieldwork for the Project began early in 1967; by 1968 the first of the many Project publications saw light; others appeared steadily in following years.

The very magnitude of the labors (and the eagerness with which many journals published Project-based monographs in a variety of oft-revised forms) has inevitably created certain difficulties for the bibliographer, who is forced in part to abandon traditional listing format so as to be able to present, in as coherent a fashion as possible, the Project's multitudinous publications, revisions, title changes, author changes, reprintings, etc.

It is not quite accurate to say that scholars interested in all pertinent information from the Bilingualism in the Barrio project (hereafter abbreviated as "BB") need look no further than the following work:

Fishman, Joshua A., Robert L. Cooper, Roxana Ma et al. Bilingualism in the Barrio. Indiana Univ. Publications Language Science Monographs, Vol. 7 (Bloomington: Indiana Univ. Research Center for the Language Sciences, and The Hague: Mouton, 1971). 696 pp. plus Errata. (Distributed in the United States and Canada by Humanities Press, New York City.)

The BB 1971 contains most of the original Project research but not all of it. However, scholars who want to consult all Project material will have to purchase the following bulky item, which even on microfilm runs to nearly $12.00 and which in soft-cover costs upwards of $60.00:

*Fishman, Joshua A., R.L. Cooper, R. Ma et al. Bilingualism in the Barrio. (Final Report, Yeshiva Univ., Contract No. OEC-1-7-062817-0297, U.S. Dept. of Health, Education and Welfare, Office of Education.) Bethesda, Maryland: U.S. Dept. of HEW/EDRS, 1968, 1232 pp. [ED 026 546.] [Annot. RIE (July 1969) 5.] (This item is referred to subsequently as "Fishman/BBFinal Report 1968.")

And for the sake of completeness they may also want to obtain another item which reported on the initial stages of Project research

Fishman, Joshua A. The Measurement and Description of Language Dominance in Bilinguals: Final Report--Phase 1. (Yeshiva Univ., Contract No. OEC-1-7-062817-0297, US Dept. of HEW.) Bethesda, Maryland: US Dept. of HEW/EDRS, 1967. 79 pp. [ED 016 954.] [Annot. RIE (Aug. 1968) 21.]

So in all probability the interested scholar will be able to limit his consultation to the BB 1971. With this in mind we will use the BB 1971 as a bibliographic baseline for describing Project material and publications. To do so requires a reverse chronology in most instances; thus initial reference is made to the chapter or section of BB 1971 in which the given material appears, and subsequent reference takes in all other printings of what is often essentially the same material. As we have not consulted the Fishman/BBFinal Report 1968 we are unable to give page or chapter references to that volume, except where Fishman himself provides them in the BB 1971.

The few Project-based publications which did not make their way into BB 1971 are listed in a separate section, following the guide to materials in the BB 1971, which appears here below:

GUIDE TO MATERIALS IN FISHMAN ET AL., 1971

PART I: INTRODUCTION

Fishman, Joshua A. "The Measurement and Description of Widespread and Relatively Stable Bilingualism." MLJ 53.152-156 (1969). Rpt., substantively rev. and retitled as "The Measurement and Description of Societal Bilingualism," Fishman/BB 1971, 3-10 ("Introduction").

CHAPTER ONE [Chs. 1-5 form "Part II: Background Studies."]

Hoffman, Gerard. "Puerto Ricans in New York: A Language-related Ethnographic Summary." Fishman/BB 1971, 13-42 (Ch. 1).

CHAPTER TWO

Fishman, Joshua A. and Heriberto Casiano. "Puerto Ricans in Our Press." MLJ 53.157-162 (1969); rpt., slightly rev., in Fishman/BB 1971, 43-55 (Ch. 2).

CHAPTER THREE

Fishman, Joshua A. "Intellectuals From the Island." LMLP 2.1-16 (1970); rpt. with minor revisions in Fishman/BB 1971, 57-73 (Ch. 3).

CHAPTER FOUR

Anon. "Individual Interview: Puerto Rican Intellectual (Tape F66)." Fishman/BB 1971, 75-104 (Ch. 4).

CHAPTER FIVE

Fishman, Joshua A. "Bilingual Attitudes and Behaviors." Fishman/BBFinal Report 1968, pp. 186-224; rpt., rev., LangS 5.5-11 (1969); also in Fishman/BB 1971, 105-116 (Ch. 5).

CHAPTER SIX

Anon. "Group Interview: High School Students (Tape F35)." Fishman/BB 1971, 117-153 (Ch. 6).

CHAPTER SEVEN [Chs. 7-11 form "Part II: Sociologically-oriented Studies."]

Fishman, Joshua A. "A Sociolinguistic Census of a Bilingual Neighborhood." In Fishman/BBFinal Report 1968, pp. 260-299. Rpt., rev., AJS 75.323-339 (1969); also in Fishman/BB 1971, 157-176 (Ch. 7).

CHAPTER EIGHT

Fishman, Joshua A. and Charles Terry. "The Validity of Census Data on Bilingualism in a Puerto Rican Neighborhood." ASRev 34.636-650 (1969). Rpt., rev., as "The Contrastive Validity of Census Data on Bilingualism in a Puerto Rican Neighborhood," Fishman/BB 1971, 177-197 (Ch. 8).

CHAPTER NINE

Hoffman, Gerard. "Life in the Neighborhood: A Factor Analytic Study of Puerto Rican Males." Fishman/BB 1971, 198-232 (Ch. 9).

CHAPTER TEN

Greenfield, Lawrence. "Spanish and English Usage Self-Ratings in Various Situational Contexts." In Fishman/BBFinal Report 1968 [n. pp. cit.]. Rpt., rev. (with J.A. Fishman), as "Situational Measures of Normative Language Views in Relation to Person, Place and Topic Among Puerto Rican Bilinguals," Anthropos 65.602-618 (1970). Rpt., with minor revisions, as "Situational Measures of Normative Language Views of Person, Place and Topic Among Puerto Rican Bilinguals," in Fishman/BB 1971, 233-252 (Ch. 10); and in Advances in the Sociology of Language, vol. 2: Selected Studies and Applications. Contributions to the Sociology of Language No. 2, edited by J. A. Fishman (The Hague: Mouton, 1972), pp. 17-35; and in Man, Language and Society: Contributions to the Sociology of Language, edited by Samir K. Ghosh, The Hague: Mouton, 1972, pp. 64-86.

CHAPTER ELEVEN

Anon. "How I talk to My Parents (Instrument-construction Try-out, Tape A, Informant P/2)." Fishman/BB 1971, 253-269 (Ch. 11).

CHAPTER TWELVE ["Part IV: Psychologically-oriented Studies"]

RONCH, Judah. "Word Naming and Usage Scores for a Sample of Yiddish-English Bilinguals." [Compares these to Jersey City Puerto Ricans.] In Fishman/BBFinal Report 1968, pp. 564-576. Rpt., rev. (with Robert L. Cooper and Joshua A. Fishman). MLJ 53.232-235 (1969); an abridged version rpt. as "Yiddish-English Bilinguals," Fishman/BB 1971, 304-307 (part of Ch. 12).

Edelman, Martin. "The Contextualization of Schoolchildren's Bilingualism." In Fishman/BBFinal Report 1968, pp. 525-537. Rpt., rev., MLJ 53.179-182 (1969)--[Abs. LLBA III-938] and also (with R.L. Cooper and J.A. Fishman) in IJE 2.109-114 (1969). An abridged version rpt. as "Young Puerto Rican Schoolchildren," Fishman/BB 1971, 298-304 (part of Ch. 12).

Berney, Tomi D. and Robert L. Cooper. "Semantic Independence and Degree of Bilingualism in Two Communities." In Fishman/BB Final Report 1968, pp. 538-548. Rpt., rev., MLJ 53.182-185 (1969) [Abs. LLBA III-939] and also (with J.A. Fishman) IJP 2.289-294 (1969). An abridged version (by T.D. Berney and R.L. Cooper) rpt. as "Semantic Independence and Degree of Bilingualism," Fishman/BB 1971, 295-297 (part of Ch. 12).

Cooper, Robert L. "Two Contextualized Measures of Degree of Bilingualism." In Fishman/BBFinal Report 1968, pp. 577-597. Rpt., rev., MLJ 53.172-179 (1969)--[Abs. LLBA III-938]. Rpt., abridged, as "Word Naming and Word Association," Fishman/BB 1971, 286-294 (part of Ch. 12).

Cooper, Robert L. and Lawrence Greenfield. [1968/69b.] "Word Frequency Estimation as a Measure of Degree of Bilingualism." In Fishman/BBFinal Report 1968, pp. 475-484. Rpt., rev., MLJ 53.163-166 (1969). [Abs. LLBA III-938.] Rpt., abridged, as "Word Frequency Estimation," Fishman/BB 1971, 283-286 (part of Ch. 12).

Cooper, Robert L. and Lawrence Greenfield. [1968/69a.] "Language Use in a Bilingual Community." In Fishman/BBFinal Report 1968, pp. 485-504. Rpt., rev., MLJ 53.166-172 (1969). [Abs. LLBA III-938.] Rpt., abridged, as "Spanish Usage Rating Scale," Fishman/BB 1971, 275-283 (part of Ch. 12).

CHAPTER THIRTEEN

Cooper, Robert L., Barbara Fowles and Abraham Givner. "Listening Comprehension in a Bilingual Community." In Fishman/BBFinal Report 1968, pp. 577-597; rpt., rev., MLJ 53.235-241 (1969). Rpt., abridged, as "The Comprehension of Bilingual Conversations," Fishman/BB 1971, 311-321 (part of Ch. 13).

Kimple, James, Jr. "Language Shift and the Interpretation of Conversations." In Fishman/BBFinal Report 1968, pp. 598-610. Rpt., rev. (with R.L. Cooper and J.A. Fishman), Lingua 23.127-134 (1969). [Annot. HLAS 34 (1972) no. 3092 (Canfield).] Rpt., abridged, Fishman/BB 1971, 321-328 (part of Ch. 13).

Silverman, Stuart H. "The Evaluation of Language Varieties." In
Fishman/BBFinal Report 1968, pp. 611-619. Rpt., rev., MLJ
53.241-244 (1969). [Abs. LLBA III-948.] Rpt., abridged (with
R.L. Cooper and J.A. Fishman), in Fishman/BB 1971, 328-333
(part of Ch. 13).

Terry, Charles E. and Robert L. Cooper. "A Note on the Perception
and Production of Phonological Variation." MLJ 53.254-255
(1969). Rpt., abridged, as "The Perception of Phonological
Variation," Fishman/BB 1971, 333-334 (part of Ch. 13).

CHAPTER FOURTEEN

Findling, Joav. "Bilingual Need Affiliation and Future Orientation
in Extragroup and Intragroup Domains." MLJ 53.227-231 (1969).
[Abs. LLBA III-947.] Rpt., slightly abbreviated, Fishman/BB
1971, 337-344 (Ch. 14), and in Advances in the Sociology of
Language. Vol. 2: Selected Studies and Applications. Contributions to the Sociology of Language No. 2, edited by J. A.
Fishman (The Hague: Mouton, 1972), pp. 150-174.

CHAPTER FIFTEEN ["Part V: Linguistically-oriented Studies"]

Ma, Roxana and Eleanor Herasimchuk. "The Linguistic Dimensions of
a Bilingual Neighbrohood." In Fishman/BBFinal Report 1968,
pp. 636-835; rpt. in Fishman/BB 1971, 347-464 (Ch. 15). Roughly
the last one-fourth of this item is reprinted in slightly revised form--see esp. the initial four-paragraphs and the brief
"conclusion"--as "Speech Styles in Puerto Rican Bilingual
Speakers: A Factor Analysis of Co-Variation of Phonological
Variables," in Advances in the Sociology of Language, Vol. 2:
Selected Studies and Applications. Contributions to the
Sociology of Language No. 2, edited by J. A. Fishman (The
Hague: Mouton, 1972), pp. 268-295. [Rev. Craddock 1973 pp.
307-309.] (Of all the multiple contributions to Fishman/BB
1971 this is the one most oriented to linguistics. It is re-
viewed separately in this Bibliography.)

CHAPTER SIXTEEN

Fishman, Joshua A. and Eleanor Herasimchuk. "The Multiple Prediction of Phonological Variables in a Bilingual Speech Community."
AmA 71.648-657 (1969). [Rev. HLAS 32 (1970) no. 3074 (D.L.
Canfield).] Rpt. with minor alterations in Fishman/BB 1971,
465-479 (Ch. 16).

CHAPTER SEVENTEEN [Summary and Conclusions]

Fishman, Joshua A. and Robert L. Cooper. "Alternative Measures of Bilingualism." In Fishman/BBFinal Report 1968, pp. 880-928; rpt., rev. JVLVB 8.276-282 (1969). Rpt., rev. (with Joshua A. Fishman, R.L. Cooper and R. Ma) in Fishman/BB 1971, 483-512 (Ch. 17).

CHAPTER EIGHTEEN [Summary and Conclusions]

Fishman, Joshua A. "Some Things Learned; Some Things Yet to Learn." MLJ 53.255-258 (1969). Rpt., rev. and expanded in Fishman/BB 1971, 513-518 (Ch. 18).

CHAPTER NINETEEN [Theoretical Addendum]

Fishman, Joshua A. "Societal Bilingualism: Stable and Transitional." In Fishman/BB 1971, 539-555 (Ch. 19). [This is a revision of Fishman, "Bilingualism With and Without Diglossia: Diglossia With and Without Bilingualism," JSI 23:2.29-38 (1967); the 1967 version contained no implicit reference to mainland Puerto Rican bilingualism.]

CHAPTER TWENTY [Theoretical Addendum]

Fishman, Joshua A. "Sociolinguistic Perspective on the Study of Bilingualism." Linguistics 39.21-49 (1968); rpt. (with minor revisions) Fishman/BB 1971, 557-582 (Ch. 20). [This article has no direct bearing on the study of mainland Puerto Rican bilingualism.]

CHAPTER TWENTY-ONE [Theoretical Addendum]

Fishman, Joshua A. "The Relationship Between Micro- and Macro-Sociolinguistics in the Study of Who Speaks What Language to Whom and When." In Fishman/BB 1971, 583-604 (Ch. 21). [This is a revision of Fishman, "Who Speaks What Language To Whom and When?," La Linguistique 2.67-88 (1965); the original version contained no reference to Fishman's work on mainland Puerto Rican bilingualism, which in any case had not yet begun as of 1965.] Rpt. as "Domains and the Relationship Between Micro- and Macro-sociolinguistics" in Directions in Sociolinguistics, edited by Dell Hymes and John J. Gumperz. New York: Holt, Rinehart and Winston, 1972. Pp. 435-453.

CHAPTER TWENTY-TWO [Theoretical Addendum]

Fishman, Joshua A. "Chairman's Summary [Session 5: 'How Can We Describe and Measure the Behaviour of Bilingual Groups?']" In Description and Measurement of Bilingualism: An International Seminar, Univ. of Moncton, June 7-14, 1967, edited by L.G. Kelly. Toronto: Univ. of Toronto Press/Canadian National Commission for UNESCO, 1969. Pp. 275-281. (This piece makes no reference to mainland Puerto Rican bilingualism.) Rpt., slightly rev., as "The Description of Societal Bilingualism," in Fishman/BB 1971, 605-611 (Ch. 22).

APPENDIX

Anon. "Appendix: Instruments." Fishman/BB 1971, 613-696.

PROJECT-BASED PUBLICATIONS NOT INCLUDED IN BB 1971

[Though absent from BB 1971, the following three items all appeared in two numbers of the Modern Language Journal dedicated largely to various Project-based articles:]

Fishman, Joshua A. "Preface [to the special 'Bilingualism in the Barrio' numbers of the MLJ 53:3,4]." MLJ 53.151 (1969). [Abs. LLBA III-937.]

Fertig, Sheldon and Joshua A. Fishman. "Some Measure of the Interaction Between Language, Domain and Semantic Dimension in Bilinguals." MLJ 53.244-249 (1969). [Abs. LLBA III-948.]

Silverman, Stuart H. "A Method for Recording and Analyzing the Prosodic Features of Language." In Fishman/BB Final Report 1968, pp. 859-873. Rpt., rev., MLJ 53.250-254 (1969). [Abs. LLBA III-1217.]

[The following two items appeared neither in the BB 1971 nor in the MLJ "Bilingualism in the Barrio" numbers:]

Cooper, Robert L. "Theme Address [Session 4: 'How Can We Measure the Roles Which a Bilingual's Languages Play in His Everyday Behaviour?']" In Description and Measurement of Bilingualism: An International Seminar, Univ. of Moncton, June 7-14, 1967, edited by L.G. Kelly. Toronto: Univ. of Toronto Press/Canadian National Commission for UNESCO, 1969. Pp. 192-208. [This is essentially a "progress report" on the Jersey City Project, then still in the research stage.]

FISHMAN, Joshua A. "Puerto Rican Intellectuals in New York: Some Intragroup and Intergroup Contrasts." CJBS 1.215-226 (1969)

Brief, Analytical Comments on the BB 1971:

Space will not permit more than a passing discussion of Fishman/BB 1971. For longer reviews of the work see: ALASH 23. 406-412 (1973) (Z. Réger), and especially the insightful review in Lingua 34.89-93 (Aug. 1973) (R. Le Page). See also Haugen 1973, Craddock 1973.

One cannot fail to be impressed by the very magnitude of the Project's task and, in general, by the importance of its findings. In one sense, however, both Project and BB 1971 have failed to live up to their own high standards. I refer here to the embarrassingly anarchic way the BB 1971 transcribes conversations in Spanish.

In particular one notes the absence of grapheme s, which in all probability the transcriber omitted (in the expected syllable-final and word-final positions) to indicate aspiration or → [∅]; the problem is that whoever did the transcriptions also included the s in many environments where aspiration would have been expected. Punctuation and orthographic accentuation are likewise anarchic. An example from Ch. 9 will prove my point (other mistranscriptions appear elsewhere as well, esp. in Ch. 6): "Si. No escribirlo; olvídate que ello no aprenden. Ahora estos muchachos que yo tengo aquí yo lo enseño aquí por ejemplo aunque no vale la pena enseñarlo pero cuando van a escuela pue el español ello no saben escribirlo. Ello no saben escribir en español ni la palabra 'papá' aunque se escribe igual en inglés, porque es que no lo saben." (p. 219) Occasionally these mistakes appear to exceed the merely fortuitous (?), and thus give rise to some serious doubts as to the transcribers' (and the researchers') knowledge of Spanish; thus the following (Ch. 13, p. 333): "Selected English and Spanish variables were also studied with respect to the respondent's ability to perceive differences . . . The respondent heard on tape three realizations of a word in which a variable was embedded. (For example, interasado, interasao, interasado [sic! 'interesado, etc.].) He was then asked . . . "

Several errors in transcription were ultimately corrected in the Errata (following p. 696); many, many others were allowed to stand as printed. In general one feels the transcription was chiefly undertaken by persons whose apparent skill in oral Spanish led staff members to presume them equally proficient in Spanish orthography and phonetic interpretation. In that sense, then, Fishman and associates would have done well to include at least one Hispanist among their otherwise impressive team of researchers. [RT]

[Fishman, Joshua A. [1968/69a.] "Bilingual Attitudes and Behaviors." 1968; 1969.] V.s. FISHM-1968/71, Ch. 5.

[Fishman, Joshua A. [1968/69b.] "A Sociolinguistic Census of a Bilingual Neighborhood." 1968; 1969.] V.s. FISHM-1968/71, Ch. 7.

[Fishman, Joshua A. [1969a.] "The Measurement and Description of Widespread and Relatively Stable Bilingualism." 1969. Abs. LLBA III-937.] V.s. FISHM-1968/71, Part I: Introduction.

[Fishman, Joshua A. [1969b.] "Preface [: 'Bilingualism in the Barrio']." 1969. Abs. LLBA III-937.] V.s. FISHM-1968/71 ("Project-Based Publications Not Included in BB 1971").

[Fishman, Joshua A. [1969d.] "Some Things Learned; Some Things Yet to Learn." 1969.] V.s. FISHM-1968/71, Ch. 18.

[Fishman, Joshua A. "Intellectuals From the Island." 1970.] V.s. FISHM-1968/71, Ch. 3.

[Fishman, Joshua A. and Robert L. Cooper. "Alternative Measures of Bilingualism." 1968; 1969.] V.s. FISHM-1968/71, Ch. 17.

[Fishman, Joshua A. and Eleanor Herasimchuk. "The Multiple Prediction of Phonological Variables in a Bilingual Speech Community." 1969.] V.s. FISHM-1968/71, Ch. 16.

[Fishman, Joshua A. and Charles Terry. "The [Contrastive] Validity of Census Data on Bilingualism in a Puerto Rican Neighborhood." 1969.] V.s. FISHM-1968/71, Ch. 8.

[Greenfield, Lawrence. "Spanish and English Usage Self-Ratings in Various Situational Contexts." 1968. "Situational Measure of Normative Language Views in Relation to Person, Place and Topic Among Puerto Rican Bilinguals." 1970.] V.s. FISHM-1968/71, Ch. 10.

*HERMENET, Argelia María Buitrago. "Ethnic Identification of Puerto Rican Seventh Graders." EdD Diss., Univ. of Massachusetts, 1971. 375 pp. [DA 32 (1972) 4350-4351-A.]

From the abstract of this important and apparently definitive work we learn that Hermenet quantified heretofore largely anecdotal "Puerto Rican resistance to the melting pot" by measuring nine indicators of ethnic identity across five groups: Puerto Rican (PR) children in Puerto Rico; in the United States as migrants; in Puerto Rico but with experience on the mainland; white non-Puerto Ricans born and living in the United States; and white immigrants (mainly Italian and Portuguese). Her chief hypotheses were that (1) preference patterns of Puerto Rican students and "Anglo" students will differ, approximating or not these three modes: Puerto Rican, "Anglo-Saxons" and mixed; (2) "the pattern of preferences approximating a Puerto Rican mode and a Mixed mode will vary according to the degree of PREI (Puerto Rican Ethnic Identification);" and (3) that "the PREI will vary according to the length of residence and education in Puerto Rico and/or the Mainland" in an inverse sense, i.e., the longer the mainland residence the lower the PREI, and vice versa. Her sample consisted of five groups of seventh graders living throughout Puerto Rico or in Springfield, Massachusetts: "1. PRPR's: 93 Puerto Ricans tested in Puerto Rico who had had no experience in the United States. 2. NON PRPR's: 12 Puerto Ricans [a rather small sampling?] tested in Puerto Rico who had had experience in the United States. 3. USPR's: 68 Puerto Ricans tested in Springfield . . . with varying degrees of experience in Puerto Rico and in the United States. 4. A control of 'Anglo Saxon' (85 'White Americans,' English-speaking). 5. A control of 'Other' [38 students born abroad, chiefly in Italy and Portugal]." The test questionnaire contained nine items related to ethnic consistency, i.e., first choice of language, of place to visit, best friend, food, parents, etc.

Hermenet's first two hypotheses were confirmed, and in general it was established that all sets of Puerto Rican students "have not been assimilating structurally" to Anglo modes and likewise indicate they do not wish to do so. Furthermore, hypothesis three was proven invalid: those students who had lived longest on the mainland showed the greatest degree of Puerto Rican ethnic identification and not the least, as hypothesized. In similar fashion "the concept of Puerto Ricans as a 'race' was made evident only by the subjects who had had experience on the mainland." Nevertheless the overall language-preference responses showed a "mixed" mode, with "PRPR's" and "NON PRPR's" preferring Spanish but "USPR's" preferring English. That language continues to be a prime indicator of ethnic solidarity, however, is shown by the following: "The hypothesized preference of White American above Black American (hypothesis 9) was hardly seen among Puerto Ricans, who seemed to make their first choice of parents or friends according to language rather than to race." [RT]

[Hoffman, Gerard. [1971a.] "Life in the Neighborhood: A Factor Analytic Study of Puerto Rican Males." 1971.] V.s. FISHM-1968 1968/71, Ch. 9.

[Hoffman, Gerard. [1971b.] "Puerto Ricans in New York: A Language-Related Ethnographic Summary." 1971.] V.s. FISHM-1968/71, Ch. 1.

*KENDLER, Karen Seed. "An Exploratory Study of Mainland Puerto
    Rican Public and Parochial High School Students: The Effects
    of Perception of Discrimination, the Main Value of Education,
    and Other Factors Upon Academic Achievement." PhD Diss.,
    Pennsylvania State Univ., 1972. 369 pp. [DA 34 (1973) 1374-
    1375-A.]

   Public and parochial high school students are systematically
compared in terms of school performance attendance and with regard
to a wide range of attitudes and behavioral patterns. Of specific
interest to socio-linguists is the following information on domain
and preference: "Students, regardless of school type and SES, tend
to have Puerto Rican friends. Students speak more Spanish [at]
home than with friends, the latter regardless of ethnicity of
friends. This and the fact that language patterns are not associated with high school average indicate language patterns [are] due
to choice and not just [school] ability. Language spoken [at]
home is associated with language spoken with friends, with parochia
school students speaking English more in both situations." In
general, parochial students had higher aspirations and did better
academically than public school students. [RT]

[KIMPLE, James, Jr. (and [1969] Robert L. Cooper and Joshua A.
    Fishman). "Language Shift and the Interpretation of Conversa-
    tions." 1968; 1969.] v.s. FISHM-1968/71, Ch. 12.

*LAYDEN, Russell Glenn. "The Relationship Between the Language
    of Instruction and the Development of Self-Concept, Classroom
    Climate and Achievement of Spanish-speaking Puerto Rican
    Children." EdD Diss., Univ. of Maryland, 1972. 191 pp. [DA
    33 (1973) 6733-A.]

   Layden asserted that "for linguistically handicapped children
to achieve maximum self-development . . . they must: 1. Retain
the strength of ethnic identity and cultural heritage. . . [and]
3. Be educated in a classroom setting where . . . transition into
a new sociocultural milieu avoids alienation." (abs.) He thus
hypothesized that "Puerto Rican children who receive instruction
in their native language (Spanish)" will demonstrate more positive
changes in self-concept than those receiving English-language
instruction and will show a greater overall achievement; he also
posited that the climate of the Spanish-language classroom would
be more democratic than would its counterpart.
   Both groups were pre-tested through the Inter-American Series
Tests (level 2, primary, reading and also general ability),
initially in Spanish and, after a "ten week interval," again in
Spanish and also in English; self-concept testing also took place
"before and after," ambi-lingual testing for classroom climate only
"after." Layden found no significant differences in self concept.
Similarly "Hypothesis II was not supported by the data and in fact

the findings were in a direction opposite to that hypothesized."
The classroom climate of the Spanish-instructed group, though, was
the more democratic of the two.

Apart from the possibility that ten weeks may be too short a
period to effect marked improvement, it is pertinent to ask whether
one can accept at face value the author's attribution of "Spanish-
speaking" status to an entire given ethnic population of a large
public school (and if so, to what degree?). One need hardly mention that sociolinguists would want to know what percentage of the
children tested were Spanish-dominant (and to what degree), and
whether this hypothesized dominance would carry over effectively
into a domain (such as "school") where English had already become
fixed in the subjects' minds as expected language of communication.
One would also have to examine the possibility that some children
were already fluent or even dominant in English. What, in short,
is meant by the term "Spanish-speaking"? For a more sophisticated
treatment of these matters see Hollomon 1973. [RT]

*LEAVITT, Ruby Rohrlich. "A Comparative Study of Sociocultural
 Variables and Stuttering Among Puerto Rican Elementary School
 Children in San Juan, Puerto Rico, and New York, New York."
 PhD Diss., New York Univ., 1969. 582 pp. [DA 31 (1970)
 1586-B.]

We will quote directly from Leavitt's well-written abstract:
"In order to test the theory held by a number of speech pathologists
that stuttering is a deviant language response to sociocultural
stress, the incidence of stuttering was investigated in a single
ethnic group, Puerto Rican elementary public school children, in
two different cultural milieus, San Juan and New York City. On the
assumption that acculturation in New York is more stressful than
urbanization in San Juan for the Puerto Rican rural migrants who
constitute the bulk of the migration stream, it was hypothesized
that socio-cultural stress evokes a greater incidence of stuttering
among Puerto Rican children in New York than in San Juan. However,
the incidence of stuttering in the sample population of San Juan
was found to be significantly greater than in the sample population
of New York, beyond the 1% confidence level."

In an attempt to explain this unexpected finding, Leavitt
examines a wide range of sociological and cultural-historical
materials which deal with Puerto Rico, the U.S., New York City,
immigrants, etc., and concludes that the lower stuttering incidence
can be attributed to the "immediate and long-range economic gains
and the long-range sociocultural benefits [which are] greater for
the migrants in New York." Initially, however, "sociocultural
stress is greater for the migrants in New York than in San Juan."

Among Rohrlich's other conclusions: "The findings not only
revealed no relationships between stuttering and bilingualism, but
indicated that knowledge of English is a source of psychological
gratification to Puerto Rican children in New York." [RT]

*LENNON, John Joseph. "A Comparative Study of the Patterns of
    Acculturation of Selected Puerto Rican Protestant and Roman
    Catholic Families in an Urban Metropolitan Area (Chicago)."
    PhD Diss., Univ. of Notre Dame, 1963. 249 pp. [DA 24
    (1963) 2613.]

This sociological study is chiefly concerned with measuring
the "extent of acculturation" of the specified families, but will
be of interest to sociolinguists because the subjects' language
preferences and (apparently subjective) measures of English performance were two of the sixteen items which Lennon tested in
his sample of one hundred married couples ("predominantly of lower
socio-economic class and resident in areas of high density of
Spanish-speaking groups"), fifty from each religious grouping.
Data were collected through Spanish-language interviews in the informants' homes; responses of more than sí or no length may have
been transcribed in the text although Lennon nowhere indicates
this.

The abstract does not give separate statistics for data assembled for each of the sixteen items but the overall conclusion
is that the respondents "have generally low acculturation scores . . .
On a scale of 0-188 points, the respondents ranged from 39-123
points with a median score of 83.5 points." Both Protestant and
Roman Catholics "preferred Puerto Rican clergymen and church services in Spanish." [RT]

LEWIS, Oscar (with the assistance of Douglas Butterworth). A
    Study of Slum Culture: Backgrounds for La Vida. New York:
    Random House, 1968. xiv, 240 pp. (See Lewis 1965, 1969.)

In this book Lewis presents the sociological analysis and the
statistics concerning communities and individual informants that
the exclusively "narrative" format of La Vida prevented him from
presenting in that volume. Pp. 109-202 give "The New York Sample."
Language usage and attitudes are discussed there in two separate
sections: briefly on p. 159 (parental complaints about New York's
public schools, including their almost exclusive use of English in
classroom teaching), and more extensively on pp. 185-191 ("The
Use of English"). As a general rule, first-generation informants
"were very conservative in replacing Spanish with English," (185)
according to information from the self-administered questionnaire
and "spoke English only when the situation absolutely demanded it."
Second-generation children, however, "often used English among themselves, and the majority of their parents were concerned about
their offsprings' [sic] ignorance of Spanish. This was particularly
true of the written language." (189) Other matters such as patterns
in naming of children and ways of "getting around" the language
barrier are also discussed. [RT]

MA, Roxana and Eleanor Herasimchuk. "The Linguistic Dimensions of a Bilingual Neighborhood." In FISHM-1968/71: BBFinal Report 1968, pp. 636-835; rpt. in Fishman/BB 1971, 347-464 (Ch. 15), q.v. [Rev. Craddock 1973, pp. 307-309.] Roughly the last one-fourth of this item is reprinted in slightly revised form -- see especially the initial four paragraphs and the brief "conclusion" -- as "Speech Styles in Puerto Rican Bilingual Speakers: A Factor Analysis of Co-Variation of Phonological Variables," in <u>Advances in the Sociology of Language, Vol. 2: Selected Studies and Applications</u>. Contributions to the Sociology of Language No. 2, edited by Joshua A. Fishman (The Hague: Mouton, 1972), pp. 268-295. (Of the many off-shoots of Fishman's "Bilingualism in the Barrio" project, MA/HERA-1968/71/72 is the one most oriented toward linguistic concerns; we thus review it separately here.)

The authors chose the most notable deviations of Puerto Rican Spanish from Western Hemisphere "standard" Spanish and then plotted the relative frequency of each variable in five specific ways designed to call forth the full "repertoire range" of the informants: reading aloud from wordlists, reading paragraphs aloud, word naming (e.g., all words used on the job, at home, etc.), "careful" conversation, and then "casual" conversation. The "notable deviations" studied were syllable-final [r] and [s], the realizations of /rr/, intervocalic /d/, word-final /n/, and the nasalization of vowels in contact with nasal consonants.

This particular approach was chosen since "phonological variables have the advantage of high frequency of occurrence in spoken text, easy codability, fair immunity to conscious suppresion by the speaker, and wide-spread distribution throughout the speech community." (1968, p. 666) Craddock argues, however, that "in the case of Spanish, the 'fair immunity . . . ' seems open to dispute" (308) since its standard orthography provides a nearly unequivocal model for correct pronunciation; "for instance, the relatively high frequency of the standard realizations [r] and [s] for syllable-final /r/ and /s/ in reading aloud from wordlists (better than 60 per cent for [r] . . . and upwards of 80 per cent for [s] . . .) has surely been induced by the spelling the informants had before their eyes. It is not easy to see how this totally artificial 'context' could correlate to any actual speech environment." (ibid.)

Of nearly equal interest to the student of "transplanted" Puerto Rican speech are the summaries the authors give of each informant's linguistic history. One learns that in general the group most faithful to Hispanic speech traditions comes from the traditionally <u>jíbaro</u> villages of the Central Highlands of Puerto Rico; <u>costeños</u> assimilate more rapidly to Anglicization. [RT]

*MAYANS, Frank, Jr. "Puerto Rican Migrant Pupils in New York City Schools: A Comparison of the Effects of Two Methods of Instructional Grouping on English Mastery and Attitudes." PhD Diss., Columbia Univ., 1953. 83 pp. [DA 14 (1954) 68.]

  This work examines the effect of environment upon second language acquisition, specifically among recently-arrived Puerto Ricans entering their first continental school at junior high levels in East Harlem. The youngsters were divided into "vestibule" classes (separate [Puerto Rican] environments with concentrated English instruction) and "a more 'American' environment with a little formal English instruction [i.e., enrollment as "regular" pupils]." (abs.) All students were pre-tested and (at the end of the school year) post-tested for ability in English reading and oral vocabulary and attitude toward surroundings (test given in Spanish).
  Mayans found that the more favorably a migrant views his surroundings, the more English he will learn. The "regular" students came to view surroundings and schoolmates favorably while "vestibule" students experienced no change in attitude; "regulars" scored higher in all three tests of English mastery and therefore "being placed with English-speaking groups is superior to separation insofar as English gains are concerned." Mayans attributes the gains to a greater motivation to become part of the peer group; similarly the "regular" pupils "have made greater strides in becoming assimilated [and] speak English more often with their friends." But regular pupils disliked school more and did not make English reading gains consonant with gains in spoken English. Mayans conjectures that both trends reveal conformity to the "tough-guy" attitudes prevalent among the subjects' U.S.-born peers. [RT]

MILLS, C. Wright, Clarence Senior and Rose Kohn Goldsen. The Puerto Rican Journey: New York's Newest Migrants. New York: Harper Brothers, 1950. xi, 238 pp.

  Of the 101 sections in the questionnaire upon which this classic study was based (see Appendix I, pp. 205-217), only four dealt with language use or language attitudes; inevitably, then, language emerges as a relatively minor concern in this otherwise major volume. Page 98 mentions the troubles that arise when children learn English "and find that they hold a whip hand over the parents who speak only Spanish, or speak English brokenly;" pp. 118-120 give valuable statistics on media preferences. In the context of a broader discussion of Puerto Ricans and American racial attitudes the authors analyze the plight of the grifo (the fairly light-skinned mulato Puerto Rican) who "finds that if he learns English, he is even more likely to lose the slight advantage he holds in New York over the American Negro." (134) Subsequently discussed (136-138) is evidence for the growth of a pan-Hispanic consciousness among New York Puerto Ricans. Language use and degrees of knowledge of English are dealt with on pp. 141-145; one conclusion is that "the reluctance of those who know English well to use it frequently in public is considerable." (144) Pp. 200-202 (part of the "Notes and Sources" to Ch. 8) set forth the processes whereby statistics on language were obtained.

All of the study's several thousand immediate informants were first-generation New Yorkers. [RT]

*OXMAN, Wendy G. "The Effects of Ethnic Identity of Experimenter, Language of Experimental Task, and Bilingual vs. Non-Bilingual School Attendance on the Verbal Task Performance of Bilingual Children of Puerto Rican Background." PhD Diss., Fordham Univ., 1972. 98 pp. [_DA_ 33 (1972) 195-A.]

While this dissertation focusses largely on matters of minimal concern to persons not directly involved with issues of Zweisprachigkeitspedagogie, it nonetheless describes the relationship between the habitual language of a given domain and the ability of a bilingual to perform in the "other" language in that domain, i.e., in the one not generally associated with it. Specifically, Oxman (who tested the effects that a variety of language-use/ethnic-identity combinations would have on the "paired-associate learning tasks" performed by 256 fourth and fifth grade Spanish-English-speaking Puerto Rican youngsters in three types of New York City schools, full-bilingual, limited-bilingual and non-bilingual [English]) found that "the scores of pupils tested by Puerto Rican experimenters in the limited bilingual school and the comparable non-bilingual school were significantly lower in Spanish vs. English" and that "in the limited bilingual school, scores were lower in Spanish for non-Puerto Rican vs. Puerto Rican experimenters." (abs.) From this one concludes that language proficiency decreases as the "unnaturalness" of the situation increases; Oxman seems partly aware of this caveat when she notes that "effects of race or ethnic identity of experimenter may reflect distraction from a verbal task rather than an attitudinal factor such as alienation."

Beyond the scope of these pages is a full analysis of Oxman's central (to her) conclusion, one guaranteed to schock advocates of bilingual education and offer much grist for future mills: "Pupils attending the bilingual school with a full bilingual program, however, scored significantly lower than did pupils attending the school with the limited bilingual program or the comparable non-bilingual school, indicating the possibility of increased, rather than reduced alienation in full bilingual schools." [RT]

PADILLA, Elena. Up From Puerto Rico. New York: Columbia Univ.
Press, 1958. xiii, 317 pp.

Never intended to address itself primarily or even incidentally
to linguistic questions, this anthropological "case study" still
sheds considerable light on various aspects of New York City
Puerto Rican language behavior, and especially upon the attitudes
of the residents of "Eastville" (which one assumes to be Spanish
Harlem) towards language use and language choice. Especially
seminal though scattered references are found in ch. 6 ("Growing
Up in Eastville," pp. 161-211); ch. 2 ("The 'We Feeling' Among
Puerto Ricans") is crucial towards the understanding of local attitudes towards such concepts as Hispanic solidarity, the essence
of being Puerto Rican, etc. Some gleanings from Padilla's research
(conducted from 1954 through 1957 by a team of Columbia fieldworkers): "Part of the learning that a recent migrant has to
accomplish right away involves acquiring words and phrases in
Spanish currently used here and not in the island." (31) "The
children . . . soon realize that if they learn conversational
English their status in the family will improve. [A child] will
now be the interpreter . . . [and] may have to miss classes to
accompany his mother to hospitals and schools, and on errands that
require the services of an interpreter." (64) Padilla notes on
p. 199 the often ambivalent parental attitude towards their
children's acquisition of English, which is usually to the detri-
ment of their Spanish. She also notes that some public schools
would "make the bilingual children monitors or place them in other
positions of leadership, because they can be helpful not only to
the non-English-speaking students, but also to non-Spanish-speaking
school personnel in communication between the two." (201) [RT]

RAMOS-PERDA, Israel. "The School Adjustment of Return Migrant
Students in Puerto Rican Junior High Schools." PhD Diss.,
Univ. of Missouri, Columbia, 1972. 237 pp. [DA 34 (1973)
2045-A.]

As if the average Puerto Rican didn't have enough trouble ad-
justing to mainland life and the English language, we now learn
from this sociological study that an equally severe set of adjustment problems awaits adolescent Puerto Ricans who "return" to the
island for what is essentially the first time, after extended or
else exclusive mainland residence. Ramos surveyed an impressive
number of subjects in a multitude of island schools ("twenty-four
schools were in turn randomly selected from the eighty-five junior
high schools composing the fifteen [selected] school districts. . .
Data were obtained from 1069 return migrants and 904 non-migrant
students" [abs.]); all were tested for personal adjustment/self-
image/perception-of-school, as well as for their ability to read
Spanish. "As expected, the data revealed that more migrant than
non-migrant students were poorly adjusted to school." While

differences persisted even after the influence of social status and ability in Spanish were controlled, more poorly- than well-adjusted returnees "had experienced high residential mobility, long length of residence in the United States, low social status, and low ability in Spanish. The last was the most influential factor in explaining variation in the migrant's school adjustment. . . All of this indicated the need for nurturing the migrant's linguistic ability to speak, write, and understand Spanish." Ramos also stressed the need for more knowledge about "the nature and extent of this limitation" in Spanish. All in all, a telling argument for comprehensive bilingual education on the mainland. [RT]

*RIVERA, Carmen Elena. "Academic Achievement, Bicultural Attitudes and Self-Concepts of Pupils in Bilingual and Non-Bilingual Programs." Ph.D., Fordham Univ., 1973. 194 pp. [DA 34 (1973) 2238-2239-A.]

This dissertation's concern appears largely pedagogical; Rivera's chief conclusion is that third and fifth grade Puerto Ricans and non-Puerto Ricans both benefitted from (or at least were not retarded by) the bilingual schooling they received. But the following conclusion may stimulate linguists to consult the manuscript itself: "5. A residue of undetected language handicap was at the base of the difference in scores between the Hispanic of the experimental group and the non-Hispanic of the control group." (abs.) No elucidation accompanies this statement. [RT]

[RONCH, Judah. "Word Naming and Usage Scores for a Sample of Yiddish-English Bilinguals." 1968; 1969.] V.s. FISHM-1968/71, Ch. 12.

[SILVERMAN, Stuart H. [1969c.] "The Evaluation of Language Varieties." 1969. Abs. LLBA III-948.] V.s. FISHM-1968/71, Ch. 13.

[SILVERMAN, Stuart H. [1969b.] "A Method for Recording and Analyzing the Prosodic Features of Language." 1969. Abs. LLBA III-1217.] V.s. FISHM-1968/71 ("Project-Based Materials Not Included in BB 1971").

[TERRY, Charles E. and Robert L. Cooper. "A Note on the Perception and Production of Phonological Variation." 1969.] V.s. FISHM-1968/71, Ch. 13.

*WEISSMAN, Julius. "An Exploratory Study of Communication Patterns of Lower-Class Negro and Puerto Rican Mothers and Pre-School Children." EdD Diss., Columbia Univ., 1966. 136 pp. [<u>DA</u> 27 (1967) 3960-A.]

From the Abstract we learn that Weissman investigated "an assumption that lower-class family life was socializing passive behavior and lack of motivation for learning in the developmental growth of lower-class children." To that end various "pairs" of mothers and children were studied (both in the home and at Head Start centers) for verbal patterns "and such sensory modes as touch contacts, auditory, visual, and related forms of non-verbal communication patterns." These pairs were observed informally and also "under structured and task controlled conditions in the formal playing of games. There were taped recordings of the verbal communications during the playing of the games;" W makes no reference to the relative amounts of Spanish and English the Puerto Rican "pairs" employed, but a linguistic study of any available tapes would probably yield valuable information. The dissertation concludes that "Puerto Rican mother-child pairs are much more active in the home than in the school setting. . . . The Puerto Rican group had higher activity rates than the Negro group in such categories as 'teaching,' in the reenforcement of verbal praise, smiles, touch contacts, and related areas." [RT]

ZIRKEL, Perry Alan. "A Sociolinguistic Survey of Puerto Rican Parents in Connecticut." Paper Presented at the 15th Annual Meeting of the American Orthopsychiatric Association, New York, May 1973. 32 pp. (Available ERIC: ED 074 191.) [Annot. <u>RIE</u> (Jul 1973) 122.]

While this well-written report's chief purpose was to develope "a data base concerning the home background of Puerto Rican pupils as it relates to present and potential educational progress," (pp. 2-3) there is much here for sociologists of language as well. Some 218 families were surveyed in their homes; Zirkel's interview instrument (Appendix I) was an adaptation of the Hoffman <u>Bilingual Background Schedule</u> (1934) and of R.E. Mosley's <u>Attitude Toward Bilingualism Scale</u> (PhD Diss., 1969). Some sociolinguistic gleanings from the report:
Parents opted for interviews in Spanish in almost all instances. "In spite of the supposed English requirements in the economic domain, [22 to 37 per cent] of the parents used Spanish as the principal language" at work. (7) The immigrant (parental) generation remained strongly attached to the homeland: thus 90 per cent "aspired to eventually return to Puerto Rico, and an even greater majority (98.9 per cent) had such aspirations for their children." (8) Trends in language proficiency and dominance reflect time-honored patterns: while self-ratings showed the parents' "relatively limited abilities in English," their offspring's ratings "revealed

a greater tendency toward bilingualism, favoring Spanish in oral skills and English in written skills," (9) the latter a likely product of the school milieu. While overall there was a "gradual movement toward English, reflecting the length of mainland residence and schooling," (10) for the present "a definite degree of Spanish dominance in the home environment" was the rule. Furthermore "the various measures of parental attitudes toward bilingualism and bilingual/bicultural education revealed an overwhelming majority of the parents to be clearly in favor of both." (12) [RT]

9.2.2 TEXTBOOKS

Major Items: (none)

See also these items elsewhere (consult Author Index for location):

(none)

BOMSE, Marguerite D. and Julián H. Alfaro. Practical Spanish for Medical and Hospital Personnel. Elmsford, New York: Pergamon Press, 1973. 176 pp.

_____. Practical Spanish for School Personnel, Firemen, Policemen and Community Agencies. Elmsford, New York: Pergamon Press, 1973. vi, 165 pp.

These two texts have been used "at Staten Island Community College in classes in child care and community assistant programs, as well as in classes for policemen, firemen and professionals dealing with the Spanish-speaking community" (to quote from the Foreword of the second volume). While nowhere do the authors specify that their situational dialogues ("El maestro/La maestra en clase," "Instrucciones para los padres," "Vivienda: quejas," "El incendio," etc.) deliberately followed Puerto Rican and Cuban models, one concludes this from the various answers to the question "Dónde nació Ud." (passim); furthermore the authors claim to be presenting "authentic spoken Spanish, recorded from the conversation of people engaged in their daily work." But persons who anticipate rich veins of "Spanglish" here will be disappointed, since for the most part the authors eschew Anglicized Spanish and present the sort of vocabulary and constructions that one would expect to hear in any part of the Hispanic world; as an example one notes the systematic avoidance of the word aplicación as sense loan of Eng. application; solicitud is consistently used instead. Occasionally, though, one finds a more "authentic" New York-type dialogue, as on p. 48 of vol. 2, "Policía: tráfico," in which an officer asks to see a driver's licencia and, after giving him a ticket because "Ud. no paró en la señal de Stop," indicates that the offender "Tendrá que comparecer en la Corte" because the fact that he did not see the stop-sign "no es excusa." [RT]

9.3 SPANISH PHONOLOGY (includes ORTHOGRAPHY)

Major Items: DECK-1952

See also these items elsewhere (consult Author Index for location):

LEAV-1969; MA/HERA-1968/71/72

DECKER, Bob Dan. "Phonology of the Puerto Rican Spanish of Lorain, Ohio: A Study in the Environmental Displacement of a Dialect." MA Thesis, Ohio State Univ., 1952. 173 pp.

Directed by Prof. Stanley Sapon, this capably executed thesis is the most thorough-going descriptive study we possess of any one brand of mainland Puerto Rican Spanish segmental phonation (though in general the topic has received little attention). Decker interviewed each of fourteen recent migrants to Lorain (a city near Cleveland) for fifteen minutes, for the most part following the questionnaires and the methodology of Tomás Navarro Tomás, with whose findings Decker constantly compares his own data. Informants were asked to describe pictures, read word lists and longer prose selections, etc., and did not engage in free conversation. All material was taped, though not subjected to machine analysis.

Allophonic variations are discussed in detail on pp. 81-152; each discussion is accompanied by charts showing incidence of variant production per individual informant. Among Decker's many conclusions (153-170): "Only four phenomena occurred in enough subjects to be considered true characteristics of [Lorain PR Spanish] rather than individual Puerto Ricans of the area examined: . . . common usage of closed palatal a, excessive use of open e, the use of open o where [standard Castilian Spanish] requires that it be closed, and the aspiration of final -s . . . . All other phenomena must be considered tendencies or potentialities [of the dialect]." (156-157) Among these "secondary characteristics" are [ey] for /e/, devoiced word-final vowels after voiceless consonants, actual use of [θ] for orthographic z, c /$\frac{e}{i}$ (most informants hailed from western interior Puerto Rican and especially the town of Lares; none was born in Spain), "lambdacism (not entirely restricted to r)" (170; see also 113-119 for a thorough treatment), and confusion of occlusives. Nine lesser tendencies (such as failure to fricativize /d/ in the usual environments) and a "partial" list of nineteen isolated traits at variance with the findings of Navarro Tomás are also presented.

While the brevity of the interviews and the relatively few informants tend to vitiate the author's claims as to the birth of a "new" dialect of Puerto Rican Spanish on the shores of Lake Erie, this thesis is nonetheless well worth consulting for the wealth of idiolectal detail it has amassed with such exemplary thoroughness. [RT]

9.4 SPANISH GRAMMAR (MORPHOLOGY AND SYNTAX)

Major Items: (none)

See also these items elsewhere (consult Author Index for location):

JESU-1952; KELL-1974; and especially ANAS/JESU-1953

GUMPERZ, John J. "On the Linguistic Markers of Bilingual Communication." JSI 23:2.48-55 (April 1967). [Abs. LLBA II-225.]

Chiefly concerned with methods of analyzing the theoretical problems of the world's Sprachbunde, Gumperz takes most of his examples from the languages of the Indian subcontinent but towards the end of the article (p. 55) he devotes several paragraphs to "New York Spanish-English" as a case study similarly illustrative of the progressive approximation of element-ordering which languages in India, the Balkans and elsewhere have experienced over the centuries. Gumperz admits that while the particular period of Spanish-English contact has hardly equalled the length of that experienced by, say, Kannada-Marathi, an alignment of syntactical structures is beginning to take place nonetheless. While one cannot disagree that New York City Puerto Rican Spanish increasingly prefers the periphrastic future to the synthetic (vamos a comer vs. comeremos--likewise a feature of other U.S. Spanish dialects but also of popular Spanish in general and thus not necessarily the product of English influence), it is very difficult to accept (as Gumperz does) the notion that in NYC Puerto Rican Spanish "the only subjunctive form which occurs with any frequency is the conditional which serves as the direct translation equivalent of English constructions with 'would.'" Gumperz ascribes this statement to no specific source; few Hispanists would accept it without direct evidence. [RT]

*PETERS, Daniel I. "A Contrastive Analysis of Selected English and Spanish Written Verb Forms Which Present Difficulty to Native Speakers of Spanish." PhD Diss., New York Univ., 1973. 109 pp. [DA 34 (1973) 3377-A.]

Undertaken "for the purpose of segregating the specific learning problems in English verb phrases that the Puerto Rican senior high school student may experience," (abs.) Peters' examples were all taken from 343 student compositions written in English. Following a preliminary analysis of "the structural differences between English and Spanish verb phrases . . . with regard to tenses, tense sequence, aspect, auxiliary verbs (have, do and be), be as a past participle, the modal would, and verb forms in the present tense," Peters attempted ("using a variety of generative transformational models") to explain why the students made the errors they did. His conclusion is that "this contrastive analysis

was not sufficiently effective in pinpointing specific reasons
for the verb phrase errors committed," and that "claims as to the
universal applicability of contrastive analysis must be substantiated by analyses of many more of the world's languages." Word
from the dissertation's director (Prof. Harvey Nadler of NYU's
School of Education) is that the work includes samples of the
student errors analyzed. [RT]

9.5 SPANISH LEXICON (includes SEMANTICS)

Major Items: (none)

See also these items elsewhere (consult Author Index for location):

ROSA-1969

HAMILTON. Carlos D. "Amenazas contra el español en Estados Unidos."
EspAct 19.23-25 (Oct. 1971).

Prof. Hamilton of Brooklyn College protests vigorously against
the abortive course in "Spanglish" which was offered briefly in
New York by the New School for Social Research. (For ancillary
information on this same course see Varo 1971, Fernández 1972).
Along the way Hamilton gives examples of the "Spanglish" lexicon
being dutifully memorized by the New School's students: rufo,
norsa, jobecito, marqueta, grocería and so forth. Hamilton is
convinced that this "well-meaning attempt to communicate" with New
York Puerto Ricans is just one more example of Anglo-Saxon patronage; he concludes: "De modo que toda la lucha de negros y porto-
rriqueños por alcanzar una educación pareja a la de los estudiantes
de otros orígenes étnicos . . . va a terminar en que se les vuelva
a 'enseñar' el 'Black English' y el 'Spanglish' que ya farfullaban
natural y espontáneamente en el barrio." (p. 24) [RT]

THOMAS, Piri. Down These Mean Streets. New York: Alfred A.
Knopf, 1967. xiii, 333 pp. (Glossary pp. 332-333.)

Standard Spanish words comprise the majority of ca. 125 entries
in the Glossary but one does find occasional terms that appear to
stand out as regional and perhaps peculiar to New York City argot,
e.g., coquís 'crickets,' cura 'shot of heroin,' embalao 'strung out
on drugs,' guiso 'angle [i.e., trick; pull, in (n.)].' The work
itself is the autobiography of a dark-skinned New York-born Puerto
Rican whose tempestuous life in the underworld of drugs is vividly
depicted. Language per se is nowhere discussed. [RT]

9.7 ENGLISH INFLUENCE ON SPANISH

Major Items: KREI-1957

See also these items elsewhere (consult Author Index for location):

FERNA-1972; GUMP-1967

CRAIG, Colette Grinevald. "La situation linguistique de la communauté Porto-ricaine de Cambridge, Massachusetts." MA Thesis ["mémoire de maîtrise"], Univ. de Paris-Nanterre [Fac. des Lettres], 1969. 105 pp. [Annot. Haugen 1973 (CTL 10) 2.2.]

Americans wanting to consult this thesis will find the task difficult if not impossible; I myself am indebted to Prof. Einar Haugen for lending me his personal copy. The thesis was directed by Bernard Pottier and deals for the most part with sociology, ethno-linguistic history (of Puerto Rico) and sociolinguistics, as the titles of chapters 2-5 will show: "La communauté de Cambridge," "Originalités de la Situation Linguistique des Porto-ricains aux U.S.A.," "La Situation Linguistique de Puerto-Rico," "Généralités Linguistiques de la Communauté de Cambridge." Chapter 4 often relies on the largely second-hand information of Germán de Granda (Transculturación e interferencia lingüística en el Puerto Rico contemporáneo [Río Piedras: 1969]). The brief Ch. 1 describes the methods of data collection; Craig first contacted and then administered a questionnaire (not reproduced) to 223 persons, 194 of them Puerto Ricans (the remainder Cubans, Dominicans, Guatemalans and "others"). Of the 223, 64 were chosen for Spanish-language oral interviews of a half an hour at least; since the interviews' purpose was chiefly sociological the questions appear oriented towards statistics. In very general terms, Craig concludes that a typical young mainland Puerto Rican requires about half a generation to enter the mainstream of language shift, and that as a rule, in the spoken Spanish of Cambridge "L'accumulation d'anglicismes n'est modérée par aucun frein." (p. 58) This is because "La conscience linguistique des Porto-Ricains reste limitée par leur attitude d'inhibition passive et d'acceptation, symptômes d'un complexe sensible d'infériorité linguistique." (ibid.)

Language itself is dealt with in the final two full chapters (6, pp. 57-77 and 7, pp. 78-97), essentially in the manner of Haugen's treatment of The Norwegian Language in America (1953). C's "interférences léxicales" are presented in narrative style according to category of topical reference ("Pour le petit déjeuner, el breakfast, ils mangent des cereals des chirios et des cornflakes et boivent du lait écrèmé el skim milk. Avant de déjeuner, lonchear, ils on . . . " [59]); there follows a more formal analysis of borrowing patterns (67-72). Next is a discussion of phonetic interference, which C finds almost non-existent and thus easy to examine descriptively ("[Les voyelles anglaises] sont assimilées

aux voyelles espagnoles les plus proches du point de vue ouverture
et localisation" [75]). Morphological miscellany appear on pp.
78-84 and syntactical Anglicisms subsequently; C gives a commendable discussion of the mainland Puerto Rican tendency to calque
many BE + past participle constructions according to their original English models and to prefer ser over estar in the process:

("las comidas son preparadas saludablemente con sus propios jugos
naturales" 'las comidas se preparan . . . ,' "aa actriz es paseada
por la factoría donde trabaja. Sus demandas son acogidas con
ferbor por sus compañeras"); other calques and putative English inroads such as the overuse of hacer + N (hacer el disparo rather than
disparar, but cf. English 'to shoot,' not *to make a shot), the
loss of obligatory conjunctive que, the deterioration of number/
gender agreement ("La paz podría muy bien ser seguido de una guerra"
--the latter taken from the New York daily El Tiempo) are also
dealt with competently. [RT]

KREIDLER, Charles W. "A Study of the Influence of English on the
    Spanish of Puerto Ricans in Jersey City, New Jersey." PhD
    Diss., Univ. of Michigan, Ann Arbor, 1957. 182 pp. [DA
    19 (1958) 527-528.] [Annot. HLAS 22 (1960) no. 4324 (D. Wogan);
    Craddock 1973 pp. 309-310.]

Kreidler's study is based on semi-guided interviews with thirty
persons ranging in age from adolescence to "over 50" and all born
in Puerto Rico; the majority had not lived on the continent for
more than five years. Operating within the structuralist bilingual
approach of Einar Haugen 1956 (The Norwegian Language in America)
and Uriel Weinreich 1953 (Languages in Contact), Kreidler was primarily interested in collecting a maximal list of English loanwords
and sense loans/loanshifts; as a consequence the questionnaire
which formed the heart of the interviews (Appendix B) is strongly
oriented towards the largely-unaccustomed artefacts and circumstances of the immigrant's new environment: the apartment building,
winter clothing, the factory job, the automobile, the world of
sports, etc.

Following a description of the local sociocultural setting
(as a means of selecting his thirty informants the author personally visited seventy Jersey City households) and a good encapsulation of the phonemes of Puerto Rican Spanish and American English,
Kreidler analyzes first the phonological (Ch. 5) and then the
morphological adaptation of his 228 borrowings (Ch. 6); Ch. 7 provides a "Semantic Classification of Borrowings." By way of
general conclusion he remarks that the phonological Hispanization
of the loanwords is progressively greater as the individual informant's knowledge of English decreases, and that by the same
token the adoption of an English phoneme is less frequent than is
its substitution (with an equivalent Spanish sound). [RT]

PORGES, Ana. "The Influence of English on the Spanish of New York City." MA Thesis, Univ. of Florida, 1949. iii, 38 pp.

More than 150 items (chiefly Anglicisms) which appeared for the most part in eight Puerto Rican newspapers and magazines are arranged here according to topic and presented not as dictionary entires but as part of a series of "narratives" which tell the reader as much about daily life and social conditions in the barrios boricuas during the first years of mass immigration as they do about the lexicon itself ("To the average Puerto Rican migrant, coming from a slum area or a remote mountain village, even a squalid New York tenement may have its attractions. It is a unique experience to sleep on el caucho provided with un matres. After he arises in the morning he pulls up el shade . . . His wife may go up on el ruf to shake out el mop since she wants to 'mopear la casa'. . . after which she will sweep la carpeta and dust la furnitura [p. 3]"). Porges limits her entries to items "not found in" the 16th (1939) edition of the DRAE or in F.J. Santamaría's dictionary of Americanisms. Her chapter titles include: "Daily Life," "Current Events in Spanish Newspapers" and "Advertisements" (both followed by two pages of direct quotations, mostly from La Prensa), "Entertainment" and "Sports." Pp. 31-37 list all lexical items alphabetically.

In her "Introduction" (i-iii) Porges explains how English elements enter New York Spanish so massively and expresses chagrin that this is so; these sentiments perhaps account for a certain overzealousness in judging an item Anglicized: thus some perfectly Hispanic forms such as algo de inglés, desoír, asalto, dramaticismo, incogible, lanzamiento del martillo, secuencias, supermercado and others are found alongside such curious and clearly English-derived entries as yopesito 'little job,' jolopear 'to stop by force in order to rob,' cuarto furnido 'furnished room,' etc. [RT]

ROSA-NIEVES, Cesáreo. "El español de Puerto Rico en Nueva York." BAACPR 5.519-529 (1969).

Another collection of the Anglicisms (perhaps 100) and the lexical miscellany that the observer has noted "in use" by Puerto Ricans in New York City. The findings are presented anecdotally and unsystematically but are usually accompanied by brief definitions (or ready equivalents) and by English etyma. As set forth on pp. 520-521 R's classification scheme is fourfold: (1) "los anglicismos violentos (palabras, oraciones y frases), traídos al español . . . a las bravas;" (2) "la mezcla de palabras hispanas con el inglés coloquial" (usually shop-names such as García Garage, Carmita Beauty Salón); (3) "los neologismos," i.e., non-borrowed forms, many already common in Puerto Rico and elsewhere (pisa y corre 'guaguita pequeña,' rajarse); and (4) "los nombres de personas y animales," many taken straight from English. The most

voluminous of these is category no. 1, which contains many old
friends: jolopero 'persona que hace atracos,' pari, chou, wikén,
fornido, marqueta . . . ; fn. 1 on p. 522 lists several English
loanwords the author has observed in New York Cuban Spanish. Only
two errors were noted: jara 'policía,' a form R claims as English
but for which no etymology is attempted (see Trejo 1968 p. 102;
the word is probably "del gitano" or else [our own suggestion] des-
cends synecdochically from jara [originally Arabic] 'palo de punta
aguzada y endurecido al fuego, que se emplea como arma arrojadiza');
and the much more obvious "donas (de donnas [sic])" 'doughnuts.'
R concludes that "dentro de algunos siglos, ese fermento hispano-
yanqui, se convertirá en una lengua neoboricua en los futuros
hombres nuevos." (529) [RT]

SECADES, Eladio. "El Spanglish, ... ¡qué horror!" ABC de las
  Américas 6.53 (11-17 noviembre, 1972). [TSBJr.]

The inevitable and by now traditional grito de alarme against
English Contamination of Spanish (New York's, in this case, and
although the author nowhere makes specific reference to the Puerto
Rican variety one recognizes quickly the dozens of Anglicisms that
have come to "typify" it such as rufo 'techo,' carpeta 'alfombra,'
grosería 'albarrotería/bodega' et al). While much of what Secades
presents is déjà vu for connoisseurs, occasional examples are
newsworthy, e.g., frisarse 'morirse de frío,' ringar 'sonar [un
teléfono],' the Anglicized syntax of street names (la cuarentiocho
calle) and so forth; one or two examples are uproarious but hopefully apochryphal: "Y si llueve, se oye también la demanda angus-
tiosa de la madre criolla que desde la ventana llama al hijo:
'Sube, Johnny, que está reinando.'" [RT]

9.8.1 ENGLISH OF THIS PARTICULAR HISPANIC GROUP

Major Items: SHIEL-1972; WOLFR-1972b; WOLFR-1973; WOLFR/et al-1971

See also these items elsewhere (consult Author Index for location):

  (none)

*KANDELL, Alice Susan. "Harlem Children's Stories: A Study of
  Expectations of Negro and Puerto Rican Boys in Two Reading-
  level Groups." EdD Diss., Harvard Univ., 1967. 184 pp. [DA
  28 (1967) 2338-A.]

In no sense can the abstract of this dissertation be interpreted to show a focus on language, but it may be of interest to
linguists if the author includes portions of the transcribed
stories of the Puerto Rican youngsters (who appear to have been
speaking in English throughout); in all other respects this is a
study of child attitudes. K used a "projective test technique com-

bined with a direct questionnaire technique" to elicit the boys'
"expectations and feelings about their capacity to master tasks
in school and in general life situations, their teachers, their
school and home environment, their mothers and father, and their
peers." Thirty informants were Puerto Rican, thirty black.
"Content analysis of the stories they told and responses they
gave revealed significantly more negative expectations and themes
for Negro boys than for Puerto Rican boys . . ." [RT]

KINDIG, Maita M. "A Phonological Study of the English Speech of
    Selected Speakers of Puerto Rican Spanish in Honolulu." MA
    Thesis, Univ. of Hawaii, 1960. iv, 211 pp.

   A well-handled structuralist study of all aspects of the
English phonology the writer obtained from "fifteen informants of
Puerto Rican-Spanish Language background . . . three each in five
families, representing three generations." (p. 12) K gives inventories and then analyses of "sound deviations," offers information on intonational as well as "idiomatic" variations
(chiefly an inventory of miscellaneous non-standard lexemes from
various sources), and devotes much space to informants' biographies
and transcriptions of the "free conversations" largely on topics
culinary or musical). Chapter 9 presents conclusions, in particular the correlations between the informants' English and Puerto
Rican Spanish but also between the former and "Hawaiian dialect,"
a de-creolized and increasingly Anglo-standardized reflex of the
once widely-spoken Hawaiian Pidgin English.
   Few of K's conclusions are new; she notes for example that
"The general PR tendency to weaken, aspirate, or omit syllable-
final /s/ is noticeable in both the Spanish and English used by
the informants," (157) and that "the influence from Spanish sounds
is considerable in the first generation, joined by influence from
Hawaiian dialect in the second, and absent from the third generation except in loan words [from Spanish]." (197)

*MARTÍNEZ, Antonio J. "An Analysis of the Present Status of the
    Teaching of English as a Second Language to Puerto Rican
    Adults in New York City." EdD Diss., New York Univ., 1970.
    226 pp. [DA 31 (1971) 5749-A.]

   The abstract informas us that data for this study were collected through questionnaires and by direct observation of 30 teachers
randomly selected from the five programs examined intensively. M
concludes that the main goal of most programs is "to increase the
English language proficiency of Spanish-speaking adults;" one thus
assumes that many students were at least partly bilingual before
enrollment. Only two of the five programs use "testing instruments
specifically designed for placing adult students . . . at different
levels of proficiency." Some facts about the teachers: 75 per
cent are native speakers of English, 20 per cent native Spanish
speakers; a depressing 55 per cent have never taken college courses

in linguistics or courses directly related to TESL; 56 per cent
said they favor "the audio-lingual method," and roughly the same
percentage of texts had an audio-lingual orientation. [RT]

*SHIELS, Marie. "Dialects in Contact: A Sociolinguistic Analysis
 of Four Phonological Variables of Puerto Rican English and
 Black English in Harlem." PhD Diss., Georgetown Univ., 1972.
 270 pp. [DA 32 (1972) 6959-A.]

From the Abstract we learn that Shiels has worked from "tape
recordings of informal interviews with forty-three adolescent boys"
and has analyzed four phonological variables: "AI, -ING, consonant
cluster simplification, and R." While "the use of Spanish in daily
communication is generally preserved, contact with the larger surrounding black community makes homogeneity of Puerto Rican contact
impossible [and thus] tends to foster assimilation of the Puerto
Ricans." Not surprisingly the English of the second-generation
Puerto Rican adolescents with the greatest black contact most
closely approximates black pronunciation; Puerto Ricans with
minimal black contact show less black assimilation. Both Puerto
Rican groups handle R in the same way, however, "thus approximating
what has been described in previous sociolinguistic study as typical
of Nonstandard Negro English, and distinct from Standard English
and White Nonstandard English. The variable R therefore appears
to be an example of nearly complete Puerto Rican assimilation to
black speech patterns." Faut du texte, one accepts this statement
on faith, but the curious will want to consult Shiels directly to
discover what she means by "White Nonstandard English" renditions
of R in order to learn how "black R" differs from New York City
working-class white "R-less" R, since if the two are indistinguish-
able then Puerto Rican replicas of that R would not, in themselves,
prove assimilation to black speech patterns. [RT]

*SILVERMAN, Stuart H. "The Effects of Peer Group Membership on
 Puerto Rican English." PhD Diss., Yeshiva Univ., 1971. 113
 pp. [DA 32 (1972) 5621-A.]

Another dissertation which quantifies the concept that Puerto
Ricans with significant numbers of black associates will come to
approximate black speech patterns. (See also Shiels 1972.)
Adolescent Puerto Ricans with black friends, without black friends,
and various blacks themselves were measured for linguistic negri-
tude "under five different Elicitation Procedures (Conversation,
Paragraph Reading, Word List, Minimal Pairs-Sentences and Minimal
Pairs-List);" for nine of the variables (which are not specified
in the Abstract) Puerto Ricans with black friends sounded significantly blacker than did their atrophobic co-ethnics; indeed they
actually surpassed blacks themselves in the production of black
forms. Silverman indicates his results "were discussed mainly in
terms of their implications for education. . . [Having] society

accept non-standard varieties of English may be more desirable
than having non-standard speakers learn the standard variety"
since in order for the latter to come about, friendship patterns
would have to be disrupted, he suggests. [RT]

WILLIAMS, George. "Some Errors in English by Spanish-Speaking
 Puerto Rican Children." In Language Research Report No. 6,
 Cambridge, Mass.: Language Research Foundation, 1972, pp.
 85-102. (Solely available through ERIC:ED 061 850.)

 This is a careful description of "the range of errors in the
spontaneous speech of [six] Puerto Rican children of intermediate
English ability" which devotes primary attention to "common pronunciation problems, many attributed to the influence of Spanish"
and also deals with unsystematic substitution of [a] for [ʌ] and
[ae]; universal absence of the "prothetic /e/" before /sC/ clusters
(e.g., all informants rendered school as [sku(1)]; vocalization
(to [U]) of English velar /l/; "the pronunciation of /r/ [as in]
English, usually even exaggeratedly so" (89); word-final stops
which "may be replaced by /h/ or by a glottal stop" (92), this
latter a small part of "the range of things which happen to word-
final obstruents [and which constitute] perhaps the most pervasive
non-native consonantal aspect" of the children's speech. Word-
final reduction affects verbal morphology in well-known ways: say
for says, use for used, did for did not, etc. While "less fluent
pupils used Spanish negation exclusively ['he no wanna go']" (98),
the more fluent ones employed the DO supports that accompany
English negations, though with a reduction of the cluster ('he
brother di' finish it'). [RT]

WOLFRAM, Walt. [1972a]. "Linguistic Assimilation in the Children
 of Immigrants." LRep 14:1.1-3 (Jan. 1972). [Abs. LLBA 6.7
 6.7204172.]

 Sums up the more salient conclusions of Wolfram et al. 1971
and Wolfram 1972b. [RT]

WOLFRAM, Walt. [1972b]. "Overlapping Influence and Linguistic
 Assimilation in Second Generation Puerto Rican English [PRE]."
 In Sociolinguistics in Cross-Cultural Analysis, edited by
 David M. Smith and Roger W. Shuy. Washington D.C.: Georgetown
 Univ. Press, 1972. Pp. 15-46. (Discussion of Wolfram on pp.
 104-105, 120 and 126-127 by Dell Hymes, Alfred E. Opubor and
 A.B. Hudson, resp.) (Wolfram 1972 can also be obtained through
 EDRS: ED 057 6650. Annot. RIE 7:4.58 [April 1972].)

 This carefully-wrought study of several phonological and grammatical features of the English of 29 Puerto Rican Teenage males
of generally below-average educational achievement (several were
functionally illiterate) from lower- or poverty-class families in
New York's East Harlem and South Bronx neighborhoods has sought to

quantify the extent to which PRE traits are the products of
Spanish interference or Black English contact. Specifically
examined were the youths' renditions of /θ/ and /d/ in morpheme-
final position. (Fifteen New York City black teenagers were also
tested for these features.) Strict attention was paid to incidence
of realization and to peer associations of the informants. W does
not differ from Shiels 1972, Silverman 1971 and others in section
9.8.1 of this Bibliography with respect to the conclusion that
the largest number of black features are found in the English of
Puerto Ricans associating frequently with blacks. Morpheme-final
/θ/, for example, was realized by PRE speakers 44.8 per cent of
the time as [f] (clearly a black trait), 39.2 per cent as standard
[θ], 12.6 per cent as ∅, i.e., "no phonetic realization or an
assimilated fricative such as [f], [s] or [s]" (?) (Table 1, p. 19),
and 3.5 per cent as "[s] or [z] when not followed by a sibilant."
(ibid.) W correctly assigns the [s] variant as "a case of vestigial interference" from Spanish but apparently does not investigate
or consider the possibility that ∅ or "assimilation" may also be
an interference product, inasmuch as the aspiration or deletion
of morpheme-final /s/ is the rule in Puerto Rican Spanish (W's explanation of ∅ is that PRE "simply shares the assimilation rule
for morpheme-final //θ// that exists for standard and other nonstandard varieties of English" [22]). Not surprisingly, PRE
speakers with extensive black contacts rendered [f] for /θ/ at
roughly twice the rate of PRE speakers with limited black contacts
(see Table 3, p. 24), although even the former group did not equal
the black production of [f] (76.6 per cent of all utterances). The
deletion of /d/, however, was "considerably more frequent in the
speech of Puerto Ricans than Blacks;" (29) this circumstance is discussed in terms of grammatical function (e.g., -ed as in treated)
vs. nongrammatical (e.g., head, dead) on pp. 24-31, and while
Wolfram posits vestigial Spanish interference as one explanation
for this, he nonetheless asserts in a general discussion of interference that "the interference variants so characteristic of first
generation Puerto Rican immigrants learning English are of minimal
significance in the speech of the second generation [and that]
straight-forward interference has not become habitualized" in that
speech. (32) Other influences are at work in PRE as well: "For
example, some speakers of PRE with restricted Black contacts show
ARE copula absence (e.g. You nice, They nice) as an integral part
of their dialect but show little or no incidence of IS deletion
(e.g. He nice). For these speakers, it seems reasonable to hypo-
thesize that ARE deletion may be related to the r-lessness which
is quite typical of both Black and white speech in New York City."
(39) Also discussed is the tendency of some PRE speakers to mark
tense pleonastically in negative sentences containing the auxiliary
didn't; this is shown to be based initially upon an analogy with
the Spanish tense marking scheme ("He no ate the food"), retained
intact with the acquisition of English didn't (thus 'He didn't
ate the food;' see pp. 40-42). [RT]

WOLFRAM, Walt. "Objective and Subjective Parameters of Language Assimilation Among Second-Generation Puerto Ricans in East Harlem." In <u>Language Attitudes: Current Trends and Prospects</u>, edited by Roger W. Shuy and Ralph W. Fasold. Washington D.C.: Georgetown Univ. Press, 1973. Pp. 148-173.

This high-quality article is based on data first presented in Wolfram 1971, and continues Wolfram 1972's analysis of linguistic and sociolinguistic material elicited from 29 Puerto Rican and 15 black teenage males. Wolfram 1973 is divided three ways. Part One adds to what we know about differing Puerto Rican assimilations to black English: additional features consistently appearing in the English of Puerto Rican teenagers with extensive black contacts (PR/BL's) are [a] for diphthong /ay/ (Table 2, p. 154) and "distributive <u>be</u>" (e.g., 'Sometimes he be at home; I know he do' [155]; see Table 3, 156). Part Two reports on variant perceptions of the black verbal jousting known as "sounding;" again it appears that PR/BL's have largely assimilated "the informal rules and cultural function of this verbal activity," (162) while familiarity with "sounding" was mostly passive among those with restricted black contacts. Part Three (165-171) informs as to "subjective level of language assimilation;" here the reportage becomes especially insightful and of major value to all students of mainland Puerto Rican language and sociolinguistic attitudes. In essence the second generation of East Harlem's Puerto Ricans appears to differ regarding relationships with blacks. Wolfram's PR/BL's clearly sought to minimize all differences (including linguistic) between themselves and blacks; this was not the case with those whose black contacts were limited. For the first group "assimilation is largely one-way; it is the Puerto Ricans who are copying the blacks. Black teen-agers do not pick up aspects of Puerto Rican English which might identify them as being Puerto Rican, such as occasional syllable-timing, the tendency not to reduce vowels in unstressed syllables, and so forth." (168)

For the most part among the first or immigrant generation "it is considered inappropriate for children to answer parents in English at all. To speak to parents in a dialect of English that is discernibly influenced by Black English is to elicit an even stronger reaction on the part of parents." (171) As one informant puts it: "'[My father] won't take it in English. I have to answer him in Spanish 'cause he says I'm not an Italian and I'm not a Negro, but I'm a Puerto Rican and have to speak to me in my language. . . . So if we speak English . . . it's like cursing right in front of him.'" (ibid.) [RT]

*WOLFRAM, Walt, Marie E. Shiels and Ralph W. Fasold. Overlapping
Influence in the English of Second Generation Puerto Rican
Teenagers in Harlem. Final Report, Office of Education (Dept.
of HEW), Washington, D.C. Cooperative Research Program,
Grant No. OEG-3-70-0033(508) (1971). 460 pp. (Available
ERIC:ED 060 159.) [Annot. RIE 7:6.106 (June 1972).] (For
more readily accessible studies based on the material see
Wolfram 1972, Wolfram 1973 and Shiels 1972.)

(From the RIE abstract:) "This research is an attempt to determine the relative influence of Black English and Puerto Rican Spanish in the speech of Puerto Ricans raised contiguous to the black community in Harlem. The first chapter provides a general introduction to the study of this variety of Puerto Rican English and a description of the sample on which this study is based. In Chapter Two, a general socio-cultural picture of various aspects of the Puerto Rican community is given, particularly as it relates to the surrounding black community. A number of selected variables in Puerto Rican English are examined in Chapter Three, building on the descriptive framework of variable rules in generative-transformational grammar. Chapter Four deals with the assimilation of linguistic features from Black English in three groups within the continuum of second generation Puerto Rican speakers in Harlem. The final chapter consists of a nontechnical description of the differences between Puerto Rican English and Standard English among second generation Puerto Ricans in Harlem, intended as a practical guide for educators . . . " [RT]

SECTION 10 (CUBANS)

10.1 BIBLIOGRAPHY

Major Items: (none)

See also these items elsewhere (consult Author Index for location): (none)

LÓPEZ MORALES, Humberto. "El español de Cuba: situación bibliográfica." RFE 51.111-137 (1968).

The author indicates that the interviewing for the Havana part of the on-going PILEI-sponsored study of "la norma culta del español hablado en las [diez] grandes ciudades del mundo hispánico" is being done in Miami, where "se han utilizado refugiados políticos recién llegados . . . con límites de permanencia [en Miami] entre unas horas--en muchos de los casos--y tres meses, para evitar la más mínima posibilidad de interferencia." (p. 131, fn. 1) Except for this on-going study, just one other work on the Spanish of the Cuban exiles is listed (Castellanos 1968), since at the time of compilation there were no other works.
The PILEI Miami/Havana project is mentioned on these pages because it is the first attempt known to us to interview immigrants who are literally "just off the boat" (or plane); see also Vallejo 1970 for a full-length study of the same population group. Thus to determine the changes wrought by a decade or more in Miami, future research might well interview the same individuals. [RT]

10.2 COMPREHENSIVE/GENERAL STUDIES; MISCELLANY; ANTHOLOGIES/FESTSCHRIFTEN

Major Items: (none)

See also these items elsewhere (consult Author Index for location):

FERN-F-1965; JACK-1952; REYN/HOUC-1971

*GOMULA, Wanda Wallace. "Common Patterns of Nonverbal Behavior Among Selected Cuban and Anglo Children." EdD Diss., Indiana Univ., Bloomington, 1973. 159 pp. [DA 34 (1974) 4957-A.]

"The specific nonverbal areas investigated were cultural uses of time, territory boundaries, and body language, as shown through gross body movements, hand gestures, facial responses, and eye contacts." (Abstract) Gomula's subjects were Anglo and Cuban elementary students in Miami. Non-verbally oriented stimulus/response lessons were "taught by the researcher to both groups" and were simultaneously videotaped for later analysis. Among the ethnicity-specific kinesic traits: "The Cuban pupils reached out and touched the teacher more frequently than the Anglo pupils [and] used hand

gestures with words and/or in place of words more frequently
than the Anglo pupils." Among Cubans it appears that teacher-
student eye contact indicates that a friendly relationship has
been established whereas the absence of eye contact is utilized
as "either a hostile reaction or a cultural sign of respect to
a teacher-territory invasion." While Anglo pupils "used gross
body movement and arm and hand motion in maintaining their own
territories from invasion by other pupils," the Cubans did not.
[RT]

HAYES, Francis G. "Anglo-Spanish in Tampa, Florida." Hispania
    32.48-52 (1949). [Annot. HLAS 15 (1949) no. 2125 (C. Kany);
    Woodbridge p. 237.] (Cf. Ortiz 1949.)

    Originally a talk presented at the 1949 meeting of the AATSP,
Hayes's paper takes its examples of "Anglo-Spanish" from the MA
thesis of his student at the Univ. of Florida, Carmelita Ortiz,
who in turn published some excerpts from her thesis (Ortiz 1949)
in a subsequent issue of Hispania. Of the two articles, Ortiz's
conforms most carefully to good lexicographic practice (her word-
list is alphabetized and its definitions are concise), while
Hayes provides various historical and sociological details not
found in Ortiz. [RT]

LINEHAN, Edward J. "Cuba's Exiles Bring New Life to Miami."
    NGeog 144.68-95 (July 1973). [TSBJr.]

    A cheery account of the Cubans in Miami and their impact
on life there. News of interest to sociolinguists appears from
time to time, e.g., "Four Cuban-run radio stations and one TV
channel now broadcast full time in Spanish. Four theaters show
only Latin films; others present films with Spanish subtitles.
One daily newspaper, Diario Las Américas, has reached a circulation of 63,000. More than a score of other Spanish newspapers
and magazines circulate through the community . . . A Cuban-
published phone book devotes the bulk of its 376 pages to Latin-
American names and businesses in the Miami area." (p. 75) It is
estimated that there are close to 300,000 Cubans in Dade County--
more than a fifth of its overall population. Says one photograph's
caption: "Absorbing the old culture, children of exiles attend
an after-school course in Cuban history at Miami's St. John Bosco
Catholic Church. Says a parish priest: 'Once we worried that the
kids wouldn't learn English. Now we worry that in a couple of
generations they won't know Spanish!" (86) [RT]

PIZZO, Anthony P. Tampa Town, 1824-1886: The Cracker Village
    With a Latin Accent. Miami: Hurricane House Publishers,
    Inc., 1968. xii, 89 pp. [TSBJr.]

    Pizzo convincingly erradicates an historical misconception,
i.e., "the general belief . . . that the Latin element came [to

Tampa] in 1886 with the advent of the cigar industry and the creation of Ybor City." (xi) The truth, says Pizzo, is that when Colonel George Mercer Brooke arrived in Tampa with his garrison of American soldiers in 1824, Cuban and Spanish fishermen were already making their homes along the shores of Tampa Bay; prominent among them was one Antonio Máximo Hernández, "turtle fancier and pilot," born of old Spanish stock in St. Augustine as were several of the signers of an 1834 petition calling for increased federal troop protection against rebellious Seminole Indians. Pizzo's history nowhere discusses language but is nonetheless of value for the apparent proof that Spanish has been spoken in Florida (at least by a handful of persons) without interruption since the establishment of the St. Augustine settlement. [RT]

10.2.2 TEXTBOOKS

Major Items: (none)

See also these items elsewhere (consult Author Index for location):

BOMS/ALFA-1973

10.2.1 SOCIOLINGUISTICS

Major Items: (none)

See also these items elsewhere (consult Author Index for location):

VALL-1970

Smith, M. Estellie. "The Spanish-Speaking Population of Florida." In Helm 1968, pp. 120-133.

This piece is a treasure trove of anthropological information about Florida's Hispanos, whom Smith classifies as (1) Old (pre-Castro) Cubans, (2) New Cubans, (3) Puerto Ricans, and (4) Mexican-Americans (chiefly migrant farmworkers). There is little here on language per se, though we learn (from a Miami Puerto Rican "broker" [patrón]) that dark-skinned Puerto Ricans "insist on retaining the use of Spanish as much as possible" to differentiate themselves from U.S. blacks; that one of the many manifestations of the strong traditionalism of New Cubans is that "except for children and teenagers outside the home [they] are loath to give up speaking Spanish;" (p. 124) and that relations between Old and New Cubans in Ybor City (Tampa) are not always harmonious ("New Cubans, it is claimed, make snide remarks about the way the Old Cubans speak and refer slightingly to what they call 'Ybor City Spanish.'" [127]). [RT]

*STEVENSON, James M. "Cuban-Americans: New Urban Class." PhD
Diss., Wayne State Univ., Detroit, 1973. 192 pp. [<u>DA</u> 34
(1974) 4440-4441-A.]

This otherwise strictly sociological study may offer something
to linguists because S discusses among other things the Miami Cuban
refugees' assimilation: "Assimilation is considered in relation
to past and present culture, . . . amalgamation with the dominant
society, and social acceptance by other Americans. Also explored
are the personal assimilation and changes in national identity of
the Cuban-American, plus the relationship between visibility, speech,
and discrimination." (abs.) Thus S appears to investigate the degree to which less-than-native English accent would elicit negative reactions from English-monolinguals. [RT]

10.3 SPANISH PHONOLOGY

<u>Major Items</u>: GUIT-1973; HAMM-1973; LAMB-1968; VALL-1970

<u>See also these items elsewhere</u> (consult Author Index for location):

CAST-1967

CANFIELD, D. Lincoln. "Tampa Spanish: Three Characters in Search
of a Pronunciation." <u>MLJ</u> 35.42-44 (1951).

Brief but erudite notes on the three types of Spanish most
commonly heard among Cubans and Asturians in the Ybor City section
of Tampa: the conservative northern peninsular pronunciation typified by palatal /l/ for <u>ll</u>, interdental /θ/, etc.; a somewhat modified peninsular pronunciation in which <u>s</u> is pronounced as a dental
sibilant and not as an apico-alveolar; and the standard "Cuban"
pronunciation characterized by aspiration of implosive /s/ and so
forth. Canfield indicates that of the three the third is easily
the most generalized and that is has "won out" in Tampa just as it
has in many other parts of the New World. [RT]

GUITART, Jorge Miguel. "Markedness and a Cuban Dialect of Spanish."
PhD Diss., Georgetown Univ., 1973. v, 190 pp. [<u>DA</u> 34 (1974)
4230-A.]

This is a masterful synopsis of and original contribution to the
debate within generative phonology concerning markedness; Guitart's
points of departure are the writings of Chomsky, Halle, Postal and
others; his own theoretical contribution is a construct he labels
"Relative Markedness." The dialect he analyzes (chiefly to prove or
disprove certain points concerning markedness) is his own, "educated
Spanish of Havana [ESH]," although incursions into ancillary sources
are also made, and features of less-educated Havana Spanish are adduced when the need arises. As Guitart's goals are ultimately theo-

retical, his description of the dialect (given chiefly in Ch. 2, pp. 40-57 but also throughout Ch. 6, 146-177) is less encyclopedic than the description of essentially the same dialect by Lamb 1968, but is still worth consulting for what it adds to our knowledge both phonetic and sociolinguistic. Among other things we learn that ESH "does not show substitution of [l] for [r] and vice versa in word-final position . . . which, on the other hand, is a common phenomenon in the speech of poor Cuban blacks and of other lower socioeconomic groups;" (43) that in ESH, /s/ is never realized as zero in utterance-internal position (contrary to what Lamb found), and thus "the phrase estas cosas . . . is usually pronounced [éhtahkósa] but is never pronounced [éhtakósa] or [étakósa], although these are common in less prestigious dialects." (ibid.) Some will be startled by G's claim that in colloquial ESH the "archiphonemes B, D, G" (products of the neutralization of all obstruents) actively tend towards velarization "and only G occurs," e.g., [aksolúto] 'absoluto,' [égniko] 'étnico,' (48-49) Other news is that "/l/ and /r/ are both realized as an unreleased, voiced dorsopalato-alveolar stop [d⁼] before dentals and alveolars other than [s]," thus arde [ad⁼de], saldo [sad⁼do]; similarly "the apico-alveolar nasal is realized instead as a dorsopalatoalveolar nasal; e.g., [kad⁼ne] for carne." (51) As can be seen, assimilation is rampant and also gives rise to copious gemination as in [eb⁼béd⁼de] 'el verde,' "[seffíno] 'ser fino'" and many other examples (see pp. 52-53). [RT]

*HAMMOND, Robert M. "An Experimental Verification of the Phonemic Status of Open and Closed Vowels in Spanish." MA Thesis, Florida Atlantic Univ., Boca Raton, 1973. 76 pp. [MAAb 12:1. 42 (March 1974).]

We shall quote in its entirety the well-written abstract of this impressive-looking thesis: "The phoneme /s/ appears as the sibilant [s] in standard Spanish and has a high functional load. In those dialects of Spanish in which /s/ → [∅], however, the question arises as to how, apart from context, those morphological distinctions carried by /s/ are maintained. This study attempts to verify experimentally the often-repeated hypothesis that a compensatory phonemic change in quality takes place in the vowel immediately preceding this [∅] allophone of /s/ in syllable-final and word-final positions. -- Speech samples were elicited from four native speakers of Cuban Spanish; a perception test was constructed from these samples and was administered to 20 test subjects. The items used on the perception test were also studied spectrographically. -- In neither the acoustic nor the perceptual portions of this study could we find evidence of any phonemicization of differences in vowel qualtiy before word-final /s/ → [∅]. A significant increase in vowel length provided the test subjects . . . with sufficient acoustic cues to correctly discriminate pairs of words such as patillas [patíyas] and pastillas [pa∅tíyas] at a rate of 91.6 per cent." [RT]

*HULME, Antonia Lala. "The Phonology of the Spanish of Tampa, Florida." MA Thesis, Florida Atlantic Univ., Boca Raton, 1973. 34 pp. [MAAb 12:2.128 (June 1974).]

The study first offers " . . . a descriptive phonological analysis of [Tampa Spanish]. Selected segmental features are then compared with those of the Castilian of Asturias and Galicia, as well as with present-day Cuban Spanish. The predominant influence in the phonology of Tampa Spanish is determined to be Cuban, rather than Castilian of Asturias or Galicia spoken by many of the early settlers of Tampa." (abs.) For an earlier attestation to the very same facts see Canfield 1951. [RT]

LAMB, Anthony J. "A Phonological Study of the Spanish of Havana, Cuba." PhD Diss., Univ. of Kansas, 1968. 171 pp. [DA 29 (1969) 2244-A.]

It was never Lamb's intent to describe a form of "United States Spanish" and indeed he hastens to assert that "the extent of the informants' present stay in this country . . . has not been found to have contributed to observable forgetfulness of the native language or interaction with English," (p. 37) except in the case of one young man who left Cuba at age 17. We review this work nevertheless since it examines the phonology of 30 Cubans who had all lived in the Chicago area at the time of the interview for about three years.
Having obtained his material through a Cubanized version of Prof. Stanley Sapon's Pictorial Linguistic Interview Manual (1957), Lamb subjects it to structuralist analysis and concludes that Havana Spanish phonemes are precisely those of general Western Hemisphere Spanish; "phonetic variation," though, is predictably rich. What sets off Lamb's allophonic discussion (Ch. 5, 72-100) from others of the genre is the author's readiness to cross-reference all findings with the observations of the few philologers who have written on the same topic, along with his attempts, Labov-style, to cite and establish social parameters for variants; this is facilitated by use of an adequate if not universal cross-section of pre-Castro Havana society encompassing everything from chambermaids to university professors ("extremes" such as illiterates or plutocrats were not included, and none of the informants was a full-blooded black).
Especially noteworthy among Lamb's variants (many of which constitute "expected" Caribbean or general dialect features such as lenition, assimilation, aspiration, etc.) are the following: (1) substitution of voiced labiodentals for [b] or [ƀ] as a prestige feature from learnèd influences at school in an attempt to differentiate words orthographically, but with very mixed success, since it is "interspersed haphazardly at any articulation for either b or v" (75); (2) "In the speech of all but the most paced and circumspect speakers" [d] not only disappears in -ado forms but in -ido ones as well (e.g., [deretía] 'derretida') (76); (3) historical

reduction of clusters to the contrary, most informants rendered the year's ninth month 'almost exclusively as either [sektiémbre] or [septiémbre], with a rare occurrence of [setiémbre]." (78) (4) [s̱] as variant of /ĉ/ "has occurred predominantly with women informants, and also seems characteristic of unemphatic speech," (79) although "the speakers do not seem to be cognizant of performing this variant, if one can gauge by the surprise and disbelief they registered when the phenomenon was later mentioned to them." (80)

Lamb's discussion of those old Caribbean trouble-makers /s/, /r/, /r̄/ and N (nasals in general) (80-93) is especially worth consulting for its lucid presentation of a wealth of information phonetic and social, although it is possible to take issue with his ideas on the perception of plurality (p. 83), which would have benefitted from a submission of data to machine analysis.

This dissertation definitely represents the very best in structuralist Hispanic dialectology and will be required reading for all who wish to acquaint themselves with any aspect of middle-brow Havana Spanish pronunciation. [RT]

VALLEJO-CLAROS, Bernardo. "La distribución y estratificación de /r/ /r̄/ y /s/ en el español cubano." PhD Diss., Univ. of Texas, Austin, 1970. xv, 173 pp. [DA 31 (1971) 6039-A.]

This is the first dissertation based on data obtained in large part from the PILEI-sponsored study of "educated" speech of the major urban centers of Spanish America (see López Morales 1968). Examined here is the (for the most part) natural speech of 27 adults resident in Greater Miami and recently arrived from Cuba (in no case more than six months removed from the island). Persons from all classes and regions were interviewed, though contacts were initially limited to individuals of the "nivel profesional" from Havana exclusively. V expertly studies, in the by now classic Labovian sociolinguistic manner, the socioeconomic as well as the situational and stylistic correlations of the three variants of /r r̄ s/; geographic distribution is also taken into account. Foremost among the conclusions (all heavily documented by an impressive number of computer-produced charts and graphs): that variants [l] and [∅] of /r/ are more frequent among lower socio-cultural groups and that in consequence they function as conscious social differentiators, though only in western and central Cuba, since the cited variants do not obtain in the eastern part of the island. The two observable variants of /r̄/ ("normal" multiple alveolar tap and the deviant "líquida fricativa alveolar alargada" [p. 27]) played little or no role as social or geographical indicators. Variant [h] for /s/ was uniform throughout the island in implosive position in all speech styles and thus did not serve as a social differentiator; however, lack of prestige is indeed attached to the variant [∅]. [RT]

10.4 SPANISH GRAMMAR (MORPHOLOGY AND SYNTAX)

Major Items: (none)

See also these items elsewhere (consult Author Index for location):

KELL-1974

10.5 SPANISH LEXICON

Major Items: NAVA-1963

See also these items elsewhere (consult Author Index for location):
(none)

CHERRY, Adrian. Tampa Spanish Slang. Tampa, Florida: Lamplight Press, 1966. 59 pp.

This volume contains several hundred dichos observed in use among the nearly 100,000 Cubans and peninsulares of Greater Tampa; naturally most of the sayings are heard in other parts of the Hispanic world as well. Cherry first lists the proverb in Spanish, then its literal translation in English, and finally its approximate equivalent in English (upon occasion a kindred proverb is sought and found), e.g., "No me pareces católico / You don't seem Catholic to me / You look sick; suspicious." (p. 7) The sayings are arranged, curiously, according to the various categories of "head words" in the proverb itself, i.e., animals, money, foods, names, parts of the body; the effect of this is that proverbs referring to sullenness, stubbornness, inebriation, idiocy, etc., are scattered throughout several different sections; a thematic arrangement would have been more logical and useful. [RT]

NAVARRO, Carlos. "An Analytical Study of Three Hundred and Sixty-One Slang Forms Collected at Random from a Heterogeneous Group of Twenty-Six Cuban Informants." MA Thesis, Univ. of Miami, Coral Gables, 1963. vi, 145 pp.

Directed by Prof. R.S. Boggs, this study seeks to record previously untapped material which it then analyzes from a variety of stylistic and semantic standpoints. Among the trends in "slang" production are word pairing for mutual emphasis, euphemism, hyperbole, augmentation and diminuition, antithesis, paragoge, and the like. Of Navarro's 26 informants, 12 are residents of Greater Miami, one of New York City and the remainder of Cuba itself (mostly Havana).

The value of this work lies chiefly in its presentation of a wealth of words and expressions with which most non-Cuban readers will not be familiar. Each main entry includes part(s) of speech, definition, usage label(s), example(s) from context, and synonymous words or expressions (most of which are given separate alphabetical listings themselves). A typical listing: "AGUA (JUGAR AGUA) To take a bath or shower. 'Bien se nota que hace un par de días que no juegas agua.' . . . SYN: bomberos (jugar a los bomberos). ANT[onym]: turno (volar el turno)."

Many entries refer to personal obnoxiousness, to unacceptable forms of behavior, to sexual attractiveness or its opposite, to copulation, and the like. Navarro's entries suggest (as does he himself, by way of conclusion [p. 141]) that much of Cuban slang belongs to "a man's world": eight forms alone refer to male homosexuality (cherna, loca, pailero, pargo and its paragoge parguera, pato, rififi, sospechoso), while none refers to lesbianism; twelve forms treat feminine ugliness (bacalao, campeona de natación, casco, chancleta, de hacho, fleje et al.), a full nineteen to feminine pulchritude, while only two bespeak male handsomeness. Occasional Anglicisms appear, such as the calque caja de pan 'barriga' in imitation of English breadbasket. [RT]

RAMÍREZ, Manuel D. "Some Semantic and Linguistic Notes on the Spanish Spoken in Tampa, Florida." RIAF 1.25-33 (1939). [Annot. Nichols no. 1148.]

An early description of Tampa's Hispanic colony and of the Spanish of its inhabitants. Ramírez carefully discusses some 80 forms "peculiar to" the local dialect(s), chiefly by comparing them with entries from Malaret's Diccionario de americanismos, Segovia's Diccionario de argentinismos and other regionalist works. Anglicisms constitute slightly more than half the items presented. Occasional Tampa variations are minor, e.g., alegar "'to argue, dispute.' (In Castilian the verb alegar simply means 'to allege, affirm, quote, maintain.' The change in meaning here may be due to the related idea of argument in the quoting of facts, citing passages, etc. . . .)" (p. 27) [RT]

10.6 ONOMASTICS (includes TOPONYMY)

Major Items: (none)

See also these items elsewhere (consult Author Index for location):
    (none)

HAMILTON, John W. "La toponimia española en el estado de la Florida, Estados Unidos." ACIH-3.431-434 (1970).

Hamilton seeks to distinguish between Spanish toponyms actually established by Spaniards during the colonial period and Spanish or (more typically) pseudo-Spanish forms subsequently produced by English speakers. Only 88 of the Rand McNally Atlas's 223 Spanish-appearing place names were judged legitimate; many were discarded as incongruous with the canons of Spanish grammar (thus Lagovista, Monte Vista and all of Florida's other Vistas) or as congruous but

demonstrably recent. The author favors San Juanito as the etymon
of the renowned Suwan(n)ee River, and makes a brief attempt at
unraveling the history of the toponym Pensacola (península + cola?
"corrupción del nombre del puerto español Peñiscola"? [p. 434]).
[RT]

10.7 ENGLISH INFLUENCE ON SPANISH

Major Items: BEAR-1972-73; ORTI-1947; VARE-1974

See also these items elsewhere (consult Author Index for location):

  RAMI-M-1939; ROSA-1969

BEARDSLEY, Theodore S., Jr. "Influencias angloamericanas en el
    español de Cayo Hueso." Exilio 6:4/7:1-4.87-100 (1972-73).
    [Issue combines five nos. from two vols. originally scheduled
    as separata but subsequently combined.] [TSBJr.]

    According to Beardsley the Hispanos of Key West (Cubans for
the most part, and representing about a third of the city's population) constitute "el grupo hispanoparlante inmigrante más antiguo
de los Estados Unidos," (p. 87) as their colony largely dates back
to 1868, the year of the exodus of Havana's entire cigar industry.
Spanish continues to be spoken in Key West (although we do not
learn to what extent or by which generation[s]), and it appears to
owe its maintenance and pureza in no small part to the longevity
and vitality of the private school El Instituto de San Carlos which
teaches largely in Spanish.
    A substantial part of the interview material derives from in-
formant identification of photographs in Tomás Navarro Tomás's
Cuestionario lingüístico hispanoamericano (Buenos Aires, 1945).
To the author's surprise nearly all five informants were noticeably
resistent to English lexical incursions, and furthermore often used
"properly Hispanic" terms for items of recent invention whose castizo equivalents had yet to be accepted by the Spanish Royal Academy
dictionary. The greater part of the Anglicisms were direct borrowings of English words whose Spanish equivalents are periphrastic
(thus rómbalsit rather than asiento posterior descubierto) or which
could appear "affected" to bilingual speakers, e.g., limpiapara-
brisas 'windshield wiper,' for which one informant produced oaipa.
One is not surprised that the bulk of Anglicisms are direct loans.
    Following the discussion of borrowing types, there appears an
analysis of "la fonética de los angloamericanismos" (94-96); "los
porcentajes de aceptación de fonemas angloamericanos para cada in-
formante" range from .11 per cent to 4.295 per cent (the last figure
is for the one informant with the least education in Spanish). Phon-
ologists of all persuasions will greatly wonder at Beardsley's statement (based on the "Guide to Pronunciation" of Webster's New International Dictionary of the English Language, whose transcriptive

system Beardsley follows) that "se distinguen para el inglés 32 alófonos principales de las cinco vocales [!], mientras que el español peninsular sólo cuenta con 18." [RT]

CASTELLANOS, Sister Mary Catherine, O.P. "English Lexical and Phonological Influences in the Spanish of Cuban Refugees Living in the Washington Metropolitan Area." M.S. Thesis, Georgetown Univ., Washington D.C., 1967. vii, 193 pp. (Sole library copy destroyed and thus not available through Georgetown; can only be obtained from author directly [1200 S. Court House Rd., Apt. 307, Arlington, Virginia, 22204.])

This thesis was directed by Prof. Charles Kreidler and resembles his own doctoral dissertation (1957) in format, method of approach and theoretical assumptions. While Castellanos' work contains much of little interest to researchers who want to learn about what the title promises to teach (lengthy résumés of Navarro Tomás, Alarcos Llorach and Stockwell/Bowen throughout Ch. 3 and parts of Ch. 5; Ch. 3 also sums up the findings of Dagmar Salcines, "A Comparative Study of the Dialects of Cuba," M.S., Georgetown, 1957, upon whom Castellanos draws heavily for her presentation of Cuban dialect traits), there is nonetheless much here that will interest students of immigrant languages willing to limit their curiosity to loanword typology (Ch. 4, "English Influences in the Lexicon"--chiefly the "corpus" itself and then a classification of borrowings) and to which English segmental phonemes and combinations appear in the "fully or partly assimilated loanwords" (Ch. 5, "English Influences in the Phonology").

In all, Castellanos used 25 informants, subjecting each to interviews both free-form and structured. (The preponderance of questions on matters domestic surely accounts for the frequent appearance of words for household articles.) The great majority of lexical Anglicisms were loanwords, although there are also six pages of loanshifts (some of them rather unique, e.g., camino libre 'freeway,' capitalizar 'escribir con mayúsculas'). Castellanos' work confirms Haugen's findings that most loanshift extension involves words exhibiting the highest degree of surface as well as semantic resemblance (aplicación 'solicitud'). Within her chosen theoretical framework Castellanos seldom errs, although occasionally an excessive formalism leads her to misinterpret the data at hand (e.g., the assertion that the changes pórch > pórchĕ and sprấy > [ĕhpréi] represent an "adaptation of stress patterns" (p. 139) along the lines of jáywâlkĭng > [yĕiguókĭn], whereas in fact the addition of an extra syllable probably indicates expansion, not adaptation). One notes with interest that some English loanwords clearly present in assimilated form in the speech of the informants prior to their departure from Cuba (bar, beisbol) are now tending toward a more English-like pronunciation. [RT]

*FERNÁNDEZ, Roberto G. "The Lexical and Syntactical Impact of
English on the Cuban Spanish Spoken in Southeastern Florida."
MA Thesis, Florida Atlantic Univ., Boca Raton, 1973. 89 pp.
[MAAb 11:4.459 (Dec. 1973).]

The author apparently uses a classificatory scheme derived
from the works of Einar Haugen (categories of analysis are "loanshifts, hybrid creation, hybrid compounds, loan translation and
syntactic interference" [abs.]) in his presentation of Anglicisms
"gathered from the following sources: native informants, newspapers, magazines, letters, radio and television programs, and
advertising." Both "formal" and "informal" levels of speech and
writing were taken into account. Loanshifts and hybrid creations
produced the most Anglic influence while "informal speech" accounted for almost 100 per cent of the borrowing. Fernández
wisely remarks that certain Anglicisms reflecting items foreign
to traditional Cuban culture may be eradicable, e.g., coger un
incompli 'to take an incomplete [grade, in an academic subject].'
[RT]

ORTIZ, Carmelita Louise. "English Influence on the Spanish of
Tampa." MA Thesis, Univ. of Florida, Gainesville, 1947.
vii, 68 pp. [Annot. Woodbridge p. 237.] (Cf. Ortiz 1949,
also Hayes 1949.)

This is a carefully-executed and well-informed study of the
Anglicisms which appeared in 150 issues of two Spanish-language
newspapers published in Tampa for the city's Hispanic colony (chiefly Cuban and Asturian). Ortiz has collected 275 examples of English
influence which she cites in context, discusses in terms of morphophonological adaptation, and categorizes as to type of borrowing,
e.g., "English Words Hispanized," "Literal Translations," "Spanish
Words With Semantic Changes," English words spelled as in English
(and often written within quotation marks as a possible indication
that they represent "interference," not "assimilation"), and "non-
English Words Adopted Through English" (chiefly from French).
Semantically the borrowings conform to well-established trends:
127 are sports terms and many others pertain to politics, fashion,
food, and U.S. customs for which Spanish has no name. Anglicismo-
philes will find many old friends here though occasional items are
surprises, e.g., viruela de pollo 'chicken pox,' el principio del
fin 'the beginning of the end,' and la caja de pan 'breadbasket'
(i.e., stomach). [RT]

ORTIZ, Carmelita Louise. "English Influence on the Spanish of Tampa."
Hispania 32.300-304 (1949). [Annot. HLAS 15 (1949) no. 2135
(C. Kany); Woodbridge p. 237.] (Cf. Hayes 1949, Ortoz 1947.)

Here Ortiz sums up her own MA thesis (1947). Inevitably much
had to be omitted, though the summary is a good one. Information
from Ortiz 1949 also appears in Hayes 1949. Readers who want the
full story will do well to stick to the MA thesis. [RT]

VARELA DE CUÉLLAR, Beatriz. "La influencia del inglés en los cubanos de Miami y Nueva Orleans." EspAct 26.16-25 (abril 1974).

This is a detailed narration of all the various types of English influence (phonological, grammatical and, to be sure, lexical) upon the mother tongue of the author's compatriots; analysis of interference and incorporation proceeds along lines established by Einar Haugen, Uriel Weinreich, and various Hispanists (such as Emilio Lorenzo, Ricardo Alfaro and Jerónimo Mallo) who have written at length of the Anglic invasion. Varela posits three types of emigré speakers: incipient bilinguals ("no son capaces de componer en inglés frases dotadas de sentido, pero en cambio emplean en su vocabulario resignar en lugar de renunciar y tronco en lugar de baúl o maletero" [p. 17]), coordinate bilinguals, and "subordinate" bilinguals; English is becoming dominant among subordinates, who commit "faltas de ortografía propias de un anglohablante," whose unstressed Spanish vowels are tending towards schwah just as their /r/'s and /r̄/'s are tending toward the English retroflex /R/, and whose grammar contains "los clásicos errores del estudiante norteamericano en el uso del subjuntivo y en la concordancia." (ibid.) Of the approximately 130 loanwords the author has gathered (through random observation? Methods of collection and frequency of use are not discussed), verbs constitute a slight plurality with nouns a close second and adjectives a very distant third; a separate list of calques appears on pp. 24-25. Cognoscenti of Anglicisms will find much that is familiar in both lists along with new and even outrageous items such as manejarle loco 'to drive one crazy' and the wild maquillarse la mente 'to make up your mind.' The preposition back has given rise to the same verbal calques among Cubans as it has among Chicanos and Puerto Ricans; thus llamar para atrás 'volver a llamar,' echar para atrás 'devolver,' etc. [RT]

SECTION 11 [ISLENOS (LOUISIANA CANARY ISLANDERS)]

11.1 BIBLIOGRAPHY

Major Items: (none)

See also these items elsewhere (consult Author Index for location):

FODY-1971

MACCURDY, Raymond R. A History and Bibliography of Spanish-Language Newspapers and Magazines in Louisiana, 1808-1949. Univ. of New Mexico Publications in Language and Literature, No. 8 (Albuquerque: Univ. of New Mexico Press, 1951). 43 pp.

This item may have some indirect interest for linguists seeking evidence for bilingual phenomena and dialectal traits in the journalistic media: pp. 34-40 contain a bibliography of Spanish-language newspapers published in Louisiana during the time span indicated, including locations of extant copies. The history of the subject is mildly entertaining (pp. 7-33); this reader was left wondering whether genuine memorabilia are as few and far between as the author's description suggests. [JC]

11.2 COMPREHENSIVE/GENERAL STUDIES; MISCELLANY; ANTHOLOGIES/FESTSCHRIFTEN

Major Items: MACC-1950b

See also these items elsewhere (consult Author Index for location):
(none)

FORTIER, Alcée. "The isleños of Louisiana." In her Louisiana Studies, New Orleans: F.F. Hansell, 1894. Pp. 197-210.

Brief sketch of the history, customs and dialect of the isleños. She quotes a brief conversation and a love poem with some trivial comments on the language they reflect. [JC]

MACCURDY, Raymond R. [1950b]. The Spanish Dialect in St. Bernard Parish, Louisiana. Univ. of New Mexico Publications in Language and Literature, No. 6 (Albuquerque: Univ. of New Mexico Press, 1950). 88 pp. (Abbreviated version of M's "The Spanish Dialect of St. Bernard Parish," PhD Diss., Univ. of North Carolina, Chapel Hill, 1948. 265 pp.) [Annot. HLAS 16 (1950) no. 2489 (C. Kany); Woodbridge p. 237; Serís no. 15524; Solé no. 1004. Rev. Filología 2.344-345 (1950) (E. Speratti Piñero); Hispania 34.221-222 (1951) (L. Kiddle); Language 27.405-411 (1951) (Y. Malkiel); RHM 17.173-174 (1951) (M. Lasley); RDTP 7.158-159 (1951) (P. Pérez Vidal); RPh 5.231-232 (1951-52) (W.A. Read); HR 19.364-367 (1951) (R. L. Predmore).]

This monograph, though already quite old-fashioned by the standards of linguistic science prevalent at the time it was published, nevertheless remains the cornerstone of our knowledge about Louisiana Spanish. A brief initial chapter (which comes after the bibliography) sketches in the history and current (as of 1950) state of St. Bernard Parish, where the isleños (lit. 'Islanders') are concentrated. There follow in close succession a phonology, morphology and vocabulary. The style of presentation is atomistic, each section containing collections of forms that deviate in some fashion from standard Spanish. This is, of course, the "classical" approach to Hispanic dialectology, and one presumes the author was in no position to overcome the restraints of that tradition. Consequently, the best part of the slender book is, beyond any doubt, the lexicon, which bears such eloquent testimony to the remarkable trilingual environment (Spanish, French and English) of rural Louisiana.

One shortcoming of this and so many other Hispanic dialect studies that drives linguistically inclined readers quite mad is the failure to employ a consistent phonetic transcription. It can be partially remedied by consulting the dissertation on which the present work is based. Pages 19-90 of the former contain narrow phonetic transcriptions of various texts, mostly folkloric in character. All but one of the folkloric texts were published (SFQ 12.129-135 [148], 13.180-191 [1949] and 16.227-250 [1952]) in a normalized orthography that masks a great deal of the phonetic reality. Compare the published version of the following sentence with MacCurdy's transcription of it (SFQ 13.187 vs. 1948:28): "Todito el mundo saludaba al rey cuando [el] rey pasaba pero Quevedo nunca ni se agachaba" / [toíto él múndo saludába a r̃éi kwánd ə r̃ei pasáọ // péro kebéọ núŋka ni sẹ a:cába]. The system employed is that of the RFE; note in particular how the loss of the voiced fricatives b, d and g, as well as l before r̃, is ignored in the printed text. What I render with schwah [ə] may actually be the mid back vowel o; the handwritten transcription sometimes leaves doubt as to which of the two sounds is meant; I have omitted intonational symbols.

A linguist must consider this wide discrepancy as bordering on the irresponsible. Why should folklorists be absolved from the duty of presenting their material as accurately as possible? No doubt the fault in this instance lay with MacCurdy's publishers.

Besides the collection of transcribed texts, the dissertation also offers more detailed phonological observations than the monography and arranged in a different manner (by mode, rather than point, of articulation). The forms cited are coded so as to allow the reader to locate them in the transcribed corpus. These advantages were sacrificed to economy in the printed version.

MacCurdy's work elicited detailed and severe criticism from Malkiel; there is no need to repeat his observations here. A Spanish translation is in the works; to my knowledge it has not yet appeared. [JC]

11.5 SPANISH LEXICON (includes SEMANTICS)

Major Items: (none)

See also these items elsewhere (consult Author Index for location):
(none)

MACCURDY, Raymond R. [1950a]. "Louisiana-French Loan Words for 'Water-fowl' in the Spanish of St. Bernard Parish, Louisiana." In Romance Studies Presented to W.M. Day. Univ. of North Carolina Studies in the Romance Languages and Literatures, No. 12 (Chapel Hill: Univ. of North Carolina Press, 1950). Pp. 139-142. [Annot. Woodbridge p. 238.]

A list of more than thirty designations that illustrate unassimilated loans (zenzen 'baldpate duck,' "pronounced in the French fashion"), phonologically adapted loanwords (bransí 'wood duck' < Louisiana French [canard] branchu), and loan translations (pato de isla 'black mallard' < Lou. Fr. canard d'île). The author provides Louisiana French etyma in standard orthography; phonetic transcriptions of both source and product would have been illuminating. [JC]

MACCURDY, Raymond R. "A Spanish Word-List of the 'Brulis' Dwellers of Louisiana." Hispania 42.547-554 (1959). [Annot. HLAS 23 (1961) no. 4450 (D. Wogan). Rev. Craddock p. 475.]

The Brulis (< Fr. brûlé 'burned,' i.e. 'cleared [land]') are descendants of Spanish-speaking colonists that occupied what are now the Ascension and Assumption parishes in Louisiana; in 1948 Spanish was still sufficiently current as to allow the author to compile a rather large lexical corpus. Here he publishes only a small selection of that corpus, having eliminated all forms coincident with the standard language or frequent in other Spanish dialects. This list is remarkable for the number of Louisiana French loanwords it reveals in Brulis Spanish; of course, loanblends and loanshifts are not wanting.

As was to be expected, many Louisiana French forms are not European but stem instead from local sources; such is the case of chaoui 'racoon' of Amerindian provenience, which I, in my brief critique (Craddock 1973) of MacCurdy's piece, too laconically labeled "French."

This reviewer regrets very much the author's failure to use a consistent phonetic transcription and even more his decision not to be inclusive. When so many inexcusable trivia pollute the bibliographies of U.S. Spanish, I find it difficult to comprehend why MacCurdy was not more encouraged in his efforts to make better known one of the most fascinating dialects in the Hispanic world. [JC]

SECTION 12 [PENINSULARES (SPANIARDS)]

12.1   BIBLIOGRAPHY (nothing to report)

12.2   COMPREHENSIVE/GENERAL STUDIES; MISCELLANY; ANTHOLOGIES/FESTSCHRIFTEN

Major Items: (none)

See also these items elsewhere (consult Author Index for location):

   HAYE-1949; PIZZ-1968

GODWIN, Parke, ed. Prose Writings of William Cullen Bryant. Vol. 2: Travels, Addresses, and Comments. New York: D. Appleton & Co., 1884. vi, 424 pp.

   Bryant's occasional remarks about the Minorcans of St. Augustine (cf. Grandoff 1940) appear on pp. 41, 43-44, 46, and 48-49; the Hymn to the Virgin of which Grandoff speaks is given on pp. 49-50. On p. 48 Bryant refers to language use: "The Minorcan language, the dialect of Mahon, el Mahones, as they call it, is spoken by more than half of the inhabitants who remained here when the country was ceded to the United States, and all of them, I believe, speak Spanish besides. Their children, however, are growing up in disuse of these languages, and in another generation the last traces of the majestic speech of Castile will have been effaced from a country which the Spaniards held for more than two hundred years." This was written in 1843. [RT]

GRANDOFF, Victor C. "Folklore Note About the Minorcans of Old Saint Augustine, Florida." RIAF 1:2.31-34 (May 1940). [TSBJr.]

   Mentions the re-establishment in St. Augustine of the colony originally located in 1768 at New Smyrna (Florida). The author reports that at the time of writing "the Minorcans have become assimilated and . . . have lost their native speech . . . " (p. 31) The article quotes from a letter of William Cullen Bryant (1843 [v.s. Godwin 1884, supra]) who remarked upon the local Minorcan folklore; the letter included a copy of an old hymn in honor of the Virgin ("Fromajardis") which young Minorcans sang from house to house the night before Easter Sunday (fromajardis 'type of cheese cake the singers demanded as reward for their efforts'). Here is a sample of Bryant's transcription of the hymn's chorus: "Disciarom lu dol / Cantarom aub'alegria / Y n'arom a dá / Las pascuas a Maria." [RT]

JACKSON, William Richard, Jr. "Florida in Early Spanish Colonial Literature." PhD Diss., Univ. of Illinois, Champaign-Urbana, 1952. 306 pp.

   This work analyzes the various literary themes of the sixteenth and seventeenth century chroniclers of Spanish Florida. Students of the language of the age of discovery will find much of value here, since Jackson freely quotes long passages from Pedro Martyr, Gonzalo Fernández de Oviedo, Juan de Castellanos, Bartolomé de Flores and various others. But unlike New Mexico, Florida did not conserve a sizeable Spanish-speaking population when the territory was transferred to the United States; as a consequence Jackson's "Florida Spanish" cannot be said to have fathered directly the Spanish spoken there today. [RT]

12.2.1 SOCIOLINGUISTICS

Major Items: (none)

See also these items elsewhere (consult Author Index for location):

GUTI-M-1971

12.3 SPANISH PHONOLOGY

Major Items: (none)

See also these items elsewhere (consult Author Index for location):

CANF-1951; and especially GUTI-M-1971

12.5 SPANISH LEXICON (includes SEMANTICS)

Major Items: (none)

See also these items elsewhere (consult Author Index for location):

CHER-1966

FRIEDMAN, Lillian. "Minorcan Dialect Words in St. Augustine, Florida." PADS 14.81 (1950). [Annot. Woodbridge p. 237.]

Friedman reports on 15 Catalan words which have survived for nearly two centures among the descendants of the 1200 Minorcans brought by the British to the east coast of Florida in 1768 to labor on plantations. Most of the items F cites are epithets indicating stupidity or ugliness, e.g., naschata 'a flat-note,' lawca 'crazy' (for which F gives the figured pronunciation [lɔ́kə]; since standard Catalan for 'crazy' is boig, foll or dement, this item may well represent a "Hispanism" in Florida Minorcan). [RT]

12.7 ENGLISH INFLUENCE ON SPANISH

Major Items: (none)

See also these items elsewhere (consult Author Index for location):

DIAS-1941; ORTI-1949; SECA-1972; and especially ORTI-1947

GUTIÉRREZ, Medardo. "A Description of the Speech of Immigrant and Second Generation Gallego-Spanish Speakers in New York City: A Study in Bilingualism." PhD Diss., Georgetown Univ., 1971. 270 pp. [DA 32 (1971) 2077-A.]

    The object of this painstakingly descriptivist study is to investigate "the interference of Gallego-Spanish and English on one another in the speech of Gallegos residing in Metropolitan New York;" (p. 1) to this end, fifty persons were interviewed. The study sought to answer seven theoretical questions, among them: "Is there more interference at phonological and/or lexical levels from the dominant language to the subordinate language, or the reverse?" (ibid.) Inevitably the answer is that "phonological interference occurs in both directions but preponderantly from the dominant language to the subordinate." (2) One also learns without surprise that "the unassimilated pure English loanword is the domain primarily of the second generation speaker while the partly and wholly assimilated pure loanwords that of the immigrant speaker." (3)

    The greatest part of G's dissertation, however, does not catalogue the results of this particular Spanish-English confrontation but instead gives very exhaustive "general phonological descriptions" of Gallego, of Castilian Spanish, of the former as contrasted with the latter, and then finally of "New York City English" (Chs. 2, 3, 4 and 5, resp., pp. 25-164). It is only in Chs. 6 and 7 that G gets around to examining the cross-currents of his informants' bilingualism (Spanish-English); for this reason one wonders why it was necessary to pay such full attention to Gallego, especially since the matter of New Yorkers' interference from Gallego to Spanish or Spanish to Gallego is never dealt with and the putative English to Gallego influence never discussed either. But perhaps G felt that only by probing these concerns could he justify including the single piece of sociolinguistic information which by all lights is his freshest contribution to our knowledge of Hispanic bilingualism: "The outstanding characteristic of the lexicon of New York City Gallego-Spanish is the almost total absence of derivative and compound loanblends quite common in [Mexican and Caribbean Spanish, e.g., lonchar, parquear, etc.] . . . Gallego-Spanish speakers make a conscious effort to avoid these, preferring . . . to switch codes and borrow outright from the English." (227-228) G suggests this is so because the realities of bilingualism in Galicia (where the state sees to it that Castilian is very much the dominant language) have conditioned Gallegos to think of Spanish as "sacred territory" not to be defiled by morphological or lexical adulterations. [RT]

SECTION 13 [SEPHARDIC JEWS (DZHUDEZMO, LADINO OR JUDEO-SPANISH)]

13.1 BIBLIOGRAPHY

Major Items: (none)

See also these items elsewhere (consult Author Index for location):
(none)

BESSO, Henry V. "Bibliografía sobre el judeo-español." BHi 54.412-422 (1952). (Also publ. in Tribuna israelita 8:93.28-32 [Aug. 1952].)

Author-alphabetical listings (134 entries that inclues numerous book reviews) with very occasional critical comments. Relevant to Judeo-Spanish in the U.S. are nos. 2, 3, 15, 18, 19, 55, 66 and 74. [JC]

13.2 COMPREHENSIVE/GENERAL STUDIES; MISCELLANY; ANTHOLOGIES/FESTSCHRIFTEN

Major Items: AGAR-1950; HIRS-1951; LEVY-1952a

See also these items elsewhere (consult Author Index for location):
(none)

AGARD, Frederick B. "Present-Day Judaeo-Spanish in the United States." Hispania 33.203-210 (1950). [Annot. Serís no. 14830; HLAS 16 (1950) no. 2462 (C. Kany).]

Useful introduction to the chief phonological, morphological and lexical traits of Judeo-Spanish. The primary data were recorded from informants living in Rochester, N.Y., and New York City. The author included three texts, the last of which, a personal letter from a father to his daughter in college, reveals considerable English interference. The analysis follows the structural canons of the 'fifties; certain curious traits are overlooked though evident in the forms recorded, for instance, the tendency of [w] to labialize preceeding consonants: mueve 'nine' (vs. st. Sp. nueve), kosfuegra 'mother-in-law' (vs. Sp. con + suegra), and the diachronic rule js > š : seš 'six' (Sp. seis), avláš 'ye speak' (Sp. habláis). Other details corrected by Besso 1951. [JC]

ARMISTEAD, S.G. and J.H. Silverman. "Hispanic Balladry Among the Sephardic Jews of the West Coast." WF 19.229-244 (1960). [Annot. Craddock 1973 p. 474.]

The authors transcribe and translate seven ballads from their vast collection that illustrate both the conservatism and the vitality of the genre among the Sephardim. Copious linguistic notes assist the reader untrained in the Balkan languages and Turkish. The texts are set down in an alphabet that permits immediate perception of the phonological structure of the dialects they represent (the majority were recorded from informants hailing from the island of Rhodes). With their abundant loanwords, the ballads are remarkable examples of bi- and pluri-lingual influences. [JC]

BENARDETE, Mair Jose. *Hispanic Culture and Character of the Sephardic Jews*. New York: The Hispanic Institute, 1953. 186 pp. (Translated into Spanish by Manuel Alvar as *Hispanismo de los sefardíes levantinos*. Madrid: Aguilar, 1963. 268 pp.)

Chapter VII ("The Sephardic Jews in the United States," pp. 135-151; pp. 154-175 in the Spanish version) provides an impressionistic account of Sephardic settlement in the U.S. There are several brief prose texts, but the Castilian orthography successfully masks most of the linguistic peculiarities one would expect to find. Benardete's judgment of Sephardic Spanish seems unduly harsh. As a professor of Spanish literature he apparently believes that it would have been preferable for the Sephardim never to have developed their curious dialects (see also pp. 103-106, "Language and Decadence"), a proposition linguists and anthropologists would surely dispute. [JC]

BESSO, Henry V. "Judeo-Spanish in the United States." *Hispania* 34.89-90 (1951).

Letter to the editor concerning Agard's essay (1950) also published in *Hispania*. Paragraph 3 presents a few linguistic data, i.e., that "kosfuegra is not 'mother-in-law' but a term used by one mother-in-law to refer to another mother-in-law in the same family," and the like. The remainder corrects and completes the background information compiled by Agard. [JC]

HIRSCH [Weinstein], Ruth. "A Study of Some Aspects of a Judeo-Spanish Dialect as Spoken by a New York Sephardic Family." PhD Diss., Univ. of Michigan, Ann Arbor, 1951. iv, 142 pp. [*DA* 11 (1951) 674-A.] [Annot. Serís no. 14832.]

Far and away the finest piece of work on U.S. Judeo-Spanish, Hirsch's dissertation describes a brief corpus recorded from two informants, the one, a septuagenarian monolingual speaker of Judeo-Spanish, the other, her daughter, conversant in French and English as well as her native tongue, both originally from Salonika, but New York City residents for some 30 years at the time the author interviewed them. There are sections devoted to phonology (pp. 5-38), including syllable struacture, morphology (pp. 39-73), both inflexional and derivational, syntax (pp. 73-

82) and lexicon (pp. 85-109). Pp. 82-84 contain samples of each informant's speech. The bibliography (pp. 118-140) is annotated and critical; a brief summary concludes the work.

Except in the lexicon, overtly comparative and historical in approach, the linguistic analysis follows Pike's methodological orientation. The first two portions are very carefully done, with charts of phonemes and verb forms. It should be noted that the author, unlike bonafide tagmemicists, was willing to go beyond the artificial limitations of the corpus in order, for instance, to fill out the verb paradigms by consulting the informants directly. The lexicon divides the vocabulary into various subsections so as to provide some notion of the nature and extent of the archaisms, dialectalisms, and foreignisms (including Anglicisms) present in the speech of the informants.

Among many interesting details that one might mention, I note that Hirsch's informants preserve the r/r̄ contrast (p. 10) so often lost in other Judeo-Spanish dialects. The author has been careful to observe sandhi phenomena such as the voicing of s/s̃ before voiced consonants (p. 37) and the development of an antihiatic glide j after stressed i even across word boundaries: [akí-j-áj] 'here there is/are' (p. 38). On p. 92, Hirsch seeks to connect ambezar 'to learn' with OSp. a-, e-nviso 'wise, prudent;' I would guess that a better starting point is Sp. avezar 'to train, accustom' with possible secondary interference from the OSp. adjective. [JC]

LEVY [Lida], Denah. [1952a]. "El sefardí esmirniano de Nueva York." PhD Diss., Univ. de México, 1952. 154 pp. Also:
LEVY [Lida], Denah. "El sefardí de Nueva York. Observaciones sobre el judeo-español de Esmirna." MA Thesis, Columbia Univ., 1944. 112 pp.

I collapse these two items since the grammatical core of the dissertation ("Ortografía," pp. 16-24, "Fonología," pp. 25-46 [see Levy 1952a], "Morfología," pp. 47-57, and "Sintaxis," pp. 58-61) is, as far as I can judge, an unaltered transcript of the corresponding material in the Masters thesis (pp. 11-57). The dissertation has a new prologue and offers a larger selection of folk literature (songs, pp. 62-80, and proverbs, pp. 81-106), though some items are carried over from the previous work. The thesis contains some folk tales and anecdotes lacking in the more advanced academic exercise. The vocabulary of the latter (pp. 109-149), alphabetical and not entirely first-hand (it borrows from Luria 1930b), is, awkwardly enough, a Spanish/Judeo-Spanish lexicon with no index of the Judeo-Spanish terms (e.g., J.-Sp. deredor 'around' appears only under Sp. rededor). The vocabulary presented in the thesis (pp. 63-83) is more imaginative, being organized by sense groups: kinship, birth, marriage, death, parts of the body, etc.; adjectives and verbs are given separate sections. An alphabetical index is also wanting.

The author, convinced that the language was on the point of

disappearing, concerned herself but little with the impact of English on the speech of the community she was studying, and concentrated instead on presenting the remarkable linguistic heritage that the Smirna Sephardim maintained over the centuries. The linguistic material is clear and orderly, though quite traditional; the chapter on the Rashi script would have greatly benefitted from illustrations containing the actual characters. I found Levy's transliterations somewhat confusing. Both works are well written, and I feel it unfortunate that the dissertation was not published in its entirety. [JC]

LURIA, Max A. "Judeo-Spanish Dialects in New York City." In [Henry Alfred] Todd Memorial Volumes: Philological Studies, edited by J.D. Fitz-Gerald and P. Taylor. 2 vols. New York: Columbia Univ. Press, 1930. Pp. 2.7-16.

One wishes Luria had found the opportunity to pursue further the project described in this all-too-brief sketch. He interviewed speakers representing dialects from 22 regions of North Africa, the Middle East, and the Balkans, and recorded their responses with regard to 26 key words in an effort to reveal basic dialect cleavages. He subjects the material to a rather atomistic diachronic analysis, without, unfortunately, attempting to draw the isoglosses that his work was presumably intended to reveal. It is curious to note how Luria's embryonic project anticipated by more than a decade Max Weinreich's monumental undertaking, the Language and Culture Atlas of Ashkenazic Jewry, likewise based on informants resident in New York City. [JC]

SOLA POOL, David de. "The Use of Portuguese and Spanish in the Historic Shearith Isreal Congregation in New York." In Studies in Honor of M.J. Benardete, edited by I.A. Langnas and B. Sholod. New York: Las Américas Publishing Co., 1966. Pp. 359-362.

The author notes certain ritualistic survivals of those two languages in this, the oldest Jewish congregation in the United States. The text of a 1683 tombstone and a passage from the prayerbook are in Spanish, while certain ritual greetings are Portuguese. The texts seem carelessly transcribed and would require verification. [JC]

13.3 SPANISH PHONOLOGY (includes ORTHOGRAPHY)

Major Items: (none)

See also these items elsewhere (consult Author Index for location): (none)

ADATTO, Emma. "A Study of the Linguistic Characteristics of the

Seattle Sefardí [sic] Folklore." MA Thesis, Univ. of
Washington, Seattle, 1935. 116 pp.

Adatto's thesis has two parts: the first comprises folkloric
texts (ballads, proverbs and stories, pp. 7-93), while the second
is an analysis of the language reflected in those texts (phonology,
pp. 94-106, morphonology, pp. 107-114). The informants are not
identified specifically other than that they invariably belong
to the oldest surviving generations in the Seattle community, since
the youth show little interest in, or knowledge of, their elders'
folklore (p. 3).

At the time Adatto was composing her thesis, there were about
500 Sephardic families residing in that city, all, or nearly all,
immigrants from Turkey who began arriving at the beginning of the
present century. She notes that the Sephardic dialect spoken in
the island of Rhodes shows some important departures from the norms
prevalent in the other areas her informants hailed from (Rodostó
[Tekirdag], Constantinople, Gallipoli and Marmora).

The texts are transcribed in a modified Castilian orthography
with frequent lexical and literary notes. While this does provide
very readable transcriptions, it may be misleading in some ways,
especially with regard to the distribution of fricative vs. occlusive d and g.

The linguistic description offers little more than a résumé
of the most familiar traints of Judeo-Spanish. The examples used
for illustration are not referred to the texts in which they occur,
nor is there an index of forms studied. Adatto's work is more
useful for the interesting texts it contains than for the rather
sketchy and inexperienced linguistic analysis presented. [JC]

BESSO, Henry V. "Situación actual del judeo-español." Arbor 55.155-
172 (1963). "Situación actual del judeo-español." PFLE 1.307-
324 (1964). "Muestras del judeo-español con ilustraciones en
cinta magnetofónica de canciones y romances sefardíes." CALE
4.410-432 (1966). [Annot. Sefarad 27.227-228 (1967) (Hassán).
Rev. Craddock 1973 p. 312.]

The textual coincidences in these three publications are so
extensive that it seemed best to treat them as one entry. Their
chief interest for the present bibliography lies in the samples
presented by the author of various texts printed, written or recorded in the United States: Arbor pp. 161 ff., 167, PFLE 314 ff., and
CALE 413-415, 418, 427. His transcription permits a reasonable
appreciation of the phonological characteristics of the language
of his informants. [JC]

LEVY [Lida], Denah. [1952b.] "La pronunciación del sefardí esmirniano de Nueva York." NRFH 6.277-281 (1952).

Extremely concentrated distillate of the chapter on phonology
contained in the author's PhD dissertation (1952b, pp. 25-46). What

we have here is an extremely swift sketch of the salient phonological characteristics found in the dialect under study, with some attempt at historical explanation. I note one shift in the author's point of view with regard to the curious development of initial s̲ before the labio-velar glide [w]: [sfwégra]/[sxwégra] = Sp. [swégra] 'mother-in-law.' Whereas the change had earlier been regarded as a property of the s̲ (Levy 1952.b, p. 39), she here declares that "la sibilante causa el ensordecimiento [de la semiconsonante w̲] hasta tal punto que se requiere el refuerzo, la aspiración o el apoyo labiodental." Since the standard Spanish glide in [swégra] undergoes some unvoicing because of the preceding voiceless sibilant without demonstrating any tendency to develop such reinforcement, I wonder whether this conjecture is genuinely illuminating. Elsewhere the labio-velar glide tends to generate a consonantal onset, i.e., [w] > [gw], and that may be what has occurred in this instance, the velar onset becoming unvoiced due to the preceding s̲-; the labio-dental articulation would be secondary in this view, a consequence of the frequent alternation of [f] and [x] before [w] (cf. [xwérte]/[fwérte] 'strong,' etc. (Levy 1952.b, p. 35). [JC]

UMPHREY, G.W. and Emma Adatto. "Linguistic Archaisms of the Seattle Sephardim." Hispania 19.255-264 (1936).

This brief essay is not particularly illuminating as far as the specific linguistic traits of the Seattle Sephardim are concerned, since the authors stress phonological characteristics common to all Judeo-Spanish dialects, esp. the b/v contrast and the preservation of the old sibilants (s̲/z̲, š/ž ~ dž). A few words on morphology are added toward the end. One interesting detail is the sandhi-voicing of final s̲ before words beginning with vowels: maz arriva 'higher.' On pp. 261-262, Umphrey and Adatto perceive an analogy between the development -ks- > š (dīxī > diše 'I said') and the more recent shift of -sk- to -šk- (moška 'fly' = Sp. mosca) that entirely escapes me. See Adatto 1935 for the project on which this note is based. [JC]

13.4 SPANISH GRAMMAR (MORPHOLOGY AND SYNTAX)

<u>Major Items</u>: (none)

<u>See also these items elsewhere</u> (consult Author Index for location):

ADAT-1935; UMPH/ADAT-1936

13.5 SPANISH LEXICON (includes SEMANTICS)

Major Items: (none)

See also these items elsewhere (consult Author Index for location):

ARMI/SILV-1960

BAR-LEWAW, Itzhak. "Aspectos del judeo-español de las comunidades sefardíes en Atlanta, Ga. y Montgomery, Ala. (EE. UU.)." ACILFR-11 [vol.] 4.2109-2124 [vols. consecutively paginated]. [Annot. Sefarad 25.465-466 (1965) (M. Romero).]

The linguistic material presented here consists of a brief recorded narration containing striking examples of English interference (pp. 2112 ff.), a vocabulary arranged according to etymological provenience (Turkish, Hebrew, Greek, Galician-Portuguese, French, Italian, Yiddish and English loanwords beside Castilian archaisms) and five ballads (the last describes the Nazi persecution of the Jews during the Second World War). Bar-Lewaw's workmanship is not always up to par. Few will accept Turkish origin for aldukera 'pocket,' a variant of archaic Sp. faltriquera, or for čamuskar 'to scorch,' identical to the Spanish Lusism chamuscar. While čapinero 'shoemaker' is attributed to the Turks, chapín 'shoe' figures as an archaism free of oriental taint. His transcription is occasionally inconsistent: one finds x both for [š] (p. 2120: Moxé, abaxar) and [x] (p. 2117: xuego, xuente). What is the value of j in mojer (p. 2120)? Despite such minor flaws, the author's ponencia arouses the hope that he will continue to gather and publish linguistic data from the two little-known communities that he has studied. [JC]

13.7 ENGLISH INFLUENCE ON SPANISH

Major Items: (none)

See also these items elsewhere (consult Author Index for location):

BARL-1968; HIRS-1951

AUTHOR INDEX

Sigla used to identify items are ordered alphabetically, as are the names of the authors themselves. The additional authors of multiple-authored items are given separate listings, alphabetically and within parentheses, thus: (Bittle, William E. V.s. HYME/BITT-1967). Multiple separate listings, alphabetically and according to husband's surname, are also given for women authors who follow Hispanic conventions for surname citation; thus while the main listing for Rosan Jordán de Caro is found alphabetically s. JORD-R-1973, cross-references also appear, parenthetically, s. Caro, Rosan Jordán de, and also s. de Caro, Rosan Jordán.

Every effort has been made to limit item-identifying sigla to four capital letters, a dash, and the four numbers of the date of publication. When dealing with author names of high frequency, however, it has usually been necessary to add one more capital letter (most typically that of the author's first name) to the siglum; see for example the multiple entries under the surnames Barker, García and González.

Siglum arrangement for multiple-editioned items has each edition's date of publication separated by a slash, thus: ADAM-1944/68; placement of a dash between figures merely indicates that the journal's volume number encompasses two or more calendar years (e.g., BEEL-1966-67).

"Location" refers to the Bibliography section where the item's annotation is found.

SIGLUM	AUTHOR AND START OF TITLE	LOCATION
AARO/etal-1969	Aarons, Alfred C., Barbara Y. Gordon and William A. Stewart, eds. Linguistic-Cultural . . .	1.2
ACOS-1951	Acosta, Vincent S. Some Surviving . . .	4.2
ADAM-1936	Adams, Ramon F. Cowboy Lingo.	2.8
ADAM-1944/68	_____. Western Words . . .	2.8
ADAT-1935	Adatto, Emma. A Study of . . .	13.3
ADKI-1966	Adkins, Patricia G. An Investigation of . . .	3.8.1
ADKI-1968	_____. Reverse Borrowings . . .	2.7
ADOR-1973	Adorno, William. The Attitudes of . . .	6.2.1
AGAR-1950	Agard, Frederick B. Present-Day Judaeo-Spanish . . .	13.2
AJUB-1943	Ajubita, María Luisa. Language in . . .	2.2.1
AKIN-1970	Akin, Johnnye. The Anglicization of . . .	3.6
	(Alatorre, Margit Frenk. V.s. FREN-1953.)	
ALAT-1955	Alatorre, Antonio. El idioma de . . .	2.7
ALON-1930	Alonso, Amado. Problemas de . . .	3.3
ALON-1951	_____. La ll y . . .	2.3
ALON/LIDA-1945	_____ and Raimundo Lida. Geografía fonética . . .	3.3
ALLR-1970	Allred, Forrest Rich. Errors in . . .	7.8.1
ALVA-1967	Alvarez, George R. Calo: The . . .	8.5
ALVA-1973	Álvarez, Salvador. The Influence of . . .	5.3

328

AMSD-1969	Amsden, Constance E. A Study of . . .	6.8.1
ANAS/JESU-1953	Anastasi, Anne and Cruz de Jesús. Language Development . . .	9.2
ANDE-1964	Anderson, John Q. Texas Stream . . .	5.6
APPL-1932	Applegate, Frank G. Native Tales . . .	3.5
AREL-1972	Arellano, Estevan. Entre verde . . .	3.5
ARMI/SILV-1960	Armistead, S.G. and J.H. Silverman. Hispanic Balldry . . .	13.2
ATWO-1953	Atwood, E. Bagby. A Preliminary Report . . .	5.8
ATWO-1958	_____. The Regional Vocabulary . . .	5.8
AUST-1933	Austin, Mary H. Geographical Terms . . .	2.8
AYER-1971	Ayer, George W. Language and . . .	2.2.1
BAKE-1953/66	Baker, Paulline. Español para . . .	2.2.2
BARB-1952	Barber, Carroll Gary. Trilingualism in . . .	4.2.1
BARB-1973	_____. Trilingualism in . . .	4.2.1
BARK-G-1947a	Barker, George C. Social Functions . . .	4.2.1
BARK-G-1947b	_____. Social Functions . . .	4.2.1
BARK-G-1950	_____. Pachuco: An . . .	8.2
BARK-G-1951	_____. Growing Up . . .	8.2
BARK-G-1972	_____. Social Functions . . .	8.2
BARK-M-1970	Barker, Marie Esman. Español para . . .	2.2.2
BARK-M-1973	_____. The Purdue Perceptual . . .	2.5
BARK-S-1942	Barker, S. Omar. Sagebrush Spanish.	2.8
BARL-1968	Bar-Lewaw, Itzhak. Aspectos del . . .	13.5
BARN-1935/60	Barnes, Will[iam] C. Arizona Place . . .	4.6
BARR-1971	Barrios, Ernie. Bibliografía de . . .	2.1
BAUG-1933	Baugh, Lila. A Study of . . .	5.5
BAXL-1972	Baxley, Dan Michael. The Utility of . . .	5.8.1
BEAR-1972-73	Beardsley, Tehodore S., Jr. Influencias anglo-americanas . . .	10.7
BEBE-1958	Beberfall, Lester. Some Linguistic . . .	5.8.1
BECK-1970	Beck, Mary Margaret. The English Influence . .	7.7
BEEL-1966-67	Beeler, Madison S. The Californian Oronym . .	6.8
BEEL-1972	_____. Inyo.	6.9
BELT-1972	Beltramo, Anthony Fred. Lexical and . . .	6.7
BENA-1953	Benardete, Mair Jose. Hispanic Culture . . .	13.2
BENI-1970	Benítez, Carrahlee. A Study of . . .	5.8.1
BENT-1932	Bentley, Harold W. A Dictionary of . . .	2.8
BERN/COOP-1968/69		
	Berney, Tomi D. and Robert L. Cooper. Semantic Independence . . .	9.2.1
BESS-1951	Besso, Henry V. Judeo-Spanish in . . .	13.2
BESS-1952	_____. Bibliografía sobre . . .	13.1
BESS-1963	_____. Situación actual . . .	13.3
BESS-1964	_____. Situación actual . . .	13.3
BESS-1966	_____. Muestras del . . . [V.s. BESS-1963.]	
BIER-1920	Bierschwale, Margaret. English of . . . (Bilataha, Jaa. V.s. PERR/etal-1972.)	5.8

BILL-1974a	Bills, Garland D. Southwest Areal . . .	2.2
BILL-1974b	_____. Review Article.	2.2.1
	(_____. V.s. SPOL/BILL-1974.)	
	(Bittle, William E. V.s. HYME/BITT-1967.)	
BLAC-1891a	Blackmar, Frank W. Spanish American . . .	2.7
BLAC-1891b	_____. Spanish Institutions . . .	2.2
BLAN-A-1971	Blanco, Antonio. La lengua española . . .	6.2
BLAN-G-1971	Blanco, George M. Teaching Spanish . . .	5.2
BLUM-1952	Blum, Owen W. Some Aspects . . .	5.2.1
BOGG-1954	Boggs, Ralph S. Phonetics of . . .	3.7
BOGG-1954-55	_____. Términos del . . .	8.5
BOMS/ALFA-1973	Bomse, Marguerite D. and Julián H. Alfaro.	
	Practical Spanish . . .	9.2.2
BOWE-1952	Bowen, J. Donald. The Spanish of . . .	3.2
BOWE-1972	_____. Local Standards . . .	3.2
BOWE-1974	_____. New Mexican . . .	3.4
BRAD-1937	Braddy, Haldeen. Cowboy Lingo . . .	5.8
BRAD-1955	_____. Narcotic Argot . . .	8.8
BRAD-1956	_____. Smugglers' Argot . . .	8.8
BRAD-1960	_____. The Pachucos and . . .	8.5
BREK-1973	Brekke, Alice M. Evaluational Reactions . . .	6.2.1
BREN-1968	Brennan, James Edward. A Study of . . .	5.2.1
BREN-1964	Brenni, Vito J. American English . . .	1.1
BRIG-1967/71	Bright, Elizabeth S. A Word Geography . . .	6.6
BRIG-1960a	Bright, William. Animals of . . .	6.9
BRIG-1960b	_____. A Note on . . .	2.9
BRIG/BRIG-1959	_____ and Elizabeth S. Bright.	
	Spanish Words . . .	6.9
BRIS-1972	Brisk, María Estela. The Spanish Syntax . . .	3.4
BRUS-1974a	_____. New Mexican . . .	3.4
BRIS-1974b	_____. A Preliminary Study . . .	3.4
BROO/etal-1970/72		
	Brooks, Bonnie S., Gary D. Brooks, Paul W. Good-	
	man and Jacob Ornstein. Sociolinguistic	
	Background . . .	2.2.1
	(Brooks, Gary D. V.s. BROO/etal-1970/72.)	
BROP-1932	Brophy, Mrs. William A. [Kathleen McKee]. The	
	Language of . . .	3.8
BROU-1972	Broussard, Neonetta Cabrera. The Spelling	
	Errors . . .	2.8.1
BROW-1970	Brown, Dolores. A Two-syllable . . .	4.3
BRÜC-1955	Brüch, Josef. Ein spanisches Wort . . .	2.8
	(Bucchioni, Eugene. V.s. CORD/etal-1972.)	
BUSS-1971	Bussey, Jo Ann Keslar. A Comparative Study . .	5.3
BUTL-1935	Butler, Susan Passmore. Usable Spanish . . .	5.2.2
CANF-1951	Canfield, D. Lincoln. Tampa Spanish: . . .	10.3
CANF-1962	_____. La pronunciación del . . .	1.3
CANF-1968	_____. East Meets . . .	1.2
CANN-1971	Cannon, Garland. Bilingual Problems . . .	1.2

CARD-1958	Cárdenas, Daniel N. The Geographic Distribution . . .	1.3
CARD-1970	_____. Dominant Spanish . . .	1.2
CARD-1972	_____. Compound and . . .	2.2
CARD-1933	Cárdenas, Juan Francisco de. Hispanic Culture . . .	1.2
	(Caro, Rosan Jordán de. V.s. JORD-R-1973.)	
CARL-1939	Carlisle, Rose Jeanne. A Southwestern Dictionary.	2.8
CARR-1973	Carrillo, Rafael Abeyta. An In-depth Survey . . .	3.2.1
CARR-1955	Carrow, Sister Mary Arthur [Elizabeth]. A Comparative Study . . .	2.8.1
CARR-1971	____, Elizabeth [Sister Mary Arthur]. Comprehension of . . .	5.5
CARR-1972	_____. Auditory Comprehension . . .	5.5
CASA-1954-55	Casagrande, Joseph B. Comanche Linguistic . .	7.9
	(Casiano, Heriberto. V.s. FISHM/CASI-1969.)	
	(Castellanos, Diego. V.s. CORD/etal-1972.)	
CAST-1967	Castellanos, Sister Mary Catherine, O.P. English Lexical . . .	10.7
	(Castillo, Lupe. V.s. RIOS/CAST-1970.)	
CAST-1936	Castillo Nájera, Francisco. Breves consideraciones . . .	5.5
CERD/etal-1953	Cerda, Gilberto, Berta Cabaza and Julieta Farias. Vocabulario español . . .	5.5
CERV-1973	Cervantes, Alfonso. A Selected Vocabulary . .	5.5
CHAC-1969	Chacón, Estelle. Pochismos.	6.7
CHAV-1950	Chávez, Fray Angélico. Some Original . . .	3.1
CHAV-1957	_____. New Names . . .	3.6
CHEN-1938	Chenault, Lawrence R. The Puerto Rican . . .	9.2.1
CHER-1966	Cherry, Adrian. Tampa Spanish . . .	10.5
CHIL-1971	Childers, Jean. Some Secondary . . .	5.2
CHRI-1973	Christian, Chester C., Jr. Criteria for . . .	2.2
CHRI/CHRI-1966	Christian, Jane MacNab and Chester C. Christian, Jr. Spanish Language . . .	2.2.1
CLAR-1959/70	Clark, Margaret. Health in . . .	6.5
CLAR-1970	Clark y Moreno, Joseph A. A Bibliography of . . .	2.1
CLAR-1972	_____. A Bibliography of . . .	2.1
CLEG-1969	Clegg, J. Halvor. Fonética y . . .	5.3
COBO-1973	Cobos, Rubén. Southwestern Spanish . . .	2.5
COHE-1970	Cohen, Andrew David. A Sociolinguistic Approach . . .	6.2.1
COHE-1973	_____. Innovative Education . . .	6.2.1
	(Cohen, Paul. V.s. LABO/etal-1968.)	
COLE/MOND-1974	Coleman, William and Antonio Mondragón. Qué Pasó?	3.5
COLT-1967	Coltharp, Lurline H. The Influence of . . .	8.5
COLT-1965	_____. The Tongue of . . .	8.5
COLT-1970a	_____. Invitation to . . .	8.5

COLT-1970b	_____. Some Additions: . . .		8.5
COLT-1973	_____. Bilingual Onomastics . . .		5.6
COOP-1968	Cooper, Robert L. Two Contextualized . . .		9.2.1
COOP-1969	_____. Theme Address . . .		9.2.1
COOP/etal-1968/69	_____, Barbara Fowles and Abraham Givner. Listening Comprehension . . .		9.2.1
COOP/GREE-1968/69a	_____ and Lawrence Greenfield. Language Use . . .		9.2.1
COOP/GREE-1968/69b	_____ and _____. Word Frequency . . .		9.2.1
	(_____ 1968/69. V.s. FISHM/COOP-1968/69.)		
	(_____ 1969. V.s. EDEL-1968.)		
	(_____ 1969/71. V.s. KIMP-1968/69/71.)		
CORD/etal-1972	Cordasco, Francesco, Eugene Bucchioni and Diego Castellanos. Puerto Ricans . . .		9.1
CORD-1972	Córdova, Gilbert Benito. Bibliography of . . .		3.1
CORN-1969	Cornejo, Ricardo J. Bilingualism: Study . . .		5.5
COST-1937	Costales, Dionisio. Spanish Games . . .		3.2
CRAD-1973	Craddock, Jerry R. Spanish in . . .		1.2
CRAI-1969	Craig, Colette Grinevald. La situation linguistique . . .		9.7
CRAI/HUMB-1938	Craigie, Sir William Alexander and James R. Hulbert. A Dictionary of . . .		2.8
CROO-1935	Crook, Alice M. Old-Time New . . .		3.5
CROW-1962	Crowley, Cornelius J. Some Remarks . . .		2.9
CRUZ-1970	Cruz-Aedo, Víctor. Español para . . .		5.2.2
CURR-1950	Currie, Mona Boyd. Problems of . . .		6.2.1
	(Davenport, Catherine D. V.s. PERR/etal-1972.)		
DAVI/KOEH-1932	Davidson, Levette J. and Olga Kazel Koehler. The Naming of . . .		3.6
DAVI-1957	Davis, Jack Emory. Teaching Spanish . . .		4.2
	(de Caro, Rosan Jordán. V.s. JORD-R-1973.)		
DECK-1952	Decker, Bob Dan. Phonology of . . .		9.3
	(de Cuéllar, Beatriz Varela. V.s. VARE-1974.)		
DELA/MAST-1952	De Lannoy, William C. and Elizabeth Masterson. Teen-age Hophead . . .		8.8
	(de Porras, Normina Wolff. V.s. WOLF-1971.)		
DIAS-1941	Días, Rosario Simón. A Vocabulary of . . .		6.7
DILL-1972	Dillard, J.L. Language Contact . . .		2.8
DILL-1973	_____. The Lingua Franca . . .		2.8
DILLO-1972	Dillon, David Andrew. An Analysis of . . .		5.8.1
DOBI-1935	Dobie, J. Frank. Puro Mexicano.		2.2
DOCK-1955	Dockstader, Frederick J. Spanish Loanwords . .		4.9
DON?-1937	Don ? . Vaquero Lingo.		2.8
DONO-1972	Donofrio, Rosalie S. Maggio. Situation and . .		3.2.1
DOSS-n.d.	Dossick, Jesse J. Doctoral Research . . .		9.1

DOZI-1956	Dozier, Edward P. Two Examples . . .	3.9	
DOZI-1967	_____. Linguistic Acculturation . .	2.9	
DUNC-1956	Duncan, Robert M. Algunas observaciones . . .	3.3	
DUNN-1973	Dunn, Edward Wesley, Jr. A Factor Analysis . .	5.2.1	
DURA-1965	Duran, Felix Leroy. A Compilation of . . .	3.7	

EDEL-1968   Edelman, Martin. The Contextualization of . .   9.2.1
             (_____, R.L. Cooper and J.A. Fish-
             man 1969. V.S. EDEL-1968.)
EDMO-1952   Edmonson, Munro S. Los Manitos: Patterns . .   3.2
EDMO-1957   _____. Los Manitos: A . . .   3.2
ELIA-1970   Elías Olivares, Lucía E. Study of . . .   5.5
ESPI-1909a   Espinosa, Aurelio Macedonio. Studies
             in . . . [I]   3.3
ESPI-1909aa _____. Studies in . . . [I]   3.3
ESPI-1909aaa _____. Studies in . . . [I]   3.3
ESPI-1910   _____. Los elementos indios . . .   2.5
ESPI-1911   _____. The Spanish Language . . .   3.2
ESPI-1911-12-13
             _____. Studies in . . . [II]   3.4
ESPI-1912   _____. Cuentitos populares . . .   3.3
ESPI-1913   _____. Nombres de . . .   3.3
ESPI-1914-15 _____. Studies in . . . [III]   3.7
ESPI-1917   _____. Speech Mixture . . .   3.7
ESPI-1925   _____. Syllabic Consonants . . .   3.3
ESPI-1930a   _____. Estudios sobre . . . [I]   3.3
ESPI-1930b   _____. Apuntaciones para . . .   3.5
ESPI-1932   _____. El desarrollo de . . .   3.9
ESPI-1934   _____. El desarrollo fonético s . . .   3.3
ESPI-1935   _____, La palabra 'Castilla' . . .   4.9
ESPI-1942   _____. Miscellaneous Materials . . .   3.9
ESPI-1946   _____. Estudios sobre . . .   3.4
ESPI-1952   _____. Spanish Tradition . . .   3.9
ESPI-J-1957 Espinosa, Aurelio Macedonio, Jr. Problemas
             lexicográficos . . .   2.5
EVAN-1971   Evans, Phyllis Joyce Howell. Word-Pair
             Discrimination . . .   5.3
EYRI-1937   Eyring, Edward. Spanish for . . .   2.2

             (Fallis. V.s. VALD-1973.)
FERNA-1972   Fernández, Micho. El Barrio Diccionario: . .   9.2
FERNA-1973   Fernández, Roberto G. The Lexical and . . .   10.7
FERN-F-1965 Fernández Flores, Darío. The Spanish Heri-
             tage . . .   1.2
FERN-S-1972 Fernández-Shaw, Carlos M. Presencia española .   1.2
FERT/FISHM-1969
             Fertig, Sheldon and Joshua A. Fishman. Some
             Measures . . .   9.2.1
FICK-1930   Fickinger, Paul Lawrence. A Study of . . .   3.2

FIND-1969	Findling, Joav. Bilingual Need . . .	9.2.1
FISH-1973	Fisher, Alan Thomas. English Proficiency . . .	5.8.1
FISHM-1966	Fishman, Joshua A. Language Loyalty . . .	1.2
FISHM-1968/71	_____. The "Bilingualism in the Barrio" Project	9.2.1
FISHM-1968/69a	_____. Bilingual Attitudes . . .	9.2.1
FISHM-1968/69b	_____. A Sociolinguistic Census . .	9.2.1
FISHM-1969a	_____. The Measurement and . . .	9.2.1
FISHM-1969b	_____. Preface [: 'Bilingualism . .	9.2.1
FISHM-1969c	_____. Puerto Rican . . .	9.2
FISHM-1969d	_____. Some Things . . .	9.2.1
FISHM-1970	_____. Intellectuals From . . .	9.2.1
FISHM/CASI-1969	_____ and Heriberto Casiano. Puerto Ricans . . .	9.2
FISHM/COOP-1968/69	_____ and Robert L. Cooper. Alternative Measures . . .	9.2.1
FISHM/HERA-1969	_____ and Eleanor Herasimchuk. The Multiple Prediction . . .	9.2.1
FISHM/TERR-1969	_____ and Charles E. Terry. The [Contrastive] Validity of . . .	9.2.1
	(_____ 1969. V.s. EDEL-1968.)	
	(_____ 1969. Vis. FERT/FISHM-1969.)	
	(_____ 1969/71. V.s. KIMP-1968/69/71.)	
FITZ-1921	Fitz-Gerald, John D. The Bilingual-Biracial .	2.2
FODY-1969	Fody III, Michael. A Glossary of . . .	5.5
FODY-1971	_____. The Spanish of . . .	2.1
FORT-1894	Fortier, Alcée. The isleños of . . .	11.2
	(Fowles, Barbara. V.s. COOP/etal-1968/69.)	
FRAU-1969	Frausto, Manuel H. Vocabulario español . . .	5.5
FREN-1953	Frenk Alatorre, Margit. Designaciones de . . .	8.5
FRIA/KELL-1949/69	Friar, John G. and George W. Kelly. A Practical Spanish . . .	2.5
FRIE-1950	Friedman, Lillian. Minorcan Dialect . . .	12.5
FRYD-1972	Frydendall, Dennis Joe. Errors in . . .	7.8.1
GAAR-1944	Gaarder, A. Bruce. Notes on . . .	8.5
GAAR-1971	_____. Language Maintenance . . .	1.2.1
GALA-1971	Galarza, Ernesto. Barrio Boy.	2.5
GALI-1969	Galíndez Suárez, Jesús de. Puerto Rico . . .	9.2
GALV-1949	Galván, Roberto A. Un estudio geográfico . . .	5.5
GALV-1955	_____. El dialecto español . . .	5.5
GALV-1966	_____. Más observaciones . . .	8.5
GALV-1970	_____. 'Chichecano,' neologismo . .	5.5
GALV-1971	_____. More on . . .	5.5
GALV-1973	_____. Chicano, vocablo . . .	2.5

GALV/MILL-1972	_____ and Damon Miller. Student Study . . .	2.2.2
GAMI-1930	Gamio, Manuel. Mexican Immigration . . .	2.5
GARC-A-1969	García, Anita H. Identification and . . .	5.2
GARC-E-1971	García, Ernest. Chicano Spanish . . .	2.2
GARC-FB-1760	García, Fr[ay] Bartolomé. Manual para . . .	5.2
GARC-M-1974	García, Maryellen. Para-pa Usage . . .	5.4
GARC-N-1971	García, Nelda C. Language Factors . . .	5.2.1
GARC-Ri-1973	García, Ricardo L. Identification and . . .	3.8.1
GARC-Ro-1972	García, Rodolfo. Language Interference . . .	2.8.1
GARC-T-1939	García, Trinidad. A Vocabulary of . . .	3.7
GERR-1964	Gerritsen, William D. An English-Spanish . . .	3.5
GILB-1967	Gilbert, Glenn G. The Linguistic Geography . .	1.2
GILB-1970	_____. Texas Studies . . .	5.2
GILP-1970	Gilpin, George H. Street Names . . .	5.6
GING-1974	Gingràs, Rosario C. Problems in . . .	6.10
	(Givner, Abraham. V.s. COOP/etal-1968/69.)	
GODW-1884	Godwin, Parke, ed. Prose Writings . . .	12.2
	(Goldsen, Rose Kohn. V.s. Mill/etal-1950.)	
GOMU-1973	Gomula, Wanda Wallace. Common Patterns . . .	10.2
	(Gonzales, James Lee. V.s. GONZ-J-1972.)	
GONZ-Ge-1973	González, George Adelberto. The Development and . . .	3.2
GONZ-Gu-1968	González, Gustavo. A Linguistic Profile . . .	5.4
GONZ-Gu-1969	_____. The Phonology of . . .	5.3
GONZ-Gu-1970	_____. The Acquisition of . . .	5.4
GONZ-Gu-1973a	_____. The Analysis of . . .	2.2
GONZ-Gu-1973b	_____. The English of . . .	5.8.1
GONZ-Gu-1974	_____. The Acquisition of . . .	5.4
GONZ-J-1972	Gonzales, James Lee. The Effects of . . .	3.2.1
	(González, José Luis. V.s. LEWI-1965.)	
GONZ-N-1967	González, Nancie L. The Spanish-Americans . .	3.2
GONZ-R-1967	González, Rafael Jesús. Pachuco: The . . .	8.5
	(Goodman, Paul W. V.s. BROO/etal-1970/72.)	
	(Gordon, Barbara Y. V.s. AARO/etal-1969.)	
GOSN-1945	Gosnell, Patria Arán. The Puerto Ricans . . .	9.2
GRAH-1962	Graham, Robert Somerville. Spanish-Language Radio . . .	7.7
GRAND-1940	Grandoff, Victor C. Folklore Note . . .	12.2
GRANG-1960	Granger, Byrd H. Grand Canyon . . .	4.6
GRANT-1942	Grant, Rena V. The Localized Vocabulary . . .	6.8
GRAY-1912	Gray, Edward Dundas McQueen. The Spanish Language . . .	3.2
GREB/etal-1970	Grebler, Leo, Joan W. Moore and Ralph C. Guzmán. The Mexican-American . . .	2.2.1
GREE-L-1968/70/71		
	Greenfield, Lawrence. Spanish and English . .	9.2.1
	(_____ 1968/69a, b. V.s. COOP/GREE-1968/69 a, b.)	
GREE-P-1971	Greenfield, Philip J. Playing Card . . .	4.9
GRIF-1947a	Griffith, Beatrice. The Pachuco Patois. . . .	8.2.1

335

GRIF-1947b	_____.	Who Are . . .	8.2.1
GRIF-1948a	_____.	American Me.	8.2.1
GRIF-1948b	_____.	Fingertip Coats . . .	8.5
GROS-1935	Gross, Stuart M. A Vocabulary of . . .		3.5
GUDD-1949/69	Gudde, Erwin G. California Place . . .		6.6
GUIT-1973	Guitart, Jorge Miguel. Markedness and . . .		10.3
GUMP-1967	Gumperz, John J. On the . . .		9.4

(_____ 1970. V.s. GUMP/HERN-1972.)
(_____ and Eduardo Hernández-Chávez 1969/70. V.s. GUMP/HERN-1972.)

GUMP/HERN-1972	_____ and _____. Bilingualism, Bidialectalism . . .		6.10
GUTI-L-1972	Gutiérrez, Lorraine Padilla. Attitudes Toward . . .		3.2.1
GUTI-M-1971	Gutiérrez, Medardo. A Description of . . .		12.7

(Guzmán, Ralph C. V.s. GREB/etal-1970.)

HALL-1947	Hall, Robert A., Jr. A Note on . . .		2.9
HAMC-1971	Hamilton, Carlos D. Amenazas contra . . .		9.5
HAMJ-1970	Hamilton, John W. La toponimia española . . .		10.6
HAMM-1932	Hamilton, Marian. California Gold-Rush . . .		6.8
HAMM-1973	Hammond, Robert M. An Experimental Verification . . .		10.3
HARD-1956	Hardman, Martha James. The Phonology of . . .		3.3
HARR-1974a	Harris, James W. Morphologization of . . .		3.3
HARR-1974b	_____. Two Morphophonemic . . .		3.3
HARR-1967	Harrison, Helene W. A Methodological Study . .		5.5
HATC-1909	Hatcher, Mattie Austin. Plan of . . .		5.2
HAUG-1956	Haugen, Einar. Bilingualism in . . .		1.1
HAUG-1973	_____. Bilingualism, Language . . .		1.1
HAYE-1961	Hayes, Alice Frazer. Acoustic Vowel . . .		5.3
HAYE-1949	Hayes, Francis G. Anglo-Spanish in . . .		10.2
HEAR-1969	Heard, Betty R. A Phonological Analysis . . .		5.8
HEFL-1941	Heflin, Woodford A. Characteristic Features .		3.8
HEIL-1966	Heiler[-Saavedra], Barbara. An Investigation of . . .		5.8.1
HELL-1967	Heller, Celia S. Mexican American . . .		2.2.1
HELM-1968	Helm, June. Spanish-Speaking People . . .		1.2
HENR-1938	Henríquez Ureña, Pedro. El español en . . .		2.2
HENS-1973	Hensey, Fritz G. Grammatical Variables . . .		5.4
HENS-1974a	_____. The Development of . . .		2.2
HENS-1974b	_____. Two Current . . .		5.5

(Herasimchuk, Eleanor. V.s. MA/HERA-1968/71.)
(_____. V.s. FISHM/HERA-1969.)

HERM-1971	Hermenet, Argelia María Buitrago. Ethnic Identification . . .		9.2.1
HERN-1970	Hernández, José Gonzales. Chicano Dictionary: . . .		8.5
HERN/etal-1975	Hernández-Chávez, Eduardo, Andrew D. Cohen and Anthony Fred Beltramo, eds. El lenguaje de . . .		2.2

                        (Hernández-Chávez, Eduardo. 1969/70. V.s.
                            GUMP/HERN-1972.)
                        (_____. 1972. V.s. GUMP/HERN-1972.)
HICK-1970   Hicks, Jerral Robert. Errors in . . .   7.8.1
HILL-1906a   Hills, Elijah Clarence. New Mexican . . .   3.2
HILL-1906aa   _____. New Mexican . . .   3.2
HILL-1929   _____. New Mexican . . .   3.2
HILL-1938   _____. El español de . . .   3.2
HIRS-1951   Hirsch [Weinstein], Ruth. A Study of . . .   13.3
HOFF-1974a   Hoffer, Bates. Bilingual Language . . .   5.8.1
HOFF/ORNS-1974   _____ and Jacob Ornstein. Sociolinguis-
                            tics in . . .   2.2.1
HOFFM-1971a   Hoffman, Gerard. Life in . . .   9.2.1
HOFFM-1971b   _____. Puerto Ricans . . .   9.2.1
HOIJ-1939   Hoijer, Harry. Chiricahua Loan-words . . .   4.9
HOIJ-1948   _____. Linguistic and . . .   4.9
HOLL-1973   Hollomon, John Wesley. Problems of . . .   3.2.1
                        (Hulbert, James R. V.s. CRAI/HULB-1938.)
HOUC-1939   Houck, Helen Phipps. [Review of] . . .   9.2
HULM-1974   Hulme, Antonia Lala. The Phonology of . . .   10.3
HUMP-1943-44   Humphrey, Norman D. The Education and . . .   7.2.1
HYME-1956   Hymes, Dell H. The Supposed Spanish . . .   4.9
HYME-1964   Hymes, Dell H. Language in . . .   2.2
HYME/BITT-1967   _____ and William E. Bittle. Studies
                            in . . .   2.2

IVEY-1927   Ivey, Alfred Joe. A Study of . . .   5.5

JABL-1973   Jablonsky, Adelaide. Mexican Americans . . .   1.2
JACK-1938   Jackson, Lucile Prim. An Analysis of . . .   5.8.1
JACK-1952   Jackson, William Richard, Jr. Florida in . . . 12.2
JANU-1970   January, William Spence, Jr. The *Chicano*
                        Dialect . . .   8.5
JATO-1961   Jato Macías, Manuel. La enseñanza del . . .   2.2
JENK-1931   Jenkins, Thelma Adams. A Study of . . .   2.8
JESU-1952   Jesús, Cruz de. A Study of . . .   9.2
                        (_____. 1953. V.s. ANAS/JESU-1953.)
JIME-1969   Jiménez Núñez, Alfredo. Panorama etnológico .   3.2
JOHN-J-1943   Johnson, Jean Bassett. A Clear Case . . .   4.9
JOHN-L-1938   Johnson, Loaz W. A Comparison of . . .   3.8.1
JOHN-1951   Johnston, Marjorie C. Spanish-Language News-
                        papers . . .   1.2
JORD-L-1973   Jordan, Lois B. Mexican Americans . . .   2.1
JORD-R-1973   Jordán de Caro, Rosan. Language Loyalty . . .   5.2.1

KAND-1967   Kandell, Alice Susan. Harlem Children's . . .   9.8.1
KANY-1945/51   Kany, Charles E. American-Spanish Syntax.   3.2
KANY-1960   _____. American-Spanish Semantics. 1.5

KATZ-1974	Katz, Linda Fine. The Evolution of . . .		8.5
KEEV/etal-1945	Keever, Mary, Alfredo Vásquez and Anna Padilla. Glossary of . . .		2.5
KELL-1974	Keller, Gary D. La norma de . . . (Kelly, George W. V.s FRIA/KELL-1949/69.)		1.4
KELL-1938	Kelly, Rex R. Vocabulary as . . .		5.5
KELL/KELL-1960	Kelly, George W. and Rex R. Kelly. Farm and . . .		5.5
KEND-1972	Kendler, Karen Seed. An Exploratory Study . .		9.2.1
KENI-1942	Keniston, Hayward. Notes on . . .		1.1
KERC-1934	Kercheville, Francis M. A Preliminary Glossary . . .		3.5
KERC-1967	_____. A Preliminary Glossary . . .		3.5
KIDD-1941	Kiddle, Lawrence B. Los nombres del . . .		3.5
KIDD-1943a	_____. A propósito . . .		1.1
KIDD-1943b	_____. Bibliografía adicional . . .		1.1
KIDD-1951-52	_____. 'Turkey' in . . .		3.5
KIDD-1952	_____. Spanish Loan . . .		2.9
KIDD-1964	_____. American Indian . . .		2.9
KIDD-1968	_____. Hispanismos en . . .		2.9
KIDD-1972	_____. Los nombres del . . .		3.5
KIMM-1952	Kimmerle, Marjorie. Bum, Poddy . . .		3.8
KIMP-1968/69/71	Kimple, James, Jr. Language Shift . . .		9.2.1
KIND-1960	Kindig, Maita M. A Phonological Study . . .		9.8.1
KREI-1957	Kreidler, Charles W. A Study of . . .		9.7
KUVL-1973	Kuvlesky, William P. Use of . . .		2.2.1
KUVL/PATE-1971	Kuvlesky, William P. and Victoria M. Patella. Degree of . . .		5.2.1
LABO/etal-1968	Labov, William, Paul Cohen, Clarence Robins and John Lewis. A Study of . . .		9.2
LAMB-1968	Lamb, Anthony J. A Phonological Study . . .		10.3
LANC-1969	Lance, Donald M. A Brief Study . . .		5.2
LANC-1970	_____. The Codes of . . .		5.2
LAND-1959	Landar, Herbert J. The Diffusion of . . .		2.9
LAND-1961	_____. The Southwestern Words . . .		2.9
LANE-1966	Lane, James Alfred. A Descriptive Study . . . (Lavignino. V.s. POTT-1969.)		6.2.1
LAWS-1969	Lawson, Jack. Bobby and . . .		6.3
LAYD-1972	Laydon, Russell Glenn. The Relationship Between . . .		9.2.1
LEAC-1971	Leach, John Nathaniel. Cultural Factors . . .		9.2
LEAV-1969	Leavitt, Ruby Rohrlich. A Comparative Study .		9.2.1
LENN-1963	Lennon, John Joseph. A Comparative Study . . .		9.2.1
LEON-1936	León, Aurelio de. Barbarismos comunes . . .		5.5
LEVI-1969	Levine, Harry. Bilingualism: Its . . . (Levy [Lida] 1944. V.s. LEVY-1952a.]		2.2.1
LEVY-1952a	Levy [Lida], Denah. El sefardí esmirniano . .		13.3
LEVY-1952b	_____. La pronunciación del . . .		13.3

                    (Lewis, John. V.s. LABO/etal-1968.)
LEWI-1965   Lewis, Oscar. La Vida: A . . .   9.2
LEWI-1968   _____. A Study of . . .   9.2.1
LIND-1971   Lindenfeld, Jacqueline. Semantic Categoriza-
                         tion . . .   4.9
LINE-1973   Linehan, Edward J. Cuba's Exiles . . .   10.2
LOPE-1968   Lope Blanch, Juan M. El español de . . .   1.2
LOPE-M-1972   López, Melitón. Bilingual-Bicultural . . . 2.2.1
LOPE-T-1972   López, Thomas R., Jr. Prospects for . . .   3.2
LOPEZ-1968   López Morales, Humberto. El español de . . . 10.1
LOSP-1949   [Anon.] Los pastores: A . . .   5.2
LOWR-1932   Lowrie, Samuel H. Culture Conflict . . .   5.2
LOZA-1961   Lozano, Anthony Girard. Intercambio de . . . 5.7
LOZA-1974   _____. Grammatical Notes . . .   2.4
LUNA-1970   Luna, Juanita J. A Selected Vocabulary . . . 5.5
LURI-1930   Luria, Max A. Judeo-Spanish Dialects . . . 13.2
LYNN-1940   Lynn, Klonda. A Phonetic Analysis . . .   4.8.1
LYNN-1945   _____. Bilingualism in . . .   4.8.1
LYNN-1950   _____. Gringoisms in . . .   4.8

MA/HERA-1968/71/72
                    Ma, Roxana and Eleanor Herasimchuk. The
                         Linguistic Dimensions . . .   9.2.1
MACC-1950a   MacCurdy, Raymond R. Louisiana-French Loan . . 11.5
MACC-1950b   _____. The Spanish Dialects . . . 11.2
MACC-1951   _____. A History and . . .   11.1
MACC-1959   _____. A Spanish Word-List . . .   11.5
MACE-1972   Mace, Betty J. A Linguistic Profile . . .   7.2.1
                    (_____. V.s. MATL/MACE-1973.)
MADS-1964   Madsen, William. Mexican-Americans of . . . 5.2.1
MAHO-1967   Mahoney, Mary Katherine. Spanish and . . . 5.2.1
MALK-1968   Malkiel, Yakov. Hispanic Philology.   1.2
MALK-1972   _____. Linguistics and . . [V.s. MALK-1968]
MALL-1971   Mallory, Gloria Griffin. Sociolinguistic
                         Considerations . . .   3.2.1
MANU-1967   Manuel, Herschel T. Spanish-Speaking Children 2.2.1
MARA-1955   Maravilla, Frederick B. Los anglicismos en . . 7.7
MARA-1970   Marambio, Juan. Vocabulario español . . .   5.5
MARR-1972   Marrocco, Mary Ann Wilkinson. The Spanish of . 5.2
MART-A-1970   Martínez, Antonio J. An Analysis of . . .   9.8.1
MART-I-1972   Martínez, Irma Herrera. A Study of . . .   5.2.1
MART-J-1972   Martínez-Bernal, Janet Ayers. Children's
                         Acquisition . . .   4.2
MATH-1951   Mathews, Mitford M. A Dictionary of . . .   2.8
MATL/MACE-1973   Matluck, Joseph H. and Betty J. Mace. Language
                         Characteristics . . .   2.2
MAY-1966   May, Darlene Rae. Notas sobre . . .   5.5
MAYA-1953   Mayans, Frank, Jr. Puerto Rican . . .   9.2.1
MAYN-1973   Maynes, J. Oscar, Jr. A Comparison of . . . 4.5
MAZE-1971   Mazeika, Edward John. A Descriptive Analysis . 5.2

MACCL-1964	McClendon, Juliette J.C. Spanish-Speaking Children . . .	5.2.1
MCCL-1972	McClinton, Johnnie W. Effectiveness of . . .	5.2
	(McDonagh, Edward C. V.s. PEÑA/MCDO-1966.)	
MCHA-1939	McHale, Carlos F. Spanish Don'ts . . .	1.7
MCKE-1955	McKee, Okla Markham. Five Hundred . . .	5.5
MCLE-1969	McLendon, Sally. Spanish Words . . .	6.9
MCME-1973	McMenamin, Jerry. Rapid Code . . .	6.10
MCSP-1932a	McSpadden, George E. Some Semantic . . .	3.2
MCSP-1934b	_____. Some Semantic . . .	3.2
MCWI-1949	McWilliams, Carey. North From . . .	2.8
MELL-1954	Mellenbruch, Julia Kda Klattenhoff. Teaching Spanish . . .	5.2
MERZ-1974	Merz, Geri W. Speech Levels . . .	4.3
METC-1972	Metcalf, Allan A. Mexican-American English . .	6.8.1
METC-1974a	_____. The Study (Or, . . .	6.8.1
METC-1974b	_____. The Study of . . .	6.8.1
MENC-1919/36	Mencken, H.L. The American Language.	2.8
MICH-1969	Michel, Joseph. A Pilot Project . . .	5.2
MICK-1969	Mickey, Barbara H. A Bibliography of . . .	2.1
	(Miller, Damon. V.s. GALV/MILL-1972.)	
MILL-1959	Miller, Wick R. Spanish Loanwords . . .	3.9
MILL/etal-1950	Mills, C. Wright, Clarence Senior and Rose Kohn Goldsen. The Puerto Rican . . .	9.2.1
	(Mondragón, Antonio. V.s. COLE/MOND-1974.)	
MONT-1966	Montemayor, Elsa Diana. A Study of . . .	5.2
	(Moore, Joan W. V.s. GREB/etal-1970.)	
MURP-M-1973	Murphy, Marilyn. The Effects of . . .	3.8.1
MURP-RP-1972	Murphy, R. Paul. Integration of . . .	3.7
MURP-RP-1974a	_____. The Extent of . . .	3.7
MURP-RP-1974b	_____. Interference, Integration . .	3.7
MYCU-1968	Mycue, Elena Ines de los Santos. Testing in . . .	5.2.1
MYER-1959	Myers, Gail Eldrige. A Study of . . .	7.2.1
NALL-1962	Nall, Frank C. II. Role Expectations . . .	2.2.1
NATA-1969	Natalicio, Eleanor Diana S. Formation of . . .	5.8.1
NAVA-1963	Navarro, Carlos. An Analytical Study . . .	10.5
NICH-1941	Nichols, Madaline W. A Bibliographical Guide . . .	1.1
NOGA-1969/71	Nogales, Luis. The Mexican American . . .	2.1
NORM-1956	Norman, Arthur M.A. A Southeast Texas . . .	5.8
NORT-1937	Northrop, Stuart A. Terms from . . .	2.8
OLIV-1970	Oliva, Félix S. Nueva York . . .	9.2
OLIV-1972	Oliver, Joseph D. Diatype Identification . . .	3.2.1
OLST-1973	Olstad, Charles. The Local Colloquial . . .	4.2
ORNS-1951	Ornstein, Jacob. The Archaic and . . .	3.2
	(_____. 1970/72. V.s. BROO/etal-1970/72.)	

ORNS-1970	_____. Sociolinguistics and . . .	2.2.1
ORNS-1971a	_____. Language Varieties . . .	2.2
ORNS-1971b	_____. Sociolinguistic Research . .	2.2.1
ORNS-1972a	_____. Mexican American Sociolinguistics . . .	2.2.1
ORNS-1972b	_____. Toward a . . .	2.2.1
ORNS-1973	_____. Toward an . . .	2.2.1
ORNS-1974	_____. The Sociolinguistic Studies .	2.2.1
ORTE-1969	Ortego, Phillip D. Perspectives in . . .	2.2
ORTE-1969-70	_____. Some Cultural . . .	2.2
ORTE-1974	_____. Sociolinguistics and . . .	2.2.1
ORTI-1947	Ortiz, Carmelita Louise. English Influence . .	10.7
ORTI-1949	_____. English Influence . . .	10.7
OSBO-1972	Osborne, Zelda L. et al. Mexican-Americans: A . . .	2.1
OXMA-1972	Oxman, Wendy G. The Effects of . . .	9.2.1
	(Padilla, Anna. V.s. KEEV/etal-1945.)	
PADI-1958	Padilla, Elena Up From . . .	9.2.1
PADI-1971	Padilla, Ray. Apuntes para . . .	2.1
PATE-1971	Patella, Victoria M. A Study in . . .	5.2.1
PATE/KUVL-1973	_____ and William P. Kuvlesky. Situational Variation . . .	5.2.1
PATT-1946	Patterson, Maurine. Some Dialectal . . .	5.4
PAUL-1970	Pauls, Leo Wayne. Errors in . . .	7.8.1
PEAR-1932	Pearce, Thomas Matthews. The English Language . . .	2.8
PEAR-1941	_____. Trader Terms . . .	2.8
PEAR-1943	_____. New Mexican . . .	3.8
PEAR-1955	_____. Spanish Place-name . . .	2.6
PEAR-1958a	_____. The New Mexico . . .	3.6
PEAR-1958b	_____. Three Rocky . . .	2.8
PEAR-1961	_____. Religious Place . . .	3.6
PEAR-1965	_____. New Mexico . . .	3.6
PEÑA-1967	Peña, Albar Antonio. A Comparative Study . . .	5.2
PEÑA-1970	_____. Spanish-Speakers.	5.4
PEÑA-F-1972	Peñalosa, Fernando. Chicano Multilingualism .	2.2.1
PEÑA/MCDO-1966	_____ and Edward C. McDonagh. Social Mobility . . .	6.2.1
PEÑU-1964	Peñuelas, Marcelino C. Lo español en . . .	2.8
PEON-1966	Peón, Máximo. Cómo viven . . .	2.5
PERR/TRIM-1971	Perren, G. E. and J.L.M. Trim. Applications of . . .	2.2
	(Perry, Corrine B. V.s. PERR/etal-1972.)	
PERR/etal-1972	Perry, Edgar (Jaa Bilataha), Canyon Z. Quintero, Sr., Catherine D. Davenport and Corrine B. Perry. Western Apache . . .	4.9
PETE-1973	Peters, Daniel I. A Contrastive Analysis . . .	9.4
PHIL-1967	Phillips, Robert N., Jr. Los Angeles Spanish .	6.3
PHIL-1972	_____. The Influence of . . .	6.3

PIAL-1973	Pialorsi, Frank Paul. The Production and . . .	4.8.1
PIZZ-1968	Pizzo, Anthony P. Tampa Town . . .	10.2
POLI/RAMI-1973	Politzer, Robert L. and Arnulfo G. Ramírez. An Error Analysis . . .	6.8.1
PORG-1949	Porges, Ana. The Influence of . . .	9.7

(Porras, Normina Wolff de. V.s. WOLF-1971.)

POST-1917	Post, Anita Calneh. The Spanish Dialect . . .	4.2
POST-1932	_____. Southern Arizona . . .	4.3
POST-1933	_____. Some Aspects . . .	4.3
POST-1934	_____. Southern Arizona . . .	4.3
POTT-1969	Potter, Helen Rose Lavignino. Social and . . .	3.1
POUL-1970	Poulter, Virgil L. Comparison of . . .	5.3
POUL-1973	_____. A Phonological Study . . .	5.3

(Putnam, Howard. V.s. SANC/PUTN-1959.)

(Quintero, Canyon Z. V.s. PERR/etal-1972.)

RAEL-1934	Rael, Juan B. <u>Cosa nada</u> . . .	3.5
RAEL-1937	_____. A Study of . . .	3.2
RAEL-1939a	_____. Alternate Forms . . .	3.5
RAEL-1939b	_____. Associative Interference . .	3.5

(Ramírez, Arnulfo G. V.s. POLI/RAMI-1973.)

RAMI-K-1971	Ramírez, Karen G. Bilingualism and . . .	5.2.1
RAMI-K-197[1?]	_____. Original Research . . .	8.5
RAMI-K-1974	_____. Socio-cultural Aspects . . .	2.2
RAMI-MD-1939	Ramírez, Manuel D. Some Semantic . . .	10.5
RAMI-MI-1971	Ramírez, María Irene. A Comparison of . . .	5.2
RAMO-1974	Ramón, Simón René. Vocabulario selecto . . .	5.5
RAMO-I-1972	Ramos-Perea, Israel. The School Adjustment . .	9.2.1
RONC-1968/69	Ronch, Judah. Word Naming . . .	9.2.1
RANS-1953	Ransom, Helen. 'Manitos' and . . .	3.2
RESE-1970	Reséndez, Víctor. Vocabulario español . . .	5.5
RESN-1968	Resnick, Melvyn C. The Coordination and . . .	1.3
REYN-1973	Reyna, José Reynaldo. Mexican-American Prose .	5.2
REYN/HOUC-1971	Reynolds, John J. and Thomas J. Houchin. A Directory for . . .	9.2
REYN-1945	Reynolds, Selma Fay. Some Aspects . . .	5.4
RIBE-1970	Ribes Tovar, Federico. El libro puertorriqueño . . .	9.2
RICH/RIST-1934	Richardson, Rupert N. and Carl C. Rister. The Greater Southwest . . .	3.2
RICH-1935	Richie, Eleanor L. Spanish Place . . .	3.6
RIOS/CAST-1970	Ríos, Herminio and Lupe Castillo. Toward a . .	2.1

(Ríos, Herminio C. V.s. ROMA/RIOS-1972.)
(Rister, Carl C. V.s. RICH/RIST-1934.)

RIVE-1973	Rivera, Carmen Elena. Academic Achievement . .	9.2.1
RIZZ-1955	Rizzo, Gino L. Lingua e . . .	6.2
ROBE-1970	Roberts, Neil Alden. Errors in . . .	7.8.1

(Robins, Clarence. V.s. LABO/etal-1968.)

RODR-1973	Rodríguez del Pino, Salvador. El idioma de . .	2.2
ROMA-1960	Romano-V., Octavio Ignacio. Donship in . . .	5.5
ROMA/RIOS-1972	_____ and Herminio Ríos C. Toward a. . .	2.1
ROME-1928a	Romero, Cecil V. A Unique American . . .	3.5
ROME-1928b	_____. Notes on . . .	3.5
ROOT-1936	Roots, Floy. Methods and . . .	5.2
ROSA-1969	Rosa-Nieves, Cesáreo. El español de . . .	9.7
ROSE-1946	Rosenblat, Ángel. Notas de . . .	3.4
RUBE-1966	Rubel, Arthur J. Across the . . .	5.2.1
RUBE-1968	_____. Some Cultural . . .	5.2.1
SAID-1970	Said, Sally Eugenia Sneed. A Descriptive Model . . .	5.4
SALA-1924	Salado Álvarez, Victoriano. Mexicanismos supervivientes . . .	2.8
SALA-1930	_____. Nuevo Méjico . . .	3.2.1
SAMO-1966	Samora, Julian. La Raza: Forgotten . . .	2.2
SANC-1966	Sánchez, George I. History, Culture . . .	2.2
SANC/EAST-1960	_____ and Charles L. Eastlack. Say It . . .	5.3
SANC/PUTN-1959	_____ and Howard Putnam. Materials Relating . . .	2.1
SANC-1972	Sánchez, Rosaura. Nuestra circunstancia . . .	5.2
SANT-1959	Santamaría, Francisco J. Diccionario de . . .	2.5
SAVI-1970	Saville-Troike, Muriel R. Spanish.	1.2
SAWY-1957	Sawyer, Janet Beck Mosely. A Dialect Study . .	5.8.1
SAWY-1959	_____. Aloofness from . . .	5.8.1
SAWY-1964	_____. Social Aspects . . .	5.8.1
SAWY-1969	_____. Spanish-English Bilingualism . . .	5.8.1
SAWY-JO-1964a	Sawyer, Jesse O. The Implications of . . .	6.9
SAWY-JO-1964b	_____. Wappo Words . . .	6.9
SCHE-1965	Scheff, Thomas J. Changes in . . . (Schutz, Noel W., Jr. V.s. VOEG/etal-1967.)	2.2.1
SCHU-1933	Schupp, Ona E. Oral and . . .	3.8.1
SCOT-1969	Scott, Carmen Casillas. Spanish Language . . .	5.2.1
SECA-1972	Secades, Eladio. El Spanglish . . . ¡qué . . . (Senior, Clarence. V.s. MILL/etal-1950.)	9.7
SERI-1964	Serís, Homero. Bibliografía de . . .	1.1
SERR-1972	Serrano, Rodolfo Gaitán. Sociocultural Influences . . .	4.2.1
SHAF-1942	Shafer, Robert. The Pronunciation of . . .	6.6
SHAR-1970	Sharp, John M. The Origin of . . .	5.5
SHEL-1935	Shelton, Wilma Loy. A Check List . . . (Shiels, Marie E. V.s. WOLFR/etal-1971.)	3.1
SHIE-1972	_____. Dialects in . . .	9.8.1
SHIP-1959	Shipley, William. Review of . . .	6.9
SHIP-1962	_____. Spanish Elements . . .	6.9
SHOB/SING-1970	Shoban, Gloria and Pita Singer. The Degeneration of . . .	3.5

SHUL-1949	Shulman, David. Some Californian . . .	6.8
SHUL-1953	_____. Spanish Words . . .	6.8
	(Silvaroli, N.J. V.s. WAKE/SILV-1969.)	
	(Silverman, J.H. V.s. ARMI/SILV-1960.)	
SILV-1969a	Silverman, Stuart H. The Evaluation . . .	9.2.1
SILV-1969b	_____. A Method for . . .	9.2.1
SILV-1971	_____. The Effects of . . .	9.8.1
SIMO-1945	Simón, Alphonse, O.M.I. Pastoral Spanish.	5.5
	(Singer, Pita. V.s. SHOB/SING-1970.)	
SKOC-1972	Skoczylas, Rudolph V. An Evaluation of . . .	6.2.1
SKRA-1967/70	Skrabanek, R.L. The Use of . . .	5.2.1
SMIT-1968	Smith, M. Estellie. The Spanish-Speaking . . .	10.2.1
SOCR-1869	Socrates, Hyacinth. Southwestern Slang.	5.8
SOLA-1966	Sola Pool, David de. The Use of . . .	13.2
SOLE-1970	Solé, Carlos A. Bibliografía sobre . . .	1.1
SOLE-1972	_____. Bibliografía sobre . . .	1.1
SORV-1952	Sorvig, Ralph W. A Topical Analysis . . .	2.8
SORV-1953	_____. Southwestern Plant . . .	2.8
SOTO-1956	Soto, Pedro Juan. Spiks: Grabado . . .	9.2
SPAN-1971	[anon.] The Spanish-Speaking . . .	1.1
SPEC-1972	Spector, Sima. Patterns of . . .	6.8.1
SPEL-1925-26	Spell, Lota M. The First Text . . .	5.2
SPEN-1947	Spencer, Robert F. Spanish Loan . . .	3.9
SPIC-1943	Spicer, Edward H. Linguistic Aspects . . .	4.9
SPIC-1954	_____. Spanish-Indian . . .	2.9
SPOL-1972	Spolsky, Bernard. The Language Education . . .	2.2
SPOL/BILL-1974	Spolsky, Bernard and Garland D. Bills. The American Southwest.	2.2
STEC-1943	Steck, Francis Borgia. A Tentative Guide . . .	1.1
STEI-1969	Steiner, Stan. La Raza: The . . .	2.2
STEV-1973	Stevenson, James M. Cuban-Americans: New . .	10.2.1
STEW-1941	Stewart, George R. Two Spanish . . .	6.5
	(Stewart, William A. V.s. AARO/etal-1969.)	
STRO-1958	Strout, Clevy Lloyd. A Linguistic Study . . .	2.5
SUAR-1947-48	Suárez, Mario. Kid Zopilote.	8.5
TALL-1896	Tallichet, H. A Contribution Towards . . .	5.8
TAYL-1962	Taylor, Allan R. Spanish manteca . . .	1.9
TEEL-1971	Teel, Tommy Lou. A Sociolinguistic Study . . .	5.8.1
TERR/COOP-1969	Terry, Charles E. and Robert L. Cooper. A Note on . . .	9.2.1
	(_____. V.s. FISHM/TERR-1969.)	
TESC-1972	Teschner, Richard V. Anglicisms in . . .	7.7
TESC-1973	_____. The Feasibility of . . .	1.2
TESC-1974a	_____. Preparing a . . .	5.5
TESC-1974b	_____. Problems of . . .	5.5
TESC-1974c	_____. Spanish-Surnamed Populations	1.1
THOM-1967	Thomas, Piri. Down These . . .	9.5
THOM-1971	Thompson, Roger M. Language Loyalty . . .	5.2.1
THOM-1974a	_____. The 1970 U.S. . . .	5.2.1
THOM-1974b	_____. Mexican Americans . . .	5.2.1

TIMM-1971	Timmins, Kathleen M. An Investigation of . . .	3.2.1
TIRE-1948a	Tireman, Loyd Spencer. Spanish Vocabulary . .	3.5
TIRE-1948b	_____. Teaching Spanish-Speaking . .	3.2.1
TITI-1946	Titiev, Mischa. Suggestions for . . .	4.9
TORO-1972	Toronto, Allan Sharp. A Developmental Spanish . . .	7.4
TOVA-1974	Tovar, Inés. The Changing Attitude . . .	2.2
TRAG-1935	Trager, George L. Some Spanish . . .	3.6
TRAG/VALD-1937	_____. English Loans . . .	3.7
TRAG-1939a	_____. 'Cottonwood' = 'Tree' . . .	3.5
TRAG-1939b	_____. The Days of . . .	3.9
TRAG-1944	_____. Spanish and . . .	3.9
TREJ-1951	Trejo, Arnulfo D. Vocablos y . . .	4.5
TREJ-1959	_____. Una contribución al . . .	8.5
TREJ-1968	_____. Diccionario etimológico . . .	8.5
	(Trim, J.L.M. V.s. PERR/TRIM-1971.)	
TROI-1968	Troike, Rudolph C. Social Dialects . . .	2.2
TRUJ-1961	Trujillo, Luis M. Diccionario del . . .	3.5
TSUZ-1963/71	Tsuzaki, Stanley M. English Influences . . .	7.7
TUCK-1946	Tuck, Ruth D. Not With . . .	2.2.1
TUCS-1951	[anon. ed.] Tucson: The . . .	4.2.1
TURN-1973	Turner, Paul R. Bilingualism in . . .	2.2
TURN-1928-29	Turney, Douglas. The Mexican Accent.	6.8.1
UMPH/ADAT-1936	Umphrey. G. W. and Emma Adatto. Linguistic Archaisms . . .	13.3
USBU-1973	[anon.] U.S. Bureau of the Census . . .	1.2.1
VALD 1973	Valdés-Fallis, Guadalupe. Spanish as . . .	2.2
	(Valdez, Genevieve. V.s. TRAG/VALD-1937.)	
VALL-1970	Vallejo-Claros, Bernardo. La distribución y .	10.3
VALL-1971	Valls, Dolores L. Linguistic Description . . .	6.4
VANM-1972	Van Metre, Patricia Downer. Syntactic Characteristics . . .	4.8.1
VARE-1974	Varela de Cuéllar, Beatriz. La influencia del . . .	10.7
VARO-1971	Varo, Carlos. Consideraciones antropológicas	9.2
	(Vásquez, Alfredo. V.s. KEEV/etal-1945.)	
VASQ-1929	Vásquez Arjona, Carlos. Spanish and . . .	6.8.1
VIVO-1973	Vivó, Paquita. The Puerto Ricans: . . .	9.1
VOEG/etal-1967	Voegelin, Carl F., Florence M. Voegelin and Noel W. Schutz, Jr. The Language Situation . .	4.2.1
WAGN-1937	Wagner, Henry R. New Mexico . . .	3.1
WAGN-1953-54	Wagner, Max Leopold. Ein Mexikanisch-amerikanischer . . .	8.5
WAKE/SILV-1969	Wakefield, Mary W. and N.J. Silvaroli. A Study of . . .	3.2

WALT-1938	Walter, Paul Alfred Francis, Jr. A Study of .	3.2
WARD-1944	Ward, Hortense Warner. Ear Marks.	5.5
WARD-1972	Ward, James H. Spanish Teachers . . .	1.2.1
WATE-1948	Waters, Lena W. Mexican Geographical . . .	5.6
WEBB-1974	Webb, John T. Investigation Problems . . . (Weinstein. V.s. HIRS-1951.)	8.2
WEIS-1966	Weissman, Julius. An Exploratory Study . . .	9.2.1
WHAT-1922	[anon.] What Do . . .	3.8
WHIT-1972	White, Opal Thurow. The Mexican American . . .	2.2
WILLA-1971	Willard, Caroline Corser. A Linguistic Analysis . . .	6.8.1
WILLC-1974	Willcott, Paul. Differences in . . .	5.8.1
WILLI-1972	Williams, George. Some Errors . . .	9.8.1
WILM-1955	Williams, Stanley T. The Spanish Background .	6.2
WOLF-1971	Wolff de Porras, Normina. Anomalías lingüísticas . . .	5.2
WOLFR-1972a	Wolfram, Walt. Linguistic Assimilation . . .	9.8.1
WOLFR-1972b	_____. Overlapping Influence . . .	9.8.1
WOLFR-1973	_____. Objective and . . .	9.8.1
WOLFR/etal-1971	_____, Marie E. Shiels and Ralph W. Fasold. Overlapping Influence . . .	9.8.1
WOOD-1954	Woodbridge, Hensley C. Spanish in . . .	1.1
WOOD-1958	_____. A Handful of . . .	5.8
YOUN-1971	Young, Rodney W. Semantics as . . .	3.2
YOUN-1973	_____. The Development of . . .	3.2
ZIRK-1973	Zirkel, Perry Alan. A Sociolinguistic Survey .	9.2.1
ZUNS-1935	Zunser, Helen. A New Mexican . . .	3.2

LIST OF ABBREVIATIONS

(Note: the following items are published in the United States unless otherwise noted.)

*	not seen by annotator
AATSP	American Association of Teachers of Spanish and Portuguese
ACIH-3	<u>Actas del Tercer Congreso Internacional de Hispanistas</u>. México D.F., 26-31 agosto 1968. Edited by Carlos H. Magis. México: El Colegio de México, 1970
ACIL-10	<u>Actes du Xe Congrès Internationale des Linguistes</u>. Bucarest, 28 août-2 sept. 1967. Edited by A. Graur, I. Iordan et al. Bucarest: Éditions de l'Acad. de la République Socialist de Roumanie, 1970. 3 vols. (I: 1969; II and III published in 1970.)
ACILFR-11	<u>Actas del XI Congreso Internacional de Lingüística y Filología Románicas</u>. Edited by Antonio Quilis. Madrid: CSIC, 1968
ActSal	<u>Acta Salmanticensia: Primeras Jornadas de Lengua y Literatura Hispanoamericana: Comunicaciones y Ponencias</u>. (Acta Salmanticensia, Filosofía y Letras, Tomo 10.) Salamanca: Univ. de Salamanca, 1956.
AdL	<u>Anuario de Letras: Revista de la Facultad de Filosofía y Letras</u>. UNAM, México.
AIL	<u>Anales del Instituto de Lingüística</u> (Univ. Nacional de Cuyo, Mendoza, Argentina)
AJS	<u>American Journal of Sociology</u>
AL	<u>Anthropological Linguistics</u>
ALASH	<u>Acta Linguistica Academiae Scientiarum Hungaricae</u> (Budapest)
AmA	<u>American Anthropologist</u>
AnCF	<u>Annuaire du Collège de France</u> (France)
AnMN	<u>Anales del Museo Nacional</u> (Mexico)
AORL	<u>Anuari de l'Oficina Romànica de Lingüística y Literatura</u> (Barcelona)
AQ	<u>Arizona Quarterly</u>
Archivum	<u>Archivum: Revista de la Facultad de Filosofía y Letras</u> (Univ. de Oviedo, Spain)
AS	<u>American Speech</u>
ASeph	<u>American Sephardi</u>
ASES	<u>Actas del Primer Simposio de Estudios Sefardíes</u>. Madrid, 1-6 junio, 1964. Edited by I.M. Hassán. Publicaciones de Estudios Sefardíes, Serie I: Colectánea No. 1 (Madrid: CSIC/Instituto "Arias Montano," 1970)
ASFM	<u>Anuario de la Sociedad Folklórica de México</u> (Mexico)
ASNS	<u>Archiv für das Studium der Neueren Sprachen</u> (West Germany)
ASRev	<u>American Sociological Review</u>
AT	<u>Arizona Teacher</u>

BAACPR	Boletín de la Academia de Artes y Ciencias de Puerto Rico
BACLS	Bulletin of the American Council of Learned Societies
BBMP	Boletín de la Biblioteca Menéndez Pelayo (Spain)
BDH	Biblioteca de Dialectología Hispanoamericana (Univ. de Buenos Aires, Argentina)
BFUCh	Boletín de Filología (Univ. de Chile [Santiago])
BHi	Bulletin Hispanique (France)
BHS	Bulletin of Hispanic Studies (Great Britain) (continues BSS, q.v., infra)
BilR	The Bilingual Review/La Revista Bilingüe
BPAU	Bulletin of the Pan American Union
BSL	Bulletin de la Société de Linguistique de Paris (France)
BSS	Bulletin of Spanish Studies (succeeded by BHS, q.v.)
CALE-2	Congreso de Academias de la Lengua Española, II. Madrid 1956. Madrid: Real Academia de la Lengua, 1956
___-3	_____, III. Bogotá 1960. Bogotá: Academia Colombiana, 1961
___-4	_____, IV. Buenos Aires 1964. Buenos Aires: Academia Argentina de Letras, 1966
CFQ	California Folklore Quarterly (succeeded by WF, q.v.)
CG	Common Ground
CJBS	Canadian Journal of Behavioural Science (Canada)
CQ	Colorado Quarterly
CR	Congressional Record [Congress of the United States]
CSIC	Consejo Superior de Investigaciones Científicas (Madrid)
CTL 4.	Current Trends in Linguistics, Vol. 4: Ibero-American and Caribbean Linguistics, edited by Thomas A. Sebeok. The Hague: Mouton, 1968
___ 10.	_____, Vol. 10: Linguistics in North America, edited by William Bright, Dell Hymes et al. The Hague: Mouton, 1973
DA	Dissertation Abstracts International (Xerox University Microfilms)
DN	Dialect Notes
DRAE	Diccionario de la Real Academia Española (Madrid, Spain [19th ed. 1970])
EDRS	ERIC [q.v.] Document Reproduction Service ([language/language pedagogy serviced by] Arlington, Virginia: Center for Applied Linguistics)
ERIC	Educational Resources Information Center [cf. EDRS]
ESL	English as a second language (standard abbreviation)
EspAct	Español actual (Spain)
ETC.	ETC.: A Review of General Semantics
Exilio	Exilio: Revista de Humanidades

FFLR	<u>Florida F[oreign] L[anguage] Reporter</u>
GLing	<u>General Linguistics</u>
GPO	<u>United States Government Printing Office</u>
GRM	<u>Germanisch-Romanische Monatsschrifte</u> (West Germany)
HAHR	<u>Hispanic American Historical Review</u>
HEW	<u>United States Department of Health, Education and Welfare</u>
Hispania	<u>Hispania: A Journal Devoted to the Interests of the Teaching of Spanish and Portuguese</u> [cf. AATSP]
HLAS	<u>Handbook of Latin American Studies</u>
HomMP	<u>Homenaje a Ramón Menéndez Pidal</u> (Madrid: 1925)
HR	<u>Hispanic Review</u>
ICCNC	<u>Instituto Caro y Cuervo: Notas Culturales</u> (Colombia)
IJAL	<u>International Journal of American Linguistics</u>
IJCS	<u>International Journal of Comparative Sociology</u> (Canada)
IJE	<u>Irish Journal of Education</u> (Ireland)
IJP	<u>Interamerican Journal of Psychology</u>
ILR	<u>International Language Reporter</u>
IntMig	<u>International Migration</u>
InvLing	<u>Investigaciones Lingüísticas</u> (Mexico)
JAP	<u>Journal of American Folklore</u>
JAUMLA	<u>Journal of the Australasian Universities Modern Language Association</u> (New Zealand)
JCLA	<u>Journal of the Canadian Linguistic Association</u> (Canada)
JEGP	<u>Journal of English and Germanic Philology</u>
JEP	<u>Journal of Educational Psychology</u>
JES	<u>Journal of Educational Sociology</u>
JFI	<u>Journal of the Folklore Institute</u> [Univ. of Indiana]
JGP	<u>Journal of Genetic Psychology</u>
JSE	<u>Journal of Secondary Education</u>
JSHR	<u>Journal of Speech and Hearing Research</u>
JSI	<u>Journal of Social Issues</u>
JSPsych	<u>Journal of School Psychology</u>
JVLVB	<u>Journal of Verbal Learning and Verbal Behavior</u>
LangS	<u>Language Sciences</u>
LBRIGN	<u>Language By Radio Interest Group Newsletter</u> [Purdue Univ., Indiana]
Lingua	<u>Lingua: Revue International de Linguistique Génerale</u> (The Netherlands)
Linguistics	<u>Linguistics: An International Review</u> (The Netherlands)
LJS	<u>Le Judaisme Sephardi</u> (France)

LL	Language Learning: A Journal of Applied Linguistics
LLBA	Language and Language Behavior Abstracts
LMLP	La Monda Lingvo-Problema (The Netherlands [editorial office: Adelphi Univ., U.S.A.])
LRep	The Linguistic Reporter [Center for Applied Linguistics]
MAAb	Masters Abstracts [Xerox University Microfilms]
MAFS	Memoirs of the American Folklore Society
MARI	Middle America Research Institute Publications
MLA	The Modern Language Association of America
MLAAB/Ling	MLA Abstracts/Linguistics Series ("Vol. III")
MLB	Modern Language Bulletin
MLF	Modern Language Forum
MLJ	Modern Language Journal
MLN	Modern Language Notes
MLR	Modern Language Review
ModPh	Modern Philology
MSLL	Monograph Series on Language and Linguistics [Georgetown Univ.]
Nation	The Nation
n.d.	no date [no date of publication given]
NGeog	National Geographic
New York	New York Magazine
NMFR	New Mexico Folklore Record
NMHR	New Mexico Historical Review
NMQ	New Mexico Quarterly
NMSR	New Mexico School Review
n.p.	no page [no page cited]
n.pl.	no place [no place of publication cited]
NRFH	Nueva Revista de Filología Hispánica (Mexico)
OFINES	Oficina Internacional de Información y Observación del Español (Spain)
Orbis	Orbis: Bulletin Internacional de Documentation Linguistique (Belgium)
PacS	The Pacific Spectator
PADS	Publications of the American Dialect Society
PFLE	Presente y future de la lengua española: Actas de la Asamblea de Filología del Primer Congreso de Instituciones Hispánicas. Madrid, June 1963. Madrid: OFINES/Ediciones Cultura Hispánica, 1964. 2 vols.
Philologica	Philologica [Supplement to Časopis Moderní Filologii] (Czechoslovakia)
PILEI	Programa Interamericana de Lingüística y Enseñanza de Idiomas

PJ	Poradnik Językowy (Poland)
PQ	Philological Quarterly
PTFS	Publicationes of the Texas Folklore Society
QJS	Quarterly Journal of Speech
QuadIb	Quaderni Iberoamericani (Italy)
RBUA	Revista Bimestral de la Universidad de los Andes (Colombia)
RCu	Revista Cubana (Cuba)
RDR	Revue de Dialectologie Romane (Belgium/Germany)
RDTP	Revista de Dialectología y Tradiciones Populares (Spain)
ReadT	The Reading Teacher
RES	Review of English Studies (Great Britain)
RevIb	Revista Iberoamericana
RevIbBA	*Revista Iberoamericana de Buenos Aires (Argentina)
RF	Romanische Forschungen (West Germany)
RFE	Revista de Filología Española (Spain)
RHisp	Revue Hispanique (France)
RHM	Revista Hispánica Moderna
RIAF	Revista Interamericana
RIB	Revista Interamericana de Bibliografía
RIE	Research in Education [1975- Resources in Education]
RIR	Revista Iberoamericana Review (Puerto Rico)
RJB	Romanistisches Jahrbuch (West Germany)
RPh	Romance Philology
rpt.	reprinted/reprint
RR	Romanic Review
RRLing	Revue Roumaine Linguistique (Rumania)
RS	Rural Sociology
SFor	Social Forces
SFQ	Southern Folklore Quarterly
SL	Studies in Linguistics
SocSQ	Social Science Quarterly
SNPh	Studia Neophilologica (Sweden)
SPh	Studies in Philology
SpT	Speech Teacher
SR	Saturday Review
SSLL	Stanford Studies in Language and Literature
SSSB	Sociolinguistic Studies in Southwest Bilingualism [ongoing project at the Univ. of Texas-El Paso, directed by Prof. Jacob Ornstein]
SWHQ	Southwestern Historical Quarterly (succeeds THAQ)
SWJA	Southwest Journal of Anthropology
SWR	Southwest Review
SWSSQ	Southwestern Social Science Quarterly

TAM	Theatre Arts Monthly
TESOLQ	T[eaching of] E[nglish to] S[peakers of] O[ther] L[anguages] Quarterly
THAQ	Texas Historical Association Quarterly (succeeded by SWHQ)
Thesaurus	Thesaurus: Boletín del Instituto Caro y Cuervo (Colombia)
TLandS	The Land of Sunshine
TOM	The Overland Monthly
TSR	The Spanish Review
UAB	Univ. of Arizona Bulletin
UASSB	Univ. of Arizona Social Science Bulletin
UCLAW/TESL	Univ. of California-Los Angeles Work Papers: Teaching of English as a Second Language
UCPL	Univ. of California Publications in Linguistics
UCS	Univ. of Colorado Studies
Univ. de Méx	Revista de la Universidad Nacional Autónoma de México
UNMBLS	Univ. of New Mexico Bulletin/Language Series
UNMBSS	Univ. of New Mexico Bulletin/Sociological Series
UTEHA	Unión Tipográfica Editorial Hispanoamericana (Mexico)
v.d.	various dates (of publication)
WF	Western Folklore (successor to CFQ)
Word	Word: Journal of the Linguistic Circle of New York
WR	Western Review
XUM	Xerox University Microfilms (Ann Arbor, Michigan)
YBAPS	Year Book of the American Philosophical Society
YR	Yale Review
ZRPh	Zeitschrift für Romanische Philologie (West Germany)